Communication in Modern Organizations

The Wiley Series in

MANAGEMENT AND ADMINISTRATION

ELWOOD S. BUFFA, Advisory Editor
University of California, Los Angeles

COMMUNICATION IN MODERN ORGANIZATIONS

George T. Vardaman
Professor of Administration and Associate Dean
College of Business Administration
University of Denver

Patricia Black Vardaman
Vice President and Senior Systems Analyst
Management Associates
Indian Hills, Colorado

JOHN WILEY & SONS, INC.
New York   London   Sydney   Toronto

Cover Photograph:

Bob Blansky, Dolphin Computer Image Corporation

Library of Congress Cataloging in Publication Data:

Vardaman, George T.
Communication in modern organizations.

Bibliography: p.
1. Communication in management.   I. Vardaman,
Patricia Black, joint author.   II. Title.

HF5718.V37   658.4   72-7391
ISBN 0-471-90300-0

Printed in the United States of America

10 9 8 7 6 5 4 3 2 1

Preface

Purpose and Approach

Succinctly stated, the purpose of this book is to give practical guidance for learning the most important communication principles, procedures, and skills for use in modern organizations. The concepts and practices presented can be used with enterprises of any size or type—business, government, professional, and educational.

The book is designed principally as a four-year or two-year college text, and it is intended to equip the student with both basic communication strategies and tactics (high-level how-to) for superior results. While emphasizing the written communication, other valuable communications resources are also included: speaking, listening, automated, and combinations of all types. A proven method for assessing, planning, and carrying out any communication is presented and applied throughout. This approach, termed PRIDE, gives a practical, systematic pattern for use in all organizational communications.

The PRIDE sequence is essentially a disciplined decision-making method to achieve effective communication. It is an acronym for the five "how-to" elements for skillfully planning and carrying out any written or oral communication:

> Purpose
> Receiver
> Impact
> Design
> Execution

The book sets forth the total organizational communications spectrum, together with a systematic way to maximize effectiveness. Thus, it gives an integrated perspective plus sharp decision-making skills for optimal control of a person's own and his organization's communications.

Materials and Presentation

This textbook combines important principles with a representative variety of organizational examples. Examples are presented as figures or specimens. *Figures* are used profusely within chapters to illustrate principles and to deepen communication understandings. *Specimens* (a total of 115) are included in a separate reference section (Part V) for further illustration and for relevant practice exercises to increase the student's understandings and skills. Moreover, both figures and specimens are interwoven with principles throughout the book. This combination of important principles with authentic examples of organizational documents furnishes a tool for sound communication decision making and execution.

The Book's Rationale and Learning Progression

As stated, PRIDE is a guide to effective personal and organizational communication, a method combining discipline with creativity. Once learned, the student has a practical, systematic way to make sound communication judgments and to put his judgments into effective action. After all, in modern real world organizations, we are required to make our own decisions about the communication tasks that confront us, then communicate to implement those decisions most effectively.

To help the student to learn disciplined, creative decision making in communication, materials are deliberately organized to optimize the mastery of understandings and skills. Part I sets forth the nine most important organizational written documents, giving essential knowledge of and skills in using these fundamental communications resources. The presentation and applications show how to know where given documents fit into the organizational scheme, how to assess strengths and weaknesses, and how to make needed improvements. Figuratively, this part gives the student the ability to *walk* briskly and directly toward his communication destination.

Part II is designed to give the student the ability to *run* rapidly and most effectively to his destination. The PRIDE method is presented in depth, taking him step-by-step through the entire sequence so that he gets it "in his bones." When so conditioned, the student has the high-level ability to use this decision-making method; he has a communication perspective and capacity far beyond that possessed at the end of Part I.

Part III discusses supplemental personal and organizational communications resources (oral, automated, and combinations). Once more the PRIDE method is used as the basis for effective communication assessment, planning, and execution. When this part is understood, then the student has true professional competence and genuine personal confidence to assess, to plan, and to carry out any communication mission, whether personal or organizational.

In sum, the learning progression of the book's basic text is to build competence in knowing about and handling important written media (Part I);

to build competence in knowing about and applying the PRIDE sequence as a disciplined, creative decision-making method for effective communication (Part II); and to build competence in knowing about and using the PRIDE method to assess, to plan, and to improve supplementary communications resources—oral, automated, and combinations (Part III).

Part IV presents important review materials for effective organizational language handling (clarity, correctness, persuasiveness). These three chapters refresh the student's memory on the parts where he needs to build greater proficiency. Furthermore, he can use all principles as basic resources as he works through Parts I to III.

Part V includes 115 specimens of actual organizational written communications. These are used throughout Parts I to IV for both illustration and practice. Exposure to and analysis of these real-world writings result in truly meaningful learning about the nature of modern organizational communications. More important, working with these representative authentic examples markedly helps the student to develop skills for rapid and accurate size-up of a given writing and to know how to reshape it for better results.

George T. Vardaman
Patricia Black Vardaman

Sources and Acknowledgments

Our ideas and approach have come from many sources. The basic concepts, of course, come from our studies and teaching of communication, management, and organizational theory. The rationale and learning progression come from our experiences as organizational managers (where we too must work with all types of communication) and as communications and management analysts (where we designed and used the book's principles, procedures, and practices in other real-world organizations).

We acknowledge our debts to (1) our academic colleagues at many educational institutions, who have been helpful in evaluation and suggestions; (2) our students in communications and management courses, who have given us opportunities to test and improve our concepts and approaches in the classroom; and (3) practitioners in all enterprises—private, public, and professional— with whom we have worked, who were especially helpful in giving valuable critiques and suggestions from their organizational perspectives. We are deeply grateful for all three groups' suggestions, which have helped to shape this volume.

G. T. V.
P. B. V.

Contents

Communication in Modern Organizations

Part I

PRIDE and Written Communication Media

In this part you will learn the essential components of PRIDE, the book's basic sequence to achieve effective communication. You will also be offered suggestions for discovering the importance and workings of communication in contemporary organizations. Moreover, you will be given guides for determining your own communication proficiency, as well as suggestions for improvements where needed. These items are covered in Chapter 1 and its related exercises.

Chapters 2 through 6 treat in depth the three types of a firm's written media: individually oriented—letters, memoranda, reports (Chapters 2 to 4); legally oriented—proposals, agreements, directives (Chapter 5); and organizationally oriented—manuals, forms, brochures (Chapter 6).

Each chapter includes a wide variety of figure examples for illustration and for better understanding of principles. Practical exercises are also suggested to achieve high-level understanding of and skill in the use of principles and procedures presented.

When you complete this section, you will understand clearly and be able to use effectively the nine most important written documents of modern organizations.

Chapter 1

PRIDE: A GUIDE TO EFFECTIVE ORGANIZATIONAL COMMUNICATION

Your Learning Objectives:

1. To know the importance of communication in today's organizations.
2. To know the effectiveness of communication in a few representative organizations.
3. To know three basic causes of different theories and practices of communication in modern organizations.
4. To know four different basic definitions (or perspectives) of organizational communication.
5. To know the general definition of PRIDE and its applications to both organizational and personal communication effectiveness.
6. To know the general definition of *disciplined creativity* in communication.
7. To know the basic learning progression to gain *disciplined creativity* in communication.
8. To know your own important communication strengths and weaknesses.
9. To know how to improve your personal communication.
10. To know how to investigate and evaluate some important dimensions of organizational communication.
11. To know how to write clear, accurate reports on findings from studying organization communication.
12. To know how to make meaningful oral reports on findings about organizational communication.

If taken seriously, organizational communication can be one of the most important subjects you will ever study—for both your college and professional career.

Why do we make this assertion? Because we have heard the same statement from hundreds of important persons in business, government, and professional organizations; and because we have also heard it from thousands of mature college students.

Even more significant, we have observed what such study has done for both practitioners and college students. In other words, we have witnessed what proper uses of sound communication principles, procedures, practices have done for people and for organizations, often transforming mediocre output (in enterprises or on campus) into excellent (often superior) performance.

So convinced are we concerning communication's importance to both practitioner and student, that we are willing to put our conclusions to the test: we invite you to find out for yourself. We shall even give you a practical way to get realistic answers. The method is simple. First, we shall present four basic questions, along with our predictions of the likely answers you will get from most respondents. At the end of the chapter, we then supply an easily used checklist questionnaire for cataloging and for interpreting these responses. You may then compare your results with our predictions.

Let us start with questions directed to organizational practitioners, after which we shall discuss slightly modified versions for college students.

Questions and Answers: Practitioners

Question 1
Is effective communication important in modern business, government, or professional organizations?
Likely Answer
"Effective communication is *extremely* important in the successful operation of every job in our organization."

Question 2
How effective is communication in today's firms, agencies, or enterprises?
Likely Answer
"Communication is less effective than it ought to be in our organization. We should be doing better." (Often the answer will be "We ought to be doing much better.")

Question 3
Is effective communication easily accomplished?
Likely Answer
A resounding "No!"

Question 4
How does one accomplish effective communication?

Likely Answers

These will range from an emphatic "I wish I knew!" to a dogmatic "I know exactly; you do thus and so. . . ." Between these extremes you will probably receive an astonishing array of different principles, procedures, and practices.

Questions and Answers: College Students

If you raise these four basic questions to serious, perceptive college or university students about effective personal communication in relation to their academic success, we predict that you will get essentially the same responses. That is, you will find their basic answers add up to the following: (1) personal communication proficiency is very important to academic success; (2) personal communication proficiency is not what it ought to be; (3) personal communication effectiveness is not easy; and (4) personal communication theories and practices vary widely.

Implications

Let us assume that you do find essentially what we have predicted. What implications can be drawn? First, answers from both practitioners and students to the first three questions generally correspond—that is, effective communication (1) is important to both organizational and academic success, (2) is not up to the right quality level in either context, and (3) is not easily attained by either group.

Question four, however, concerning "how to do it" is where you will likely see a great divergence in responses from both groups. There are basic reasons for the disagreement concerning communication practices. Let us now look at three of the more important.

Reasons for Differences in Communication Practices

First, people have *different definitions* or concepts of "effective communication." Some look on it as purely *results-centered*; that is, if the sender gets the response he is after, his communication is thereby effective (regardless of the means employed). Others view effective communication in terms of its *palatability to receivers*—that is, to the extent that people accept a given message, it is to that degree effective. Still another outlook concerns the *quality of verbal and graphic dimensions* of presentation—that is, the excellence (or the opposite) of factors such as format, language usage, visual aids, and general appearance is concomitant with effectiveness of communication. Finally, a fairly widely accepted perspective is that the *technology* of communication (both machine and medium) is the key to whether communication is adequate or inadequate.

Second, and growing out of the divergent perspectives described, people have had *different conditioning*. That is, the education, training, and experience of people make for different values, methods, techniques, and approaches. Only a cursory study of the hundreds of books on the subject will demonstrate the countless diverse ways in which communication is preached and practiced. Even schools differ widely in emphasis and approach. Some colleges and universities do not even require formal communication courses; most do demand some instruction, but the lack of uniformity in content and teaching method (even when using the same text in the same school) is apparent to even the casual observer. This leads to the next reason for differences in communication approach and practice.

Third, *insufficient emphasis* has been given *to communication as integral to managerial and organizational success.* (Unfortunately, this often includes the student, who is actually a *manager of* his own *learning in* the context of a *university organization* with all its pressures and demands.) Not nearly enough emphasis has been placed on the importance of organizational and managerial communication; and certainly not enough sound, realistic principles, procedures, and practices have been presented to either practitioners or students.

These three basic causes of the fragmented state of existing managerial and organizational communication practices point to a real need to present *integrated* communication principles, procedures, and practices to give both the practitioner and student sound guidance and direct help.

The Book's Approach

This book is written to make communication a significant and useful part of your real world—your present academic, and your future career life—so that you can see more clearly what effective communication is and what it can do for you.

We start with a basic assumption: *the most important outcome* from studying this book and the course you are taking is *to give you the ability to quickly and accurately size up and to effectively execute your personal communication and that of any organization in which you may work.* To do this, the book's central focus is on developing communication sensitivity and competence so that you can pinpoint communication strengths and weaknesses and then make needed improvements. What we are really talking about is that *you develop* communication *judgment* and *competence.* When approached this way, communication becomes a continuing creative challenge to you and, in turn, it will reap rich rewards for both you and your organization.

How does this book help you to develop creative communication sensitivity and competence? This is done in several ways. For one thing, we deliberately use a representative cross section of actual communication examples and specimens from the world of business, government, professional, and academic organizations as bases for learning. Second, we present concise principles (drawn from the most valuable elements of all different views discussed before), followed by a series of these real world examples so that you can readily understand what we are saying. Third, at strategic points, we suggest exercises that permit your application of what you have learned. These exercises are designed for use in both classroom and in outside administered firms. This three-step approach facilitates your putting theory into practice to get productive results.

However, let us be clear: effective communication is not an easy accomplishment, for despite popular preachments to the contrary, communication is not a simple discipline. It is both an art and a science (some say a "soft" science and a "hard" art), one with its own technical principles, which must be correctly understood and properly applied. Furthermore, even with high-level understanding, effective communication output is almost always the result of some hard work—in both thought and action. All the great communicators of history and all superior ones managing and working in current up-to-date enterprises attest to this fact.

On the other hand, communication is no mysterious or supernatural area. It is open for all to explore and to learn. We believe that the learning pattern set forth in this book can result in real improvement for any industrious and intelligent student. And when you have mastered what is presented, your communication will be more effective and easier to accomplish.

Our teaching of thousands of business students and work with hundreds of business, government, and professional organizations has produced a straightforward sequence for learning how to communicate effectively. Called PRIDE, it is an acronym for (P) purpose of the communication; (R) receiver roles; (I) impact desired; (D) design of the communication; and (E) execution of the communication.

Each component will be discussed in detail in later chapters, but for now let us look at a brief description of each and its importance to effective communication.

P. The *purpose* you the sender are trying to achieve: the target or mission of the communication. Unless you know your exact purpose, communication failure is automatic.

R. The *receiver* (or receivers) to whom the communication is directed: the willingness and ability of the reader or listener to understand and accept your message. You must know the psychology and competence of the receiver in order to get anything across to him.

I. The *impact* which is needed: how your communication must affect the receiver if you are to achieve your purpose and influence him as needed. In other words, you must know what picture you want to get into the receiver's head.

D. The *design* of the communication: how it should be organized and developed to achieve the desired impact. Obviously, you must design your communication in light of the specific situation you confront.

E. The *execution* of the communication: the actual carrying out of your plan (from the four preceding steps) to a successful conclusion. Even if you have succeeded in planning purpose, recognizing the receiver, knowing the needed impact, and constructing an appropriate design, communication will fail unless it is properly carried out.

The Book's Objective: Disciplined Creativity

Proper use of PRIDE will give you a life-long, invaluable method, for once learned, the sequence becomes habitual, an automatic way to size up any communication task and to carry it out to get the results you want. In other words, PRIDE is a communication discipline.

But the discipline can be no better than the quality of judgment and creative imagination that *you* bring to it. Therefore, this book throughout focuses on *building your ability* to make *proper judgments* and to exercise your best *creative talents* as you use the PRIDE sequence. In short, this *book's* whole *purpose* is to give you a method that permits you to *develop* to the fullest *your own disciplined communication creativity*.

The "How-to" of Effective Communication

To help you develop disciplined creativity, this book deliberately presents "how-to-do-it" guidance at both the strategic and tactical levels. The PRIDE sequence is actually a *decision making strategy* for planning and producing effective communication. As such it is a "how-to" *method*. Stated another way, PRIDE gives you step-by-step guidance to proper assessment and execution of any writing or speaking. Once you get this method "in your bones," you have a conceptual "how-to" tool for universal application to communication.

We also present "how-to-do-it" at the tactical level—that is, *guidance in the assessment and skillful execution* of the most *important personal and organizational forms of communication*. First, you are exposed to a wide variety of figures and specimens (both "good" and "bad") drawn from real world organizations. This representative cross section gives you an "under the skin" sensitivity to modern organizational communications. Second, at the end of selected chapters, we provide practical (but comprehensive) checklists ("Communication Quality Control") for translating principles into effective action. Third, at the end of each text chapter, we present exercises and case situations that further help you to transform principles into effective communication output. As you work through them, you will see that these exercises are both realistic and relevant—not mere academic "busy work." Fourth, we furnish specific direction in basic writing principles in a separate reference section (Part IV). Three chapters (15 to 17) succinctly present the most frequently needed principles and guides of clarity, correctness, and persuasiveness. Since it is largely self-scoring, you can use this section for self-diagnosis and review, concentrating on areas needing most improvement. Its greatest value may be for continuing reference as you go through the text.

In sum, the entire book can be viewed as a practical "how-to-do-it" spectrum —ranging from practical guides to effective grammar to methods for effective communication decision making. This is as it should be, for ultimately all effective communication is a product of skillful use of sound strategic and tactical "how-to" principles, procedures, and practices.

Sequence of Presentation

Why is the book organized as it is? There is a deliberate learning progression. Part I presents an overview of the most important organizational communications (media), giving you an insight into an organization's operation as reflected by its written documents. Furthermore, the progression permits you to see where and how specific documents fit into the total organizational scheme. Specifically, the next five chapters (2 through 6) treat three general important types of managerial written media: individually oriented (letters, memoranda, and reports—Chapters 2 to 4); legally oriented (proposals, agreements, and directives—Chapter 5); and organizationally oriented (manuals, forms, and brochures—Chapter 6).

Once you know the nature of organizational documents, you are then ready for Part II, "Applying PRIDE to Written Communications." Here you study modern organizational communication planning and decision making through an in-depth application of the PRIDE sequence to the media studied. You learn about three general purposes (and their subsets) as they relate to different receiver roles (Chapters 7 to 9); then you learn how to recognize and apply principles to achieve important impacts and designs in communications

(Chapter 10); last, you learn how to carry out (execute) effective communications (Chapter 11).

You are now ready to look beyond written communications to other organizational communication means. Part III, "Related Communication Resources," contains three chapters dealing with important complementary communications and modes; Chapter 12 covers oral communications (both speaking and listening); Chapter 13 is concerned with automating written communications; and Chapter 14 deals with principles and guides for selection of the right communication resources for optimal results.

The first three parts are essential textual materials for effective communication planning and decision making; the last two parts (IV and V) are reference sections.

Part IV, "Reference Materials: Effective Language in Organizations," is an important section for refreshing yourself on basic principles of language handling. Chapter 15 is concerned with clarity; Chapter 16 presents guides for correct language usage; Chapter 17 deals with principles of persuasiveness.

Suggestion: you may wish to start your study of the book with a thorough review of Part IV. It can be used for self-diagnosis of strengths and weaknesses (much of it includes self-scoring exercises for this purpose). Also, you can use the materials as language resources as you work through exercises in textual chapters. Indeed, you are expected to know these principles and procedures and to be able to apply them starting with exercises at the end of this chapter.

Part V, "Reference Materials: Specimens," is a representative collection of 115 communication specimens—good and bad—which are used throughout the book for illustration and practice. The samples are deliberately drawn from both academic organizations and outside administered firms.

Special Notes on Figures and Specimens

Figures are short actual communication examples used for illustrating principles. These are numbered and presented within the text of each chapter. They are also used for exercises at pivotal points. In illustrating letters, content of the figures is limited to the salutation and body of the communication; memoranda include only the "subject" and message. Because unnecessary, the other components (e.g., date, address, closing) do not appear.

Specimens are also actual communication examples, but they are either complete writings or excerpts from longer documents. Since they are used throughout the book for illustration and for several types of exercises, they are numbered consecutively in a separate division (Part V). You can easily turn to each specimen as needed. In illustrating letter and memoranda specimens, all components (except letterhead printing) are shown so that you may judge style and appearance in addition to the message.

Note on Names, Organizations, and Locations/With few exceptions, both figures and specimens, while real, are either anonymous or use fictious names for persons, organizations, and locations. Why? Because this permits you to make candid, objective appraisals without fear of offending the originating or receiving organization and people. For convenience, where names and places are needed, we have substituted the following:

Sender: Robert M. Jones
Receiver: William S. Miller
Wilma S. Miller
Third Parties: Donald B. Thompson
Verna N. Thomas
Organizations: Star-X
City University
Locations: Spencer, Transylvania
Widespot, Texakana
University Park, Nohio

To reiterate, all the above persons and organizations are fictitious, and are in no respects to be identified with any similarly named actual persons or organizations.

Notes on Specimen Reference Numbers/For easy reference, a simple scheme is followed. The specimen number, together with paragraph and sentence order are given. For example 62:1.2 means *specimen* number 62, *paragraph* 1 *sentence* 2 (in paragraph 1). If more than one paragraph or sentence, these are indicated by 62:1-2 (paragraphs 1 and 2) and 62:1.1-2 (paragraph 1, sentences 1 and 2).

EXERCISES

exercise 1   Using the three questionnaire forms below, find how (1.1) practitioners, (1.2) educators, (1.3) other students evaluate communication.

1.1 PRACTITIONERS (business, government, or professional)
1. How important is effective communication to your organization?
Very high ☐ High ☐ Average ☐ Low ☐ Very low ☐

2. How effective is communication in your organization?
   Very high ☐ High ☐ Average ☐ Low ☐ Very low ☐
3. Is effective communication easily accomplished in your organization?
   Very easy ☐ Easy ☐ Average ☐ Difficult ☐ Very difficult ☐
4. What are the principal communication strengths of your organization?
5. What are your organization's principal communication weaknesses, and how can each be improved?

1.2 EDUCATORS (college classroom professors other than business communication)

1. How important is effective student communication in the conduct of your classes?
   Very high ☐ High ☐ Average ☐ Low ☐ Very low ☐
2. How do you rate the communication proficiency of your students?
   Very high ☐ High ☐ Average ☐ Low ☐ Very low ☐
3. Is effective communication easy for your students to accomplish in their classroom work?
   Very easy ☐ Easy ☐ Average ☐ Difficult ☐ Very difficult ☐
4. What are the principal communication strengths of your students?
5. What are your students' principal communication weaknesses, and how can each be improved?

1.3 STUDENTS (college/university)

1. How important is effective communication to your studies?
   Very high ☐ High ☐ Average ☐ Low ☐ Very low ☐
2. How effective is your personal communication for academic studies?
   Very high ☐ High ☐ Average ☐ Low ☐ Very low ☐
3. Is effective communication easy for you?
   Very easy ☐ Easy ☐ Average ☐ Difficult ☐ Very difficult ☐

exercise 2 Prepare a written report on your findings, using this format:

2.1 Comparing each group by items.
2.2 Comparing group to group similarities and differences.
2.3 Comparing to likely answers predicted by the authors.
2.4 Concluding with your own evaluation of findings, with reasons.
2.5 Attaching all response sheets as an appendix.

exercise 3 Analyze your own or your organization's communication.

3.1 If personal, follow the student form (1.3); if employed, follow the practitioner form (1.1).

3.2 Write a brief report of your findings and a specific plan for improvement of weaknesses noted.

exercise 4 Use your findings from exercises 2 and 3 to determine:

4.1 Which of the four different definitions of communication (discussed under the first "Reasons for Different Communication Practices") most closely fits each of the persons (or organizations) studied and why.
4.2 Which of the different definitions most closely fits your own outlook and why.

exercise 5 Make an oral or written report on how the PRIDE sequence can improve:

5.1 Your personal communication.
5.2 The communication of the organization studied (or if none analyzed, a hypothetical firm).
5.3 The communication in courses you are taking or have taken.
5.4 What are your principal communication strengths?
5.5 What are your principal communication weaknesses, and how can each be improved?

exercise 6 Suggestions for interviewing

6.1 Question three to five representative persons from each group.
6.2 Briefly explain to each respondent: that you are taking a course in organizational communication; that you want his candid answers to each question; that, if he wishes, his answers will remain anonymous. (However, you should identify the type of organization and the person's position or status.)
6.3 Give each respondent a copy of the questionnaire for his use as he answers your questions.
6.4 Give the respondent the option of completing the questionnaire himself or having you fill it out. If the latter, let him review your product, making any corrections he feels needed.
6.5 For use in this exercise, "effective communication" means high-level proficiency and application of writing, reading, speaking, and listening, both personal and organizational.

Chapter 2

INDIVIDUALLY ORIENTED MEDIA: LETTERS

Your Learning Objectives:

1. To know the definition of a letter.
2. To know some common purposes of letters in organizations.
3. To know how to recognize letter purposes.
4. To know basic components of letters.
5. To know situational notations of letters.
6. To know how to identify different basic components and situational notations.
7. To know how to use the different components and notations.
8. To know basic style formats of letters.
9. To know how to identify the different style formats.
10. To know how to use the different style formats.
11. To know how to check letter appearance for maximum effectiveness.
12. To know the definition and uses for *nonroutine* letters.
13. To know the definition and uses for *routine—prepared parts* letters.
14. To know the definition and uses for *routine—complete* letters.
15. To know the definition and uses for *mass distribution* letters.
16. To know the advantages and disadvantages of all four basic letter types.
17. To know how to use a checklist for ready, accurate analysis of letter components and notations.

18. To know how to use a checklist for ready, valid analysis of letter communication quality.

Let us now consider the first individual written medium, letters.

What are letters? They are so familiar that a definition may labor the obvious. However to take a common perspective, let us define a letter as a written medium which (1) is personally addressed; (2) can meet a broad spectrum of purposes; and (3) can be used both intra-organizationally and extra-organizationally.

Granting the breadth of definition, it does give the distinguishing qualities of a letter: its personalism, its capacity to attain diverse objectives, and its potential for both internal and external communication.

Let us next consider some important components of letters. In so doing we shall use both figures and specimens to illustrate ideas.

Special note/As we have stated in the introduction, we shall assume your working understanding of basic language usage—clarity, correctness, and persuasiveness. If you need review on any of these, refer to the appropriate section in Part IV.

The purpose of Chapters 2 through 6 is to give you understanding of essentials in each of the nine basic written media. In Chapters 2 through 4 we shall focus on four dimensions: (1) common purposes or general types, (2) components, (3) styles and appearance, and (4) special communication features. (Chapters 5 and 6 use a slightly different pattern.)

Let us now consider these with respect to letters.

Common Purposes

Purpose refers to the objective or mission of a letter, out of which its essential message emerges. Recognition of your letter's purpose and writing to meet that purpose is, of course, fundamental to effective communication. Obvious as it is, not following this principle is one of the most common causes of failure of a letter. In too many cases, a letter is a random, slapdash putting blobs of ink on paper, rather than a conscious, deliberate pinpointing of target and communicating ideas that hit the bull's eye. You can always distinguish the poor from the good writer of letters by whether or not the communication is written to achieve a specific, known purpose; the poor writer will know only dimly, if at all, but the good communicator will know exactly.

We shall deal in depth with specific written communication purposes in Chapters 7 to 9. At this point we shall look at some familiar ones in letters.

Dear Star-X Customer:

On Sunday, October 4th, from 11:00 a.m. to 5:00 p.m., all three Star-X appliance Centers are having a very special Private Warehouse Sale for you, our valued customer. This Sale is being held only for those customers who ˙ have bought from us in the past . . . before any announcement to the general public.

This is a wonderful opportunity for you to save on famous brand names in every department, including televisions, appliances, stereos, radios and housewares.

You'll also find fantastic buys on floor samples, one-of-a-kind demonstrators, railroad damaged and discontinued models at all three stores. In addition, we are clearing out all last year's stock to make room for the new models. These will be further reduced to offer you even greater savings.

Mark your calendar for this special date . . . Sunday, October 4th . . . we look forward to seeing you again. Refreshments will be served.

Fig. 2.1 / Letter—special inducements.

Figure 2.1 is an example of a very common letter purpose, that is, to *sell*. To be more exact, it is a "special inducements" letter. Why is it a special inducements letter? Can you see the inducements offered to the reader? Are they clear and persuasive?

Another frequently used type can be seen in Figure 2.2, the letter of *transmittal*. In fact, the letter also implies another purpose: that of *seeking information* (because it asks the reader to fill out an enclosed questionnaire). Sometimes more than a single purpose may be sought in a given letter, but the writer must be careful (and skillful) so that his objectives are not blurred (both to himself and to the receiver). Is the writer completely clear on his purposes? If not, what could he do to improve the letter?

We are sure that you have had experience with the type of letter exemplifying the next purpose. It is, of course, a response to a request for admissions information from a university. Specifically, this shows an *answer to inquiry* purpose. How does this letter strike you? Does it achieve its purpose and, at the same time, satisfy you?

You have no doubt received many letters similar to Figure 2.4. Any purpose that "hits the pocketbook" or asks you to give resources (money, goods or services) is what we call *seeking contributions*. How would you respond to this document? Would you give? Why or why not? Could this letter be improved? In what ways?

Still another purpose with which you have had experience (as a sender or

Dear Sir:

I am a student at City University. In order to fulfill the requirements of my Business Communications course, I am writing a report on the policies of graduate business schools concerning comprehensive examinations.

In order to research this report, I am taking a survey of fifty graduate business schools that are accredited by the American Association of Collegiate Schools of Business. Therefore, would you please complete the enclosed questionnaire? Part I of the questionnaire should be answered by all schools; Part II should be completed by those schools that administer a comprehensive examination; Part III should be answered by those schools that do not administer the examination. Part IV asks purely for personal opinion and can be answered if you desire.

I will appreciate any additional information you can send me. All information furnished will be kept in the strictest confidence. If requested, I will send you the results of this interesting survey.

Fig. 2.2/ Letter of transmittal.

receiver) is the *complaint.* In Figure 2.5 you can see this purpose used by a student who felt he had been unfairly treated, as he viewed it, when the University reversed its position on his retaking courses when he failed. Unfortunately this merely reinforced the University's position. Can you imagine why? What glaring defects need correction? What more subtle factors need improvement if the letter is to get a more favorable response?

The "dun" is one of the most commonly used purposes in business letters. Figure 2.6 shows this purpose, commonly known as *collection,* in correspon-

Dear Mr. Miller:

This is in answer to your letter of January 23, regarding your admission to City University. In regard to your question of which program would be more desirable, the B.S. or the B.A., the major which holds your strongest interest should determine your choice. Both of the programs are outstanding at this University. I would hesitate at this point in time, without further discussion with you, to recommend a specific program.

Under separate cover I am sending our latest catalogue on the programs offered by this University. If you have more specific questions regarding the University, you may write directly to Dr. Donald B. Thompson, Admission's Counselor.

Fig. 2.3/ Letter answering an inquiry.

Dear Bill:

Thus far in our Fraternity's long and proud history requests for contributions have been few and far between, and then only to selected individuals. Now, for the first time, we are making an appeal to all members to lend a hand.

This is your Fraternity and we need your help. Think what can be accomplished if each of you contribute an amount which would demonstrate your continuing interest and lifetime commitment to the principles of our Brotherhood.

Fig. 2.4 / Letter seeking contributions.

dence from a professional society asking for a member to renew. Of course the enclosure referred to is a renewal card stating the fee that the "delinquent" respondent is asked to remit. Would you renew? Why? What could be done to make a better impact on the reader?

Yet another purpose, acknowledgment, can be viewed in Figure 2.7. Here the manager of a hotel is confirming (or acknowledging) the reservation dates and charges for a room. Does this letter have a positive ring? Are there some changes that could strengthen its impact? What changes?

Finally, Figure 2.8 shows how a hotel communicates *refusal* to a request for reservation. Saying "No" is another frequent mission in business letters. All too frequently, it is poorly handled, resulting in untold adverse effects for the sender and his organization. Compare the tone of this letter with that of Figure 2.7. For example, could it have a more positive tone? What changes could be made to do this?

Dear Dean Miller:

Thank you for looking in to my records and discusing it with Dean Thompson and others. Respectfully, I must point out that you didn't consider the question I raise.

Last term the University told me I could retake the corses I failed and now you told me that University policys prohibit me doing this. That my indefinite suspension remains in affect.

There is not only the basic essential important practical question of the Degree, but there is morale and ethical questions envolved. The university gave me permission to retake corses, than after the fact, they took away the permission.

Fig. 2.5 / Letter of complaint.

Dear Colleague:

Our records indicate that you have allowed your membership in the Association to lapse. Won't you take this opportunity to renew?

Events of recent years have underscored the need for a strong, active professional organization. We have attempted to meet this need through such means as the recent conference on social relevance; the national project on research; the addition to the national office staff of a full-time Director of Research.

Membership is at an all-time high. But we need your support. There *is* strength in numbers.

A membership application form is enclosed. We look forward to welcoming you again as a strong supporter of the organization.

Fig. 2.6/Letter of collection.

Dear Mr. Miller:

Thank you so much for your letter of January 13th and especially for the welcome news that Mrs. Miller will join you here at Star-X Motel. We shall gladly arrange a room so that Mrs. Miller will not need to climb stairs.

Your understanding of our charges is exactly correct. Although our double motel units are not large, your room contains a dressing room, deluxe bath, color TV, and direct dial telephone for your convenience in keeping in touch with your home office.

We are continuing to anticipate your arrival February 24, with departure the afternoon of February 27. Please do not hesitate to request of me whatever additional information you may require and be sure to advise us of any way we can facilitate your arrival here.

Fig. 2.7/Letter of acknowledgment.

Dear Mr. Miller:

Thank you for your request regarding accomodation for October 3-5.

We regret we will be unable to make the reservations requested, because due to previous commitments we are booked to capacity during this period.

We appreciate your thought of our hotel and hope we may have the pleasure of serving you at some other time in the near future.

Fig. 2.8/Letter of refusal.

Components

Let us now take a closer look at letters. Specifically, we are now ready to examine the *parts* of a business letter. We realize that some view this aspect as "mere mechanics," or as "elementary." Perhaps you are already sufficiently knowledgeable about the subject; if so, you may wish to skip this section or, perhaps, to quickly review it. We recognize, too, that many organizations have detailed "style manuals" or guides concerning component requirements. Certainly you should be able to judge whether the guidelines are what they ought to be—whether they are up-to-date, whether they are proper, whether they fit the firm's real communication needs, and whether they need improvement. Remember, this book is meant to help you judge and to be sensitive to the organization's communication, as well as to be a better communicator yourself.

For those who want to learn in this light, we present a concise (but what we think is a very useful), overview of letter components, one which can help you to improve your organization's and your personal communication.

In Figure 2.9 you can see nine basic items and six situational notations that may be included in a business letter.

Basic Items	Situational Notations
1. Letterhead	1. Mailing
2. Date	2. Attention
3. Address	3. Reference
4. Salutation	4. Enclosure
5. Message	5. Carbon copy
6. Complimentary closing	6. Postscript
7. Signature area	
8. Signer's identity	
9. Typist's identity	

Fig. 2.9 / Letter components.

Figures 2.10 through 2.18 show each basic item in order, including a brief description and illustration, and, in some cases, a specimen reference.

Figure 2.19 lists the possible uses of situation notations together with reference to specimen numbers of letters which illustrate usage.

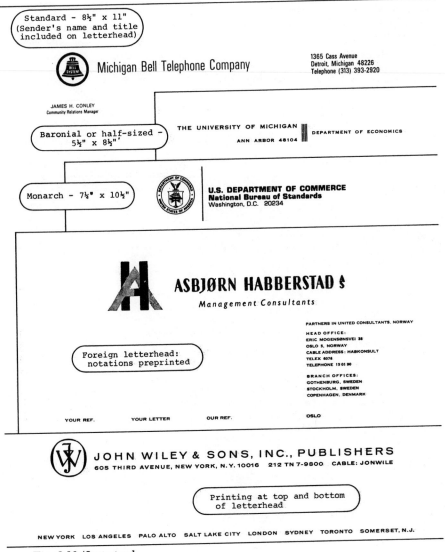

Fig. 2.10 / Letterhead.

	DATE	
Sequence		Specimen No.
(a) Traditional	(a) June 12, 19—	2
(b) Government or European	(b) 12 June 19—	16
Placement		
(a) Pure block: flush with left margin	(a)	5
(b) Centered	(b)	2
(c) Aligned with closing	(c)	22
(d) Optional: aligned to end at right margin; aligned with letterhead printing	(d)	28
(e) None: often used for pre-printed mailings which go out at different times		39

Fig. 2.11 / Date.

ADDRESS	
(a) Three lines; no street address	(a) Mr. William S. Miller Spencer, Transylvania 54321
(b) Three lines with street address	(b) Mr. William S. Miller 1200 Central Avenue Spencer, Transylvania 54321
(c) Four lines: name, company, complete address	(c) Mr. William S. Miller Star-X 1200 Central Avenue Spencer, Transylvania 54321
(d) Five lines, name, full title, company name, address	(d) Dr. William S. Miller Dean of Students City University 400 College Street University Park, Nohio 98765
(e) Foreign address	(e) Copenhagen School of Business 10, Jul. Thomsens Plads DK-1925 Copenhagen V DENMARK
(f) Special forms	(f) See note under "Salutation"

Fig. 2.12 / Address.

SALUTATION	
(a) Individual	(a) Dear Mr. Miller
	Dear Miss Thomas
	Dear Mrs. Thomas
	Dear Ms. Thomas
	Dear Bill
	Dear Verna
(b) Organization	(b) Gentlemen
	Ladies
(c) Mass distribution	(c) varies
(d) Simplified	(d) None; see Specimen 6

Note: Public officials, the clergy, the military, and other professional persons often require special forms of salutation (which may also include a unique mode of address). A comprehensive listing of accepted types may be found in unabridged dictionaries such as *Webster's New International Dictionary.* Many abridged dictionaries have abbreviated versions.

Fig. 2.13 / Salutation.

MESSAGE
See "Style and Appearance" and
"Special Communication Features"

Fig. 2.14 / Message.

COMPLIMENTARY CLOSING

Types

(a) Formal	(a)	Yours very truly, Very truly yours,
(b) Less formal	(b)	Sincerely, Sincerely yours, Yours very sincerely,
(c) More personal and friendly	(c)	Cordially, Cordially yours, Yours very cordially,
(d) To show great respect	(d)	Respectfully, Respectfully yours, Very respectfully yours,
(e) Simplified	(e)	None; see Specimen 6

Placement

Specimen No.

(a) Pure block; flush
   with left margin
(a)   5

(b) Aligned with date
(b)   22

(c) Two signatures
(c)   48

(d) Not aligned with
   date but typed
   in area between
   center and
   right margin
(d)   19

Fig. 2.15 / Complimentary closing.

SIGNATURE AREA

Types

(a) Formal

(b) Informal

(c) Initials (by some
not considered in good
taste; however, often
used on copy for
authentication)

(a) *Robert M. Jones*

(b) *Bob*

(c) *RMJ*

Placement

Customarily, the typist will
space down 3 or 4 spaces
between closing and signer's
identity

(a) Between closing and
signer's identity

(b) Below closing (no
signer identity as
preprinted on letter-
head)

(a) Complimentary closing,
s/
Robert M. Jones

(b) Complimentary closing,
s/

Fig. 2.16 / Signature area.

SIGNER'S IDENTITY

Types

(a) Name

(b) Name
  Title (unless part
  of letterhead)

(c) Name
  Title, department
  (unless part of
  letterhead)

(d) Company name
  Name, title

(f) None: preprinted
  on letterhead

(a) Robert M. Jones
  (Mrs.) Gerald P. Thomas
  (Miss) Verna N. Thomas
  (Ms.) Verna N. Thomas

(b) Robert M. Jones
  Vice President
  Robert M. Jones, Dean

(c) Robert M. Jones
  Manager
  Service Department
  (Mrs.) Gerald P. Thomas
  Dean, School of Art

(d) Star-X Hotel, Inc.
  Robert M. Jones
  Credit Manager

Placement

Generally parallel with complimentary closing

Fig. 2.17 / Signer's identity.

TYPIST'S IDENTITY

None: see Specimen 8 (official business) and 7 (personal)

ti	R.M. Jones/ti
TI	RMJ/ti
RMJ:TI	rmj/ti
rmj:ti	RMJ:3

Fig. 2.18 / Typist's identity.

SITUATIONAL NOTATIONS

Mailing	Specimen No.	Enclosure	Specimen No.
Certified Mail	75	Enclosure	50
Personal	31	Enclosures	38
Air Mail	24	Encl.	28
Special Delivery	70	Encl: 2	6
Registered Mail		Encs.	37
(used when mailing		2 Enclosures	28
valuables—stocks,		Enclosure(s):	24
money, etc.)		Item(s)	

Attention		Carbon copy	
Attention: Position	32	Copy to Donald B. Thompson	32
		CC: Donald B. Thompson	38
Attention of Mr. Miller	19	cc: Donald B. Thompson	

Reference		bcc: Donald B. Thompson	
Subject	19	(noted on copy to recipient;	
Re	60	not on original letter)	

Reference	2	Postscript	
Preprinted (See		P.S.	18
Figure 2.10, foreign		May be used to add an	
letterhead)		afterthought (often hand-	
		written by sender); more	
		commonly used to give	
		special emphasis to a major	
		point of the letter.	

Fig. 2.19 / Situational notations.

Styles and Appearance

Having considered the several parts, we are now ready to see how they fit together, how they are shaped, and how they appear as output. It is clear that even though you know all letter parts, their relationship to one another and their appropriate usage can make or break a business letter.

Once more, many firms or agencies prescribe formats and configurations of correspondence (e.g., government agencies). However, as stated before, this review can help you to judge the adequacy or inadequacy of these requirements, as well as the what and how of any needed improvements.

Figures 2.20 through 2.24 show five different commonly used styles of letter format: full block, modified block, semiblock, official business, and personal business. Figure 2.25 shows the use of a distinctive style format. Note: the

LETTERHEAD

June 12, 19--

Mr. William S. Miller
Spencer,
Transylvania 54321

Dear Mr. Miller:

This is an example of a letter typed using a full block
style (sometimes called pure block).

As you can see, all lines are flush with the left margin
so there is no need to indent. The lack of indentation
will increase a typist's speed. The left margin may be
aligned with the letterhead printing; or, if the letter
is short, it may be centered beneath the letterhead so
that the typing is spaced equally between the edges of
the stationery.

The components included in this letter are letterhead,
date, address (three lines, no street address), a salutation (formal), message, complimentary closing (formal),
signature area, the signer's identity, the typist's
identity, and copy and postscript notations.

Yours very truly,

Robert M. Jones
Manager

RMJ:ti
Copy to Mr. D.B. Thompson

P.S. The full block can also be used in the simplified
letter style, except that there is no salutation or
complimentary closing. Furthermore, the sender's identity
is typed in caps and only the typist's initials appear
(see Specimen 6).

Fig. 2.20 / Full block.

LETTERHEAD

June 12, 19--

Personal

Mr. William S. Miller
1200 Central Avenue
Spencer, Transylvania   54321

Dear Bill:

Here you see an example of a letter using the modified block
style--sometimes referred to as blocked.

Except for the date, complimentary closing, and signature
line, all lines are flush with the left margin. The date
is centered under the letterhead printing; the closing and
signature lines are aligned to end at the right margin.
These three components could have been aligned vertically
--all to parallel the letterhead printing or to end at the
right margin.

The components included are letterhead, date, mailing
notation (which would also be noted on the envelope),
address, salutation (informal) message, complimentary
closing (personal), signature area, signer's identity, and
typist's identity.

                                        Cordially yours,

                                        Robert M. Jones

RMJ/TI

Fig. 2.21/Modified block.

LETTERHEAD

June 12, 19--

Dr. William S. Miller
Professor of Management
City University
University Park, Nohio 98765

Dear Professor Miller:

This letter is typed using a semiblock style, very
frequently referred to as a modified block with indented
paragraphs.

The address and salutation are aligned with the left
margin, as is the typist's identity. The date, closing,
and signer's identity end at the right margin. The paragraphs are indented five spaces.

Components included are letterhead, date, address,
salutation, message, closing, signature area, sender's
identity, typist's identity, and enclosure notation.

Sincerely yours,

Robert M. Jones
Dean

rmj/ti
Enc.

Fig. 2.22 / Semiblock.

LETTERHEAD

June 12, 19--

Dear Judge Miller:

   Official business letters are often used in writing
letters of personal congratulations or thanks. This
style is particularly useful when one wishes to ask a
public official, president of an organization, or member
of the clergy to give a speech.

   The main difference is that the address is to the
left and below the signer's identity and not between the
date and salutation, as is shown in the other styles.
The overall style of this letter is semiblock; a modified
block could also be used.

   Components included are letterhead, date, salutation,
message, closing, signature area, signer's identity, and
address of receiver. The typist's identity is not shown
in this letter, but this is optional on the part of the
sender.

                              Sincerely,

                              Robert M. Jones

The Honorable William S. Miller
Judge of the District Court
1200 Central Avenue
Spencer, Transylvania 54321

Fig. 2.23 / Official business.

300 South Main Street
Widespot, Texakana 24680
June 12, 19--

Mr. William S. Miller
1200 Central Avenue
Spencer, Transylvania 54321

Dear Mr. Miller:

The personal business letter is very often used by those
wishing to write a business letter but who do not have
letterhead stationery.

The return address of the sender and the date appear in
the upper right corner. The rest of the letter, in this
instance, is modified block; any of the other styles could
be used.

Components included are return address (in lieu of letterhead), date, address, salutation, message, closing,
signature area, signer's identity, and enclosure notation
(with specific description). The typist's identity is
not necessary if the sender has typed the letter himself.

Sincerely yours,

Robert M. Jones

Enc: Order form
     Check ($25.00)

Fig. 2.24 / Personal business.

LETTERHEAD

Gentlemen:

Distinctive style (sometimes called "hanging indentation")
      is used to draw special attention to the layout of
      the letter and particularly to the first few words
      in each paragraph.

Generally limited to sales and promotion letters, this
      unusual format does attract the reader's attention
      because of its unique use of indentation. However,
      the different style is not too often palatable to
      those wishing a more conventional mode.

Components included in this "mass distribution" letter
      are letterhead, salutation, message, complimentary
      closing, and sender's identity.

                         Sincerely yours,

                         STAR-X AUTOMOBILE SALES

Fig. 2.25 / Distinctive.

message of each letter points out the salient features of the style being illustrated.

Appearance plays a very important part in the impression a letter makes on the receiver. Figure 2.26 is a checklist of important questions and suggestions for action.

Special Communication Features

Letters can be viewed many ways, but a useful classification is:

Nonroutine
Routine—prepared parts
Routine—complete
Mass distribution

Some letters may fit into more than one category as we shall see.

We can use the previous figures to illustrate types; we shall also refer to some specimens for further exemplification.

Nonroutine letters are the most frequently used in the majority of organizations. Essentially these are *situational,* that is, directed to a given person (or

APPEARANCE CHECKLIST

Questions	Suggestions
1. Are names and addresses accurate?	Verify with related correspondence, file, person making assignment, dictator of letter, or appropriate directory.
2. Are spelling, word division, and punctuation correct throughout?	Consult dictionary, company style manual, or appropriate reference (e.g., glossary for technical terms).
3. Are all dates and days correct? (E.g., is Wednesday, July 23, actually a Wednesday? Are referenced dates accurate?)	Check calendar, persons, or related documents. Don't guess!
4. Is the meaning of the letter clear?	If not, substitute words or revise message until exact.
5. Is paragraphing arranged for both appearance and reading ease?	If not, reshape.
6. Is style proper and consistent?	Refer to company style manual, previous correspondence, or a reputable style guide.
7. Do mechanical errors stand out?	Clean up sloppy typing, corrections, strikeovers, and obvious flaws.
8. Where needed, is special handling indicated (on letter and envelope) and carried out?	Check situation; follow through.
9. Where needed, are copies and enclosures properly indicated and distributed?	Check letter, related documents, sender, and follow through.

10. *Above all:* Remember that the sender's signature means official approval, in other words, that *he* is responsible for the product and its consequences. Act accordingly.

Fig. 2.26 / Appearance checklist.

persons) to meet a specific purpose in a unique circumstance. Figure 2.5 (a student complaint about his suspension) and Figure 2.7 (confirming a reservation and answering special questions) are examples.

The major advantages of this letter type are obvious: it can be tailored to meet the exact needs of the situation at hand. This leads to the second advantage: you can, with competent communication, get predictably good results. But there is a basic disadvantage: they are the most costly per unit, because each takes more resources per letter (more time to plan, compose, and carry out, plus additional clerical transcription and processing) than do the other three.

Moreover, it goes without saying that this type requires competent communicators, something not always existent throughout an organization. All the principles of written communication presented in this book bear upon letters of this sort.

Routine—prepared parts refers to letters that have "canned" paragraphs or sections that may be put together to handle a variety of frequent, anticipated situations. In essence, they are "packaged" form letters. An example of this type can be seen in Figure 2.3 (answer to an inquiry about university programs). Both paragraphs are already written and numbered (in this instance numbers 3 and 15 respectively) in the Admissions Office Manual. The Director merely indicates on a "buck slip" which paragraphs are to be used and in what order, which is then given to a secretary for typing. Specimens 2 and 69 are also examples.

Routine—prepared parts letters are advantageous to handle efficiently many anticipated *similar* situations. They are quickly "composed" and processed, reducing per unit costs. However, disadvantages are several, the most important of which are (1) that the situation confronted may not fit the circumstances for which the parts are prepared and assembled; (2) that, if parts are not competently written and skillfully assembled, these letters may not meet their intended purposes, and indeed they may do irreparable damage; and (3) that, unless judiciously written and used, they may be perceived as nothing more than a typical "form letter," something most readers will resent (especially if they are expecting a *personal* letter).

Routine—complete letters are those prepared as units to handle the most common important anticipated situations. These are true form letters in that they are complete communications, already planned to handle recurring circumstances, conditions, or problems. They may be already produced and ready for filling in names, dates, and the like; or they may be already composed (and put in a manual or file), then typed or reproduced as the occasion arises. Figure 2.2 is an example (a student soliciting information through a questionnaire from fifty graduate schools of business, all of which were sent the same letter). Figure 2.6 is also this type (letter of collection automatically sent to members whose expiration dates exceed one month). Figure 2.8 is an example of an already-composed, typed-for-the-occasion form letter (letter turning down a request for hotel reservation). Specimens 9 and 12 also exemplify routine—complete letters.

Form letters of this type are advantageous in that (1) they are less costly per unit than even the routine—prepared parts, because they can be produced in economical volumes; (2) they can be quickly and easily dispatched. Properly planned, composed, produced, and distributed, these letters can be real communication assets.

Disadvantages are similar to those discussed in routine—prepared parts. There is an even greater hazard here in that (1) if care and competence are not exercised, complete form letters may be used for conditions for which they were not designed; (2) if not carefully controlled and managed, correspondence of this type can become outdated or inapplicable due to policy, procedure or personnel changes. Thus, the management of routine—complete letters is of utmost importance.

Mass distribution letters are, of course, "form" letters in that they are already prepared for distribution. Therefore they partake of the qualities described in the prior group. However, as we use the term, they differ in that they are "broadcast" rather than "drilled." In other words, broad segments or groups (rather than individuals as such) are the objects of communication. We grant that these can overlap with routine—complete, and it is not our intent to make a hard and fast distinction between the two. However, the general characteristics differ: the routine—complete is addressed to people as persons; the mass distribution letter is sent to segments or groups, the individual entering in only as a member (e.g., name and address) in that group. Figure 2.1 (mailing to a customer group about a special sale) and Figure 2.4 (solicitation of contributions from fraternity members) are clear examples of mass distribution.

The advantages of mass distribution mailings are obvious: (1) they are the least costly (monetarily) per unit because they can be produced in volumes geared to the number of intended readers; (2) they can be distributed economically, both within and outside the firm. Normal channels can be employed internally, whether existing mail services, distribution to managerial heads for departmental dissemination, or even pickup by employees. External mailings can be second or third class, rather than the more costly first class; furthermore, (3) uniformity and timeliness of message to a large readership can be assured. These are the more important assets.

However, mass distributions entail some real risks that you should remember: (1) they can be very costly psychologically. At best they are still seen by most receivers as "form letters," or "junk" mail, resulting in negative impact. You may be surprised how many are discarded without ever being read or, if "read," only cursorily. For example, a great number of letters from a "philanthropic" or "service" organization soliciting contributions may engender receiver hostility because a perceptive reader wonders what proportion of monetary returns are being spent on the generation, processing, and distribution of the "junk" solicitations as opposed to that going to the charitable purpose. Our experience indicates that upwards of one-half of the total returns may be spent on the mail alone. This does not include all other administrative costs that go into the whole operation. In any event, both psychological and monetary costs can be high indeed. This negative impact can result from both internal and external mass distribution documents; (2) they can result in suboptimal performance or response. This grows out of the first liability. Even though superbly written, if readers ignore or misunderstand messages because they do not (or carelessly) read mass distribution letters, less-than-adequate results are built in; (3) they can make for *ultimate higher costs* (if results 1 and 2 obtain). It is clear why this can be true: the costs of "cleaning up messes" made by inappropriate or poorly executed mass distribution letters. This should give you pause before you decide to use them. If not properly handled, both monetary and psychological costs can be enormous, and the costs of repairing the damage may be beyond calculation.

Summary Chart: Types of Letters

Figure 2.27 summarizes the four types of letters, together with their uses, advantages, and disadvantages.

TYPE	USE	ADVANTAGES	DISADVANTAGES
Nonroutine	Nonroutine cases Special situations Important occasions	1. Can meet exact situational needs 2. Can produce predictably good results	1. Most costly per unit 2. Requires competent communicators
Routine— Prepared Parts	Anticipated partially similar situations	1. Can be packaged to handle specific differences 2. Can be processed and distributed quickly and economically 3. Less costly than nonroutine	1. May not fit situation 2. May not meet intended purpose 3. May be seen as "form" letters

Fig. 2.27 / Summary—types of letters.

Fig. 2.27 (continued)

Routine—Complete	Anticipated essentially similar situations	1. Less costly than routine—prepared parts 2. Can be dispatched quickly, easily	1. Same as routine—prepared parts, plus 2. May be used for wrong conditions 3. Can become outdated or inapplicable
Mass Distribution	Uniform messages to broad readership groups	1. Least costly per unit 2. Economical distribution 3. Can assure message uniformity and timeliness	1. Can result in high psychological costs 2. Can produce suboptimal performance/response 3. Can produce ultimate higher costs to repair damages

EXERCISES

exercise 1 Using the letter checklist, fill in appropriate items for specimens indicated. (Specimen 2 is done as a guide for your completion of the other five.)

LETTER CHECKLIST

	Spec. 2	Spec. 5	Spec. 8	Spec. 12	Spec. 20	Spec. 84
Letter Style						
Full block						
Modified block						
Semiblock	√					
Official business						
Personal business						
Distinctive						
Basic Items						
Letterhead	√					
Date	√					
Address	√					
Salutation	√					
Message	√					
Comp. closing	√					
Signature area	√					
Signer's iden.	√					
Typist's iden.	√					
Situational Notations						
Mailing						
Attention						
Reference	√					
Enclosure						
Copy						
Postscript						

exercise 2 Using the Communication Quality Control checklist as a guide, rate each of the six letters listed in exercise 1.

exercise 3 From your analyses in exercise 2, rewrite one of the specimens judged unsatisfactory or marginal in one or more of the *Letter Dimensions*.

exercise 4 From exercise 1, rewrite one of the specimens judged unsatisfactory or marginal in one or more of the *Basic Dimensions*.

exercise 5 Using the Communication Quality Control sheet, rate Specimen 31. In light of your analysis, rewrite the letter, using a different, but appropriate, letter style.

exercise 6 Using a different letter style for each, rewrite Figures 2.2, 2.3, and 2.5. Include all necessary letter components. In planning and rewriting, you may use the Communication Quality Control sheet as a guide.

CASE PROBLEMS

1. Re: Figure 2.4. As a member of the fraternity, you have received this letter from the national office. (If you are female substitute sorority.) The letter antagonizes you for several reasons:

(1) Both local and national fees were recently increased 25%;

(2) During the last year, you feel that the organization's national newsletter has degenerated in coverage and quality of reporting;

(3) You feel that recent local chapter business meetings have been nothing more than drinking social occasions;

(4) You have heard that last month two local chapter officers went on a so-called business trip (paid for by the local chapter), but that it was nothing more than a personal pleasure junket.

Your Mission: Based on the facts and your feelings, write to the national president (William S. or Wilma S. Miller) to express your opposition to the solicitation of special contributions and to the poor state of both national and local units. Make the letter positive and constructive—not a diatribe. You also want the local chapter president (Donald S. Thompson or Verna N. Thomas) to know your feelings, so you will send him (or her) a copy of your letter. Use an appropriate style and include necessary letter components; use the Letter Communication Quality Control to check your final product.

2. Re: Figure 2.5. Assume that you are Dean Miller, and that you have received this letter from Robert M. Jones. You again discuss the case with Dean Thompson and the Academic Standards Committee and all reaffirm the original decision to suspend Jones. Furthermore, investigation confirms that Jones' suspension was correct and that his allegations concerning university "promises" have no foundation.

Your Mission: Based on the facts, write a letter to Jones reaffirming his suspension. Avoid further antagonizing of Jones, but make the "no" message clear. Also, since you want the case closed, write the letter so as to shut off further communications from him about this subject. Use an appropriate style and include necessary letter components; use the Letter Communication Quality Control to check final product.

LETTER

Communication Quality Control

Explanatory key

U—**Unsatisfactory:** Major correction(s) needed

M—**Marginal:** Minor correction(s) needed

S—**Satisfactory:** No corrections needed

Needed Corrections: If marginal or unsatisfactory, note incorrect items or inappropriate usages.

Letter Dimensions	U	M	S	Needed Corrections
Purpose: propriety/ clarity				
Components				
Style and Appearance				
Special communication features: propriety/adequacy				

Basic Dimensions	U	M	S	Needed Corrections
Clarity (See Chapter 15)				
Correctness (See Chapter 16)				
Persuasiveness (See Chapter 17)				

Chapter 3

INDIVIDUALLY ORIENTED MEDIA: MEMORANDA

Your Learning Objectives:

1. To know the definition of a memorandum.
2. To know some common purposes of memoranda in organizations.
3. To know how to recognize memorandum purposes.
4. To know basic components of memoranda.
5. To know optional items and situational notations of memoranda.
6. To know how to identify different basic components, optional items, and situational notations.
7. To know how to use the different components, optional items, and notations.
8. To know how to check memorandum appearance for maximum effectiveness.
9. To know different receiver types and uses.
10. To know different sender types and uses.
11. To know how to present proper memorandum subject statements.
12. To know how to present communicative memorandum messages.
13. To know how to use a checklist for ready, accurate analysis of memorandum components, optional items, and notations.
14. To know how to use a checklist for ready, valid analysis of memorandum communication quality.

Now that we have studied letters, the most common managerial internal-external written medium, let us turn to memoranda.

Memoranda are *essentially internal letters*. As mentioned before, letters are used internally for special occasions (e.g., holiday greetings to employees from the President; commendations from the boss to workers for jobs well done). In a broad sense, such letters could be classed as memoranda. However, this correspondence usually is issued in letter style and appearance in order to achieve a more personal impact.

Certain memoranda may also be circulated outside the company. For example, a sales manager may answer a complaining customer by letter. However, in order to give the complaining customer evidence that he has taken affirmative action, the sales manager may also enclose a copy of the memo he wrote to the production chief about the alleged poor quality of the company product.

However, the essential focus of memoranda is in-house. Let us now look at some possible purposes.

Common Purposes

Among the more frequent memoranda purposes are: (1) transmittals, (2) policies, (3) procedures, (4) reports, (5) confirmations, (6) recommendations, (7) commendations or reprimands, and (8) special situations. As you shall see, sometimes a single memorandum will include more than one purpose. A detailed treatment is given to memoranda and other media purposes in Chapters 7 to 9.

Let us now turn to examples of the foregoing purposes. Note: Raise your own questions about the communication quality of each memorandum (using basic principles from Part IV); later in the chapter, we shall analyze special communication features of selected memoranda. An example of a *transmittal* memo (transmittal of a booklet on the objectives of a government agency) is seen in Figure 3.1. Actually, it can be considered a combination of *transmittal* and *policy* in that "objectives" are synonymous with "basic policies" for this agency. In Figure 3.2 you see another combination of transmittal and policy, except that this memo highlights the policy (law) within the transmittal document and its implications for the organization.

SUBJECT: Booklet

The new booklet on our organization's objectives has just come off the press. We are sending you this copy for your information. You are sure to find much of real interest in it. Later your Division Director will hold staff meetings to answer questions and to clarify any points you want discussed.

Fig. 3.1 / Memorandum—transmittal.

SUBJECT: Hiring Policy

In line with the attached newly enacted Equal Opportunity Employment Law, the Company will hire people soley on merit. No applicant will be turned down because of race, riligion or sex. The attached directive spells out this policy in detail.

While equal opportunity employment has been an understood policy of the Company for many years, this makes the practice official.

Routine: William Miller _____   John Browne _____
         Donald Thompson _____   Julian Williams _____
         Verna Thomas _____   Copy to all
                                    Department Heads

Fig. 3.2 / Memorandum—transmittal and policy.

Specimens 45, 66, and 79 also illustrate policy memoranda.

A *change in procedures* is the subject of Figure 3.3 (change of due dates for monthly financial reports).

Introduction of a *new procedure* is shown in Figure 3.4 (requirement of safety hats and reports on work-related accidents).

See Specimen 57 for another memorandum suggesting a change in procedure (screening job applicants).

Examples of *memo reports* are shown in Figures 3.5 (production report) and 3.6 (report on accident rate increase).

Specimens 80 and 88 also exemplify memo reports.

Confirmations generally are followups to prior communications (e.g., oral agreements; for the record summaries of meetings) of which Figure 3.7 is an example.

SUBJECT: Monthly Financial Report

In order to plan and control more effectively our Divisional budget allocations, I would like you to get the Monthly Financial Report to my office by the 15th, rather than the present 22nd, of the month date. I know this will mean a change in your procedures, and if you need any additional people to help, I'll make necessary arrangements.

This will permit us to make more optimal shifts of resources in light of changing conditions. I'll certainly appreciate your cooperation in meeting the new deadline.

Fig. 3.3 / Memorandum—change in procedure.

SUBJECT: New Safety Procedure

We have had a 45% increase in on-the-job accidents during last year as opposed to the preceding year. Over one-half (24%) of these accidents have resulted in head injuries, some very serious.

Effective immediately all production personnel (including supervisors and foremen) shall wear safety hats on the job. I expect each of you to see that all workers under your supervision comply with this new procedure.

Furthermore, I want weekly reports on accidents in your divisions, with special notes on those resulting in head injuries.

If this new procedure does not result in a significant decrease in head injuries, we shall be forced to take further action.

Fig. 3.4/Memorandum—new procedure.

SUBJECT: Increased Output

I am glad to report that our total production output increased 75 units in April over March. Even more gratifying, we did this in spite of the two-day shutdown of the production line because of the power failure caused by the April storm. Let's keep this momentum!

Fig. 3.5/Memorandum report.

FROM THE DESK OF ROBERT JONES

Traffic Manager

Bill,

I'm sorry to say that we had an increase of more than 10% in traffic accidents for the first six months of this year against the same period last year. Totals were 68 for the first half of this year as opposed to 60 for the same period last year.

I don't know why this increase occurred. However, I'm studying the situation and I'll let you know as soon as possible what I find and what I plan to do.

Bob

Fig. 3.6/Memorandum report.

SUBJECT: Highlights of November 25 Staff Meeting

After much discussion we agreed that:

1. The Department will appoint a task force to study possible untapped markets.
2. Our advertising and promotion activities will be carefully reviewed by the Advertising Director and me.
3. The Department will hold weekly meetings for the next two months (Wednesdays, 2:00 to 4:00 p.m.) to review our whole sales effort and how we can improve it.

If I have left out something or if my notes do not accurately reflect what we agreed to, let me know right away.

Fig. 3.7 / Memorandum—confirmation.

Specimen 74 (putting in writing the conditions of a prior agreement on termination of employment) is another example of a memo of confirmation.

Recommendations as memos are very common. Figure 3.8 is an example of a manager recommending personnel for a training course.

SUBJECT: Candidates for Management Development Seminar

I appreciate your note concerning the management seminar to be given in September. In line with your request, I would like to see the following persons from our Department attend: Donald Thompson, Publicity; Verna Thomas, Customer Relations.

Fig. 3.8 / Memorandum—recommendation.

Specimen 23 is an example of self-recommendation (for a higher company position) in memo form; Specimen 33 concerns recommendations for reshaping responsibilities of two departments (computer and controller's office) for better coordination and control.

Commendation is represented in Figure 3.9; a not-so-polite *reprimand* can be seen in Specimen 78.

SUBJECT: Your article: *Professional Quarterly,* June

Yours was an excellent presentation, Bill. I consider myself knowledgeable on the subject, but your exposition of what is needed to assure a successful total organizational communication system opened my eyes to things I've never even thought about. Congratulations on a job well done!

Fig. 3.9 / Memorandum—commendation.

Figure 3.10 is a double-purpose memo in that it solicits some annual reports from company employees, but it is also a polite reprimand (note the last sentence).

SUBJECT: Annual Report Collection

If you are about to throw away those annual reports received from other companies, please don't. Bring or send them to the Library. We are trying to build up our collection. We are also trying to replace some which have a habit of walking out of your Library.

Fig. 3.10 / Memorandum—solicitation and reprimand.

Special situations (e.g., one-of-a-kind, one-time, important events) are also frequently communicated via memo. Figure 3.11 shows a one-of-a-kind situation.

SUBJECT: Research Technicians

Last Wednesday I talked with the Comptroller, Donald Thompson, concerning the problem resulting from his cutting us back on funds for hiring the three new Research Technicians. I explained to him our problems in having already offered three persons jobs and that all three had accepted. While he wasn't happy, he asked that we send him their names and he would take care of us. He apologized for his delay in getting the word to us on the budget decrease, but he said that unexpected circumstances had arisen which prevented earlier confirmation of allocations. In any event, I would appreciate your sending him immediately the names of these three people so that he will have official notification to act. Thanks.

Fig. 3.11 / Memorandum—special situations.

Specimen 35 (communicating a discrepancy in the printing of a schedule) is an example of a one-time situation. Specimens 30 and 40 exemplify important situations.

We have now examined the nature of memoranda and some common purposes for which used. Let us now turn to other dimensions of memoranda: components and appearance.

Components and Appearance

We shall consider memoranda components and appearance together in this single section. First we shall discuss components, followed by a succinct, easy-to-use "Appearance Checklist."

As with letters, if you feel that you already know about memoranda components and appearance, you may wish to go ahead to "Special Communication Features" (or to quickly review what we discuss here).

Remember that memoranda are "internal" letters, therefore many principles given in Chapter 2 apply to them. We shall focus here primarily on differences. Figure 3.12 sets out essential memoranda components. Figures 3.13 through 3.19 show and explain each item in order, including figure references in some instances.

Figure 3.20 then presents the appearance checklist to which we alluded before.

MEMORANDA COMPONENTS		
Basic Items	**Optional Items**	**Situational Notations**
1. Stationery	1. Typist's Identity	1. Processing
2. Date	2. Signature	2. Enclosure
3. Receiver's Identity	3. Signer's Identity	3. Carbon Copy
4. Sender's Identity		
5. Subject Statement		
6. Message		

Fig. 3.12 / Memoranda components.

Special Communication Features

Well-written memoranda embody most principles, procedures, and practices of good letters. However, because they are essentially directed to organization membership, and because their generation and processing must fit a given company's missions and traditions, memoranda should always be written with your firm's (not some communication expert's) demands in mind.

But there are some general guidelines that can produce better written memos, as well as their better utilization, within any organization. Let us focus on some essential memorandum parts as our discussion sequence: (1) *to* whom written, (2) *from* whom sent, (3) *subject* statement, and (4) *message* sent.

To Whom Written

This is most often the first major item in a memo, and, of course, refers to the document's receiver or receivers.

Receivers can be designated in several ways: a single name; two or more

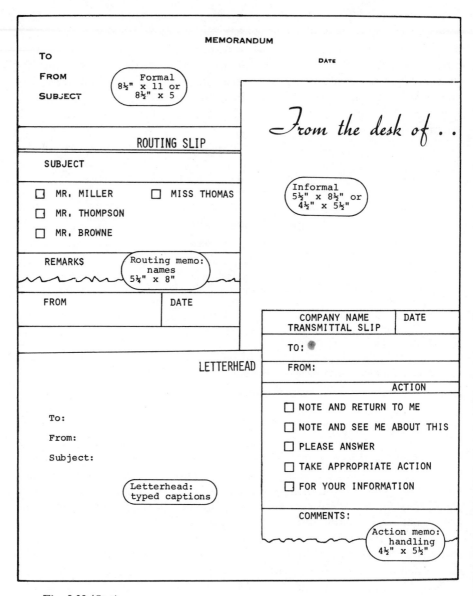

Fig. 3.13 / Stationery.

Date	
(a) Traditional	(a) June 12, 19—
(b) Government	(b) 12 June 19—
(c) Informal (often used	(c) 6/12/—
in handwritten notes)	

Fig. 3.14 / Date.

Receiver's Identity	
(a) Name	(a) William S. Miller
(b) Name, position	(b) William S. Miller, President
(c) Name, position, department	(c) William S. Miller, Manager,
or division	Sales Department
(d) Name, position, department	(d) William S. Miller, Manager,
or division, address	Sales Department,
	Building "C"
(e) Position, department	(e) Manager, Service Department
(f) Division or department	(f) Payroll Office
(g) General	(g) All Employees; Department
	and Division Heads

Fig. 3.15 / Receiver's identity.

Sender's Identity	
(a) Name	(a) Robert M. Jones
(b) Name, position	(b) Robert M. Jones, Director
(c) Name, position, department	(c) Robert M. Jones, Director,
or division	Personnel Office
(d) Position, department	(d) Director of Personnel
(e) Department or division	(e) Payroll Department

Fig. 3.16 / Sender's identity.

Subject	Statement
(a) General	(a) Personnel Policies
(b) Specific	(b) Termination of Donald B. Thompson
(c) None	

Fig. 3.17 / Subject of memorandum.

Message
Placement Determined largely by pre-printed memo or letterhead format; two common styles are:
(a) Left-margin block (e.g., Specimens 1, 35, 42)
(b) Indented (e.g., Specimens 11, 23)
Content
See "Special Communication Features"

Fig. 3.18 / Message of memorandum.

Optional Items	Situational Notations

1. Typist's identity
  (a) None
  (b) Same as letters:
    see Figure 2.18
	1. Processing (pre-printed instructions as shown in Figure 3.13)
	  (a) Routing: names of receivers
	  (b) Actions: necessary handling

2. Signature
Placement
  (a) None
  (b) Following sender's identity
  (c) Following message
Types
  (a) Initials
  (b) Informal
  (c) Formal
	2. Enclosure
	Same as letters:
	  see Figure 2.19

3. Signer's identity Name (and possibly position) typed following message	3. Carbon copy Same as letters: see Figure 2.19

Fig. 3.19 / Optional items and situational notations.

APPEARANCE CHECKLIST

Questions	Suggestions
1. Are names, positions, and addresses (if needed) accurate?	Verify with related correspondence or company directory.
2. Are spelling, word division, and punctuation correct throughout?	Consult dictionary, company style manual, or appropriate reference (e.g., glossary for technical terms).
3. Are all dates and days correct? (E.g., is Wednesday, July 23, actually a Wednesday? Are referenced dates accurate?)	Check calendar, persons, or related documents. Don't guess!
4. Is the meaning of the memorandum clear?	If not, substitute words or revise message until exact.
5. Are reader cues used to advantage?	If not, paragraph, underline, enumerate, or capitalize as needed.
6. Is style proper and consistent?	Refer to company style manual, previous correspondence, or a reputable style guide.
7. Do mechanical errors stand out?	Clean up sloppy typing, corrections, strikeovers, and obvious flaws.
8. Is personal delivery of memorandum necessary?	If so, follow through.
9. Where needed are copies and enclosures properly indicated and distributed?	Check memorandum, related documents, sender, and follow through.

10. *Above all:* Remember that your approval means that you are attesting to the worth and validity of the memo's ideas, in other words, that it represents your character and competence in the eyes of the receivers.

Fig. 3.20/ Memorandum checklist.

names; specific position(s); specific department(s); and "all" of a population (e.g., company employees or staff of a particular department).

Single name is addressed to one name person as the recipient: "William S. Miller," "Donald B. Thompson," or "Verna N. Thomas" are examples.

The single name is used when you are targeting one person, either because he is officially responsible for his and/or other person's actions (e.g., manager of a department or project) or because he is *the* person with whom you want to communicate about a special condition or situation.

Sometimes the receiver's title may be included along with his name (e.g., William S. Miller, Executive Vice President). In many companies, however, personnel and titles are so familiar that the name only is sufficient, especially in smaller, more intimate companies or in intradepartmental memos. Furthermore names only are most often permissible in informal situations, especially "From the Desk of" types of memoranda.

Two or more names obviously means a memo listing more than one person as recipients. Although there are exceptions, the number of receivers generally does not exceed four or five. Beyond this number, you should consider one of the succeeding modes (e.g., department or committee, possibly with copies to affected persons).

A memo to several persons may be used when you want information to reach all receivers simultaneously, when you want all concerned to know that others have received the same information or when you want "on-the-record" authentication or confirmation (e.g., prior oral agreements or summaries or meetings).

Specific position(s) is addressed to the person's (or persons') *functions* or *job* or *title*. Rather than "Mr. William S. Miller, Chief of Production" you direct the memo to "Chief of Production." If directed to plural positions, all are similarly listed.

This mode is often used when *impersonality* is the object. For example, task-oriented communications such as policies and procedures frequently exclude personal elements for an important reason: job and organizational continuity are of uppermost concern in such documents. Jobs must be done, and the company must survive apart from the presence of specific people; people come and go, but ongoing tasks and the firm remain. For this reason, impersonality is the desired tone; and addressing such memoranda by position is one way to facilitate this mood.

Specific department(s) means that the memo is targeted to one or more company units. Here, too, impersonality is most frequently the end. In addition, you may wish to focus on *unit*, rather than *individual*, responsibilities and duties. When impersonality and departmental operations are to be emphasized, this is an appropriate way to address memoranda.

All of a population refers to memoranda directed to every member in a particular unit(s) or in the entire firm. In other words, such memoranda are "mass distribution," with the same advantages and disadvantages given under letters of the same type. These should be used when all receivers should get the same information at the same time.

Purposes are many, among the more important are: circulation of directives on policy and procedure; announcements of special events; commendations for exceptional employee performance; changes of key personnel; and changes in organizational structure.

Properly used, memos of this sort are quick, convenient, and economical communication vehicles. Improperly used, they can result in organizational conflicts and upheavals that may take many hours and many dollars to overcome.

From Whom Sent

Referring to the originator(s) of the document, this is commonly the second major item in memoranda.

Although practices differ from organization to organization, the more often listed senders are: single name(s); position(s); department(s); and special group(s).

Single name(s) means the same as that discussed under *"To whom written"* —one or more named originators are listed. If the person (or persons) occupies an important position or is well known, the name only may suffice. Otherwise titles should also be included.

Again names help to personalize, and, thereby, to make memos more communicative. Care should be exercised, however, that the personality of the sender(s) is not unduly emphasized to the exclusion of the subject and message of the memorandum.

Position(s) again refers to the same dimension discussed under receivers of memos. As an originator, you should use it for the same reason: to make the memo impersonal in order to emphasize ongoing organizational activities. For the opposite caution given above, you should be sure that impersonalization and emphasis on task is what you should be communicating. If you need the persuasive impact of the personal, you should carefully consider the use of specific names of the right people.

Department(s), again, is referring to an originating unit or units within the firm. Departmental designation is important for authentication of documents affecting important segments of or the entire company. Policy, procedural, and other directive communications frequently indicate departmental origin.

As with positional designation, departmental origin is also impersonal with its possible attendant dysfunctional characteristics. In addition, care must be exercised that the originating units do have official sanction to issue the memoranda generated. This means that clear authority and responsibility must be set forth by the organization regarding the what, who, and how of departmental memoranda.

Special groups include ad hoc collectivities such as task forces, committees, and staff specialists. Generally memoranda come from special groups as reports, recommendations, inquiries, and the like. Since most are ephemeral or temporary, special groups must rely on either (1) administrative support from higher management or (2) expert influence of membership.

With adequate administrative support, the group name only may suffice. However, if expert influence is the primary leverage, then names and positions of members may also be needed.

Memoranda from special groups run several risks: (1) managerial support may be more "lip service" than real. If true, memoranda may not carry much influence with receivers who know this fact; (2) some receivers may look on such groups as "passing fancies," consequently their memoranda (even though well-written) may not produce the desired results (because receivers attach little long run importance to them); (3) if either condition 1 or 2 exists, replies to memoranda may be superficial, inaccurate, or even deliberately misleading. Why? Because respondents may merely "go through the motions" or, if opposed to a special group's mission, may select answers to sabotage its efforts; (4) often special groups must communicate with peers and superiors, with obvious hazards. It is often difficult to get desired responses to memoranda written to people at the same level or above.

All this means that designating the origin of memoranda from special groups must be carefully considered and phrased in light of the situation at hand.

Subject Statement

The third major item, subject statement, is crucial to effective memoranda. The subject statement should guide the receiver as accurately as possible to your essential memorandum message. Indeed, at times it may serve as an abbreviated thesis statement.

The best way to communicate about subject statement is by evaluation of specific cases. Therefore, let us use some figure examples discussed earlier in this chapter, starting with Figure 3.1. Note that the subject statement is "Booklet." Careful reading of the message shows this to be far too broad to guide the reader as intended. Would not a more exact statement be something like "New Booklet on Organization Objectives" or "Organization Objectives: New Booklet"?

Now turn to Figure 3.2. Read the message, then compare what you think is the subject with that given ("Hiring Policy"). Is this not another misleading subject statement? Again it needs more exactness. While there are several alternatives, something like "Equal Opportunity Hiring Policy" is a more helpful, precise guide to the reader.

Figure 3.3 is clearly deficient as are the two preceding examples. The subject statement "Monthly Financial Report" could cover a multitude of possibilities. The memo is focusing on the new due date of the report, so something similar to "New Due Date: Monthly Financial Report" would be better.

Examine Figures 3.4, 3.5, and 3.6. Are not 3.4 and 3.5 deficient in the same respects as the foregoing? However, 3.6 measures up well in stating a more exact subject so that the reader will be led to get the right message.

To repeat, the subject statement of a memorandum is key to proper reader understanding of your message. The following are general guidelines in writing it:

1. Use the fewest number of words commensurate with clarity.
2. Use words that get the reader's attention and move him to read the message.
3. Where helpful, use names, departments, dates, occasions, and other relevant detail (e.g., Figure 3.7, "Highlights of the November 25 Staff Meeting").
4. Balance generality and specificity of subject statement. In other words, your subject statement should be broad enough to cover your ideas, but at the same time precise enough to put "sideboards" on the discussion.
5. Use language appropriate to the readers. If directed to an expert in a discipline, terminology in that field can be used; however, if a "layman" or relatively unsophisticated receiver, simple nontechnical language is more appropriate. Of course, if the memo is directed to a plurality, then you select language that most (or the most influential) readers readily understand.

Message Sent

Memoranda messages conform to all sound communication principles, most of which will be treated in detail in subsequent chapters. However, there are some special features that you should bear in mind when writing memoranda:

1. Know and emphasize the *essential* message you want to communicate; confine your remarks to this. If you have adequately stated your subject, you have already given your reader the key to your basic message. As an example of subject-message mismatch, let us return to Figure 3.1. "Booklet" (the stated subject) is certainly not the intended message. Although it does not clearly emerge in the message, you can properly infer that the writer wanted receivers to *read and understand* the new booklet on the organization's objectives. In other words, the essential message actually is never really stated (much less emphasized) in this example.

On the other hand, if in Figure 3.2 the writer had more exactly stated the subject (e.g., "Equal Opportunity Hiring Policy" rather than merely "Hiring Policy"), this memorandum would emphasize the intended ideas. In this case, the writer's message is essentially clear and to the point (in spite of—not because of—the too general subject statement).

2. Organize ideas in relation to subject and situation. As a general rule, you

should organize the message as simply as possible, but do not oversimplify. Simple issues can be simply presented; complex problems may require more elaborate structure (e.g., a technical report).

Here are some general suggestions for organizing memoranda messages:

a. Determine the *basic sequence* to be used. Possibilities include time-order (for instructions), essential elements (for analysis of important issues), order of importance (for recommendations), and problem-solution (for analysis and recommendation). In some cases (e.g., simple acknowledgment), one clear, straightforward sentence may be sufficient. In this instance the *sentence sequence* (syntax) must be proper to assure communication of your intended message.

b. Use appropriate *headings* and *captions*. These are often very effective in helping your reader grasp your essential message quickly and accurately.

c. Use proper *paragraphing* and *division* of ideas. A long rambling, incoherent "paragraph" can completely confuse a memo reader. A better practice is the use of pithy, concise idea units to convey each main point.

d. Use *enumerative* (as exemplified in this section) and *typographical devices* (e.g., underlining, indentation, dingbats) to guide the reader (as exemplified in this section).

3. Use *proper language* and *tone* for the situation. This subject is discussed in depth in Chapter 17, "Principles of Persuasive Writing"; therefore we shall merely highlight some elements peculiar to memoranda.

In informal memos (e.g., "From the Desk of" types) you may almost "write as you talk," that is, use a chatty conversational style and tone (even handwritten in some cases). But in formal memoranda (official policy communications or job instructions), an impersonal style and authoritative tone are more proper. In between these extremes, you must judge how best to phrase your ideas and what mood you want to convey. Where practicable, informality and warmth should be communicated. However, in official or crucial situations, you should convey necessary seriousness, which means a sacrifice of informality for more formal language and tone.

Summary

Let us summarize special communication features in four tables (Figures 3.21 to 3.24). These summary sheets can be used as helpful checklists in evaluating, rewriting, and composing memoranda of all types.

TO WHOM WRITTEN:

Receiver	Uses
Single name	To get message to only one person To meet special conditions or situations
Two or more names	To get message to several persons To get simultaneous message receipt To let all receivers know others have same message To get authentication or confirmation
Specific position(s)	To achieve impersonality To focus on jobs and the organization
Specific department(s)	To meet conditions listed in specific positions—plus To focus on unit responsibility

All of a population	To meet most conditions of "mass
	   distribution" letters
	To circulate information bearing
	   upon all members of a given
	   segment or the entire organization

Fig. 3.21 / To whom written.

FROM WHOM SENT:

Sender	Uses	Cautions and Risks
Single name	To personalize	Avoid overemphasis on personal to exclusion of subject and message
Position(s)	To achieve impersonality To focus on organizational activities	Be sure you wish impersonality
Department(s)	To authenticate sources To make documents official in tone	Same as in "Position(s)" Be sure originating units have official sanction to issue
Special groups	To communicate objectives, activities, or output of ad hoc or temporary collectivities	Be sure managerial support is real Some receivers may perceive the special group as unimportant, causing the memos to be seen in the same light Response to group memo may be wrong/misleading Communicating with peers and superiors may be difficult

Fig. 3.22 / From whom sent.

Subject Statement—Guidelines

1. Use minimum wording consonant with clarity
2. Use words to get reader attention and to move to message
3. Use relevant detail (names, departments, dates, and occasions) where helpful
4. Balance generality and specificity in statement
5. Use language attuned to reader

Fig. 3.23 / Subject statement guidelines.

Message Sent—Guidelines

1. Know and emphasize your essential message
2. Organize ideas in relation to subject and situation
3. Use language and tone appropriate to the situation

Fig. 3.24 / Message sent guidelines.

EXERCISES

exercise 1 Using the memorandum checklist, fill in appropriate items for specimens indicated. (Specimen 23 is done as a guide for your completion of the other six.)

Memorandum Checklist

	Spec. 23	Spec. 33	Spec. 35	Spec. 42	Spec. 45	Spec. 46	Spec. 65
Basic Items Stationery	√						
Date	√						
Receiver: Name							
Name, position	√						
Name, position, dep't or div.							
Name, position, dep't or div., address							
Position, dep't							
Division or dep't							
General (all of a population							
Sender: Name							
Name, position							
Name, position, dep't or div.	√						
Position, dep't							
Division or dep't							
Subject statement	√						
Message	√						
Optional items Typist's identity							

Memorandum Checklist (continued)

	Spec. 23	Spec. 33	Spec. 35	Spec. 42	Spec. 45	Spec. 46	Spec. 65
Signature							
Signer's identity							
Situational notations Processing							
Enclosure							
Carbon copy	✓						

exercise 2 Using the Communication Quality Control sheet, rate each of the seven memoranda in exercise 1.

exercise 3 From your analyses in exercise 2, rewrite one of the specimens judged unsatisfactory or marginal in *Memorandum Dimensions*.

exercise 4 From your analyses in exercise 3, rewrite one of the specimens judged unsatisfactory or marginal in *Basic Dimensions*.

exercise 5 Using the Communication Quality Control sheet, rate Specimen 99. Rewrite it for improvement.

exercise 6 Using *formal* memorandum style, rewrite Figures 3.5, 3.6, and 3.11. Include all necessary components in your revisions.

CASE PROBLEMS

1. Re: Figure 3.2. As William S. Miller, President of the Company, you have received this memo from Robert M. Jones, Director of Personnel. While you agree with the memo's message (on abiding by the Equal Opportunity Employment law), you are concerned about misspellings in the document. In fact, you have received calls from other company officials who feel that such deficiencies detract from the memo's message and impact. You are also concerned that such errors reflect managerial carelessness, thereby damaging the image of the entire company.

Your Mission: Based on the facts and your feelings, write a memo to all department heads supporting the message of the memo, but, at the same time, pointing out the need for correct and clear communications, citing the three misspellings as an example of managerial carelessness. Use the appropriate memo style and include necessary components; use the memo Communication Quality Control to check final product.

2. Re: Figure 3.7. As William S. Miller, Sales Manager, you have received this memo from Robert M. Jones, Director of Marketing. Item 2 of the memo fails to include you in the review activities, and it was your understanding from the meeting that you were to be part of the review team.

Your Mission: Based on your understanding, write a memo to the Director of Marketing pointing out your belief that you are to be part of the review team. Try to persuade him to your viewpoint. Send a copy to the Advertising Director, Donald B. Thompson. Use the appropriate memo style and include necessary components; use the memo Communication Quality Control to check final product.

MEMORANDUM
Communication Quality Control

Explanatory key
U—**Unsatisfactory:** Major correction(s) needed
M—**Marginal:** Minor correction(s) needed
S—**Satisfactory:** No corrections needed

Needed Corrections: If marginal or unsatisfactory, note incorrect items or inappropriate usages.

Memorandum Dimensions	U	M	S	Needed Corrections
Purpose: propriety/ clarity				
Components and Appearance				
Special Communication features: propriety/adequacy				
Basic Dimensions				
Clarity (See Chapter 15)				
Correctness (See Chapter 16)				
Persuasiveness (See Chapter 17)				

Chapter 4

INDIVIDUALLY ORIENTED MEDIA: REPORTS

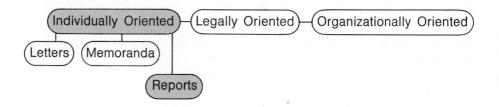

Your Learning Objectives:

1. To know the importance of reports in organizations.
2. To know the definition of written reports.
3. To know the general types of reports.
4. To know time perspectives in reports.
5. To know thinking perspectives in reports.
6. To know how to identify time and thinking perspectives in reports.
7. To know basic components of reports.
8. To know common styles of reports.
9. To know how to present verbal and graphic information in reports.
10. To know how to check appearance of graphics and tables for maximum effectiveness.
11. To know important organizational yardsticks for reports.
12. To know important planning guides for reports.
13. To know important guides for writing reports.
14. To know how to use a checklist for ready, accurate analysis of report components and styles.
15. To know how to use a checklist for ready, valid analysis of report communication quality.

Importance of Reports

We now come to reports, the final individually oriented written medium. Any experienced manager will attest to the importance of report documents. Why? Not just because they are one of his most painful daily tasks (i.e., completing ones required of him as well as interpreting and processing the multitude that cross his desk), but more important, they constitute one of the most significant vehicles for carrying crucial information for job success. Indeed the quality of reports in an organization in large measure determines the quality of the firm's operations and outputs. Why is this so? Because key managers and staff at all company levels are basically *information processors,* and their sources of the most *reliable information* are written reports *from others.*

It follows that a given manager's report *to others* (superiors, peers, subordinates) will be the inputs that influence the quality of decisions made and actions taken by them. Written reports, then, are key communication tools for the manager and the entire organization.

The Nature of Reports

What is a written report? Essentially, it is a personally oriented document that communicates one, two, or all of (1) What has happened? (2) What is happening? and (3) What will or should happen? Phrased another way, written reports are documents that convey the state or condition of past, present, or future events, relations, objects, persons, or things.

Depending on purpose and situation, reports may range from very restricted to very broad perspectives. As you can see from the definition, they can cover almost any topic or subject matter.

Furthermore, written reports can be carried by a variety of other media. Letters and memoranda, which we have already discussed, are frequent vehicles for reporting. You may well ask, "What, then, differentiates a report from a letter or memorandum?" The answer to this very pertinent question is that when letters and memoranda convey reports, they are the *carriers* of the report. When a letter is used as the carrier medium, its *body* is the actual report; when the memorandum is employed as the vehicle, the *message* is the report. Likewise, as we shall see in later chapters, brochures and forms are common carriers of reports. In other words a report can be a medium unto itself or, as is often the case, carried by other types of media. In such cases the important point to remember is that the *basic* medium is the report; other media (letter, memorandum, brochure, form) are merely convenient conveyers.

The reason we treat reports as a separate medium is that there are special types with unique formats. Let us now examine some.

General Types

Reports can be classed in numerous ways, including: internal or external; formal or informal; official or unofficial; short or long; simple or complex; routine or nonroutine; special or regular; solicited or unsolicited; and narrative or problem. Each of these categories has utility, and we shall draw upon all in our presentation.

However, here we shall focus on basic elements common to any type; these are: (1) time perspectives and (2) thinking perspectives.

Time perspectives include three foci: the past, the present, and the future. All reports are concerned with at least one, and more often, two, or all three. Let us clarify these and look at examples.

The *past* focus answers the basic question, "What happened?" It is historical in emphasis, recording events that have already taken place. Sometimes a report's basic mission is solely this; often the past is included as a part of a document with either present or future focus. Some specific report types concerned with the past are: important developments or accomplishments (e.g., meeting a special production goal), highlighting events of a given period (e.g., an annual report), background of a study or investigation (e.g., why past events are affecting present or future operations or what others have done prior to a study to be undertaken), minutes of meetings, a listing of observations made (e.g., an analyst's recording of a company's symptoms of trouble), and explanations of past events (e.g., what caused a company's sales decline).

As an example of *important developments* look at Figure 4.1. It is a report (an excerpt from a newsletter of an international education society) of both past and present events. Items 1 and 3 concern important events that have happened; item 2 focuses on a present development. Apply critical judgment to this report. Is it clear? Correct? Persuasive? (Note: Use these indices as you read all the figures and specimens included in this chapter.)

Another example of a document *highlighting yearly events* is shown in Figure 4.2 (an excerpt of an annual report to participants in an annuity-based retirement plan). In addition this report also enumerates related events that took place in preceding periods.

Background of a study is illustrated in Figure 4.3 (an excerpt from a directive sent by a company president to all department heads).

See also Specimen 109 (the section "Why The Review Was Made") as another example of background reporting.

Minutes of Meetings can be seen in Specimens 104 and 105. *Listing observations* is demonstrated in Specimen 110 (the "Symptom" section); note also that the "Problem" section of this report deals with both past and existing conditions.

Explanation of past events is exemplified in Specimen 111 (the section

EAST ASIA

1. For the first time in history, the government of the Kingdom of Thailand has authorized the development of private degree-granting colleges. Bangkok College was the first institution to apply for licensing under the new act. Applicants must be licensed by the Private College Commission to give instruction and accredited by the National Education Council to award degrees. Both academic and administrative activities of the new colleges are supervised by the National Education Council and the Ministry of Education.

2. Plans for the establishment of the Polytechnic Institute in Hong Kong are slowly moving ahead. There is great concern in Hong Kong about the failure of the educational system there to provide opportunities for higher-level technical training and for employment thereafter.

3. Hong Kong received more than 300 applications for between 15 and 20 scholarships made available by nine U.S. institutions through our Direct Placement Program. We submitted the names of 21 semi-finalists to the nine institutions.

Fig. 4.1 / Report—important developments.

"Analysis of Star-X Communications Hardware"). Note that the "Solutions" section of this report is focusing on the future.

A *present* perspective answers "What *is* happening?" In other words, it focuses on existing situations, conditions, problems, or statuses. Some important present perspectives include: explaining findings, communicating stand-

The annuity unit value, and thus the amounts received by retired participants, declined 11.0 per cent last year. A year earlier the annuity unit value had risen 8.7 per cent.

The decline in the annuitant's income during a time when consumer prices were rising at a 6 per cent annual rate must have been disappointing to those who were receiving annuity income.

The recent experience is not unique. There have been a number of periods when common stock prices fell while consumer prices were rising, as between 1916 and 1920, between 1939 and 1942, and between 1946 and 1948. It has worked the other way too, as during the upward surge in common stock prices in the 1920's, when consumer prices drifted down. And a sharp upswing in common stock prices took place between 1952 and 1965. . . .

Fig. 4.2 / Report—highlights.

Why This Management Study? Why has Star-X decided to invest $50,000 in determining its important managerial problems? These are the major reasons:

1. Last year the Company had a turnover of 35% in personnel below the supervisory level.

2. Production has levelled off during the last three years despite an investment of more than $2,000,000 in new equipment and an increase of 10% in the working force.

3. Last month our management auditor did a survey of two key departments in which he found, among other deficiencies: (1) low morale; (2) low understanding of Company objectives and purposes; and (3) low understanding of where the workers' own units fitted into the Company scheme.

. . .

Fig. 4.3 / Report—background.

---

ings or rankings, reporting problems to be solved, and giving information about a company's existing resources (men, money, materials).

An *explanation of findings* is exemplified in Figure 4.4 (an excerpt of a report on the reading habits by executives in large companies).

In Specimen 108 you can see another example of explanation of findings (note especially the last paragraph).

Communication of *rankings* is exemplified in Figure 4.5 (a memo from an Executive Vice President to Division Heads indicating weekly standings in a company-wide safety contest; standings are based on divisional percentage decreases in on-the-job accidents; that is, the division with the largest percentage from the previous week is ranked first).

Our study reveals that the rapid expansion of knowledge is burying top businessmen in an avalanche of books, pamphlets, reports and countless other written communications. Knowledge is expanding so rapidly and communications are increasing in so great numbers that the average executive cannot begin to cope with all the additional materials coming across his desk. There are two important adverse consequences: (1) more frustrated executives—because they realize their inability to process adequately all the communications they receive; and (2) more and more "outdated" executives—because they cannot keep up with all the new ideas, concepts, principles and practices so necessary to increasingly complex modern enterprises.

Fig. 4.4 / Report—explanation of findings.

SUBJECT: Safety Contest Standings

I am pleased to say that all Divisions significantly decreased accidents during this last week, resulting in important percentage decreases from the previous week. Congratulations to the Production Division for moving from second to first! Let's keep up the good work.

Division	Percentage Decrease
Production	21.2%
Maintenance	15.5%
Shipping and Receiving	10.4%
Transportation	5.1%

Fig. 4.5 / Report—rankings.

Figure 4.6 (sources of urban garbage types in rank order) is another report of this kind.

Reporting existing problems is one of the most frequently employed types. As one sample, look at Figure 4.7 (an excerpt from an analytical report concerning the writing quality of professional writers).

Another example is shown in Figure 4.8 (an excerpt from a report on management problems in a scientific organization).

Many specimens exemplify reporting existing problems, among them: 106, 107 (section "Observations"), 110, and 111.

Giving information about resources is the most commonly used present-focus report. Financial, sales, production, personnel, and systems information are

Urban Garbage

	Percent
Paper	47
Boxes—6%	
Newspapers, books,	
magazines—15%	
All other—26%	
Glass and ceramics	12
Dirt, grass, leaves	11
Food	10
Metal	10
Textiles, rubber, leather	4
Plastics	3
Wood	3
	100%

Fig. 4.6 / Report—rankings.

We analyzed sixty-five reports written by veteran technical writers from a representative sample of scientific and engineering firms. The following major problems were appallingly evident:

1. *No clear statement of purpose or problem.* In forty-four of the reports examined, we could find *no statement or other clue* which explicated what the report was supposed to communicate.

2. *Lack of discernible organization in the report proper.* In thirty-two of the reports no clear, perceptible organizational structure could be seen. True, some of the thirty-two did state a "presummary" of an intended organizational pattern, but even these did not follow through.

3. *Grammatical errors and wrong language usages.* This was the most surprising problem uncovered. In thirty-seven reports, we found a minimum of five errors (and in one, fifty-two!), even when we used the most liberal and "permissive" standards.

. . .

Fig. 4.7 / Report—existing problems.

some of the more familiar. A unique financial report (balance sheet) is British Overseas Airways Corporation's 1970 document in Figure 4.9. Rather than present additional examples of this type here, you will find a variety in Chapter 9.

A *future* report focus addresses the question, "What *should* happen?" Predictive in emphasis, it will often be preceded (or at least supported) by past and existing modes in a given report. Some significant future orientations encompass recommendations, solutions, and forecasts.

Figure 4.10 is an excerpt of a study report that ends with *recommendations.*

Our study revealed the following major weaknesses in managers at all levels: (1) a failure to understand their role *as managers.* Many understand and carry out superbly their professional responsibilities as scientists, but not as supervisors of the work of their subordinates; (2) a failure to know what other research units are supposed to do in relation to their own. Some (but not all) understand very well what is expected of their own units, but have little or no comprehension of how they relate to other Star-X entities; (3) a failure to communicate—both oral and written—with superiors, peers, and subordinates about problems both human and job. This was the most pronounced of all problems found.

Fig. 4.8 / Report—existing problems.

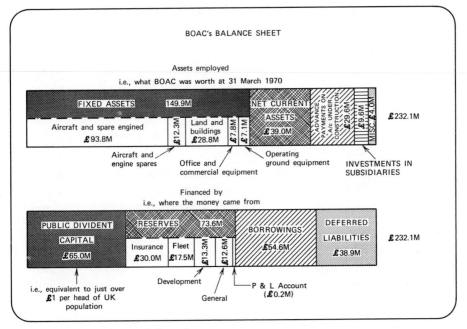

Fig. 4.9 / Report—resources information.

Before launching an international branch, we proposed that Star-X study these factors: (1) the financial capability of the firm to raise sufficient funds for the required capital investment (approximately $150,000,000). Our domestic operations should not be jeopardized because of a potential financial squeeze from spreading the Company too thinly; (2) the managerial capability of the Company to staff a major overseas operation. We have had some major managerial problems in our U.S. branches. Securing competent managers for international business can be even more difficult; (3) the market potential of the proposed international branch. The original plan gives no firm data; rather it contains only a series of sweeping generalizations about ". . . the tremendous opportunities and challenges for Star-X." This is no basis upon which to invest Company resources.

In short, much more study should be done before we make a decision to go ahead with an international branch.

Fig. 4.10 / Report—recommendations.

Specimen 107 also exemplifies recommendations (in several parts explicitly; elsewhere implicitly).

An example of *solutions* is seen in Figure 4.11 (an excerpt from a President's confidential report to the Company Board of Directors).

We are going to solve the Company's crucial problems by some specific actions: cutting all non-essential personnel; cutting our unprofitable departments and operations, emphasizing new product development; and recruiting new talent to replace our weaker managers.

I am confident these actions can result in a complete turnaround in our efficiency, effectiveness, and profitability within six months.

Fig. 4.11 / Report—solutions.

Another example is Specimen 111, an analytical report ending with solutions to deficiencies uncovered.

Forecasts are very familiar predictive reports. These are frequently statistical extrapolations as in Figure 4.12 (an excerpt from a report of a university's financial future).

Forecasts may also be more general predictions. Specimen 109 (parts of the section, "Findings and Conclusions") gives both generalized and statistical projections.

Summary: Time Perspectives

Time perspectives embrace three foci: the past, the present, and the future. One, two, or all may be included in a particular report. We have discussed each perspective, together with its common types. We have also supplied numerous figure and specimen examples.

Thinking perspectives embrace two basic modes: the *descriptive* and the *evaluative*.

The descriptive mode reports *observations* or *generalizations of observations*. When reporting *observations*, your document is *confined to* communicating only those events, relations, objects, persons, or things *perceived*. Sometimes observations may be your own (primary); often they will be those made by other persons (secondary).

Generalizations of observations are *extended perceptions*. In other words, these go beyond observed cases to infer that what you have perceived is also true of unobserved similar cases. (We discuss this in detail in Chapter 9, section on "Status Communications.")

You can see that both observations and generalizations of observations are

PROJECTED FINANCIAL INFORMATION
Selected Years

Financial Needs	19-9	% Base	19-1	% of 19-9	19-3	% of 19-9
Expenditures*						
Educational & General	$14,749		$14,749		$17,846	
Increased Costs for Preceding Level of Programs—6% compounded	—		1,858		2,249	
	$14,749	100	$16,607	113	$20,095	136
Increased Costs for Improvement of Programs—4% compounded	—		1,239		1,499	
Total E&G Expenditures	$14,749	100	$17,846	121	$21,594	146
Income*						
Tuition Income	$11,551	100	$13,568	118	$15,994	139
Endowment Income	515		515		515	
Restricted Grants	1,900		1,900		1,900	
Other sources	673		673		673	
Total	$14,639	100	$16,656	114	$19,082	130
Req. Additional Income	$ 110		$ 1,190		$ 2,512	

* Thousands of dollars.

Fig. 4.12 / Report—forecasts.

concerned with either past or present time perspectives. Let us now examine some examples of each, using foregoing figures and specimen references.

Observation is exemplified in several figures. Go back to Figure 4.1. You can see that section 1 contains both past and present; however, section 3 is concerned with the past. Now turn to Figure 4.2. Which paragraphs are observations? Clearly the first and last are reporting past observable events. (The second is more evaluative than descriptive.)

What is the focus of Figure 4.3? It is definitely observation in that it is reporting past and present events (the past decisions made and the present decision to act on them). Look through the other figures to determine where each does or does not report observations and, if so, where. Also, examine specimens in this light. For example, see Specimens 104, 105, and 107 (scrutinizing the last very carefully—you will find a mixing of descriptive and evaluative, even under the section labelled "Observations").

Generalizations of observations can be seen in Specimen 109 (under "Findings and Conclusions," especially the ideas following "Studies have shown that:").

Almost all "Symptoms" in Specimen 110 are generalized observations. However, a few are observations. Can you distinguish between the two in this report?

Specimen 111 is an example combining present and past generalizations. The first section, "The Types of Output Systems" is giving the generalized definitions of the different systems. This is followed by the section, "Analysis of Star-X Communications Hardware," which is a generalized statement of what the study group observed in its investigation.

What is the significance of all this to reporting? The competent reporter *knows* when he is describing observations as opposed to when he is generalizing observations. He must be as accurate in both perception and description in the former; in addition to accuracy, he must use clarity and proper inference in the latter. When these differences are known and carefully handled, your reporting will be given credence by even the most critical reader.

The *evaluative* mode reports *inferences* either as *reasons, values,* or *predictions.* It can be concerned with any of past, present, or future time perspectives. You can see that any evaluation can be no better than the descriptive base from which it starts, which is why we have first discussed it.

Reasons are either causal (*why* something happened) or theoretical (*what* has happened or is happening). While causes and theories are technically different, we are not going to distinguish them here. Essentially both are concerned with why events are taking place or did take place (e.g., the sequence of events leading to a sales decline; or why morale among company employees is low).

Sometimes a report is a confusing admixture of description and reasons. Specimen 107 is a report promiscuously intermingling description with evaluation, including reasons (e.g., note sections on "Limitations" and "Observations"). Such a document is anathema to a critical reader: it is neither clear nor credible because of failure to accurately describe and to properly infer reasons.

As a contrast Specimens 106 and 110 are far better in reporting reasons. Specimen 106 clearly labels and communicates reasons (see initial section "Assumptions and Basic Problem"—again bearing in mind that problems and reasons are used synonymously); Specimen 110 directly relates generalized description (symptoms) to problems (reasons). In this instance, the reader can clearly follow the writer's descriptive and evaluative thinking.

Values are judgments made about the importance, rightness or worth of objectives, events, persons or things. These may be very broad (e.g., The human species must survive) or very specific (e.g., The Company must make a net profit of 6 percent to meet its obligations to shareholders). In other words, values may range from intangible and abstract to tangible and concrete. In any event, they are very important to business reporting (a statement which is a value judgment itself).

Look once more at Specimen 107 as an example of poor use of value statements, because they are haphazardly mixed with "description" and "reasons." (Note especially the first statement under "Observations.") In contrast Specimen 108 combines descriptive and value statements more properly; note the handling of the first and last paragraphs as well-stated, value-centered reporting.

Predictions are judgments about the future. Although always future-oriented, well-founded predictions are always based on the past or present.

Predictive reports can be classed in some ways as listed under future perspectives (i.e., recommendations, solutions, forecasts), so we shall not duplicate that discussion. Another useful way to look at these is to examine the factual bases upon which the prediction (or predictions) is made, that is, whether (1) unstated or (2) stated.

Unstated factual predictions are those made without explication of the basis or bases used to forecast the future. Needless to say, if you are a reader this may be a tenuous foundation for giving credence to a report. And as a writer, you should be aware that you run a risk in inviting censure or nonacceptance of the report if your factual foundations are not presented.

Nevertheless there are situations where such reports may be appropriate, that is, where readers already believe sufficiently in you or your company or your ideas. In such instances, you may be "laboring the obvious" to include an abundance of factual detail. However, you should be sure that this is the actual report circumstance you confront, else you invite failure. An example of an unstated factual prediction report is Specimen 107 (if you can stomach it once more) where the writer under the first section, "Scope" is actually predicting what can be done to overcome problems resulting from a prior systems failure. The rest of the report is much the same: predicting without any factual basis.

Stated factual predictions are those with clearly explicated foundations, whether observations, generalized observations, reasons, or values. Whether they are true or false, valid or invalid, these report the basis or bases of your predictions. Certainly good reporting requires accuracy and validity (to the extent you can be reasonably expected to know them) but, in any event, the reader is given clues as to how you arrive at your predictions; he can then judge for himself whether your prediction is faulty or correct.

Specimen 109 (an excerpt of a government agency's report on alcoholism) is a clear example of setting forth factual background for the predicted benefits —monetary and social—resulting from a concerted attack on the problem. Specimen 114 (report of anticipated income from membership dues of a professional society) is a step-by-step factually based document. The reader knows exactly how the projected income figure is derived.

Summary: Thinking Perspectives

Thinking perspectives include descriptive and evaluative modes. Some reports emphasize one mode; others present both. Each perspective has subsets, which we have discussed and illustrated by use of figures and specimens.

Visual and Narrative Reporting: Components, Numeric Information, and Appearance

Rather than detailed expositions on report components, we present essentials in two concise, ready-to-use tables (Figures 4.13 and 4.14). Figure 4.13 presents the essential parts of short expository reports; Figure 4.14 gives components of complex/technical documents. Incidentally, these principles can be directly applied to the use of visuals in oral reporting and other spoken communications.

Following the tabular presentation of components, we then highlight the fundamentals of communicating numeric information. Figures 4.15 through 4.19 treat this most important topic.

Why is proper communication of numeric information so important in organizational reports? Because proper numeric presentation constitutes the heart of reportorial documents. Any worthwhile report contains some data. To the extent data are put in communicative quantitative form are they more

---

SHORT EXPOSITORY REPORTS

Descriptive	Evaluative
—Transmittal document (unless self-contained)	All listed under Descriptive plus:
—Introduction Purpose Background Methods and procedures used Sources of data*	—Criteria for evaluation —Conclusions or implications —Recommendations
—Body of report (including findings)	

* May require attached detailed supportive data for authentication and validation.

Fig. 4.13 / Components of short expository reports.

COMPONENTS AND NATURE OF COMPLEX/TECHNICAL REPORTS

Basic Items	Nature

Transmittal Document	Memorandum (internal) or letter (external) giving:
	  title
	  date of submission
	  acknowledgment/authorization

Title Page	title author(s), position(s) department or division (internal and external) company name and address (external)

Table of Contents	Enumeration of:
	  basic parts
	  subdivisions
	  supporting documents
	  related pagination

Body of Report	Format alternatives:
	  chronological
	  locational
	  essential elements (categorical or coordinate ideas)
	  combinations of above
	    (see also "Special Communication Features" and
	    Chapter 10, "Impacts and Designs")

Optional Items	
Cover	standard preprinted cover furnished by company for all long reports plain cover for convenience of binding

Abstract
(Presummary)
	abbreviated purpose and background
	methodology and sources
	  (interviews, questionnaires, company records,
	  reference and professional materials, personal
	  experience)
	findings
	conclusions
	recommendations

Introduction
(Preface or Background)
	authorization
	acknowledgments
	  (persons, departments or divisions, external
	  contributors)

Footnotes	Styles:
	  within text
	  at end of report or major sections
	    (e.g., chapter)

Fig. 4.14/Components and nature of complex/technical reports.

Fig. 4.14 (continued)

Optional Items (continued)	
Summary	findings
(Synopsis)	conclusions
	recommendations
Bibliography	Styles:
	at end of report or major sections
Appendix	Types: (within body or at end of report)
	photographs
	related correspondence
	detailed numeric information
	(see Figure 4.15 and subsequent figures)
Index	alphabetical listing of important items covered in a
	very long report

meaningful and trustworthy. You should, therefore, acquaint yourself with the basic modes discussed.

Three basic modes for reporting numeric information (graphics, tables, text) are set forth in Figure 4.15. Applications of the first two, graphics and tables, are then given in Figure 4.16. Statistical graphs, one of the most important graphics, are then highlighted and exemplified in Figures 4.17 and 4.18, respectively. Finally, Figure 4.19 gives a complete practical checklist for assuring communicative appearance of graphics and tables. We confine our discussion of appearance to graphics and tables, because these are so important in many reports. Indeed, putting information into communicative graphic or tabular form is a very caustic yardstick to apply to your own reporting. Why? It forces you to think through all informational ideas, eliminating the irrelevant or unnecessary and making emphatic and clearer the important. Graphics and tables can, therefore, serve as excellent disciplines to make your own ideas more communicative and valid.

When you understand and properly use these tabular references (Figures 4.13 through 4.19) your report information will communicate both efficiently and effectively.

MODES FOR REPORTING NUMERIC INFORMATION

Types	Advantages	Disadvantages	Spec. and Fig. Examples
Graphics	Visual means of illustrating a multitude of data in a number of relationships	A poorly designed or inappropriately chosen chart may negate intended purpose; takes time to prepare	Fig. 4.9, 4.18
Tables	Clarity through logical arrangement and concise description; use of columns and rows facilitates comparisons	Recognition by reader requires familiarity with legends and relationships; difficult to portray trends	Spec. 109, 114 Fig. 4.5, 4.6 4.12
Text	Narrative and mathematical manipulation: common form of expression chosen because of economy of time, space, and cost	Mass of data in narrative may be difficult to comprehend and to make necessary comparisons; mathematical symbols normally restricted to specialists	Spec. 113 Fig. 4.2

Fig. 4.15 / Modes for reporting numeric information.

APPLICATIONS OF GRAPHICS AND TABLES

Use	Possible misuse
1. Clarify complex data	1. May oversimplify
2. Separate important numbers from massive data	2. May omit significant items
3. Illustrate number magnitude	3. Quantitative emphasis may overshadow qualitative
4. Emphasize number differences	4. Differences may becloud salient points
5. Identify trends	5. Trend may be focus rather than specific or discrete elements comprising trend
6. Demonstrate relationships	6. Relationships shown may appear biased (maximized or minimized)

Fig. 4.16 / Applications of graphics and tables.

BASIC TYPES OF STATISTICAL GRAPHS
(Each is exemplified in Figure 4.18)

Types	Advantages	Disadvantages
Area	Simple breakdown for nontechnical viewers	Difficult to shade for differentiation or to label parts; unsuitable for comparison with like graphs
Bar	Versatile single scale graph; easy comparison of amounts, subdivisions, relations	Limited to single scale; must limit subdivision to avoid confusion
Column	Features two scales; easy comparison of related items having different measurement units	Time needed to prepare; special skills needed to scale relationships of unlike units
Curve	Most flexible of all types; emphasizes and compares trends; illustrates plotted points; can be used to extrapolate information	May attempt to include too many concepts hence distort or miss significance of numerical data
Surface	Can be used to give special emphasis to a single, overall, or particular aspect of a trend	Fewer uses because of limitation in arrangement of elements; screening may confuse reader or create optical illusion

Fig. 4.17 / Basic types of statistical graphs.

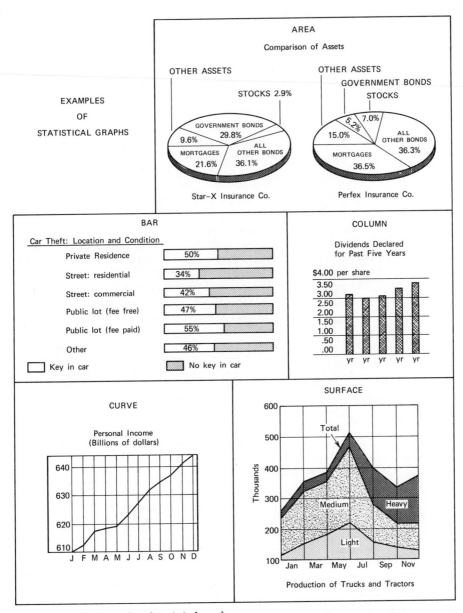

Fig. 4.18/ Examples of statistical graphs.

APPEARANCE OF GRAPHICS AND TABLES

Design Details	Suggestions
1. Message	Visual should be clear, concise, and designed for easy reader understanding of the point being emphasized. Caution: avoid oversimplification.
2. Title	Keep brief, make descriptive; if necessary, use subtitle.
3. Dimension Identification	Limit explanations to essentials; if necessary, expand in text proper or in concise terms beneath illustration.
4. Captions	Allow adequate space for: columnar and marginal headings; captions denoting scale values; labels for lines and curves.
5. Lettering	Make compatible with size: neither too small (unreadable) nor too large (distracting).
6. Symbols and Abbreviations	Use keys as appropriate (in corner or below visual) to identify uncommon symbols or abbreviations.
7. Visual Numbering	Set up a clear consistent system of numbering for quick reference in narrative. (Number is usually placed beneath visual followed by title.)
8. Documentation	Give credits in text or footnotes to support data from other printed sources (e.g., other reports, directories, government statistics, books).
9. Mode and Style	Achieve a balance between simplicity and completeness: (1) visual should achieve purpose through proper mode; and (2) spatial allowance should create an honest representation of information depicted.
10. Final Check	When in final form (whether self- or professionally prepared), re-examine in light of all foregoing. If necessary, redesign or omit. Be sure the visual is achieving efficient and effective communication of ideas.

Fig. 4.19 / Appearance of graphics and tables.

Special Communication Features

We have discussed general types, components, and styles and appearance of reports. We come now to the important communication factors to be kept in mind for assessing the situation and for writing a report.

We shall consider three report dimensions: (1) important organizational yardsticks, (2) important planning guides, and (3) important writing guides.

Important Organizational Yardsticks

We have already mentioned several report attributes. Let us now explore these in depth in relation to principles of effective reports in the organization as a whole.

The first significant principle is that a report *meets a legitimate need for organizational information*. In other words, there must be some defensible, rational reason why you make a given report or ask for one from others.

Routine reports (e.g., monthly sales, weekly inventory) answer recurring important company needs; nonroutine documents respond to special requests or unique demands. In any event, there must be some recognized, sanctioned, task-related reason for any report. All too frequently, we have found that when the question, "What real need does this report satisfy?" is asked about all reports in a firm, many can be eliminated or combined. Why? Because in most organizations a great number contribute nothing significant, either because they had no original legitimate mission, or the need has changed or no longer exists.

On the other hand, this question also frequently reveals needs for additional (or modified) reports. Often we have found that there are basic organizational information gaps because of inadequate report mechanisms. In this case the organization must generate—rather than eliminate—documents to meet the newly recognized need or needs.

Assuming a legitimate need, the second yardstick is that a report is *aimed at a clearly defined purpose*. Lack of a clear-cut objective builds in report failure. Is the document to give information? If so, what kind? In what form (e.g., narrative or statistical or both)? It is obvious that if the writer does not know his exact purpose, the reader of a report cannot know (except by accident). Again, when we have raised this caustic question, twenty-five to fifty percent of report originators cannot clearly articulate what their reports are supposed to do. And when receivers of the same reports are interrogated, the range runs from sixty to seventy-five percent. Is it any wonder that most organizations get so little mileage out of their reports? And is it any wonder that most organizational personnel take such a dim view of them—whether as originators, processors, or receivers?

Assuming positive responses to the first and second questions (i.e., respecting need and purpose), the third yardstick is that an organizational report is directed *to receiver willingness and ability to understand and respond*. A report is a document for communicating ideas, which means that company writers must address receivers in terms of their willingness and capacity to understand and respond to the message. If the report is for highly specialized professionals, *their* ability to understand technical terminology and their knowledge of certain essentials may be assumed. On the other hand, if the receiver (even if the specialist's boss) lacks these qualities, the writer must put his ideas in terms the receiver can readily handle. This yardstick is another "obvious" one, but it is so frequently violated in organizations (at all levels) that we are compelled to spell it out here. You can certainly see that if not followed in practice, report failure is almost automatic.

The fourth yardstick of effectiveness is that a report *employs proper format*. We have already delved into this topic a little, and we shall discuss it in detail later in this chapter, as well as in Chapter 10. At this point we shall deal only with format in relation to organization goals.

Formats for routine organizational reports are most often prescribed; the most common mechanism is a report form. A well-conceived form will get the needed information economically and efficiently. A standardized format is built into the report form, making it easy to complete by the originator and easy to process and understand by the receiver.

Formats for nonroutine reports are, of course, more flexible. Since we do elaborate on format (design) later, let us merely present a few salient things to remember about this subject in relation to reports: (1) keep the format as simple as possible; exclude any nonessentials; (2) make the format clearly discernible to your receiver; use sufficient reader cues (e.g., headings, numbers, typographical aids) so that the reader can follow your ideas with ease; (3) for complex, lengthy reports, use digests or transmittals (letters or memos) to present highlights; these then become operational formats for the receiver to use in reading the report wholly or in part.

The fifth yardstick is that *description and evaluation are clearly differentiated* in company reports. In other media, this separation is seldom important, but in reports the distinction is fundamental. We have already treated descriptive and evaluative elements in this chapter, so we shall not discuss this dimension further here.

The sixth yardstick is that reports focus on *accuracy and validity*. We have already discussed this dimension under "thinking perspectives." We mention it here merely to remind you that unless company reports meet these criteria, they cause irreparable harm: since they are the major carriers of vital organizational information, incorrect, sloppily prepared reports can create havoc in the firm.

The seventh yardstick is that organizational reports *are properly coordinated*. Unless all the firm's reports are designed to fit together to get the total organization's jobs done properly, the company suffers a severe deficiency. This means that reports must be properly planned to meet their individual objectives, but each must blend harmoniously with all others. It means also that adequate report monitoring and updating mechanisms must be part of the company's scheme.

Important Planning Guides

Let us now turn to principles for use in preparing reports for which you are personally responsible. (The organizational criteria we have presented, of course, constitute the matrix within which you report; what follows must be judged within the particular organization as to whether or not it adequately measures up to the yardsticks enumerated.)

First, *allow sufficient time* to do the right job. The "right job" of course is relative to report importance, requirements for accuracy, data detail, and the receiver for whom written. You should remember that, as with any other form of communication, planning, preparing, and processing reports cost money, so you should allocate *optimal* time to get the right result for the circumstance you confront.

Second, know the *exact purpose and* the *receiver* of the report. We have already discussed purpose and receiver under organizational yardsticks. The principles presented are directly translatable to your personal reporting. Furthermore, Chapters 7 to 9 elaborate exact purposes and receivers for all media.

Third, determine the *needed information and sources.* "What key information do I need?" and "Where do I get the needed information?" are the questions to be raised and answered here. For routine reports, your own memory or your records and files (which may include reports from others to you) should probably be sufficient. For nonroutine or special requests, you may be required to do a careful analysis of data requirements, followed by intensive and extensive intracompany and extracompany search.

Fourth, determine a *communicative format.* What basic organizational pattern should be used? This is the basic question here. If a short, simple report, a straightforward narrative sequence may be sufficient. If a lengthy, complex, technical exposition, very careful arrangement of ideas is required. If your company prescribes the format, the decision is already made (assuming, of course, that you agree the "prescription" will effect the "cure"). If preset patterns are not given, then you must come up with one you deem best to do the job. Some of the more common formats for reports are: (1) Background→Problem→Reasons→Solutions; (2) Problems→Recommendations→Implementation; (3) Problem→Limitations→Methods (procedures) for study→Findings (results)→Conclusions→Recommendations; (4) Past (information or records) →Present (information or status)→Future (what will or should happen); (5) Presentation of essential elements→Conclusions or implications; (6) Presentation of important ideas (in ascending or descending order)→Conclusions→Recommendations; (7) A one-for-one answering of questions or requests made (a very common pattern when disparate ideas are involved and where this paralleling is helpful to the receiver).

Many permutations of the seven patterns are possible, and still other formats are sometimes used. We shall deal more with organization of ideas in Chapter 10, "Communication Impacts and Designs."

Important Writing Guides

We are now ready to look at how you put the report on paper, which, of course, becomes your written output.

Again, if your company has a reporting style manual (which you judge satisfactory), it gives the guidance you need. More often, however, how the actual writing is to be done is left to the individual. We present the more important things to consider in reporting (for details of writing, see Part IV).

What we shall present here is a nine-step sequence, a pattern we have found to be sound checkpoints for important communications, which, of course, includes most reports. In some cases you may wish to skip certain steps (e.g., when you have an emergency deadline, it may not be possible to pretest your written output). And, of course, you may have or, through experience, discover a more productive approach for yourself. By all means use whatever works best for you.

With these provisions in mind, let us now look at the nine-step sequence for writing reports.

1. Reconsider Your Reader (or Readers) and the Situation/Was your original assessment accurate? Have you come across some new ideas or facts that change your perception of the report task? Have additional requirements been imposed? Have your informational findings put the situation in a new light? These are typical questions you should consider. Often, you will find that you see the receiver and circumstances quite differently from your initial size-up. If so, you may want to return to some or all of the steps enumerated under "Important Planning Guides."

2. Determine Needed Types and Quantity of Supporting Materials/Do you need only straightforward narration (in an appropriate format)? Or will you need to supplement narration with other backup data—statistical, tabular, or chart? Will graphics (with minimum verbal exposition) better communicate your ideas? Will extensive and intensive supporting data or merely highlighting information be required? These are the kinds of questions that should be considered here.

3. Determine the Proper Written Style/Is a formal, impersonal tone desired? If so, you should use a conservative and authoritative style. However, if you wish to convey an informal, personal mood, the use of a more conversational and human style is in order. Is traditional syntax desired, or could a more telegraphic or topical style be profitably employed? Writing style is vital to receiver impact; be sure you choose the best style to achieve the impact you want.

4. Write the Initial Draft/At this point, do not be overly concerned with the polished product. Get your ideas on paper, without too much attention to grammatical usage, spelling, and the like. Furthermore, start with the part that seems easiest. As a suggestion, begin with the body of the report—or some segment of the essential message—then go to introductory and concluding parts. In short, get started in whatever way is easiest for you to get your original thinking on paper.

5. Let Your First Draft "Cool"/Of course, no exact duration can be given, because this depends on circumstances. However, putting your writing aside for an optimal period gives you a chance to review your initial output with a fresh perspective. It is often surprising to find that in the cold dawn of the next day our original fervid outpouring of lucid and cogent ideas is not nearly as clear and persuasive as we thought.

6. Rewrite and Polish the Draft/Here you give attention to details—down to items such as spelling, punctuation, and precision of wording. In some instances, it is wise to go over materials several times to get the desired finished product.

7. In Important Reports, Pretest Your Product on Representative Readers/Possibilities include your secretary, your peers, or even better, readers of the type to which your report is addressed. If feasible, it may be wise to check with the receiver himself to see if you are on the right track. You can see that pretesting can be very helpful to know whether the report is on- or off-target.

8. If Necessary, Do Another Rewrite (or Rewrites) of Your Report/Sometimes, your pretest will show a need for a total recasting. More often, only certain segments will need revision. In any event, make the needed modifications and send out your finished document.

9. Follow-up to Determine Understanding and Response/While beyond the writing proper, it is clear that unless the report results in proper understanding and response, it fails. This is one of the most important, but unfortunately, one of the most neglected activities in managerial and organizational reporting.

Summary: Special Communication Features

Let us summarize what we have discussed in this section in tabular form (Figures 4.20 to 4.22). Used together with principles discussed in this chapter, you can make critical evaluations and rewrites of the reports of others. Moreover, you can initiate and compose effective reports on your own.

Organizational Yardsticks for Reports

1. Each meets a legitimate informational need.
2. Each has a clear purpose.
3. Each is aimed at receiver willingness and ability.
4. Each uses proper format.
5. Each differentiates description and evaluation.
6. Each focuses on accuracy and validity.
7. All are properly coordinated.

Fig. 4.20 / Organizational yardsticks for reports.

Planning Guides for Reports

1. Allow sufficient time.
2. Know exact purposes and the receiver.
3. Determine needed information and sources.
4. Determine a communicative format.

Fig. 4.21 / Planning guides for reports.

Writing Guides for Reports

1. Reconsider reader and situation.
2. Determine types and quantity of supporting materials.
3. Determine style.
4. Write initial draft.
5. Let draft "cool."
6. Rewrite/polish draft.
7. Pretest on representative readers.
8. Rewrite as needed.
9. Follow-up on reader understanding and response.

Fig. 4.22 / Writing guides for reports.

EXERCISES

exercise 1 State the three possible time elements in a report, giving a sentence example of each.

exercise 2 Give the (1) two basic perspectives of reports and (2) the foci or modes of each perspective.

exercise 3 Using the following checklist, examine Specimen 109 (a digest preceding a full report). Some components are explicit, others implicit. Like-wise, descriptive and evaluative modes may not always be clearly differentiated. For your guidance, the introduction and purpose are already checked, which sets the pattern for your analysis of other items. Study of Specimen 109 indicates why "Introduction" and "Purpose" are rated "implicit": neither is explicitly captioned or stated. Careful examination, however, shows that paragraphs 1 through 3 are actually introductory, and that the second half of paragraph 1 points to the purpose of the study.

REPORT DIMENSIONS CHECKLIST

	Exist? Yes/No	Location Para. No.	Explicit/ Implicit	Descriptive/ Evaluative	Clear/ Marginal/ Unclear
Introduction	yes	1, 2, 3	implicit	descriptive	clear
Purpose	yes	1	implicit	descriptive	clear
Background					
Methods/procedures used					
Sources of data					
Body (including findings)					
Criteria for evaluation					
Conclusions/implications					
Recommendations					

exercise 4 Now analyze Specimen 109 using the **Basic Dimension** checklist.

BASIC DIMENSIONS	U	M	S	Needed Corrections
Clarity (See Chapter 15)				
Correctness (See Chapter 16)				
Persuasiveness (See Chapter 17)				

exercise 5 Using your findings from both the *Report Dimensions* and *Basic Dimensions*, rewrite the total report as a better document.

CASE PROBLEMS

1. Re: Figure 4.6: You are Robert M. Jones, Chief of the Sanitation Department, Widespot, Texakana. At the request of the City Council, you have gathered these data on urban garbage pickup in Widespot. The City Council wants a brief, but clear, report on your findings.

Your Mission: (1) Write a one page expository report using the data in Figure 4.6. (2) Convert the data into an appropriate statistical graph from one of the types depicted in Figure 4.18. Include necessary components and check your final products using the report and basic dimensions checklists for the narrative report and the "Appearance of Graphs and Tables" checklist, Figure 4.19.

2. Re: Figure 4.6: You have made your report (Problem 1) which was well-received by Council members. They now want an in-depth report on the following:

(1) Feasibility of recycling each item;
(2) Cost/benefit ratios (cost estimates for recycling as opposed to traditional pickup and disposal; cost recovery potential from recycling);
(3) Probable technological developments within the next five years (for better recycling and/or lower costs);
(4) Other alternatives.

Your Mission: Do whatever research is necessary (e.g., library, discussions with experts, interviews with city officials) to determine the best answers for the four items. Write an appropriately lengthy report detailing answers that you find and the most valid inferences you can make from your findings. Include a minimum of two appropriate statistical graphs or tables as supportive documents. Cite important sources using appropriate footnote and documentation form. (If needed, consult library reference sources for proper documentation form.) In your report, include necessary report components and follow an appropriate format (see Figure 4.14). Check your final product using the report and basic dimensions checklists, as well as related principles in Chapter 4.

Chapter 5

LEGALLY ORIENTED MEDIA: PROPOSALS, AGREEMENTS, AND DIRECTIVES

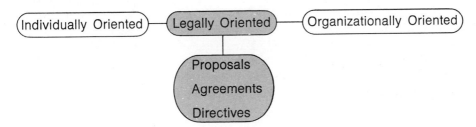

Your Learning Objectives:

1. To know the nature of legally oriented media.
2. To know the general application of PRIDE to legally oriented media.
3. To know the definition of proposals.
4. To know common purposes of proposals.
5. To know receiver considerations for proposals.
6. To know impact considerations for proposals.
7. To know design considerations for proposals.
8. To know different means for executing proposals.
9. To know the definition of agreements.
10. To know common agreement purposes.
11. To know receiver considerations for agreements.
12. To know impact considerations for agreements.
13. To know design and execution means for agreements.
14. To know the definition of directives.
15. To know common purposes of directives.
16. To know how to apply PRIDE to directive planning and presentation.
17. To know how to use checklists for ready, valid analysis of legally oriented media communication quality.

Having covered the organization's three basic individually oriented documents (letters, memoranda, and reports), we are now ready to examine the next major grouping, legally oriented media.

The Nature of Legally Oriented Media

Whereas each of the individually oriented media was considered independently (because of their numerous uses), we shall look at all three legal types together. This is done because all focus on and are used within a "legal" context. We consider the term "legal" broadly, that is, referring to media that are essentially concerned with impersonal legislative or regulatory constraints (mostly coming from outside the organization) as well as company, agency or professional policies, guidelines or codes (largely originating within the organization). In other words, both extra-organizational (legislative and regulatory) and intra-organizational (administrative) legal overlays directly and indirectly affect media considered in this chapter. Moreover, as you will see, these three documents interrelate in unique ways. For example, a proposal can result in a subsequent agreement; the agreement may produce a directive for implementation.

PRIDE as the Analytical Pattern

The three most important legally oriented documents are proposals, agreements, and directives. In considering the three, we shall depart from the pattern used for letters, memoranda, and reports. Because of their extensive uses, it was necessary to deal in depth with special characteristics of each individually oriented medium. However, since proposals, agreements, and directives are more restricted in focus, and since we are concerned primarily in showing their general utilization, we shall employ the PRIDE sequence in analysis of each.

As you recall, PRIDE is an acronym for Purpose, Receiver, Impact, Design, and Execution. Our use of the sequence here is only introductory. We shall use it differently and in-depth in Part II. With this background in mind, let us now proceed to the first legally oriented medium, proposals.

Proposals

Written proposals are documents that present plans, actions, or alternatives for consideration or adoption. They may range from simple and short to highly complex and lengthy.

Purposes

Proposals meet a variety of purposes, some of the more important of which are: bids, personnel, organization, and product or service. As you have probably surmised, these goals are not necessarily independent, because some proposals encompass more than one (e.g., personnel and organization). However, discussing them separately permits you to readily recognize the one or ones to be considered in a given situation.

Bids, as used here, refer to proposals offering specified goods and services at quoted prices. These are usually directed to customers outside the company. In many cases these are made in response to requests for proposals (RFP's). Specimen 28 quotes a price on a training course; Specimen 27 is "boiler plate" for all major proposals going out of a large manufacturing firm. While not a bid as such, this material is included to make the actual bid more persuasive to the reader.

In more technical bids (e.g., a highly complex aerospace project, or some part of it), the document must spell out all the detailed plans and operations to meet the criteria and specifications given in the request for proposal. In these instances highly intricate legislative and administrative constraints must be carefully followed.

Personnel proposals are directed to organization *member* shifts, promotions, hirings, replacements, or terminations. They can be both external and in-house. One of the most common external proposals is a job application. Examples can be seen in Specimen 22 (application from a recent university graduate); Specimen 21 (a resume accompanying an application); Specimen 24 (an application for a teaching position from an experienced university professor); and Specimen 25 (the vita for Specimen 24). However, applications for positions can originate internally. Specimen 23 (application from an employee for a higher company position) is an example.

As stated, personnel proposals can also be recommendations for shifts of people to other jobs or units or for hiring new personnel to fill actual or anticipated vacancies (e.g., Specimen 42).

Organization proposals are those recommending unit shifts or redesign and creation or elimination of policies, procedures, or practices. In addition, organizational short- and long-range planning are included in this type. They can come from both internal and external sources.

An example of an internal proposal for unit shift and redesign is seen in Specimen 33 (recommendations for integrating company computer facilities and relocating accounting responsibility). An external proposal (from an outside consultant) for creating new policies and procedures is exemplified in Specimen 34 (recommendations for assuring communication responsibility in a government agency). Specimen 34 also implies long- and short-range organizational planning in order to attain the objectives outlined.

Product or service proposals are those recommending changes or innovations in organizational outputs. Commonly technical in nature, these often require specialist expertise (e.g., science, engineering, accounting). Each discipline has its special proposal requirements; therefore, we shall not delve into this type. In product or service proposals, you should follow the legalities (laws, regulations, codes) of the discipline or disciplines involved, in addition to your company's administrative constraints (policies, procedures, practices).

Summary/Figure 5.1 summarizes the proposal purposes.

Proposal Purposes

Bids
Personnel
Organization
Product/Service

Fig. 5.1/Summary—proposal purposes.

Receivers

Recipients of proposals can be analyzed from two perspectives: (1) status and (2) psychology.

Status refers to any of the receiver's expertise, position, and organizational leverage. In writing a proposal, you should take all these into account. Why? Because a proposal is fundamentally a persuasive document, and your persuasion can be no better than your handling of these factors.

Clearly the recipient's *expertise* (specialized knowledge of the proposal's contents) affects how the document must be thought through and communicated. A receiver of profound background will be addressed accordingly; on the other hand, one with relatively meager knowledge should be given only those concepts he can readily understand. One of the surest ways to alienate the unsophisticated receiver is to try to "snow" him with technical concepts and details.

The receiver's *position* is of obvious relevance. Generally technical proposals will be addressed to technical managerial receivers (e.g., an engineering proposal will be for another engineer in a management position). Nontechnical documents, however, could go to almost any position in the receiving organization. The point is that the author of the proposal should know for what position he is addressing the document, and thereby design the document for it.

Organizational leverage refers to a receiver's real power or influence in a company. The proposal may be formally addressed to a top manager, who may, in turn, refer it to his assistant for a decision. Or, lacking specialized background, a manager may go to a company (sometimes outside) specialist for advice. This means that the writer must be aware of the real leverage points in the organization (that is, those persons or units that make or influence proposal decisions). Otherwise all the valuable time and money spent in preparation may be wasted.

Psychology refers to the attitude or state of mind of the proposal's receiver or receivers. Items covered under status may be classed as "logical," and these certainly must be properly known and handled. However, once again, let us remember that a proposal is a document to persuade, which means that you must properly consider and control receiver psychology.

We discuss this dimension in depth in Chapters 7 to 9, so we shall mention only the general idea at this point. Essentially receivers may be looked on as either unfavorable or favorable. *Unfavorable receivers* are those who are initially either opposed or neutral to you, your ideas, or your firm. Whether justified or not, if a receiver of your proposal is unfavorably disposed, you must do what is necessary to soften or eliminate his hostility (if he is opposed) or to properly direct his attention (if he is neutral).

Favorable receivers are those who are initially *for* you, your ideas, or your firm. Most often these are prospects with whom you have had good and trust-worthy past relations. In handling favorable receivers, you try to strengthen already positive attitudes and belief, which is entirely different from the methods to handle hostility or neutrality. (Methods for handling both favorable and unfavorable receivers will be detailed in Chapter 10.)

Summary: Receivers/Figure 5.2 summarizes receivers in relation to proposals.

Receiver Perspectives	
Status	expertise
	position
	organizational leverage
Psychology	unfavorable
	favorable

Fig. 5.2 / Summary—proposal receivers.

Impacts

Impact refers to the intended effect of your proposal on its receiver or receivers. In other words, impact is the "under-the-skin" reactions you want to achieve on the part of the readers of your document. Let us distinguish purpose from impact. *Purpose* is what *you* want to accomplish (e.g., get the bid, get acceptance of your plan for reshaping your department); *impact* is *what you must do to the receiver* in order to accomplish your purpose.

This dimension will be spelled out in detail in Chapter 10. At this point, let us give some salient impact features in proposals.

1. Know the precise proposal purpose. Are you trying to persuade the receiver to some idea? Or is your purpose to get a favorable decision? Or does your mission call for adoption of a plan of action? Without knowledge of exact purpose, you have no criterion for gauging impact.

2. Know your receiver's (or receivers') status and psychology. This goes back to our discussion in the previous section; it goes without saying that this information is essential to successful size-up of your impact requirements.

3. In light of 1 and 2, build your competence and credibility to carry out the proposal's objectives. This is a crucial item. In accepting your proposal, the receiver is "putting his chips" on you and your firm. You must assure him that this credence is warranted.

4. Select and include only data and information to accomplish 1, 2, and 3. In worthy proposals, quality—not quantity—of information strikes the right chord with receivers. On the other hand, you must include all pertinent ideas. In other words, you neither underdo nor overdo; you *rightly do* with respect to proposal data and information in order to get the right receiver impact.

5. Clearly and cogently state your way of implementing your plan or scheme (if action is called for), which means that you spell out the what, why, when, where, and how of execution. This is the cutting edge of an action-oriented proposal, and perceptive receivers (consciously or unconsciously) know at this point whether a proposal makes sense or nonsense, and whether you really know what you are about.

6. Keep essential ideas foremost in the receiver's mind; put supportive ideas in backup materials. In other words, highlight the important things you want to get across; use supplementary means (e.g., appendices and other attachments) to give details. This permits your reader to know quickly the essence of your proposal. In addition, it gives him the option of scrutinizing all supporting materials as much as he wants. If properly presented, this combination generally is one of the most important means to get favorable receiver impact for a proposal.

Summary: Impacts/Figure 5.3 summarizes the salient features to get favorable proposal impacts.

Designs

Design refers to the proposal's format or sequence of ideas; design should be such that it achieves the right impact with your receiver to achieve your desired

---

To Get Favorable Proposal Impacts:

1. Know your precise purpose
2. Know your receiver
3. Build your competence and credibility to carry out proposal objectives
4. Use only necessary data and information
5. Clearly, cogently state your plan to achieve (if action-oriented)
6. Highlight essentials, use supplements for supportive details

---

Fig. 5.3 / Summary—proposal impact features.

purpose. In other words, there are no "pat answers" or "cookbook recipes" that are magical guides to proposal design; rather a given proposal's format should properly fit the situation or condition. This means that you must make your best judgment about the design in each proposal instance.

However, some proposal patterns are common, and, if used with discretion (which sometimes means modification), these can be helpful in shaping the document to achieve its intended purpose. In order to give you a quick and ready reference for proposal designs, these are presented in tabular form. Figure 5.4 presents simple proposal designs and uses; Figure 5.5 sets forth complex proposal patterns; and Figure 5.6 gives dimensions and types of supporting materials (generally used with the more complex proposals).

We have listed prescribed patterns in both complex and simple proposals. Figure 5.7 exemplifies a format prescribed for all proposals submitted to a foundation (complex documents). Figure 5.8 is a company directive for suggestion system proposals (mostly simple documents).

Execution

Execution refers to the medium (or media) for conveying a proposal's basic and supportive message. As you have already seen, some organizations (originating or receiving) require specific formats (prescribed patterns). Some also dictate the medium or media to be used (e.g., a special form provided). Most organizations, however, do not exercise stringent controls, especially for simple, internal proposals. It is to these, which are by far the most frequently used by organizational personnel, that we shall primarily address ourselves.

Letters are common carriers to outsiders. For short, simple proposals, letters are efficient and effective. They are also the most common mechanism for transmitting longer or complex documents (often highlighting or creating reader interest in the proposal). Specimens 20 and 22 are examples of job applications of graduating university students. Specimen 28 is a letter quote (bid) on services and products.

SIMPLE PROPOSAL DESIGNS (commonly brief, nontechnical)

Design	Nature	Use	Spec. References and Examples
1. Prescribed Pattern	Follows predetermined standard forms or format	Routine, recurring situations	Examples: job application forms; suggestion system forms
2. Problem— Recommendations	Exposition of problem or trouble followed by solution or solutions	Relatively clear or simple troubles and actions	Spec. 33 (integrating company computer facilities and re-assigning accounting responsibility)
3. Problem— Alternatives	Exposition of problem or trouble followed by two or more possible solutions (frequently recommending one)	Controversial troubles or actions when final decision should be made by the receiver	Spec. 42 (offers two possible solutions, but favors one)
4. Solution— Reasons	Exposition of solution followed by supportive data	Directly telling receiver the answer and why; good for receivers who think inductively	Spec. 23 (implicitly suggests that the "solution" to the job vacancy is to hire the applicant for the reasons given); Spec. 28 (training course is "solution" for reasons given)
5. Recommendations	Elaborates solutions to "obvious" or known problems, frequently involving a series of proposed actions	To focus on getting things done rather than "rehashing" troubles or problems	Spec. 34 (a series of policy and procedural recommendations)
6. Problem—Request for More Information	Specifies data gaps or the need for additional information before proceeding further	To clarify, better understand problem or conditions to be met	Spec. 24 (asks for more information concerning a university teaching position)

Fig. 5.4 / Simple proposal designs.

COMPLEX PROPOSAL DESIGNS (frequently lengthy, technical)

Design	Nature	Use	Possible Examples and Receiver Orientations
1. Prescribed Pattern	Follows predetermined standard forms or format	Routine, recurring situations	Project proposals; requests for budgetary increases; Figure 5.7 (format for proposal submission to a foundation); can be critical or noncritical orientation
2. Problem—Purpose —Scope— Procedures— Findings— Conclusions— Recommendations	An in-depth analysis of a complex problem by skilled professionals for other skilled professionals	Investigative proposals (often assigned or solicited)	Studying why company sales are decreasing and what can be done about the problem or problems discovered; critically oriented
3. Purpose— Uniqueness— Applications— Plan of Action	Similar to #2 except more emphasis on "selling" the plan of action	Same as #2 except generally a more persuasive note	Seeking funding for project in which competitors are bidding; seeking approval for action; critical or noncritical orientation
4. Hypothesis— Procedures for Testing—Results —Conclusions— Recommendations	Generally tends toward basic or conceptual research	In situations with theoretical unknowns or without "hard" data	Research and development activities; new product or service development (e.g., market testing); critical orientation
5. Proposed Methods —Criteria— Recommended Changes—Stages of Program— Schedule	Generally solicited proposals with predetermined problem, product or service specified	When the firm knows generally or exactly what it wants and desires bids or quotations to get the job done	Development of a new piece of hardware; planning and conducting a training program; technical proposals (e.g., aerospace projects); critical orientation

Fig. 5.5 / Complex proposal designs.

99

SUPPORTING MATERIALS FOR PROPOSALS
(for complex and technical proposals)

Item	Nature	Specimens and Possible Examples
1. Experience	Company and people background in similar or related activities; professional/technical skills and background	Spec. 21 (resume); Spec. 25 (vita)
2. Organization	Both administrative and technical structure and capability	Technical capability of people; how organized (e.g., traditional, project, program); Spec. 27 (contract maintenance and surveillance of an engineering firm) is an example
3. Equipment/ Facilities/ Support	Special machines, buildings, lands, monies	Computer capability; laboratory equipment and physical plant; special government or foundation funding
4. Allocation of Manpower and Facilities	Detailed breakdown of who, when, what, and how much (costs)	Total and segmented manhours for project and its several stages; what exact equipment and physical facilities are available and what are needed; costs—total and part-by-part
5. Methodology	Technical or professional approach to be taken	Assumptions and conceptual bases; how job is to be done (e.g., laboratory experiment, empirical, intuitive, experiential)
6. Other Related Ideas	Special organizational capabilities; elaboration of any of 1-5; special inducements	Unique experience and background of personnel; financial strength of firm; guarantees, warrantees; financial incentives (e.g., permission to conduct special audits); cooperative relationships (e.g., offer to work closely by frequent meetings, progress reports, etc.); Spec. 27

Fig. 5.6/ Supportive materials for proposals.

The following information should be supplied, in triplicate, on no more than two typewritten, letter-size pages, using the numbered captions and sequence indicated. *Do not submit any other information unless specifically requested by the Foundation.*

1. Official name of institution or association, address, and phone number.
2. Name and title of chief administrative officer.
3. Name of dean of unit or head of department in which demonstration is to be undertaken.
4. Name, title, address, and phone number of person to be in charge of project.
5. Area of resource to be improved. (Use one of the italicized categories listed under *General Information.*)
6. Brief descriptive title of project for which support is sought.
7. Brief analysis of the resource problem and objective of the proposed demonstration.
8. Brief description of the demonstration and method of evaluation.
9. Cost of project. (Give estimates of the cost of staff, equipment, miscellaneous expenses, and total expenses.)
10. Date when project could be begun and date when it could be completed. (Give month and year only in each case.)
11. Signature of chief administrative officer.
12. Date of application.

Fig. 5.7 / Example of prescribed pattern—complex proposal.

TO: All Star-X Employees

FROM: Robert M. Jones, President

SUBJECT: Suggestion Proposals

Star-X welcomes your suggestions. In order to process them in the most rapid and effective manner, submit all proposals using this format:

1. The exact description of the idea or product
2. The benefits (e.g., financial, psychological)
3. The costs of developing and implementing
4. The way or ways the proposal can be implemented (who, what, how)
5. Other special remarks

Fig. 5.8 / Example of prescribed pattern—simple proposal.

Memoranda are often used for simple, brief proposals to insiders. They are also frequent devices for transmitting longer or complex in-house documents. Like transmittal letters, they may be used to highlight and draw reader interest to the proposal proper. Specimen 23, a job application (from an employee requesting promotion to a different position), is an example of a brief proposal in memo form. Specimen 33 (recommending computer integration and reassignment of accounting responsibility) is a longer proposal in memo form. Actually, as you can see, Specimen 33 is really more a proposal proper even though it uses traditional memo headings. It would have been better communication practice had a memo been used to highlight the document. Even better, however, would have been a much clearer, shorter proposal sent as a memorandum. (Close examination of this document will reveal much "verbal garbage" that only confuses the reader and probably alienates him.)

Proposals proper are self-evident. This is the basic document that spells out the ideas, plan, scheme, or recommendations you are advocating. As stated, Specimen 33 is really an example of this sort. Specimen 34 (which was transmitted by letter) is an excerpt from a longer proposal. Specimen 107 is another "overdone" proposal. The whole document could be easily reduced to a single page memorandum. As discussed before, proposals proper (especially complex, technical types) often must be communicated in a prescribed format or form (the next medium).

Forms are predetermined, shaped vehicles for presenting proposals. Job application forms, suggestion forms, and technical proposal forms are typical examples. Specimen 51 suggests the format and substance for proposing suggestions. Specimen 105 (minutes of a faculty meeting) contains proposals that must be communicated in this descriptive form and format (following rules of order).

Forms are also commonly used as supportive mechanisms for proposals. For example, Specimen 23 refers to the company personnel record (a detailed form) to support the memorandum application. Technical proposals are almost always supported by several required forms (e.g., certification for meeting the Fair Labor Standards Act, performance bond certification, financial statement).

Brochures are specially prepared documents (often professionally prepared and printed) for distribution to groups or population segments. Standard supportive materials (called "boiler plate") are often in brochure form; Specimen 27 is an example. Resumes and vitae for job applications can also be classed as brochures. These can range from a simple, typed copy to a slick, professional printed product. Another use of brochures is to give details of the proposal or the company and people. Specimen 50 mentions an enclosure, which is a brochure proposal to be sent out to the business community. Other types of brochure proposals are catalogues, prospectuses and special offerings.

Summary: Proposal Execution/Figure 5.9 summarizes proposal execution.

PROPOSAL EXECUTION		
Medium	Uses	Specimen References
1. Letter	Short, simple pro-posals to outsiders; transmittals	Specimens 20, 22, 28
2. Memorandum	Short, simple in-house proposals; transmittals	Specimens 23, 33
3. Proposal (proper)	To present partial or complete proposal message (short, simple; lengthy, complex)	Specimens 34, 107
4. Form (implicit or explicit format)	To present proposals in standardized patterns (brief or detailed) To present supportive data (brief or detailed)	Specimen 17
5. Brochure	To present proposal—highlights or details To present supportive data	Specimens 21, 25, 27

Fig. 5.9 / Summary—proposal execution.

Summary: Proposals

Proposals, the first of three legally oriented managerial media, are documents that present plans, actions, or alternatives for consideration or adoption. We have applied the PRIDE sequence as our analytical approach—that is, we have examined proposal purposes, receivers, impacts, designs, and execution, together with presenting principles and examples of each element. Using the principles discussed will help you to determine good or poor proposals of others, to know where improvements are needed, to know how to write better proposals, and to know where all fit in the organization's communication scheme.

Agreements

The second of the legally oriented written media, agreements, are documents binding persons, groups, or organizations to actions, conditions, tasks, or codes of conduct. Agreements range from simple, informal acknowledgments to complex, formal contracts. (You can see that many agreements result from proposals, the first legally oriented medium.)

Purposes

Six of the more important agreement purposes are: formal contracts; acceptance of official proposals; commitments to sell or purchase; commitments to conditions or actions; commitments to assignments or jobs; and commitments to codes of conduct.

However, before discussing these purposes, let us issue a warning. As stated, agreements may involve individuals, groups, or organizations. You should always be aware which one (or more) of these is affected by any agreement. To commit solely yourself is one thing; to act as an agent for a larger group or a total organization is quite another matter. Many people—and organizations—have come to grief (some to bankruptcy) from not being completely clear on requisite responsibilities for and consequences—individually or collectively—of a seemingly simple agreement.

With this admonition in mind, let us now examine the purposes mentioned.

Formal contracts are often outcomes of informal, complex proposals. The knowledgeable manager or nonlegal professional can handle some with competence. Many, however, are so intricate and technical that they require legal and other specialist interpretation. If you have the slightest *doubt, consult a competent attorney and substantive professional specialist.* Most large firms have legal departments or retain legal counsel; by all means use these resources or obtain outside legal services if none is retained, and certainly competent specialists in the field are in the company or available as consultants. As with the legal expert, get needed professional advice. Therefore, because it is normally a field for legal experts and specialists, we shall say no more about formal contracts.

Acceptance of official proposals can result from any of the proposal purposes mentioned earlier (i.e., bids, personnel, organization, or product/service). Many of these may be straightforward and simple. In fact, most organizations have standardized forms or formats for use with common, recurring situations. (Caution: be sure that existing forms fit the situation you confront; also be sure that each meets all current external legal and internal administrative constraints—all too often laws and policies change, but the standardized forms do not.)

In relatively simple, routine cases with which you are familiar, you are probably free to act, but in more complex and technical acceptances, seek competent legal, as well as specialist consultation (e.g., engineering, operations research, computer technology). In other words, the same admonitions given under formal contracts obtain.

Commitments to sell or purchase are respectively vendor or buyer offerings.

While these, too, can be very complex and technical, let us assume that you have sufficient expertise to negotiate seller/buyer commitments and turn to specimens and examples of this purpose.

Commitments to sell are exemplified in Specimens 3, 16, 39, and 70. Specimen 3 is a sales commitment on two counts: a promise to deliver (sell) some of the goods ordered and a promise to deliver the remainder when available. Specimen 16 is a commitment to reserve a hotel room, providing the "buyer" meets certain conditions. Specimen 39 is a "mass" commitment to "sell" the bank's services (by offering 100 gallons of gasoline free) if the "buyer" finances a new car through the firm. Specimen 70 is different from the preceding in that it makes a counteroffer to a buyer's request for credit purchases by offering to sell goods for cash.

A commitment to purchase is seen in Specimen 14, an offer to buy a new automobile, with a provision for possible price adjustment at time of delivery.

Commitments to conditions or actions include acceptances of specified circumstances or responses. Acceptance of conditions are evidenced in Specimens 5, 15, and 19. Specimen 5 is an acceptance (although reluctant) of conditions (interest rate) on a bank loan; Specimen 15 is documenting a previous oral agreement that specifies prices, food, and services for catering a dinner; and Specimen 19 is acceptance of a request for an audit of company books.

Commitments to assignments or jobs can be seen in Specimens 75, 76, and 92.

Specimen 75 assigns a one year suspension to a student (who has not fulfilled conditions of scholarship); Specimen 76 terminates a contract because the vendor has supplied defective materials and inferior service; Specimen 92 specifies job requirements for the superintendent of a manufacturing plant. In accepting this explication of conditions for doing his job, the superintendent is committing himself to perform accordingly.

Commitments to codes of conduct pertain to ethical or professional standards to which organizational members subscribe. Such oganizations normally are either voluntary or professional societies. Of course in a broader sense codes of conduct also apply to any administered firm as policy or procedural guides. Specimen 93 is an explicit mandate on conduct and appearance as company policies. Specimen 99 is also an example of a code of behavior for receiving patients coming into a medical clinic (an instance of professional persons working in an administered organization).

Summary: Agreement Purposes/Figure 5.10 summarizes agreement purposes.

Receivers

Receivers of agreements may be analyzed using the same dimensions discussed under proposals, that is, status and psychology. As with proposals, examination

---

Agreement Purposes

1. Formal contracts
2. Acceptances of official proposals
3. Commitments to sell/purchase
4. Commitments to conditions/actions
5. Commitments to assignments/jobs
6. Commitments to codes of conduct

Fig. 5.10 / Summary—Agreement purposes.

of the psychological element will be withheld until Chapters 7 to 9. We shall focus here on agreement receiver status.

Status elements in relation to agreement purposes are shown in Figure 5.11. The purposes discussed in the preceding section are set against three important constraints: legal, technical, and administrative. *Legal* refers to laws and regulations, largely external to the organization; *technical* refers to professional or

RECEIVER STATUS HIERARCHIES
(Related to Purposes)

Purpose	Expertise	Positions	Organizational Leverage
Formal contracts	#1 legal #2 technical #3 administrative	technical legal administrative	technical administrative legal
Acceptance of official proposals (technical/ complex: same as formal contracts)	#1 technical #2 administrative #3 legal	administrative technical legal	technical administrative legal
Commitments to sell/purchase	#1 technical #2 administrative #3 legal	administrative technical legal	technical administrative legal
Commitments to conditions or actions	#1 technical #2 legal #3 administrative	administrative technical legal	administrative technical legal
Commitments to assignments/ jobs	#1 administrative #2 technical #3 legal	administrative technical legal	administrative technical legal
Commitments to codes of conduct	#1 technical #2 legal #3 administrative	technical administrative legal	technical administrative legal

Fig. 5.11 / Receiver status hierarchies.

specialist knowledge or skill, which can be within or outside the firm; *administrative* refers to the policies, procedures, and practices of the organization, which, of course, are internal.

Since these three constraints cut across all three status variables (expertise, position, organizational leverage), they are related to each in the table.

The three constraints are listed in descending order of importance (i.e., #1 is the most important; #3 is the least important). We do not pretend that our rankings obtain in every case, but this package is a general guide to assess the majority of agreements. (Once again, that precious commodity called *judgment* must be exercised in each instance.) Used with discretion and prudence, the guide can be very helpful as a ready reference in assessing agreements in relation to receiver needs and perceptions.

Impacts

Since you know already the nature of impacts, and since the three constraints, legal, technical, and administrative, relate directly to how the agreement will strike the receiver, we show what must be considered in assessing impact on each of the three in Figure 5.12.

Design and Execution

Because of the many differences in agreements (e.g., complexity, technicality, applicability) and because they frequently grow out of proposals of similar nature, we shall not duplicate our previous discussion of design. Clearly complex proposals produce concomitantly complex designs for resulting agreements. Simple documents can be short and straightforward. For example, Figure 5.13 exemplifies a simple agreement proper (excerpt from a computerized billing statement).

We shall combine agreement design and execution by focusing on the media of execution and giving related salient features of agreement format and composition. Figure 5.14 summarizes these relationships.

Summary: Agreements

Agreements, the second important legally oriented managerial media are documents binding persons or groups or organizations to actions, conditions, tasks or codes of conduct. Like proposals, to which they directly relate, agreements range from informal to formal, simple to complex, and nontechnical to technical. Using PRIDE as the analytical basis, you can examine important agreements and with proper precautions, know their right uses and limitations. Moreover you know when to call on experts for assistance, as well as when you can use agreements yourself.

AGREEMENT CONSTRAINTS AND MAJOR IMPACT FACTORS

Constraint (together with area of little or no concern)	Major Impact Factors
Legal	
(Little concern with administrative needs; often some concern with technical)	Substantive clarity: Do we understand fully what the agreement calls for? Conformance with law: Does the agreement meet all relevant legislative and regulatory requirements? Protection of organization: What are possible *external* consequences (good and bad)?
Technical	
(Often little concern with legal demands; sometimes a little more concern with administrative)	Substantive validity: Are adequate product/service specifications spelled out? Conformance with professional/specialist codes: Does the agreement call for proper professional capability and performance? Protection of specialist: What are possible *internal* and *external* professional consequences (good and bad)?
Administrative	
(Varies, but more often weighted in favor of legal)	Organizational survival: Is the agreement compatible with and contributory to important organizational goals and needs? Conformance with organization shape and policies: Does the agreement fit existing or anticipated organizational structure and guidelines? Protection of organization: What are possible *internal* consequences (good and bad)?

Fig. 5.12 / Agreement constraints and major impact factors.

IMPORTANT INFORMATION

The **FINANCE CHARGE** shown is computed by a periodic rate of 1½% for that part of your previous balance under $500.01 and by a periodic rate of 1% for that part of your previous balance exceeding $500.00 (or a minimum charge of $.50 for balances under $33.33), which correspond to annual percentage rates of 18% and 12%, respectively. Current payments and/or credits appearing on this statement are not deducted from your previous balance before computation of the finance charge.

An asterisk (*) accompanying the finance charge on this statement indicates application of the minimum finance charge.

Fig. 5.13 / Agreement proper—form.

AGREEMENT DESIGN AND EXECUTION

Medium	Receiver Location	Length	Complexity	Technicality	Major Constraints	Common Uses
1. Letters	External	Short	Relatively simple	Nontechnical	Technical Administrative	Transmittal; Highlights more lengthy, complex documents
2. Memoranda	Internal	Short	Simple	Nontechnical	Technical Administrative	Transmittal; Highlights more lengthy, complex documents
3. Agreements Proper	Internal and external	Short to lengthy	Simple to complex	Technical to nontechnical	Legal Technical Administrative	Explicates all pertinent details, conditions; Becomes the basic agreement document
4. Directives	Internal	Short to lengthy	Simple to complex	Technical to nontechnical	Administrative Technical Legal	Explicates all pertinent details; Becomes basic document; Highlights other documents
5. Manuals	Internal	Relatively lengthy	Relatively simple	Technical to nontechnical	Technical Administrative	Basic agreement document for task performance
6. Forms	Internal and external	Short to lengthy	Complex to simple	Technical to nontechnical	Legal Technical Administrative	Basic agreement document for standardized handling; Supportive or detailed data for basic document
7. Brochures	Internal and external	Short to lengthy	Complex to simple	Technical to nontechnical	Technical Administrative Legal	Highlights detailed basic document; Supportive or back-up for basic document

Fig. 5.14 / Agreement design and execution.

Directives

The last of the legally oriented documents, directives, explicate guidelines for accomplishing organizational objectives and tasks. Like the other legal media, directives vary from complex and lengthy to simple and terse; from technical to nontechnical; from general to specific.

You can also see that directives may result from either (or both) a proposal (e.g., recommendation for a policy change) or agreement (e.g., a new contract calling for special product requirements).

Purposes

Directives embrace two main purposes: (1) policies and (2) procedures. Since policies and procedures are discussed in detail as purposes in Chapter 9, we shall only highlight these objectives here, emphasizing how they appear in directive media.

Policies include organizational goals, objectives, and general guidelines. These can best be understood by referring to some specimen examples. Look at Specimen 92 as a directive describing the position responsibilities and operations of a plant superintendent. Specimen 93 sets forth the guidelines for appearance of company employees.

Specimen 94 is different. Its title, "New R. & D. Department Office Policies," is a misnomer; the document is actually a sloppy admixture of ambiguous "policies" and "procedures." It represents an all-too-frequent confounding of policy and procedure, something we explore at length in Chapter 9.

These examples give you a glimpse of some of the more common policy purposes you will encounter. Since we give intensive treatment to the subject in Chapter 9, we shall forego further discussion at this point.

Procedures encompass the "how to" (ways, methods, processes, routines) to accomplish policy objectives or goals. As with policy, let us examine two specimens in order to gain a better understanding.

The subject stated in Specimen 99 ("Public Relations: On Being Available and Receptive") is not exact. Careful reading shows the document to be a directive presenting generalized procedures for communicating with medical clinic patients. As an aside, note the reason (given in the introductory sentence) for issuing the directive: three complaints over a period of seven years!

Specimen 100 ("Dangerous Weapon Policy") is certainly a misnomer, because the directive is wholly concerned with procedures. The parenthetical "Supplement to Directive No. 10" following the capitalized subject statement is a key for knowing that policy and procedure are confused: Directive No. 10 is actually the guiding policy. And certainly the judgment is confirmed in the last introductory sentence, which starts, "The following procedures. . . ."

Summary: Directive Purposes/General purposes of directives are twofold: policy and procedure. Policies encompass organizational objectives and guidelines; procedures are "how to do it" directives to attain policy ends. We have presented specimen examples of the two types, together with brief analyses of each. The illustrations show a common error in many directives: the failure to clearly distinguish policies from procedures. This flaw can cause untold problems in an organization, and we shall concern ourselves with ways to overcome it in later sections of the book.

PRIDE Applied

Let us now apply PRIDE to directives in a different way from the methods used with proposals. Since you now have a better feeling for what each PRIDE element means and how used to examine documents, we shall unify all in a succinct tabular presentation respecting directives.

First, however, let us explain the terms used for receiver orientations: administrative, specialist, innovator, and social. (Other concepts used for the remaining PRIDE dimensions are self-explanatory.)

Administrative refers to the manager (at any level) in the traditional organization structure (e.g., comptroller, personnel manager). Managers with *administrative* positions (or outlooks) are *concerned* primarily with *maintaining* the *organization*. This group is sometimes disparagingly termed the "bureaucracy." However, as you no doubt see, any viable organization must have effective administrative stabilization; otherwise it will cease to exist.

Specialist is used in the same sense discussed under proposals and agreements, that is, as the professional or skilled manager or worker. Specialists are essentially *task-oriented*, with basic *allegiance* to their *professional organizations* and attendant *codes*. (Often these people have little understanding or appreciation of the administratively oriented manager in keeping the organization going.) The specialist's major contribution is his expertise, which is, of course, necessary to any modern organization to get its different jobs done and to keep in contact with the outside world.

Innovator is a more slippery category. However, this person is *essentially* concerned with *problem solving*. He may be a researcher, member of a special task force, or a project leader. Or he may be an innovator in basic thought and action (a generalized state of mind), even though he occupies an official administrative position or is working as a specialist. It is clear that this type of person is also necessary for the organization to develop, to grow, and to change to meet new conditions and problems.

Social refers to nonjob member needs and interactions (e.g., a luncheon group, members of the company baseball team, and special friendship groupings). Social groups exist apart from administrative position, specialist skill, or

PRIDE APPLIED TO DIRECTIVES

Pur-pose	Receiver Orientation	Impact Foci	Design Factors	Execution Emphasis
POLICY or **PROCEDURE**	Adminis-trative	Conformance: organizational policies, procedures ⟶	Assure compatibility	Largely written media
		Major concern: enforcement ⟶	Spell out how done	
		Benefit: organization survival ⟶	Point out contribution	
	Specialist	Conformance: professional codes and practices ⟶	Assure no violation	Balance of written and oral media
		Major concern: impact on professional task ⟶	Spell out where a help (rather than hin-drance)	
		Benefit: professional enhancement ⟶	Point out contributions	
	Innovator	Conformance: applicability to problem solving ⟶	Assure need for continuing activity	Largely oral media, sup-plemented by confirm-ing written media
		Major concern: avoidance of restrictions on creativity and problem solving ⟶	Spell out where helpful rather than restric-tive	
		Benefit: possible additional resource for creativity and problem solving ⟶	Point out contribution	
	Social	Conformance: social code and peer group perspectives ⟶	Assure no restrictions or violations	Largely oral media, minor emphasis on written for authentica-tion and record
		Major concern: avoidance of restrictions on social interactions ⟶	Spell out where better for members	
		Benefit: personal rewards, psychic satisfactions ⟶	Point out contribution	

Fig. 5.15 / PRIDE applied to directives.

innovative capability. Ephemeral (transient, subject to rapid change) in nature, social groups fulfill membership needs that cannot be met by the job or the organization's goals. As such, you can see that they create member collective cohesion not otherwise possible. No organization can long survive without effectively functioning social groups. The table in Figure 5.15 can be used for convenient reference to size up the planning and execution of a directive. Together with this chapter's background, you can readily assess directives for their fit within the organization's scheme. Furthermore you can critically examine directives for improvement, as well as write your own clear and appropriate directive documents.

Summary: Legally Oriented Media

The three important legally oriented media are proposals, agreements, and directives. Proposals present plans, actions, or alternatives for consideration or adoption; agreements bind persons, groups, or organizations to actions, conditions, tasks or codes of conduct; and directives present guidelines for achieving organizational goals and jobs.

Using modifications of the PRIDE sequence, this chapter presents principles for analysis and execution of each type, together with specimen and figure examples for illustration.

We are now ready to turn to the last significant category of written media, the organizationally oriented.

EXERCISES

exercise 1 What are the foci of legally oriented media? Give examples of each focus.

exercise 2 Distinguish between proposals, agreements, and directives. Include two examples of each document type.

exercise 3 Write a letter of application (proposal) to a firm, agency or institution for which you would like to work. Emphasize all elements of a communicative, persuasive letter. (Refer to letter Communication Quality Control, end of Chapter 2.) Also include an informative, persuasive resume as supportive material.

exercise 4 Obtain a copy (or copies) of an agreement (e.g., contract, financial agreement) from some organization. Using Figure 5.14 as a guide, write a critique of the document (or documents) pointing out specific possible improvements.

exercise 5 Obtain a copy (or copies) of an organization's directives (e.g., university catalogue or handbook, company manual). Using Figure 5.15 as a guide, analyze some policy or procedure, pointing out specific possible improvements.

exercise 6 Using Figure 5.15 as a guide, analyze and rewrite Specimen 93—a directive.

exercise 7 Write a memorandum (following the criteria in memorandum Communication Quality Control, Chapter 3) transmitting the revised directive. Emphasize clarity and persuasiveness in the communication. ·

CASE PROBLEMS

1. Re: Specimen 28: You are Robert M. Jones, Director of the management consulting firm that is quoting on the training program for Star-X Engineering Consultants. Mr. Miller has called you about the letter of March 15. In the call, these ideas were brought out: You agreed that the $18,000 cost included your supplying training facilities. Mr. Miller asked for a written detailed breakdown on the $18,000 total using his firm's cost categories, which are: Administrative; Facilities; Instruction; Materials; Miscellaneous. You have the following data under your cost categories, which are: Clerical costs—$1,000; Computer terminal time—$1,500; Instructors: 8 @ $1,000 each; Management fee—$2,000; Room rental—$1,000; Texts and workbooks—$2,000; Video tape rental—$2,500.

Your Mission: Write the basic proposal in tabular form using Mr. Miller's categories for cost breakdown. Also write a transmittal letter that highlights and makes attractive your revised training proposal. Check the tabular report against Figure 4.19, "Appearance of Graphs and Tables." Examine the transmittal letter against Figure 4.5, "Simple Proposal Designs," and the letter Communication Quality Control.

2. Re: Specimen 94: You are Robert M. Jones, the originator of this directive. Your superior, the Executive Vice President, Mr. William S. Miller, has called you telling of complaints he has received that the memo is dictatorial in tone and sloppily written. Moreover, Mr. Miller pointed out that the memo is really a mixture of policy and procedures.

Your Mission: Rewrite the directive, clearly distinguishing policies from procedures, together with a brief, but persuasive presentation on legitimate reasons for the changes dictated. Refer to Figure 5.15 as a guide in your document. Also check the final product against the memorandum Communication Quality Control.

Chapter 6

ORGANIZATIONALLY ORIENTED MEDIA: MANUALS, FORMS, AND BROCHURES

Your Learning Objectives:

1. To know the nature of organizationally oriented media.
2. To know the general application of PRIDE to organizationally oriented media.
3. To know the definition of manuals.
4. To know common purposes of manuals.
5. To know how to apply PRIDE to manual planning and presentation.
6. To know the definition of forms.
7. To know common purposes of forms.
8. To know how to apply PRIDE to forms planning and presentation.
9. To know the definition of brochures.
10. To know common purposes of brochures.
11. To know how to apply PRIDE to brochure planning and presentation.

The last major grouping of managerial written media, organizationally oriented documents, includes manuals, forms, and brochures.

The Nature of Organizationally Oriented Media

Manuals, forms, and brochures are highly structured and stylized documents directed to or used by selected receiver populations within or outside the firm. Whether internal or external, they serve basic organization (rather than member) goals and needs. Moreover, as you will see when you come to Chapter 11, these three documents are essentially *media carriers,* whereas the previous six (letters, memoranda, reports, proposals, agreements, and directives) have specified *media objectives.* For this and other important reasons, we treat these three media together in this chapter.

Generally impersonal, manuals, forms, and brochures relate to all of the media previously discussed. Indeed, many manuals and brochures include all types: letters, memos, reports, proposals, agreements, and directives.

Forms may also be included in manuals and brochures. However, when considered independently, forms are the basic carriers of an organization's vital information. With this background, let us now turn to each of the organizationally oriented media.

Manuals

Manuals are basically guides to action, in other words documents that communicate "how to do it" to specific target readers. They may range from general and abstract to very specific and concrete. Moreover, they may be highly complex or relatively simple, depending on the intended user-receiver group.

Our analysis will follow the same pattern used with directives, that is, first presenting purposes (with specimen examples), after which we shall put all PRIDE elements into a reference table.

Purposes

You have no doubt already inferred that manuals are actually *collective directives*—that is, bound (e.g., booklets, pamphlets, tractates) or unbound (e.g., loose-leaf, binder, or file) ways for achieving organization objectives and carrying out its tasks.

Both bound and unbound manuals can be examined under these purpose classifications: managerial, specialist, general information, and customer.

You will recognize that some of the specimen examples given in this section were previously used as illustrations of directives. (Remember that manuals are *collective directives.*) In most instances these duplications are excerpts from bound or unbound manuals. We are using them here to demonstrate the different manual types from which they come.

Managerial manuals (often called "policy" or "administrative" manuals or handbooks) are internal documents directed to administrators at all levels of the organization (e.g., top executive, middle manager, foreman). In large organizations, each level may have a custom-designed document for its unique needs; in smaller firms, all echelons may be lumped together.

An excerpt from a manufacturing firm's "Management Guide" is seen in Specimen 92, a position description of a plant superintendent. This is one of the common components of a managerial manual.

Another frequent section of managerial manuals concerns benefits and opportunities. A hypothetical example is the file copy of a memorandum that restates the manual's section on opportunities for managerial personnel to take certain training courses. Another possibility is an explanation of a university's administrative policy on sabbatical leave for faculty.

Objectives and standards are almost always included in managerial manuals. Specimen 91 (an excerpt from an accrediting association's standards manual for use by academic administrators) sets out "Common Body of Knowledge" objectives for accredited collegiate schools of business.

Specialist manuals (often called "procedures" or "instructions" manuals, guides, or handbooks) are both internal and external documents. Specialist manuals may be directed to receivers ranging from high-level professionals (e.g., personnel officers, engineers, scientists) to the lowest worker levels (e.g., machine operator, janitor) within or outside an organization.

Technical procedures are also commonly included in specialist manuals. Specimen 97 is a memorandum changing a drug order procedure from a loose-leaf hospital staff manual. Note the specimen also as an example of confusing policy and procedure. The document is dealing with procedure even though it is called policy.

Nontechnical procedures (often called "instructions") are frequently part of external specialist manuals. Specimen 101 is an example of this sort. Note the abundance of details given in the ten steps enumerated for handling the organization's mail. Since the persons processing the mail are outside the mail service division and since many are unfamiliar with specific requirements for completion, the originating mail department felt it necessary to present this elaborate set of instructions to get desired results.

General information manuals (often called "company" or "employee" handbooks or manuals) are internal documents for dissemination of ideas common to all members of the firm. Sometimes these manuals are restricted to certain employee levels (e.g., foremen and below).

A common component of these documents is an introductory statement by a top official as an introduction to the "Company Handbook" in the form of a letter from the President. The basic purpose of this device is, of course, to encourage employees to read the handbook.

Codes of conduct are also frequent inclusions in employee manuals. Specimen 93, "Your Conduct and Appearance," sets forth general guidelines for company personnel at all levels.

Benefits and opportunities are also important parts of most general information manuals. Specimen 95 (an excerpt from a bound employee handbook of a large service firm) gives details of the "Employees' Credit Union."

Organization structure and department operations are also often included in general information manuals. An example is a graphic description of how a large distribution firm's Public Relations Department operates. In addition to schematics, company division and department organization charts are very frequently components of employee handbooks.

Customer manuals (often called something akin to "instructions" or "suggestions for use" or "reference" manual) are generally external documents concerning the "how to" of company policies, procedures, products, or services. "Customer" as used here includes both the supplier of inputs as well as the buyer of company outputs. Modern managers take the view that the supplier needs to know how to sell or service the organization just as much as the customer needs to know how to use its product. Specimen 98 is a letter restating a manufacturing firm's policies on not permitting employees to accept gifts from suppliers. While already in the bound customer manual, this letter is a reminder of the long-standing policy.

Examples of Manuals

Let us now look at other examples of the four types. Figures 6.1(a) through 6.1(d) are excerpts (both covers and contents) of the four types of manuals.

Summary: Manual Purposes

Figure 6.2 summarizes the four basic purposes of organizational manuals.

PRIDE Applied to Manuals

Let us now apply the total PRIDE sequence to organization manuals. Figure 6.3 does this in highlighted form. (Remember we shall deal in depth with all PRIDE elements in Chapters 7 to 11.) You can effectively use this table to identify and to evaluate the various manual types. You can judge both good and bad ones, as well as know the where and how for improvement.

Forms

As stated, forms are the organization's carriers of its vital information. Essentially a form is a prescribed written medium for shaping routinized information

EMPLOYEE ORIENTATION BY IMMEDIATE SUPERVISOR

Name: _____   Department: _____

Regulations: procedural guidelines

Check When
Completed   FIRST DAY

_____   1. Working Hours
                     a. Summer
                     b. Winter
_____   2. Tardiness Procedure
_____   3. Absence
                     a. Must call if absent — 3 day lim
                  4. Coffee Break
                     a. Time and Rules
_____   5. Lunch Period
                     a. Time and Rules
                  6. Coke Break
                     a. Time and Rules
_____   7. Location of Rest Rooms
_____   8. Location of Drinking Fountain
_____   9. Assignment of Locker (If required)
_____   10. Smoking Rules
                     a. Cleanliness Particularly

Benefits

what is the plan

The Plan is split approximately equally into an annual cash distribution and into the deferred trust portion, provided the deferred portion is not greater than 15% of the total compensation of those eligible to participate in the Plan. This 15% restriction is established by Federal Law, and any amounts in excess of this 15% will be placed in the cash portion.

Position description

PERSONNEL DEPARTMENT
Job Description

Department ____Engineering____   Page __1__ of __2__

Title ____Senior Engineer____   Issued _____

Grades __KES__
       _____
       _____

EDUCATION:

BS degree in one of the major engineering
An advanced degree or specialized study w
graduate with specialized training, signi
aptitude for accomplishment of advanced d

CAPABILITIES:

Must have ability to perform design work
specialization with some competence also
leadership capability.

EXPERIENCE:

Administrative objectives or policies

PURCHASING

POLICIES

Fig. 6.1(a) / Manuals—managerial.

NUMBER G-28

(Specialist policy)

FINANCE BULLETIN

PAGE 18   OF

EFFECTIVE DATE	TITLE:	UNIVERSITY-WIDE FILE
		285-10P
AUTHORIZED BY	Regulations Governing Travel	LOCAL FILE REFE
C. J. Hitch		

and board costs may be authorized for reimbursement.
Such authorization can be granted only by the Chancellor,
Vice President or University-wide Dean and must be given
in advance of the trip.

g. Calculation of Total Per Diem Due - Total reimbursement due
will be calculated in multiples of the per diem rates given
above, based on the total number of elapsed hours between
time of departure and time of return from the trip. For
partial days, per diem rates are prorated by quarters to
the nearest quarter (i.e. 26 hours would represent 1 day
for per diem but 27 hours to 32 hours would be 1 1/4 days).

SUGGESTED SAFE PRACTICES

FOR   (Non-technical procedure)

GAS DISTRIBUTION MEN

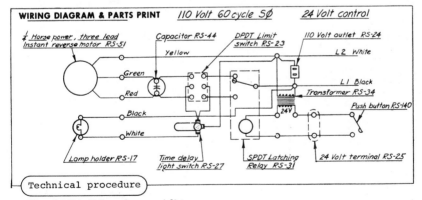

(Technical procedure)

Fig. 6.1(b) / Manuals—specialist.

Employee benefits

(Introductory statement)

It is a pleasure to extend to you a hearty welcome as a new member of the University Family. As a member of the Staff, you are an important part of an outstanding educational institution which has a three-fold purpose: Education, Research and Community Service.

This booklet contains a variety of information for your reading and reference. It will explain the benefits, rights, and privileges that are yours as a member of the University Staff. Although this booklet is primarily designed for members of the Staff, some of the information in this booklet, particularly pages 11, 13, and 14, will be of interest to members of the Faculty.

As in any organization of people working together, it is expected that you will learn your job, perform it satisfactorily and observe certain rules necessary to govern our working together. In return it is hoped that you will find here a community of common interests, affording the satisfaction of worthwhile work and a meaningfulness in your association with the University of Denver.

We are glad to have you with us.

Table of Contents

(Organization chart)

ACCOUNTING DEPARTMENT

VICE PRESIDENT
General Administration
&
Accounting

Auditor MANAGER TAXES & STAFF ASSISTANT TREASURER	Manager PURCHASING, STORES, TRAFFIC & INSURANCE	Director GENERAL ACCOUNTING ASSISTANT TREASURER	Director REAL ESTATE
Auditing	Purchasing	General Accounting	Real Estate
Methods & Procedures	Stores		
Data Processing	Traffic		
Corporate Taxes	Insurance		
Property Taxes	Headquarters Office Building		
	Arvada Service Center		

Supervision and standardization of methods
and procedures for these functions in
Divisions and Subsidiary Companies

Fig. 6.1(c) / Manuals—general information.

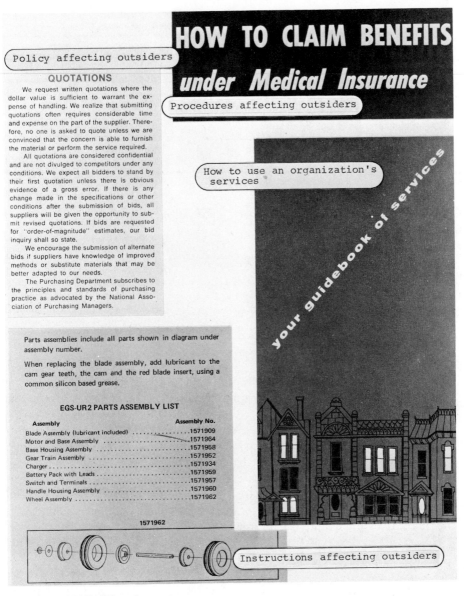

HOW TO CLAIM BENEFITS
under *Medical Insurance*

Policy affecting outsiders

QUOTATIONS

We request written quotations where the dollar value is sufficient to warrant the expense of handling. We realize that submitting quotations often requires considerable time and expense on the part of the supplier. Therefore, no one is asked to quote unless we are convinced that the concern is able to furnish the material or perform the service required.

All quotations are considered confidential and are not divulged to competitors under any conditions. We expect all bidders to stand by their first quotation unless there is obvious evidence of a gross error. If there is any change made in the specifications or other conditions after the submission of bids, all suppliers will be given the opportunity to submit revised quotations. If bids are requested for "order-of-magnitude" estimates, our bid inquiry shall so state.

We encourage the submission of alternate bids if suppliers have knowledge of improved methods or substitute materials that may be better adapted to our needs.

The Purchasing Department subscribes to the principles and standards of purchasing practice as advocated by the National Association of Purchasing Managers.

Procedures affecting outsiders

How to use an organization's services

your guidebook of services

Parts assemblies include all parts shown in diagram under assembly number.

When replacing the blade assembly, add lubricant to the cam gear teeth, the cam and the red blade insert, using a common silicon based grease.

EGS-UR2 PARTS ASSEMBLY LIST

Assembly	Assembly No.
Blade Assembly (lubricant included)	1571909
Motor and Base Assembly	1571964
Base Housing Assembly	1571958
Gear Train Assembly	1571952
Charger	1571934
Battery Pack with Leads	1571959
Switch and Terminals	1571957
Handle Housing Assembly	1571960
Wheel Assembly	1571962

1571962

Instructions affecting outsiders

Fig. 6.1(d) / Manuals—customer.

PURPOSES OF ORGANIZATIONAL MANUALS		
Type	Common Synonyms	Common Components
Managerial (internal)	Policy Manuals Administrative Handbooks Management Guides	Position descriptions Benefits and opportunities Objectives and standards Regulations and rules
Specialist (internal and external)	Procedures Manual Instructional Guides "How to" titles	Policy statements related to tasks Technical procedures Nontechnical procedures (for nonspecialists)
General Information (internal)	Company Manuals Employee Handbooks "Knowing Your Company" titles	Introductory statement Codes of conduct Benefits and opportunities Organization structure Department operations Organization charts
Customer (external)	"Instructions for" titles "Suggestions for" titles Reference manuals "How to" titles	Policies affecting outsiders Procedures affecting outsiders Instructions affecting outsiders How to use organization goods or services

Fig. 6.2 / Summary—purposes of manuals.

for communication of ideas. "Routinized information" refers to recurring important data or ideas necessary for carrying out some significant organizational operation or function.

Forms are very versatile media: they can collect data (e.g., questionnaire); record data (e.g., production record); transmit data (e.g., statement); request action (e.g., work order); report data (e.g., financial audit); instruct (e.g., checklist procedural guide); evaluate data (e.g., attitude survey); and store/retrieve machine-processed data (e.g., punched card—store; computer printout—retrieve). Indeed, a modern organization's quality of operations can be no better than the quality of its forms.

Purposes and Types

Forms may be classed as five: (1) production, (2) personnel, (3) marketing, (4) financial, and (5) machine-related.

Production forms are directly related to the output (goods, services, or both) of the organization. For example, in a manufacturing firm all forms are primarily related to man-machine-materials elements for output of goods. In a service enterprise (e.g., advertising firm, accounting organization, educational

PRIDE APPLIED TO MANUALS

Purpose	Receivers	Impacts	Designs	Executions
Managerial	Organization managers at all levels (internal)	*Clarification of:* → organization structure and goals → individual manager's position → where individual manager fits in organization (dep't and total firm) → member obligations and opportunities → Gain sufficient belief in importance of all foregoing	*Explication of:* → structure and policies → what and how of job → relation to other members and units → codes of conduct and organizational benefits → Induce conviction to or reinforcement of all elements	Formal written mode for authentication; informal and formal written and oral communications to supplement (clarify, persuade, get needed actions)
Specialist	Highly professional/technical to lowest level workers (internal and external)	*Clarification of:* → individual specialist job responsibilities operations of individual specialist job → individual specialist relation in administered organization → individual specialist relation to professional codes and associations → Gain sufficient belief in importance of all foregoing	*Explication of:* → what is expected of individual specialist → how to do the individual specialist job → where job fits in total scheme → organizational expectations in relation to professional expectations → Induce conviction to or reinforcement of all elements	Formal written mode for higher levels; informal written mode for lower levels; informal and formal oral communications to supplement (clarify, get needed actions)

Fig. 6.3 / PRIDE applied to manuals.

Fig. 6.3 (continued)

Purpose	Receivers	Impacts	Designs	Executions
General Information	Organization employees at all or selected levels (internal)	Clarification of: individual member benefits and opportunities → what and how of individual member job → department function → total organization's missions and goals → member relation to organization structure and mission → Gain sufficient belief in importance of all foregoing →	Explication of: relation to member needs, specific responsibilities and operations, specific operations, general objectives in relation to individual departments, specific fit of member job to general firm's objectives, Induce conviction to or reinforcement of all elements	Formal and informal written modes for authentication and persuasion; informal and formal oral communications to supplement (clarify, persuade, get needed actions)
Customer	Outsiders who make inputs (sell or supply) or who get organization outputs (buyers, users, consumers)	Clarification of: organizational expectations and warranties → the what and how of organization and functions → the what and how of processing organization inputs and using organization outputs → how dissatisfactions are handled → Gain sufficient belief in organization →	Explication of: guidelines for what is allowed/not allowed by customer, highlights of organization structure, specific steps to be followed by customer, exactly how remedies are processed by organization, Induce conviction to or reinforcement of organization's worth and trustworthiness	Formal and informal written modes, dependent on receiver orientation and background; informal oral communications to supplement (clarify, persuade, get needed actions)

institution, government agency), forms are more likely related to production based on persons and processes (rather than on materials); in a goods-services organization (e.g., appliance repair; engineering contractor) both persons-process-product and persons-process-services types of production forms are important.

Remember, production forms are related to *organizational output*; therefore, a given enterprise must shape these with its unique products, services, or product-services in mind. What this means is that an organization's production forms must be designed and processed in light of its unique people, policies, procedures, and practices. For this reason, rarely will one firm's production forms rightly serve another seemingly similar organization—there are always enough differences to require different instruments.

Let us now examine only a few specimens and a figure (out of the countless possibilities) of production forms.

A frequently used production form is for inventory control. Figure 6.4 is a form used by an airline for proper accounting of in-flight liquor transactions (primarily goods). This is a relatively simple, but effective document; in large production firms inventory control instruments are often lengthy, intricate, and technical.

ENROUTE LIQUOR INVENTORY
CONTROL RECORD

LIQUOR CHEST NO.______ AIRCRAFT TYPE______ SN NO.______ FIRST CLASS___ DELUXE COACH___ COACH___

SCHEDULE FLIGHT NO.______ CHARTER FLIGHT______ OTHER______

DATE______	BEER	SEAL NO.	LIQUOR	SEAL NO.	DEPOSIT	SIGNATURES
BEGINNING INVENTORY						CHEST PREPARED By X
ISSUED - SALES	—		—			VERIFIED By X
SUBTOTAL						RECEIVED By X
ISSUED - COMPLIMENTARY	—		—			FOR STATION USE ONLY DEPOSIT RECEIVED
ENDING INVENTORY	*		*			By X______

BANK DEPOSIT PREPARED

By X______

DATE______

COMPLIMENTARY LIQUOR SERVED BY SEGMENT AND CLASS

SEGMENT FLOWN		ISSUED CLASS F/A	Y

REPORT AND EXPLAIN ALL DISCREPANCIES:

*STEWARDESS:
CARRY ENDING INVENTORY INFORMATION FORWARD TO "BEGINNING INVENTORY" LINE OF NEW FORM AR 3505 AT TRIP TERMINATION OTHER THAN PROVISIONING STATION/S OR UPON TRANSFER OF KIT BETWEEN STEWARDESSES — SIGN "CHEST PREPARED BY" ON NEW FORM.

COPY 1 - REMAINS IN LIQUOR KIT

COPY 2 - ATTACH TO DUPLICATE COPY OF DEPOSIT COLLECTION REPORT

COPY 3 - RETAINED BY STATION MAKING BANK DEPOSIT

COPY 4 - RETAINED BY ORIGINATING STEWARDESS

Fig. 6.4 / Example—production form.

```
                        STAR-X REPORTS, INC.
                                         May 19, 19--

City University
University Park, Nohio

                             Re:  Thompson, Donald B.
                                  D/O/B  5/9/44
                                  Receiver M.B.A. degree

Dear Sirs:

The person named above has made application with one of
our clients for a position.  We have been requested to
verify the applicant's enrollment at your school.  We
will appreciate your furnishing us with the verification
and other information requested, which will be handled in
a confidential manner.
                             Very truly yours,

                             Special Representative
Dates of Attendance: _____
Major Course of Study: _____
Degree/Diploma/Certificates: _____
Rank in Class: _____
Average: _____
Extra Curricular: _____
Comments: _____
_____
_____
Authority_____ Title_____
```

Fig. 6.5 / Example—personnel form.

Shipping and receiving forms are almost always existent in organizations supplying goods. Specimen 3 is a shipping form for a partial delivery of goods. Another form is used for complete deliveries.

A less common production form (but a very useful one in many firms) is an operational audit instrument. Translated, this means a form for analysis of an organization's works and procedures.

Personnel forms deal with information about persons, whether employee data or applications or requests for personnel information. An example of a request for employment information is seen in Figure 6.5, a turnaround form used by a personnel agency to verify student status. How would you evaluate this form as a communication document?

Figure 6.6 is another personnel form for verifying an employee's completion of a university course. The company uses the information to pay (or not) for the employee's tuition and book expenses. Satisfactory completion entitles the

---

COURSE COMPLETION

Name of Student_____

Name of School where course is
                   being studied_____

Course Title_____

Will the student's completion of the above-named course
be:
    Satisfactory?_____
       OR   Date_____
    Unsatisfactory?_____

        Instructor's Signature_____

Form A 570-64-9778

Fig. 6.6 / Example—personnel form.

employee to ninety percent reimbursement; an unsatisfactory rating results in no payment. What about this form? For example, where could it be improved in terms of design, wording, and format to get better responses?

Figure 6.7, an application form for employment (used by a large manufacturer for applicants holding undergraduate or graduate degrees), is an excerpt from a longer document. Note the detailed information called for under each of the categories on the left. How does this application form strike you? Good or bad? Why?

Marketing forms promote the sale of goods or services or both. These include solicitation of information (e.g., market surveys) which may lead to sales. (Marketing forms in relation to people are concerned with aggregates or "body counts." Thus, they differ from personnel forms, which deal with information about specific individuals.) Many and varied, we shall illustrate only a few types here.

Figure 6.8 is a catalog order form of a mail-order house. It combines space for ordering items, together with instructions with simplified methods for computing shipping costs and taxes. Is this not a good example of an effective, communicative form?

Figure 6.9 and Specimen 41 represent two ways to survey attitudes. Figure 6.9 is an airline's form for getting quick passenger responses to service from time of reservation until arrival at destination airport. Note that it is almost completely based on a checklist of items. Specimen 41, on the other hand, is

PERSONAL INFORMATION
For Use of Bachelor's and Master's Degree
Candidates — All Academic Disciplines

USE BLACK INK OR TYPEWRITER

AN EQUAL OPPORTUNITY EMPLOYER
New York State Law Against Discrimination prohibits discrimination because of age.

Name _____ Social Security No. _____
      Last   First   Middle Initial

PRESENT mailing address. Street_____ Phone: Area_____ No._____

City_____ State_____ Zip_____
PERMANENT address where you can always be reached. Street_____ Phone: Area_____ No._____

City_____ State_____ Zip_____
Date_____ Dates available for pre-employment visits:_____ Date ready for work:_____

EDUCATION

List in chronological order all educational institutions attended. Start with last high school and include military service schools:

	Degree	Major	Minor	Cumulative Grade Point Average & Base, e.g.: 3.2 /4.0	Class Standing, e.g.: Top 1/10, ¼, ½; or 25/80	Attendance From (Mo./Yr.) To (Mo./Yr.)	Anticipated or Actual Graduation (Mo./Yr.)
High School:							
Colleges:							

Made best grades in (course names): _____
College grade point averages by years (not cumulative): 1st____ 2nd____ 3rd____ 4th____ 5th____ 6th____

Future education interests (check): Strong____ Moderate____ Indefinite____; Part Time____ Full Time____; Master's____ Doctor's____ Degree.

HONORS AND ACTIVITIES

College honors, honorary fraternities, scholarships, other awards: Honor or Award	Duties and Offices	Year	Hobbies, societies, publications, athletics, social fraternities, other organizations: Activity	Duties and Offices	Year

WORK EXPERIENCE

List chronologically all work— full time, military, summer, cooperative (number and length), and part-time:

(Mo./Yr.) to (Mo./Yr.)	Employing Organization & Location	Describe Duties	Hrs./ Wk.

MILITARY

Reserve/draft status_____ Active duty: requested___, ordered___, fulfilled___; Mo./Yr._____ to Mo./Yr._____ Highest rank_____
Branch_____ Significant activities/experience_____

PERSONAL DATA

Date of birth_____ Height_____ Weight_____ Marital Status: single_____, engaged_____, married_____, Number of children_____

Have you had or do you now have any physical and/or mental health problems such as tuberculosis; epilepsy; fainting spells; hernia; nervous, mental or emotional diseases/trouble; diabetes; back ailments; heart condition; amputations; limitations in sight, speech, hearing or limb; or any other physical/mental health problems?

No____ Yes____ If yes, explain (so we can tailor employment consideration) :_____

Fig. 6.7 / Example—personnel form.

a more lengthy combination of four items to be checked and one to be completed in essay fashion. Figure 6.9 is an external form, while Specimen 41 is internal. Both serve useful purposes. How would you rate each relative to effectiveness of communication impact to get right responses?

Financial forms treat monetary data. They are used extensively both internally and externally. Internal examples are payroll forms and internal operating forms (e.g., budget, capital expenditures). External kinds are represented by statements, invoices, and applications for credit.

Figure 6.10 shows an example of application for credit. How does this form strike you? Would you willingly fill it out? Why or why not? Could it be improved? Where and how?

HANDY ORDER FORM

CAT. NO.	QUAN.	DESC'.IPTION	PRICE EACH	TOTAL COST
			$	$

SHIPPING COST CHART:
This chart tells you how much should be included in your remittance for postage and handling as determined by total cost of merchandise ordered. This only partially covers our expense —we pay the rest.

TOTAL OF ABOVE ORDER	$
N.Y.S. RESIDENTS ADD TAX (FOOD EXEMPT)	$
SHIPPING COST OF ABOVE ORDERS	$
TOTAL AMOUNT	$

IF YOUR ORDER IS...		UP TO $3.00	$3.01 to $5.00	$5.01 to $7.00	$7.01 to $9.00	$ 9.01 to $11.00	$11.01 to $15.00	$15.01 to $20.00	OVER $20.00
EAST OF MISSISSIPPI RIVER	A D D	49¢	69¢	83¢	99¢	$1.09	$1.13	$1.29	$1.39
WEST OF MISSISSIPPI RIVER		59¢	83¢	99¢	$1.19	$1.33	$1.39	$1.53	$1.69

FOR GIFT ORDER FORM, SEE OTHER SIDE

Fig. 6.8 / Example—marketing form.

Specimen 72 is a large retail store's form for acknowledgment to inquiries on accounts due. Note that it has standardized answers to handle anticipated questions or problems for most inquiries.

Machine-related forms are those which deal with men-machine data. Actually they cut across all four preceding types (production, personnel, marketing, and financial).

Figure 6.11 is a machine-related application for membership in a professional society. Note the limited spaces allowed in order to facilitate automated processing. Does it communicate effectively? What changes could make it better? Why?

Figure 6.12 is a government agency's machine-related change of address form, a punch card for easy completion and processing. How do you rate this document in terms of clarity, correctness, and persuasiveness? Is it designed to get the right answers and for user convenience?

Originating station: BOS

Check one. Did we make you: Happy? O.K.? Unhappy?

	Happy	O.K.	Unhappy
Reservation Service	◯	◯	◯
Service at departure airport	◯	◯	◯
In-Flight Service (total flight performance)	◯	◯	◯
Meal Quality (only if meal or snack served)	◯	◯	◯
Service at arrival airport	◯	◯	◯

Date

Flight No.

Read from ticket.

☐ Leaving home.   ☐ Returning home.   ☐ Other.

Fig. 6.9 / Example—marketing form.

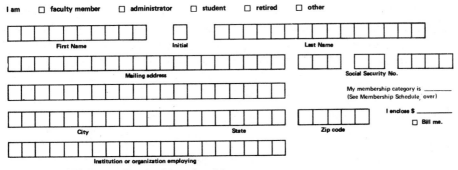

Fig. 6.10 / Example—financial form.

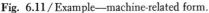

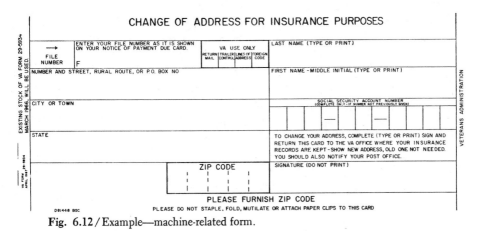

Fig. 6.11 / Example—machine-related form.

Fig. 6.12 / Example—machine-related form.

Summary: Forms Purposes and Types

Figure 6.13 summarizes the five major organizational forms purposes.

Forms—Purposes

---
1. Production
2. Personnel
3. Marketing
4. Financial
5. Machine-related

Fig. 6.13 / Summary—forms—purposes and types.

PRIDE Applied to Forms

Following the pattern used with manuals, let us now apply the total PRIDE sequence to organization forms. Figure 6.14 puts all elements together for ready reference. Since forms can function across the total media spectrum (independently or in conjunction with other types), we do not consider this aspect in the execution phase. Bear in mind, this presentation will not make you a forms design expert. It will, however, alert you to the importance and functions of forms as important organizational communications vehicles.

Brochures

The last of the organizationally oriented media, brochures, are directed to both internal and external market segments or customer groups. They appear in many modes, ranging from simple, "amateurish" mimeographed single sheets to slick, multipaged, professionally prepared documents.

Types of brochures are many, among them folders, pamphlets, posters, mail enclosures, university catalogs, annual reports, house organs, and professional articles. You may wonder why the last three are included as brochures.

Annual reports are basically a compendium of several other media types (e.g., letter from the President, directives—for example, changes in policy or procedure—and a highlighted financial report) which are directed to stockholders and other market segments (often company employees) to induce greater confidence in the organization and its purposes.

House organs are both internal and external documents covering a wide range of receiver segments—internal administrative, specialist, and social orientations, and external customers, stockholders, professional associates, and prospects. For example, they may include letters, directives, agreements, and forms of several

PRIDE APPLIED TO FORMS

Purpose	Likely Major Receivers	Desired Impacts	Patterns for Design and Execution
Production	*Internal* Line/staff output specialists Middle/upper administrative managers Workers at lower levels *External* Vendors and customers with specialist expertise	To get clarity, validity, and authenticity of information given or sought (for both internal and external)	Focus on logical format with sufficient, accurate data Assure authoritativeness of information (sources, quality, reasoning)
Personnel	*Internal* Key personnel managers and staff Middle/upper line managers *External* Organization employees—all levels Applicants and others with little or no knowledge of organization or its products	*Internal* → Clarity, validity, authenticity of data → Adequacy for handling membership management → Cogency to meet individual needs and expectations *External* → Balance of clarity and cogency; selling organization	Focus on logical format with sufficient data to demonstrate validity Focus on psychological format, using information to get credibility
Marketing	*Internal* Key marketing and staff Middle/upper administrative managers *External* Range from sophisticated to those with little or no knowledge of firm	*Internal* → Clarity, validity, authenticity of data → Conformance to organization requirements and needs *External* → Make above distinctions	→ Focus on logical format with sufficient data to demonstrate validity → Focus on logical format with selected data to show organizational compatibility → Focus on psychological format, using information to sell, but exercising care to use right information with the right level of external receiver

Fig. 6.14/PRIDE applied to forms.

Fig. 6.14 (continued)

136

Purpose	Likely Major Receivers	Desired Impacts	Patterns for Design and Execution
Financial	Internal	Internal	Internal
	Key financial managers and staff	→ Clarity, validity, authenticity of data	Focus on logical format with sufficient, accurate data to demonstrate validity
	Middle/upper administrative managers	→ Conformance to organization requirements and needs	
	Middle/upper discipline managers	→ Conformance to discipline requirements and needs	Focus on psychological format, using data to gain belief and acceptance
	Organization employees at all levels	→ Credibility of data	
	External	External	External
	Range from sophisticated to those with little or no knowledge of firm	→ Make above distinctions	→ Use same approaches as above
Machine-related	Internal	Internal	Internal
	Key and operator ADP managers and staff specialists	→ Conformance to appropriate ADP software and hardware requirements	Focus on ADP requirements for data inputs, processing, and outputs
	Middle and upper administrative managers	→ Conformance to organization requirements, needs, and understanding	Focus on organization demands for data inputs and outputs
	Discipline managers and operators in all four foregoing areas	→ Conformance to discipline requirements, needs, and understandings	Focus on discipline demands for data inputs and outputs
	Organization employees at all levels	→ Conformance to member needs and understandings	Focus on member demands for data inputs and outputs
	External	External	External
	Range from very sophisticated specialists to level of little or no knowledge of machine processing or of the firm or its products	→ Make above distinctions	→ Use same approaches as above

types. Their most common purpose is to induce greater belief in the organization, although they may also call for action.

Professional articles can be viewed as brochures (some organizations even publish periodic journals with a distinct professional aura) because they are directed to specialists inside and outside the firm. Rightly presented, they enhance both the author's and the organization's stature and image by communicating worthy information.

Therefore, as you can see, brochures are often a bringing together of several different media, which are directed to selected receiver segments. Let us now consider possible basic purposes.

Purposes

Actually, in the introductory remarks we have already mentioned examples of the three basic brochure purposes: (1) informing, (2) building belief, and (3) selling. Since they can include all other types of media, we shall use some previously mentioned and some new specimens drawn from brochures as illustrative.

Informing through brochures is a "soft-sell" approach. Frequently this is the purpose of brochures from professional organizations (accounting, engineering, law, medicine) because their codes of conduct prohibit more directly persuasive or "selling" methods.

Specimen 59 ("A Friendly Suggestion About Income Taxes") is a brochure enclosure in a monthly statement to patient-customers of a medical clinic. It is a "soft sell" in that it merely plants the idea of possible income tax deductions the customer may take by paying his bill before the end of the tax year. The information given is the basis for medical deductions allowed by the Internal Revenue Service. How does this document affect you? What are its communication strengths? Weaknesses?

Specimen 89 is a "soft-sell" student-oriented brochure (written by other students) giving factual information on drugs. It states that the pamphlet's purpose is not to pass judgment on drug users, but ". . . to inform and make more aware those who contemplate the use of drugs." Does it do the job? Do you see possible ways to improve it? Where and how?

Specimen 90 is a client newsletter (house organ) of an accounting firm. A single mimeographed sheet, it is sent periodically to the firm's clients giving new information on tax laws and related matters. In this instance, the reader is told about death taxes, with possible options for savings. How do you rate this relative to its purpose and communicability?

Specimen 96 is an excerpt from a social security booklet listing types of cash benefits for certain classes of eligible receivers. Does it communicate to its intended readership clearly, correctly, persuasively? Why?

Thus, *informing* brochures are "soft-sell" documents that stick largely to factual, reasoned expositions. It is assumed the reader will be persuaded by this type of presentation.

Building belief through brochures aims at getting mental assent, prestige enhancement, or image building. Brochures of this type are deliberately persuasive, but they do not in themselves ask for specific action. They may, however, be used as supplements to documents that sell (the next purpose to be discussed).

Specimen 25 is a vita (resume) of a university professor. In this case, the document is used to supplement his "sales" letter (application for another teaching position). Does the document really "sell?" Where could improvements be made?

Specimen 77 is not a brochure in itself, but it transmits this medium. It was sent with the last issue of a research firm's house organ to announce its cessation. Does this brochure communicate effectively to its intended readers? What changes would improve it?

Another supplementary belief-building document for a brochure is seen in Specimen 27, boilerplate for a proposal. How persuasive is this specimen? Does it make you want to read the rest of the proposal? Why?

Specimen 83 does not, at first glance, qualify as a brochure. However, this reproduction of a letter of commendation to a professional organization was displayed on the bulletin board for employees to view. It was assumed that it would induce greater employee belief in the organization and inspire better performance. Does it achieve its intended purpose? If not, why? How would you use this document—if at all?

Specimen 87 is a unique printed card mailed to customers and prospects by an international marketing firm. It tells of the death of the managing director, but at the same time, announces his successor. The purpose of this brochure is clearly one of keeping (or building) confidence in the continuity of the company. What about this specimen's communication effectiveness? Would you use such a document for this purpose? Why?

As evidenced by these illustrations, you can see that belief-building brochures are supposed to be persuasive, that is, directed to gain mental assent to ideas.

Selling through brochures is directed to get specific action response (e.g., the customer buys, the employee performs). Frequently using informing and belief-building devices as bases, the selling brochure goes beyond both to get explicitly stated action.

Specimen 6 is an example of using a belief-building letter of transmittal for a selling brochure (getting registrants for seminars). Does this document really sell you? Why? What changes would you make in it?

Specimen 17 is an excerpt from a brochure (form for seminar registration). It has been preceded by both informing and belief-building devices to induce reader action, namely, getting his name on the line as a registrant. Does it make you want to register? If not, why? How could it be more sales-centered?

Specimen 29 is a letter circular (for posting on bulletin boards) announcing an examination for a civil service job. The "Apply With" section is the action focus; preceding informing and belief-building elements presumably will persuade qualified readers to make application for the examination. What does it do to you? Are you ready to apply? Why or why not?

Brochure Purposes Applied

To give a practical demonstration of how different media may be used to achieve the three different brochure purposes, let us relate what we have discussed to a document with which you are familiar: a university bulletin (also called "catalogue"). (Note: The bulletin used for illustration is a very short one; therefore a few media are not included. More voluminous bulletins often contain all types.) Figure 6.15 applies these relationships in tabular form.

CITY UNIVERSITY BULLETIN

TABLE OF CONTENTS

Major Item	Subitem—Nature and Purpose	Medium Used
1. General Information	1.1 Welcome from President—belief building	Letter
	1.2 History of school—belief building	Proposal (boilerplate)
	1.3 Facilities/buildings—belief building	Proposal (boilerplate)
2. Student Services	2.1 Counseling services—belief building	Proposal (boilerplate)
	2.2 Dormitories and housing—belief building	Proposal (boilerplate)
	2.3 Tearout application: housing—selling	Form*
3. Admissions and Academic Standards	3.1 Admission requirements—informing	Directive/manual
	3.2 Academic standards—informing	Directive/manual
	3.3 Tearout application for admission—selling	Form*
4. Financial and Other Aids	4.1 Types—informing	Directive/manual
	4.2 Requirements—informing	Directive/manual
	4.3 Tearout application—selling	Form*

* When completed by applicant and accepted by university, each becomes an ⟶ Agreement

Fig. 6.15 / Example—application of brochure principles.

Examples of Brochure Covers and Titles

Figures 6.16(a) through 6.16(c) give a montage of several typical brochure covers and titles. While by no means exhaustive, these suggest some of the more common.

Fig. 6.16(a) / Brochures—informing.

Fig. 6.16(b) / Brochures—building belief.

Fig. 6.16(c)/Brochures—selling.

PRIDE APPLIED TO BROCHURES

Purpose	Likely Major Receivers	Desired Impacts	Patterns for Design and Execution
Informing	Professionals Specialists Critically oriented readers	"Soft-sell" through presentation of ⟶ worthy data and proper reasoning	Focus on logical format with sufficient accurate data; use proper supplementary media, careful reasoning, and "open" presentation made to assure acceptance of validity and worth. (Help reader to "sell" himself)
	Noncritical ⟶ readers of all types	Persuasive handling of information to build toward belief and selling	⟶ Focus on psychological format, using information and proper media to get reader attention and interest (make the reader want to know what is communicated)
Belief-Building	Professionals Specialists Critically oriented readers	Minimum of emotional appeal ⟶ maximum of reasoned appeal to deepen beliefs and attitudes	Focus on selected valid data and media; use proper reasoning; let reader draw the "right" conclusions on his own
	Noncritical ⟶ readers of all types	Maximum proper dramatic appeal to deepen beliefs and attitudes	⟶ Focus on selected dramatic data and media; use emotional appeals; carry reader to "right" conclusions
Selling	Professionals Specialists Critically oriented readers	Same approach as for "belief-building." (These readers will act only on basis of "reasoned" persuasion)	Same as for "belief-building" ⟶
	Noncritical ⟶ readers of all types	Gain maximum reader desire to act. (These readers must be "triggered" to respond as desired)	⟶ Focus on moving reader to act through most appropriate psychological methods, techniques, and devices

Fig. 6.17/PRIDE applied to brochures.

PRIDE Applied to Brochures

As with the two other organizationally oriented media, let us now relate the total PRIDE sequence to brochures. Figure 6.17 makes this application.

Summary: Brochures

Brochures are organizationally oriented media directed to both intra- and extra-organizational markets or customer groups. Varying widely in makeup, quality, and volume, they meet three basic purposes: informing, building belief, and selling.

By knowing the different types and applying the PRIDE sequence, you will have a viable method for size-up and presentation of brochure documents in your organization.

Summary: Organizationally Oriented Media

Organizationally oriented written media are specially designed to meet job and company goals (as opposed to membership needs). We have discussed the three basic types: manuals, forms, and brochures. In each, we applied the PRIDE sequence, using numerous figure and specimen references and easy-to-use reference tables for ready assessment and execution.

Conclusion: Written Media

This completes our discussion of the nine important written media for personal, legal, and organizational use. Figure 6.18 summarizes these, together with chapter references.

IMPORTANT WRITTEN MEDIA		
Orientation	Type	Chapter
Personal	Letter	2
	Memorandum	3
	Report	4
Legal	Proposal	5
	Agreement	5
	Directive	5
Organizational	Manual	6
	Form	6
	Brochure	6

Fig. 6.18 / Summary—Important written media.

The preceding discussion gives you grounding for the next step: an in-depth application of the PRIDE sequence to all these documents. You are now ready for Part II, "Applying PRIDE to Written Communication," which presents a sharper and even more useful method for analysis and execution.

EXERCISES

exercise 1 What is an organizational manual? List types and give two examples of each.

exercise 2 What is an organizational form? List types and give two examples of each.

exercise 3 What is an organization brochure? List purposes, giving two examples of each.

exercise 4 Obtain a copy of an organizational manual exemplifying one of the purpose types. Using Figure 6.3, write a critique indicating specific possible improvements in the document.

exercise 5 Obtain a copy of an organizational form exemplifying one of the purpose types. Using Figure 6.14, write a critique indicating specific possible improvements in the document.

exercise 6 Obtain a copy of an organizational brochure exemplifying one of the purpose types. Using Figure 6.17, write a critique indicating specific possible improvements in the document.

CASE PROBLEM

1. Re: Figure 6.15. The Dean of Students has appointed you Chairman of the Student Publications Committee of your college. Your Committee has been assigned the task of drafting a summary outline of a brochure to be sent to incoming freshmen.

Your Mission: Using Figure 6.15 as reference, select appropriate items (and add any additional ones that you think are needed) and outline the proposed brochure. Under "Nature and Purpose," give a capsule summary of what is to be included for each item. Check against Figure 6.17 for proper brochure execution.

Part II

Communicating
With PRIDE

(Purposes)——(Receivers)——(Impacts)——(Design)——(Execution)

As you recall, we discussed the PRIDE sequence in general in Chapter 1, and we used it as a general format for Chapters 5 and 6. We are now ready to spell out this pattern in greater detail so that you can better understand and use it. Properly applied, it is a very effective decision making method for planning and carrying out your communications, both oral and written.

To review, PRIDE is an acronym for the following:

P. The Purpose of your communication
R. The Receiver of your communication
I. The Impact you want to make on your receiver
D. The Design of your communication
E. The Execution of your communication

Let us now examine these. Because of special interrelationships, we will consider the five elements in five chapters: Chapters 7 to 9 will treat *purposes* and *receivers*; Chapter 10 will deal with *impacts* and *designs*; and, Chapter 11 is concerned with *execution*.

You have studied in detail the important written communication media. While you now know some general uses and features of each, we did not present an elaborate analysis of purposes and receivers. We will now examine in depth specific purposes and general receiver roles for any type of communication, whether written, oral, or automated.

Communication *purpose* is the sender's *target* or *goal*. Stated another way, purpose is the objective to which the writer or speaker directs his communication. Purposes can be very general (e.g., to satisfy human needs), or specific (e.g., to inform customers of a price increase). In organizational communication, the specific purpose is operationally the more useful; therefore it will be the focus of Chapters 7 to 9. Also, because specific purposes cannot be separated from *receiver perspectives*, we will discuss them together.

In these three chapters, we will view receivers simply as *unfavorable* or *favorable*. (In later chapters we will treat this topic in greater depth.) In relation to communication purpose, *unfavorable* receivers includes those whose perspectives are either in opposition, neutral, or unknown with respect to the sender and message. *Favorable* receiver outlooks refer to those in agreement. With this background, let us now turn to an examination of the important specific purposes.

Specific Communication Purposes

Most treatments of communication purposes are concerned with either very abstract goals (e.g., informational, action) or, at the other extreme, too trivial ends (e.g., a "yes" letter or "applying the Golden Rule" brochures). Neither approach is very helpful to the business writer or speaker.

After more than 20 years of work with business and professional practitioners and students, we have come up with three groupings of specific purposes that cut across any important business communication situation that you will confront. Proper understanding and use of these three will give you the keys to effective communication planning and execution. Once learned, you will find that you can rapidly size up what objective you are after. This permits efficient and effective use of the selected purpose to plan and to carry out your communication. After sufficient practice, recognition and use will become habitual so that you can use these purposes accurately, rapidly, and easily.

Let us now look at the three groupings and their subsets which will be covered in the next three chapters.

Chapter 7. Personal Purposes: Receiver Role Situational
    Acknowledgment/Acceptance
    Offering
    Solicitation

Chapter 8. Personal Purposes: Receiver Role Predetermined
    Complaint/Adjustment
    Rejection/Reprimand
    Goodwill

Chapter 9. Task Purposes: Receiver Role Situational
    Policy Communication
    Procedural Communication
    Status Communication

Chapter 7

PERSONAL PURPOSES:
SITUATIONAL RECEIVER ROLES

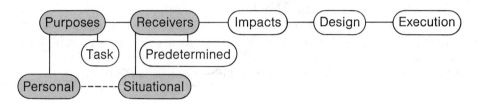

Your Learning Objectives:

1. To know the definition of personal purposes.
2. To know the definition of situational receiver roles.
3. To know the three basic personal situationally determined purposes.
4. To know the specific situational purposes for acknowledgment/acceptance to unfavorable receivers.
5. To know the specific situational purposes for acknowledgment/acceptance to favorable receivers.
6. To know the specific situational purposes for offering to unfavorable receivers.
7. To know the specific situational purposes for offering to favorable receivers.
8. To know the specific situational purposes for solicitation to unfavorable receivers.
9. To know the specific situational purposes for solicitation to favorable receivers.
10. To know how to identify and apply all situational purposes to specific personal communications.

Special Note on Specific Purposes and Receivers

In the next three chapters on purposes and receivers, we will not always raise evaluative questions concerning communication quality of figures and specimens. With your background from previous chapters, you are by now equipped to make your own evaluation of effectiveness. To encourage your raising questions on your own, we deliberately continue to include both good and bad examples and allusions.

The focus here is on an in-depth explanation of specific communication purposes and receivers. To help you get genuine understanding of these basic PRIDE dimensions, we present a new and systematic perspective for their identification and use.

To clarify ideas, we present several figure and specimen examples of each. If you understand a given purpose and receiver role without going through all examples, so much the better. In other words, proceed through the next three chapters in light of *your* understanding of each specific purpose and role, concentrating on those where you feel the greatest need for reinforcement.

In personal purposes communications are directed to the receiver as an individual. Although he may not be addressed personally (e.g., mass mailings with a "Dear Customer" salutation), the receiver's needs and aspirations are paramount. Situational means that circumstances will determine the receiver's perspective or outlook (role). In other words, the sender must know the conditions (situation) in order to predict accurately the role to which he should direct his communication.

The three specific situationally determined personal purposes under this heading are:

1. Acknowledgment/Acceptance
2. Offering
3. Solicitation

Acknowledgment/Acceptance

Simply stated, this purpose means approval of and/or making known the receipt of other communications, goods, or services. Generally, acceptance is concerned with the immediate, whereas acknowledgment involves some "holding operation" (e.g., referral of a letter to another person for answer or communication about a pending situation). This purpose can be directed to either unfavorable or favorable receivers. Let us start with situations where the unfavorable perspective prevails.

Unfavorable Receivers

Remember, unfavorable receiver perspectives may include initial opposition or neutrality or an unknown outlook. One of three different important situations usually obtains:

1. Receivers wrong
2. Apologies for sender wrongdoing
3. Answers to inquiries

Receivers are wrong simply means that you must communicate with persons whom you think have erred or are "off base." A warning: make sure that you, the sender, are right and that the recipient is wrong; otherwise you invite serious trouble.

Look at the example in Figure 7.1 (written in answer to a letter from Mr. Miller, whose organization had been inadvertently omitted from a directory).

Dear Mr. Miller:

Thank you for your letter about the *Marketing Directory.* Our records show your firm to be listed (see page 61, line 19 of the current edition).

I am sending a copy of your letter to Mr. Donald Thompson, our Editor-in-Chief, so that he will be aware of your complaint. I am also asking Mr. Thompson to write to you about the matter so that any misunderstandings can be corrected.

Fig. 7.1 / Acknowledgment—receiver wrong.

This is an acknowledgment in that Mr. Jones' letter is being referred to another person for answer. Clearly Figure 7.1 is an example of acknowledgment-centered communication to an unfavorable receiver (since Mr. Jones is allegedly wrong). For another example, see Specimen 1.

Apologies for sender wrongdoing is the reverse of the preceding, for it is an implicit or explicit admission of actual or possible sender error or inability to perform to a receiver whose reaction may be either hostile or unknown. Consider the example in Figure 7.2 as a letter admitting wrongdoing to a party whose probable response is unknown (therefore, unfavorable).

See Specimen 2 as an example of *possible* wrongdoing. Specimen 3 is an example of temporary *inability to satisfy* the customer. Specimen 4 is a tongue-in-cheek "apology," an effective approach if used discreetly.

Answers to inquiries refers to replies to either standard or special requests for information, goods, or services. This is one of the most common purposes in organizational or professional communication. Here, it is very important to

---

Dear Mr. Miller:

We goofed in billing you for $500 rather than the correct $50 figure.

Please forgive our error. I'm sure you understand how computer billings can be wrong from misplacement of a decimal point!

I am enclosing a corrected statement for $50. Please destroy the wrong one sent to you.

We'll make every attempt to avoid any future incorrect billings. Thanks for your patience.

Fig. 7.2 / Acknowledgment—apology.

distinguish between unfavorable and favorable situations, for unless this is done, communication failure can result.

Obviously the writer of the example in Figure 7.3 did not realize that he was

---

Dear Professor Miller:

You are right. The royalty checks will be paid as soon as the final payment comes in from various bookstores on the first printing.

   (A) Eastern State College   5275 copies
   (B) Polytechnic Institute   1625 copies

These are the other two principal schools using your book now.

Fig. 7.3 / Acknowledgment—special inquiry.

addressing an unfavorable reader. Certainly, however, he should have known, because in his letter to Jones, Professor Miller had indicated implicit displeasure at his not having received a past due royalty check. Unfortunately, the casual reply you see here angered Professor Miller to the point that he changed to another publisher when he wrote his next book.

Let us now turn to examples of acceptance in unfavorable situations. You can see that acceptance in unfavorable situations applies largely to inquiries, because the first two conditions (receivers wrong and apologies) are essentially acknowledgment-centered. As you recall, unfavorable may include either an opposing or neutral or unknown receiver view. In Figure 7.4, Jones, in accepting what to him is an unpleasant task, cannot be sure what reaction his candid reply may bring from Miller. He therefore is directing his communication to an unknown (unfavorable) receiver outlook.

Specimen 5 is an example of a communication addressed to either a neutral

---

SUBJECT: Community Chest Assignment

As you well know, my time is very limited for the next two months because of the demands of our new promotional campaign. And while I feel that I cannot do justice to the task, I will act as chairman of our company's Community Chest Drive, if you can find no one else to do it.

Fig. 7.4 / Acceptance—special inquiry.

or unknown receiver perspective. It can be neutral in that the bank may not be overly concerned about Jones' negative attitude; or, Jones simply may not know exactly what the bank thinks about his expression of displeasure. The latter case could produce unfortunate results for Jones. For example, what if, in light of Jones' open hostility, the bank decided to try to cancel the loan agreement? Since he was in a serious financial pinch, this could have put Jones in a real bind. In any event, Jones is running a risk in addressing this "acceptance" communication to an unknown receiver perspective.

Favorable Receivers

Since the sender is communicating with a harmonious (or agreeable) perspective, this means that different situations prevail. Among the most important:

1. Receivers right
2. Apologies to receiver
3. Sender appreciation
4. Answers to inquiries
5. Assents to offers

Receivers are right refers to cases such as the sender admitting an error or acknowledging the receiver's correctness in thought or action. Figure 7.5 ex-

---

FROM THE DESK OF

Robert Jones

Bill,

You were right and I was wrong. As you told me, our sales did decrease nearly $70,000 during the last quarter of the year. I don't know why I thought we'd had an increase.

In any event, since I lost the bet, I owe you a steak dinner. This ought to teach me to engage my brain before putting my mouth in gear!

Fig. 7.5 / Acknowledgment—"right" receiver.

Dear Mr. Miller:

On behalf of our Company, I want to express my sincere regret for the inexcusable behavior of one of our servicemen when you brought your car into our shop for repair.

Mr. Thompson, our Service Manager, tells me that he personally apologized to you. This letter is to add my own apology. If it is any satisfaction to you, we fired the guilty repairman on the day he insulted you, and we have taken steps to see that no customer is ever again subjected to such treatment.

You have been a valued customer and friend for more than ten years. We want to continue that relationship for the years to come.

Fig. 7.6 / Acknowledgment—apology.

emplifies the writer admitting an error as well as acknowledging the reader's rightness.

Apologies to receivers is self-evident. The sender openly expresses regret and often asks "forgiveness" for an adverse happening to a usually favorably disposed receiver. Often the communication will also assure the receiver that the untoward event will not happen again. Figure 7.6 includes all elements.

Specimen 6 is an apology for not anticipating or planning for the large number of persons who would wish to enroll in a seminar.

Sender appreciation can go in either direction: from the sender as appreciation (acknowledgment) and from the one who has been "appreciated" or thanked (acknowledgment or acceptance). Figure 7.7 is a note exemplifying the former; Figure 7.8 is an example of the latter.

See Specimen 7 as an example of a sender expressing appreciation; Specimen 8 is a letter in reply to a letter of thanks.

Other examples of favorable acknowledgment or acceptance of appreciation are Specimens 9 to 11. Expressions of appreciation can be transmitted through several types of written media. In addition, many such communications are done orally (e.g., face-to-face, telephone); while we have not discussed exam-

FROM THE DESK OF

Robert Jones

Dear Mr. Thompson,

Thank you for your prompt and informative reply about your firm's services.

Fig. 7.7 / Acknowledgment—sender appreciation.

Dear Mr. Miller,

Thank you for your kind comments about my presentation to your group on May 25.

I thoroughly enjoyed the association with your members; all were most courteous and friendly.

Please feel free to call on me again if you want to hear more about investments.

Fig. 7.8 / Acknowledgment/acceptance—sender appreciation.

ples, you should remember that the oral modes are often more appropriate than written means.

Answers to inquiries has already been defined in the discussion of unfavorable perspectives. In favorable outlooks this is an even more common situation. Figure 7.9 is an example of a short, but completely adequate, answer to a special inquiry concerning where a newly published book can be purchased.

Dear Mr. Miller:

In answer to your letter of April 8, if no major bookstore in Miami has "Effective Communication of Ideas," you may get it from the publisher:

Star-X Publishers
1200 Central Avenue
Spencer, Transylvania 54321

Fig. 7.9 / Acknowledgment—special inquiry.

A standard (routine) letter of acknowledgment is seen in Figure 7.10.
Specimen 12 is another example of acknowledgment of a standard inquiry from a prospective student. Even though from another school, note its remark-

Dear Mr. Miller:

Thank you for your inquiry about our University. We welcome the opportunity to help you in any way possible. The enclosed materials will give answers to most of your questions. If you want additional information, write or call this office.

Thank you again for your interest. If we can be of any further service, please do not hesitate to let us know.

Fig. 7.10 / Acknowledgment—standard inquiry.

able substantive similarity to Figure 7.10. Specimen 13 is a cablegram acknowl-edgment to a special inquiry. This means is useful when time is important, when you want a record of the communication, and when you want to mini-mize costs (since the cablegram is much less expensive than a trans-Atlantic telephone call).

Assenting to offers means accepting or agreeing to a proposal, suggestion, or quotation. More broadly, it refers to ordering, buying, or accepting any type of information, goods or services.

Dear Sirs:

Please send me, without obligation, your booklet on Med-Co Insurance Plan.

Name _____

Address _____

City, State _____

Fig. 7.11 / Acceptance—information.

Figure 7.11 is a form (reverse side of a business reply card) for use in ac-cepting the offer of a booklet giving information on an insurance plan. As with answers to inquiries, forms are very commonly used in ordering information, goods, or services.

Specimen 14 exemplifies the contractual acceptance section of an offer to purchase. When signed, the offer becomes a legal acceptance by both parties. In complex or intricate situations, a contract such as this is the best way to assure that all parties are clear on the agreement.

Specimen 15 is a written confirmation of a prior oral acceptance; it authenti-cates the earlier agreement and, in effect, becomes an informal contract.

Another example of putting a prior oral acceptance into writing is Figure 7.12. Again, this becomes an informal contractual agreement.

Dear Bill,

Many thanks for your call. I'm delighted you've chosen our location for your executive seminar next June. Since you have a tight budget, we will agree to a flat cost of $20 a day per person for double occupancy at the lodges. This, of course, means that you will have a minimum of 30 attendees.

Thanks again and if there is any additional information you need, do not hesitate to let me know.

Fig. 7.12 / Acceptance—services.

As you recall, foreign communications have different styles. An example is Specimen 16, in which the motel, in reserving a room, is accepting Professor Miller's "offer," that is, his request for a reservation. More commonly, a good form is much more efficient and effective for handling this kind of acceptance.

An effective form for acceptance of the company's offer is seen in Specimen 17. While this form provides for acceptance of services, the approach is also widely used in ordering goods or information. The value of well-designed company forms is that they provide a convenient means for the customer to communicate his acceptance.

Suggestions can also be accepted. Figure 7.13 is a memo in which the boss accepts an employee suggestion.

FROM THE DESK OF

Robert Jones

Your suggestion to consolidate our three different invoice forms into one is excellent. I am asking the Systems Control Department to draw up a form to satisfy our departments' needs.

Fig. 7.13 / Acceptance—suggestion.

Specimen 18 exemplifies assenting to a meeting time and place. An acceptance to an audit is seen in Specimen 19.

Figure 7.14 summarizes unfavorable and favorable situations in acceptance/acknowledgment, the first of the personal situationally determined purposes.

ACKNOWLEDGMENT/ACCEPTANCE	
Unfavorable	Favorable
1. Receivers wrong	1. Receivers right
2. Apologies	2. Apologies
3. Answers to inquiries	3. Sender appreciation
	4. Answers to inquiries
	5. Assents to offers

Fig. 7.14 / Summary—Acknowledgment/acceptance.

Offering

This refers to proposing or setting forth some service, goods, other communications, or other tangible items for receiver consideration. In offerings, the receiver has an implicit or explicit promise of some tangible benefit. Frequently, offerings are *quid pro quo* (e.g., buying a commodity for a given price).

Examples of offerings include an employment application (e.g., services of a person); a pricelist (e.g., catalogue on equipment); transmittals of a report (i.e. enclosing another communication for the receiver).

Bear in mind that in all cases the offering is for receiver consideration. You can see that this is a very significant and very frequently used specific purpose; and it is one that must be handled with proper caution and competence, else you and your company invite communication failure.

As with acknowledgment/acceptance, this purpose must be examined with respect to both unfavorable or favorable receiver views. Let us start with the unfavorable.

Unfavorable Receivers

In this purpose unfavorable perspectives more often include doubtful or neutral attitudes (rather than a known opposing view). Remember that doubtful perspectives are operationally unfavorable because you, the sender, are running a risk in not knowing exactly what your receiver feels or thinks about your communication. Neutral outlooks are unfavorable in that you must overcome the receiver's inertia, then move him in the direction you want.

Six important offering situations to unfavorable perspectives are:

1. Applications
2. Quotations
3. Special inducements
4. Recommendations
5. Changes/corrections
6. Transmittals

Applications are offerings, formal or informal, oral or written, for items such as jobs, admissions, credit, or services (e.g., a request for new telephone service). We need not spell out the importance and frequency of their use. While not always addressed to completely unfavorable receivers, it is best to look on most as either doubtful or neutral.

Figure 7.15 exemplifies an application for university admission.

As we mentioned before, forms constitute some of the most important documents in a firm's communication system. Most applications are forms furnished by the company. However, we are primarily concerned here with developing your personal communication competence in applications. Therefore our focus will be on the relatively "open" or unstructured, that is, documents such as letters of application, resumes, and "backup" materials for the more commonly used application forms.

Figure 7.16 is an example of a supportive letter to a credit application form that the writer filled out. Feeling that the form did not ask for sufficient salient

---

APPLICATION FOR ADMISSION IN SEPTEMBER 19—

(Please fill out in ink.)

DATE_____

Name of Candidate_____
                (Last)   (First)   (Middle)

Permanent Address_____
             (Street Address)   (City)   (State)   (Zip Code)

Present Address_____Until_____

Date of Birth_____Place of Birth_____

Marital Status_____Number of Children_____

                (their ages)_____

Are you a Citizen of the United States?_____

   If not, of what country are you a Citizen?_____

Father's Name (If father is not living or if his address is not known please give data for nearest relative and indicate relationship.)

   Name_____

   Address_____

   Occupation (be specific)_____

Below, please list chronologically the names of all Colleges or Universities which you have attended:

School	Location	Dates	Major Subjects	Degree

Fig. 7.15 / Offering—applying.

information about his personal background, the writer attached this letter to help get conviction on the part of the lending institution.

Often letters of application are "cold turkey," that is, unsolicited. In such cases, the applicant has not filled out any form; he is merely trying one or more prospective firms. His letter, then, becomes the basic means for attracting attention so that the door will be opened to him. Sometimes, also, the letter will be an answer to an advertisement in a newspaper or from a lead given by a friend or acquaintance (e.g., a professor may know of an opening about which he tells the student). This last type is seen in Figure 7.17.

Dear Mr. Miller:

I have filled out the loan application and supplied you with all the information that it calls for.

However, I feel that you need some additional information. First, I am a veteran with 5 years military service. Furthermore, I have six years experience as a manager of a machine shop in Chicago (prior to my military service). While I am a newcomer to this city, I feel that this additional background information will tell you that I am a person with some maturity and experience.

Actually, one of the best ways for you to know me is for us to talk together. Would it be possible to see you on Wednesday morning, June 12, at 9:00?

Fig. 7.16 / Offering—applying.

Specimen 20 is a letter of application from a student just graduating from college; Specimen 21 is the resume which accompanied Specimen 20. Sometimes applicants combine a letter of application with a resume. This is seen in Specimen 22.

In addition to getting an initial job, an employee may write a memorandum to upgrade himself within the company or he may correspond with another firm. Specimen 23 is an example of an in-house memorandum; Specimen 24 exemplifies an experienced professional person communicating to an outside organization. Specimen 25 is the supporting vita for Specimen 24.

Of real importance to many undergraduates is a letter applying for graduate study. Most institutions require the standard application form; therefore, the letter is supportive. An example is seen in Specimen 26.

Dear Mr. Miller:

Professor Donald Thompson of the School of Business at City University has told me about an opening for a management trainee in your company. My attached resume gives my academic and work background. You will note that I have worked my way through business school in a sales job. You will also see that I graduated with honors and am a member of Beta Gamma Sigma, honorary business society.

I would like to come in for an interview next week if it is convenient for you. I shall call your office to arrange a time when I could talk with you.

Fig. 7.17 / Offering—applying.

Quotations refer to offers to provide services, goods, or people for a given price or other specific considerations. They may be solicited or unsolicited. It is wise to consider most quotations as addressed to unfavorable receivers because you must convince them that your quotation should be accepted over others.

Specimen 27 is part of the "boiler plate" or front matter for a solicited proposal. Note that it does not deal with specific contractual considerations, but rather with conviction-centered information about the bidding firm. Such information is included to help build the company's case and hopefully to help win the contract.

Another solicited quotation is seen in Specimen 28 (price on a training course). Note again, most of the letter is devoted to build up the company; the $18,000 quotation is almost last. Figure 7.18 is a quotation on a computer equipment installation (a job that includes both goods and services).

Dear Mr. Miller:

You have asked us to bid on a terminal installation for your Purchasing Department. On behalf of our company, I would like to quote you a figure of $5,500 for the job.

I would also like to thank you for an enlightening afternoon yesterday. I was very impressed with what you plan to do. Your company is obviously a leader in its field. We certainly look forward to doing business with you.

Hoping to hear from you in the near future, I am,

Fig. 7.18 / Offering—quotation.

The above quotations are directed to a specific person in a specific organization. A more common use of quotations is by direct mail to masses. Sales letters and circulars are often used to offer goods or services to customers.

Figure 7.19 is an excerpt from a prospectus offering mutual fund shares. A prospectus offering mutual fund shares is distinctive in that it must conform with certain Security and Exchange Commission regulations.

Special inducements to unfavorable (doubtful or neutral) receivers include uncommon incentives or offerings to employees, customers, or organizational members. Specimen 29 is an announcement of a job offer to employees of the organization. Note that it is basically descriptive, giving duties and requirements of the position in addition to examination criteria and the place to apply. Specimen 30 is another announcement to employees.

House organs are common media to transmit inducements to employees. Figure 7.20 is an excerpt from a company newsletter.

PROSPECTUS

STAR-X FUND, INC.

SHARES OF THE FUND ARE OFFERED TO INVESTORS AT NET ASSET VALUE. THERE IS NO SALES OR REDEMPTION CHARGE.

THESE ARE SPECULATIVE SECURITIES

The primary objective of the Fund is to seek maximum possible growth of capital. The Fund is designed for investors who, aware of the risks, seek the possibility of obtaining capital appreciation over a period of years.

. . .

PRICE OF SHARES

The public offering price per share is determined at least once daily and is equal to net asset value. No initial subscriptions for less than $250 will be accepted from or on behalf of any investor. The Fund reserves the right to reject any subscription in whole or in part.

THESE SECURITIES HAVE NOT BEEN APPROVED OR DISAPPROVED BY THE SECURITIES AND EXCHANGE COMMISSION NOR HAS THE COMMISSION PASSED UPON THE ACCURACY OR ADEQUACY OF THIS PROSPECTUS. ANY REPRESENTATION TO THE CONTRARY IS A CRIMINAL OFFENSE

. . .

Fig. 7.19 / Offering—quotation.

Recommendations to unfavorable receivers give support to people or actions. One of the most common uses of this purpose is the letter of recommendation for either college admission or for a job. Specimen 31 is the former; Specimen 32 is the latter.

Recommendations for actions are normally for doubtful or neutral receivers —in other words, people who must be convinced of the worth of the recom-

---

The Company has set up a Suggestion System. All employees are invited to participate in order to make ours a better organization.

And there's something in it for everyone who comes up with ideas that either cut costs or increase profits. The Company will give you 10% of the first year's savings or profits directly attributable to your suggestion. So let's get with it: Let's get those brain cells in operation!

Fig. 7.20 / Offering—special inducements.

mendation. Specimen 33 is an example of a recommendation from a middle manager to top management. Specimen 34 is another recommendation from an outside consultant to the top management of a government agency.

Changes/corrections offer modifications of schedules or contracts. Note that we are not including price adjustments in this purpose. (Price adjustments are included under complaints/adjustments in Chapter 8.) Most changes to previously announced activities will engender some hostility because they disrupt a person's schedule or plans. Figure 7.21 announces to managers a change of date for a training program in which they are to participate.

Notice to Participants: Management Improvement Program

The session originally scheduled for June 11 in Room 52, "Planning and Managing Work," has been rescheduled for June 23 in Room 117. As soon as a time has been set up, you will be notified.

Fig. 7.21 / Offering—change.

Figure 7.22 is a rider or endorsement to a contract listing exclusions.

Specimen 35 is a memorandum concerning corrections about a previously printed examination schedule.

Transmittals are media that relay (offer) goods or other communications. In unfavorable circumstances, the receiver's outlook is either neutral or unknown. An example of the unknown outlook can be seen in Figure 7.23, a brochure accompanying an invitation to subscribe.

In Figure 7.24 you can see an example of another letter transmitting other communications (a brochure on a graduate school of business).

Sound-Reproducing or Recording Equipment Excluded

It is agreed that such insurance as is afforded by the policy under the Physical Damage Coverages is subject to the following additional exclusions:

The insurance does not apply:

- (u) to loss of or damage to any device or instrument designed for the recording, reproduction, or recording and reproduction of sound unless such device or instrument is permanently installed in the automobile;

- (v) to loss of or damage to any tape, wire, record disc or other medium for use with any device or instrument designed for the recording, reproduction, or recording and reproduction of sound.

Fig. 7.22 / Offering—change.

Please Forgive Us . . .

. . . if you are already a SPACE subscriber—or receive more than one of these invitations.

This invitation has been mailed to selected lists which cannot always be checked to eliminate duplication. We hope you will understand and pass this invitation along to an interested friend.

Fig. 7.23 / Offering—transmittal.

Dear Librarian:

Enclosed please find a catalogue of the Graduate School of Business of City University. I thought you might like a copy for your files. If you desire additional copies, please let me know.

Fig. 7.24 / Offering—transmittal.

Specimens 36 and 37 are relaying brochures: the first about advantages of membership in a society, and the second about a new home protection insurance for company employees.

Specimen 38 is supposedly a letter transmitting application materials to a university. You will note that the sender is also using the letter to support his application. In this case, the letter is a combination of a transmittal and a self-recommendation, which fits within the broad purpose of an offering to unfavorable receivers. It also illustrates how a sender has combined two situations that fall under the same purpose.

Favorable Receivers

As we mentioned before, most offering communications are sent to unfavorable receivers. However, there are situations where the receiver may look on your communication as agreeable (e.g., where he has orally agreed to a contractual arrangement and your written document is a followup for the record or where the receiver is a regular customer and puts trust in what you say and do).

Applications, the first item discussed above, are almost always sent to unfavorable receivers. But the last five can be sent to favorable receivers; therefore we shall focus only on these:

1. Quotations
2. Special inducements
3. Recommendations
4. Changes/corrections
5. Transmittals

Dear Mr. Miller:

This will confirm our phone conversation where we agreed to a price of $500 for the complete job of installing two outdoor lights in your front yard. The job will include all labor and materials including wiring, conduit, and two wrought iron 5 foot light poles and fixtures (Catalogue #2897). We will complete the installation no later than April 29.

Fig. 7.25 / Offering—quotation.

Dear Mr. Miller:

We are pleased that spring is nearly here so that we can renew our long term window cleaning service for your building. We are also pleased to tell you that in spite of rising costs, we will not increase our prices over the last year. As you recall, we gave you a quote of $500 for the spring and summer season (March 21 through September 20).

Again, we look forward to serving you.

Fig. 7.26 / Offering—quotation.

Quotations to favorable receivers are seen in Figures 7.25 and 7.26 which are respectively quotations on goods and services and a quotation renewal. Specimen 39 is a letter offering (quoting) some special goods and services to the bank's depositors.

Inducements to favorably disposed readers are exemplified in Specimens 40 and 41 (respectively a compensatory benefit for company employees and an exhortation to support a company club). Figures 7.27 and 7.28 are other ex-

Dear Mr. Miller:

The enclosed questionnaire is part of our effort to leave no ground unturned to promote effectively the sale of your book.

Please submit the information requested on a separate sheet of paper following the numbered sequence in the questionnaire. We shall use the information submitted with discretion. Therefore, do not hesitate to answer our questions candidly and as completely as possible.

A prompt reply will be appreciated.

Fig. 7.27 / Offering—inducement and transmittal.

Dear Fellow Employee:

Governor Donald B. Thompson, the first professional economist ever appointed to the President's Advisory Board, will be speaking on August 12 in Room 322 at 9:00 a.m. This is not only an honor for our Company, but something that anyone interested in the economy should not miss. It would be appreciated if you would attend and would urge others to do likewise.

Fig. 7.28 / Offering—inducement.

amples. Figure 7.27 is both an inducement and a transmittal; Figure 7.28 is an inducement in that it is an invitation to employees to attend company-sponsored special occasions.

Recommendations are seen in Specimens 42 and 43 (respectively a recommendation for people and action and a personal recommendation). Figure 7.29 is recommending a person for promotion.

SUBJECT: Promotion of Donald Thompson

This will confirm our discussion about recommending Donald Thompson to be manager of production. Although, as you know, I dislike losing him as my assistant, he has performed in a superior way for the five years that he has been in his present position.

But I know that he will serve the company even more in this new job. You have my strongest support for this action.

Fig. 7.29 / Offering—recommendation.

Changes/corrections can be sent to favorable receivers depending on the circumstances. Specimen 44 is a letter confirming a prior oral agreement to change a schedule. Figures 7.30 and 7.31 respectively exemplify rescheduling a seminar and a correction of spelling on an insurance policy.

Dear Bill:

Thanks for your letter of August 26. I am sorry to learn that you felt it necessary to postpone the Yellow Springs Seminar until May next year. We will be happy to work with you to make new arrangements for the Seminar.

Fig. 7.30 / Offering—change.

Dear Mr. Miller:

In response to your telephone call, I am sending you a new policy correcting the spelling of your name on your homeowner's policy. Please keep this as it is an important part of your insurance records.

Fig. 7.31 / Offering—correction.

Transmittals are frequently addressed to favorable receivers. Often they serve dual purposes. Note that Figure 7.31 in addition to confirming a change is also relaying the endorsement to an insurance policy. Figures 7.32 and 7.33 are both transmittal slips (brochures) for other communications.

Thank you!

With this policy you have purchased:

Sound policy coverage backed by . . .
Top financial strength
Readiness to serve you promptly anywhere in the United States or Canada.

Fig. 7.32 / Offering—transmittal.

Enclosed is the current edition of STAR-X Annual Report. It includes facts and figures on administration, financial structure, membership, company list, and information and research services. We hope you find it of interest.

Fig. 7.33 / Offering—transmittal.

Specimen 45 is a transmittal slip accompanying a training manual to employees.

Offering situations are summarized in Figure 7.34.

OFFERING	
Unfavorable	Favorable
1. Applications	1. Quotations
2. Quotations	2. Special inducements
3. Special inducements	3. Recommendations
4. Recommendations	4. Changes/corrections
5. Changes/corrections	5. Transmittals
6. Transmittals	

Fig. 7.34 / Summary—offering.

Solicitation

The last of the situational personal purposes, solicitations ask for *voluntary* responses from receivers. For example, whereas offerings are addressed to potential buyers of goods or services (for which something tangible in return is promised), solicitations are sent to people asking for their contributions (for which they may get no direct tangible goods or services). The solicitor may seek information, money, goods, services, or attitudinal support or approval. Very frequently, you may be soliciting monies, goods, or services as a representative of a charitable organization. Often information may be sought within the administered organization as well as from outside firms.

As with the two preceding purposes (acknowledgment/acceptance and offering), you must deal with both unfavorable and favorable receivers.

Unfavorable Receivers

The two important situations in solicitations are:

1. Seeking information
2. Seeking contributions

Seeking information refers to the solicitation of ideas ranging from tightly structured data to loosely structured comments. Often, the entire range may be sought in certain questionnaires or requests.

Figure 7.35 is a customer survey form in which both general and specific information are sought. Figure 7.36 asks only for general information.

Specimen 46 is a commonly used intracompany means in that it requests operating departments to supply information on their procedures. Another intracompany request is seen in Figure 7.37 in that it is trying to jog a laggard division to supply inputs for the company newsletter.

To please you more thru better "service" please complete

1. How much time do you have for this meal? _____

2. Did you come to eat from:
   A. Work _____ B. Shopping _____ C. Travel _____
   D. Home just to eat out _____ E. Other _____

3. How far did you come to eat? _____

4. How many in your group? _____

Suggestions _____

Fig. 7.35 / Solicitation—seeking information.

Dear Customer:

We want to improve our service to you. We want your suggestions. Please comment in the space below.

Fig. 7.36 / Solicitation—seeking information.

During the last three months, we have received no information about your Division for inclusion in our Newsletter.

I am sure some important things are happening which are of interest to other employees. Can you get your Division's inputs to us by March 1 so that you can be in the next issue?

Fig. 7.37 / Solicitation—seeking information.

Another type of informational request is that in Specimen 47. Here a former student is asking for a recommendation (information about his qualifications for graduate study). In this case he is asking for general information. Sometimes this request may be asked for on forms supplied by the institution to which the student is applying. This last type also differs from the preceding in that the information requested goes to a third party rather than the originator of the request.

Seeking contributions refers to requests for voluntary monies, goods, services, or attitudinal support. Sometimes all of these may be included in a single solicitation. More frequently, one or two are sought.

Figure 7.38 is from an envelope form soliciting money. Note that the

Here is my contribution to support the work of ASA in bringing military budgets under control and in its fight for social justice.

I enclose _____ $500 _____ $100 _____ $50 $_____

Name _____

Address _____

City, State, Zip _____

Please make your check payable to Americans for Social Action

Fig. 7.38 / Solicitation—seeking contributions.

SUMMARY OF PROPOSED SURVEY

City University, through Professor Donald B. Thompson, Ph.D., of the Department of Zoology, has proposed studying Spencer Lake as a "model of a high altitude artificial lake: so as "to develop guidelines for the future use of the lake and its environs." The study would be conducted for a minimum of one year, and would analyze not only the lake proper, but the Creek above and below the lake and the surrounding watershed.

To give an idea of the breadth of the project, the major areas to be explored are:

1. Population of vertebrate and invertebrate animals in the waters;
2. Collection and analysis of floating organisms and bottom samples;
3. Siltation;
4. Runoff—chemical and biological characteristics;
5. Census of wild mammals and other vertebrates living within the watershed;
6. Census of domestic animals in the watershed;
7. Meteorological data and water temperatures;
8. Chemical analysis of the water.

These data would be collected at various intervals to reflect the significant changes: some daily, some monthly, some quarterly, and so forth.

A graduate student from City University would be a full-time resident and would collect the data. It is hoped that local high school science classes and other interested people could participate in the project.

To fund this project for one year will require $5,000: $3,600 stipend for resident student; $400 travel; and $1,000 for laboratory supplies and rentals. Housing for the student will be provided rent-free by a local resident.

Research Area

Fig. 7.39 / Solicitation—seeking contribution.

solicitation message is combined with the envelope for sending the contribution.

Another solicitation for financial support is Figure 7.39.

A solicitation of monies is Specimen 48, which is authored by two well-known regional businessmen, goes out on the charitable organization's stationery.

A request for goods is Figure 7.40, an excerpt from a church newsletter.

Our church is making its annual request for contributions of your no-longer-needed clothing for our mission in Nigeria. Bring your old clothes to the church next Sunday, May 3. You can help!

Fig. 7.40 / Solicitation—seeking contribution.

A solicitation of services is seen in Specimen 49, while a request for support of a proposed idea is exemplified in Specimen 50.

Favorable Receivers

You can see that most solicitations are addressed to unfavorable receivers. However, in certain cases (e.g., prior trust or agreement), your solicitations may be to favorable receivers. The following demonstrate a few cases.

Seeking information from a favorable receiver can be seen in Specimen 51 and Figure 7.41. Specimen 51 is favorable in that a professional person is being

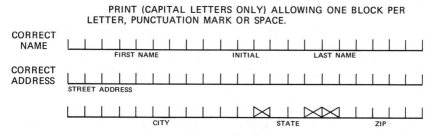

— NAME AND ADDRESS CORRECTION CARD —

Each designated block shown below represents ONE available letter position, punctuation mark or space between words. If your name, as normally written, is too long to fit – – please show us the abbreviation you prefer.

PRINT (CAPITAL LETTERS ONLY) ALLOWING ONE BLOCK PER LETTER, PUNCTUATION MARK OR SPACE.

CORRECT NAME

FIRST NAME   INITIAL   LAST NAME

CORRECT ADDRESS

STREET ADDRESS

CITY   STATE   ZIP

Fig. 7.41 / Solicitation—seeking information.

asked to give advice about a problem on which his opinion is valued and the results of which can be directly beneficial to him. Figure 7.41 is asking for a name or address correction of a member of a professional organization. It is viewed favorably in that the receiver knows that the information will be listed in the directory of the organization and he wishes it to be correct.

Seeking contributions from favorable receivers are shown in four examples: Figures 7.42 and 7.43 and Specimens 52 and 53. Figure 7.42 is soliciting money (renewal of membership in a women's organization).

Rx for a Happy year—for you

Renew your membership in the Women's Literary Association.

Take regular doses of the "Program on Current Thought."

Exercise your brain on the problems of today and the future—and limber up your thought process on the solutions.

Rest your pen on your checkbook—and send your membership renewal TODAY!

Recovery will be swift with your support.

Fig. 7.42 / Solicitation—seeking contribution.

As a member of a strong ecologically oriented organization, we know that you support anything that helps the betterment of our community habitat. As many of you mentioned at our recent meeting, trash is one of the most troublesome problems facing our region.

In answer to your suggestions, we have set up a Recycling Center. Start saving all newspapers and aluminum cans and bring them to the Recycling Center at Cypress and Pine Streets each Saturday. This is an important first step in improving our environment by minimizing the volume of trash normally dumped or burned.

Fig. 7.43 / Solicitation—seeking contribution.

Specimen 52 is asking for services in that it is requesting managers to designate people for a training course to which the managers have already agreed is important. An example of asking for attitudinal support from favorable receivers is given in Specimen 53. It should be noted that Specimen 53 is initially concerned with getting sufficient interest for the receiver to attend the function. Upon attending, he will be then asked for his ideas and reactions. In this sense, Specimen 53 is an example of combining a solicitation of both information and contribution (attitudinal support).

Figure 7.44 summarizes unfavorable and favorable circumstances in solicitation, the last of the personal situational purposes.

SOLICITATION	
Unfavorable	Favorable
1. Seeking information	1. Seeking information
2. Seeking contributions	2. Seeking contributions

Fig. 7.44 / Summary—solicitations.

Let us now view our three personal purposes and attendant situationally determined receiver roles in tabular form. Figure 7.45 summarizes these.

PURPOSE: PERSONAL	RECEIVER: SITUATIONALLY DETERMINED	
	Unfavorable	Favorable
ACKNOWLEDGMENT/ ACCEPTANCE	1. receivers wrong 2. apologies 3. answers to inquiries	1. receivers right 2. apologies 3. sender appreciation 4. answers to inquiries 5. assents to offers
OFFERING	1. applications 2. quotations 3. special inducements 4. recommendations 5. changes/corrections 6. transmittals	1. quotations 2. special inducements 3. recommendations 4. changes/corrections 5. transmittals
SOLICITATION	1. seeking information 2. seeking contributions	1. seeking information 2. seeking contributions

Fig. 7.45 / Summary—Chapter 7.

EXERCISES

exercise 1   Define each of the three situational personal purposes.

exercise 2   Using both unfavorable and favorable receiver perspectives, list specific purposes for each situational personal purpose.

exercise 3   Assuming a receiver perspective, examine each of the following figures: 7.1; 7.8; 7.16; 7.28; 7.35; 7.39. In your evaluation, state (1) the purpose (e.g., acknowledgment); (2) the receiver perspective (e.g., unfavorable, receiver wrong); (3) where the document does or does not meet the specific purpose and receiver perspective; and (4) the quality of clarity, correctness, and persuasiveness of each communication.

exercise 4 From the list of figures in exercise 3, rewrite one for each of the three situational personal purposes. In your rewrites, follow appropriate media guidelines, plus principles for clear, correct, persuasive communication.

exercise 5 Using instructions in exercise 3, evaluate one of Specimens: 15, 38, or 52. After evaluation, rewrite your specimen choice following the pattern in exercise 4.

CASE PROBLEMS

1. Re: Specimen 23. You are William S. Miller, Personnel Director, and you have received this memo from Robert M. Jones. After receipt, you discussed the promotion of Jones to Manager of Research with other Department Heads and all agree that he is completely acceptable. Furthermore, you have talked with Jones about the job and promised him you would give him an answer within a week. You have now decided that Jones is the man for the job.

Your Mission: Write a memo telling Jones that he has been promoted to the job as of May 1 at a salary of $32,500. At the top of the memo specify the exact specific purpose (e.g., acknowledgment—receiver right) and the receiver role to be addressed. Use an appropriate style and include necessary components; use the memorandum Communication Quality Control as a guide to check final product.

2. Re: Figure 7.2. You are Mr. Miller responding to Mr. Jones' letter of apology. You are pleased that the error has been corrected and want to acknowledge receipt of his message.

Your Mission: Write a letter to Mr. Jones. At the top of the letter, specify the exact specific purpose and the receiver role to be addressed. Use an appropriate style and include necessary components; use the letter Communication Quality Control as a guide to check final product.

Chapter 8

PERSONAL PURPOSES: PREDETERMINED RECEIVER ROLES

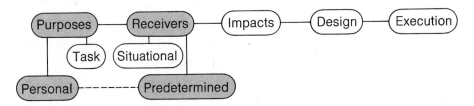

Your Learning Objectives:

1. To know the definition of predetermined receiver roles.
2. To know the three basic predetermined purposes.
3. To know the specific situational purposes for complaint/adjustment.
4. To know the specific situational purposes for rejection/reprimand.
5. To know the specific situational purposes of goodwill.
6. To know how to identify and apply all predetermined purposes to specific personal communications.

This chapter will deal with personal purposes to receivers whose outlooks are already fixed, whether favorable or unfavorable. Whereas Chapter 7 was concerned with situations in which receivers could be both unfavorable or favorable, those treated in this chapter build in one or the other—unfavorable or favorable; in other words, the receiver's attitude is predetermined by the purpose inherent in the situation. Once more, make your own evaluation of communication effectiveness; our essential focus is the explanation of specific purposes.

The three specific predetermined personal purposes are:

1. Complaint/adjustment
2. Rejection/reprimand
3. Goodwill

As you can see, the first two are automatically unfavorable; the third creates a favorable receiver attitude.

Complaint/Adjustment

This purpose embraces situations of objection or opposition, actual or potential. Three different important situations are:

1. Commodity/service/policy dissatisfaction
2. Due/past due account
3. Price increase/budget cut

Commodity/service/policy dissatisfaction refers to sender displeasure with goods, performance, or constraints. Bear in mind that we have already dealt with handling dissatisfactions in Chapter 7 (unfavorable acknowledgment/acceptance).

Remember that complaint/adjustment automatically engenders unfavorable receiver attitudes. With this in mind, let us now examine examples of communications of this type. Specimen 54 exemplifies a letter expressing dissatisfaction about the commodity (food). Figure 8.1 is another example of a complaint about goods (company product).

During last week's trip, I received four complaints from four different customers on the motors we put on our lathe No. 756. In essence, all are saying that the new motor is underpowered, causing the machine to operate too slowly and to throw circuit breakers because of power overloading.

Perhaps you are already aware of this difficulty and are taking steps to correct the problem. Would you please give me any information which could help in my communicating with these dissatisfied customers?

Fig. 8.1 / Complaint—commodity dissatisfaction.

Complaints about services can be seen in Specimens 55 and 56 and in Figure 8.2.

Dear Sir,

Due to your computer having been struck by lightning, my schedule is conflicting. More specifically, both my General English and Arts and Ideas meet at 1:00 on Mon., Wed., and Fri. Please adjust if necessary.

Fig. 8.2 / Complaint—service dissatisfaction.

Specimen 55 also is a complaint about a policy (university regulation), showing that a given communication may express dissatisfaction with more than one of commodity, service, or policy.

Figure 8.3 is fundamentally concerned with dissatisfaction about a manufacturer's policy, but it also includes an expression of displeasure about goods and services tendered (a computer installation).

Dear Mr. Miller:

I am writing to you as division manager to complain about the handling of a recent computer terminal installation at our company.

I know your policy is that parts and service are guaranteed for sixty days from the time of delivery. This is certainly a reasonable policy, and under normal circumstances, I would not object. However, in this case, your installation department did not get around to installing the equipment until March 15, which was 45 days after delivery. On April 20, the machine failed to work. When I called your service department, I was informed that the 60 day guarantee period had expired and that our company would have to pay for the necessary replacement parts and labor.

Candidly, I feel that your company should recognize the date of installation rather than date of delivery as the starting time for the guarantee to apply. I would appreciate your prompt attention to this matter.

Fig. 8.3 / Complaint—commodity/service/policy dissatisfaction.

Specimen 57 is basically a complaint about policy, but it is also communicating dissatisfaction with the consequences (services) of that policy.

Due/past due accounts means either current or delinquent payments owed. In most cases, the commodity has been delivered or the service performed. If the money due is not beyond the agreed payment time, it is current. If beyond the agreed payment time, it is delinquent.

A current due payment is shown in Figure 8.4. The reader (subscriber) is reminded of the need for renewal because of an approaching expiration of his subscription.

Specimen 58 is an example of a preprinted form collection letter in which the name and address of the "delinquent" are filled in by typewriter. Another reminder is shown in Specimen 59. Note that it only indirectly requests payment. Its literal emphasis is on the tax advantages to the receiver by paying early. Note also that it is put in the form of a holiday greeting to the reader. Specimen 60 is an example of a past due account (overdrawn amount, $.47). Note that it also demonstrates the use of "canned" paragraphs discussed under letters in Chapter 2.

YOUR SUBSCRIPTION EXPIRES SOON

Dear Subscriber:

The days do slip by virtually unnoticed. Your subscription to the Star-X Journal will expire surprisingly soon.

As a subscriber who has renewed, when previous terms have expired, we are sure you will want to take care of this important detail right now. In renewing right now, you are assured of continuous, uninterrupted service.

Fig. 8.4 / Complaint—due account.

Figure 8.5 is a particularly interesting example of a notice sent by a collection agency concerning a past due account. Read the message.

Guillermo Morales
1200 Central
Spencer, Trans.

Total Bill owed — Bal #498.00

I would be ashame if I was you
you are going to have to pay this
bill some time. you should thank
god you live in this country. People
like you should be deported. this
country can do with out people like
you. May God have mercy on you
worthless Sole.

Mrs. Jones

Fig. 8.5 / Complaint—past due account.

Clearly the impact of this is an affront to any human being. But the ironic part in this case is that the receiver (to be "deported") was an American Indian!

Specimen 61 is another example of an affront to reader intelligence. It pretends to be a personally handwritten collection letter when it is obviously an offset printed letter. The crime was compounded in this case in that it was even sent to the wrong person. Specimen 62 is a follow-up letter to two preceding requests for payment for membership renewal in a professional organization.

Price increase/budget cut refers to possible or actual commodity or service cost rises and fiscal or resource decrements. Figure 8.6 is an announcement of a rate increase for trash removal.

DUE TO RISING COSTS, INCREASED VOLUME OF TRASH, AND DUMPING FEES, EFFECTIVE JUNE 1, WE ARE CHANGING OUR RATE STRUCTURE.

ALL RESIDENTIAL CUSTOMERS will be $4.50 per mo., once a week pick up on curb or road.

ANY TRASH THAT IS CARRIED OUT will constitute a $6.00 per mo. charge.

EXTRA CHARGES will be placed on pine needles, building material, rocks, sod, grass, etc.

CONTAINERS should not weigh over 50 lbs. or more than one man can lift. Overweight will cause your trash to be left.

ALL BILLING will be 2 months in advance. No one shall be carried longer than 4 months.

Thank you for your cooperation.

Fig. 8.6 / Adjustment—price increase.

In Specimen 63, you will recognize something you or your parents may have confronted before: a letter informing the reader of an increase in university tuition. Specimen 64 is an announcement required by law in which a utility firm is announcing its intent to ask for an increase in rates to customers.

Another cost increase to employees is exemplified in Figure 8.7 (announcement of increase in insurance rates).

We have been informed that the premium charges for the Group Total Disability Benefits insurance are being raised from $4.32 to $5.18.

Effective April 1 (to be reflected in the paychecks issued May 1 and after) the following will be deducted from the checks of those employees participating in this insurance:

	Salary under $10,000	Salary of $10,000 or over
For Income Benefit	$1.80	$2.10
For Waiver Benefit	.30	.30

Fig. 8.7 / Adjustment—price increase.

Budget cuts are announced in Specimen 65 and Figure 8.8. Specimen 65 informs department heads of a 10 percent budget reduction for the company

---

In order to meet a $275,000 deficit which resulted from an 18% rise in costs and a decrease of 10% in anticipated revenues, we are forced to discontinue temporarily the replacement of any terminating employees. Our normal employee attrition should result in making up the $275,000 within six months. If this does not happen, we may be forced to the more drastic step of closing down some operations and departments. I hope the latter is unnecessary.

Fig. 8.8 / Adjustment—budget cut.

with a possible reduction in telephone service to their units. Figure 8.8 announces a company deficit with a resulting effect of nonreplacement of employees. While not a direct specific budget cut for a given department, all units are potentially affected in that no new hires are allowed company-wide, which is an actual resource loss.

A specific department budget cut can be seen in Specimen 66, a directive requiring a 5% reduction in department funds. Whereas the two preceding examples were potential cuts, Specimen 66 directly affects the department to which the communication is addressed.

Figure 8.9 summarizes complaint/adjustment, the first of the personal predetermined purposes.

Complaint/Adjustment—Unfavorable

1. Commodity/service/policy dissatisfaction
2. Due/past due account
3. Price increase/budget cut

Fig. 8.9 / Summary—complaint/adjustment.

Rejection/Reprimand

This purpose includes communications that are used to turn down, to end, or to reprove. The different significant situations in this predetermined unfavorable role are:

1. Refusal
2. Termination
3. Censure

Refusals can relate to job or school turndowns, credit denials, or service/accommodation rejections. In Figure 8.10, you see an implicit job turndown.

Note that the writer never explicitly rejects the reader's application, but the message is clearly "no."

Dear Mr. Miller:

There are no current openings on my staff nor do I contemplate any in the foreseeable future. I think your job goals are very realistic for a person with your background, but they do somewhat limit the possibilities. I am unaware of any situations, currently open, that would match your desires.

Best of luck to you.

Fig. 8.10 / Rejection/reprimand—refusal.

Another implicit turndown is shown in Specimen 67, a letter answering an inquiry concerning a professional position. Figure 8.11 is an explicit job turndown, as is Specimen 68. Note in both instances the direct, terse refusal.

Dear Mr. Miller:

Your credentials given in your letter of February 17 are impressive. However, we have had five applicants for this job and we have selected the person whom we feel best qualified for this specific position.

I am sure that one of your qualifications will find it easy to locate employment somewhere else. I wish you the very best.

Fig. 8.11 / Rejection/reprimand—refusal.

Let us now look at examples of school admission denials. Figure 8.12 is a short, direct denial.

Dear Mr. Miller:

Thank you for submitting your application for admission to City University.

Unfortunately, we received many more applications from well-qualified candidates than we can accommodate. Thus we must regretfully inform you that we have not been able to admit you.

Thank you again for your interest. We hope that you will still find it possible to carry out your plans of attending another university.

Fig. 8.12 / Rejection/reprimand—refusal.

Whereas Figure 8.12 is a denial for initial admission, Specimen 90 is a denial to a student wishing to transfer to City University.

Turning to credit refusals, Specimen 70 is a letter denying a company credit for goods. Figure 8.13 is also a letter denying credit. Note the terseness and abruptness in handling this credit refusal.

Dear Mr. Miller:

I am sorry to inform you that we cannot grant credit to you. The company will gladly sell you goods C.O.D. We look forward to serving you.

Fig. 8.13 / Rejection/reprimand—refusal.

Several examples of denying services or accommodations follow. Specimen 71 is a refusal to serve (e.g., that is, to furnish the information requested). Forms are sometimes used to communicate refusals of services. Specimen 72 is turning down a request for advance payment on a contract; Figure 8.14 is another form, a notice of intent not to renew an insurance policy.

NOTICE OF INTENT NOT TO RENEW

Your agent is no longer placing private passenger automobile business with our Company, and we will be unable to renew your automobile insurance policy No. _____ . All coverage afforded by this policy ceases as of 12:01 a.m. Standard time (at your address) on _____ 19___ . We suggest you contact your insurance agent _____ since he has adequate facilities to handle your insurance needs.

Fig. 8.14 / Rejection/reprimand—refusal.

Specimen 73 is a letter denying a request for magazines to be freely distributed to students. An accommodation denial (a letter) can be seen in Figure 8.15. This represents a frequently used "canned" answer to turn down requests for accommodations.

Dear Sir(s)/Madam(s),

We have received your letter and we regret to inform you that we are fully booked for the period you mention.

Fig. 8.15 / Rejection/reprimand—refusal.

Terminations most commonly relate to job or school, contract, or services. Figure 8.16 is a letter terminating employment; Specimen 75 is a memorandum accomplishing the same end.

Dear Mr. Miller:

As you know, economic conditions have brought our company to a crisis, forcing us to eliminate certain jobs. Regretfully, your position is one of these. This was done only after careful deliberation and consultation with your supervisor, Mr. Thompson.

We hope that the economy improves in the near future so that we could consider you for another position should one become available. We wish you every success and on behalf of the company, I want to thank you for serving us so well.

Fig. 8.16 / Rejection/reprimand—termination.

Student dismissals from school are seen in Figure 8.17 and Specimen 75.

Dear Mr. Miller:

Your total grade record has been reviewed by the Academic Standards Committee. Since your overall grade point average is 1.50 (as opposed to the required 2.0), we are forced to give you an indefinite suspension from City University. We have done this with regret, but we know that you understand the need to maintain academic standards in reputable universities. We feel this action is in your best interest.

Fig. 8.17 / Rejection/reprimand—termination.

A contract abrogation is exemplified in Specimen 76, which ends an agreement for supplying goods to a factory. Terminations of services are shown in Specimen 77 (discontinuance of a journal) and Figure 8.18 (ending delivery services supplied to a firm).

Censures include reprimands about faulty information, faulty performance, or a "slap on the wrist" recommendation for improvement. A reprimand concerning faulty information is shown in Specimen 78 (a failure to reconcile disbursement figures). Figure 8.19 also exemplifies a reprimand concerning faulty information (inaccurate production reports).

In Figure 8.20, you see a clever and subtle reprimand on faulty job performance (after all, faculty people do have a responsibility to see that the buildings are kept clean).

Dear Mr. Miller:

Our accounting department has made an intensive study of delivery costs to the company. After careful consideration, it has determined that savings of more than $10,000 per year can be made by setting up our own delivery facilities. Therefore, as of July 1, 19____, we will no longer need your company's services.

We have been completely satisfied with our arrangements. Rest assured that the only reason we are terminating your services is because of the dollar savings to our company in that we can optimize use of existing personnel and equipment more efficiently.

We will be glad to recommend Star-X Delivery Services most highly. Thanks for your courtesy and efficient handling of our deliveries.

Fig. 8.18 / Rejection/reprimand—termination.

SUBJECT: Production report procedure

Since most of the suggestions for getting more accurate production reports supplied in my memo of May 26 have not been used, in spite of Mr. Thompson's assurance that they had been used, and since he asked in the last staff meeting to be informed of shortcomings, I am writing this memo to you. Some items of my earlier memo are pertinent at this time and copies of these are available to you (if you can't locate the copy sent to you earlier).

I will make no further effort to communicate my misgivings about this venture. Obviously, Mr. Thompson really does not want constructive criticism.

Fig. 8.19 / Rejection/reprimand—censure.

SUBJECT: Dogs

An oft-quoted phrase is "A man's best friend is his dog." Nearly everybody likes dogs and we do, too. Even our building custodians like dogs, but they don't like to have to clean up after them in their buildings. Would you please ask your students to leave their dogs outside the buildings? Our custodians thank you.

Fig. 8.20 / Rejection/reprimand—censure.

Specimen 79 is a caustic directive from the company president to employees concerning the need to shape up their personal appearance, which, in his eyes, affects their job performance. Figure 8.21 is a more oblique reprimand concerning job performance. In fact, it overlaps indirectly with the next grouping of recommendations for improvement. Note the suggestion for a meeting to discuss the problem.

Doctor, we should very much appreciate the opportunity of discussing with you the coverage of the X-Ray-Laboratory waiting area by personnel from within the X-Ray Department. We should very much appreciate mutual sharing of thoughts and ideas which would contribute to the success of this plan. Please feel free to make arrangements directly with us for a meeting as soon as you find it possible to do so in your busy schedule.

Thank you!

Fig. 8.21 / Rejection/reprimand—censure.

Figure 8.22 is a kind "slap on the wrist" with a specific suggestion for improvement. Specimen 80 is a stinging reprimand that embraces all of the dimensions discussed under censure (faulty information, faulty job performance, and ways for improvement). Incidentally, this is the memorandum that precipitated the acknowledgment seen in Specimen 1.

During the course of our inspection we noted the oxygen tanks which were set on the floor of the work area, and noted also that there is smoking in a fairly proximal distance of the oxygen tanks. We know what the reaction of the Fire Department would be about smoking in an area with oxygen, and wonder if you have thought of a solution for this. I don't know whether the following suggestion can work or not, but I wonder if your oxygen should not be on call from the oxygen inhalation therapy department. At any rate, we do not think that the present method of storage is a safe one, and it will have to be remedied.

Thank you!

Fig. 8.22 / Rejection/reprimand—censure.

A summary of rejection/reprimand, the second of the personal predetermined purposes, is seen in Figure 8.23.

Rejection/Reprimand—Unfavorable

1. Refusal
2. Termination
3. Censure

Fig. 8.23 / Summary—rejection/reprimand.

Goodwill

This is a predetermined *favorable* role. Essentially, there are three different situations:

1. Commendation
2. Social relations
3. Inside information

Commendations take the form of appreciations and congratulations recognizing past accomplishments or benefits to the organization. Frequently, appreciation and a congratulatory element are combined in the same communication as seen in Figure 8.24. Note the first paragraph is a congratulation (compliment) and paragraph two expresses appreciation.

Gentlemen:

We want to compliment you for your performance on this project. Early completion and costs within the estimate are the results of a good team effort between our companies.

Please convey our appreciation to all those involved in the project.

Fig. 8.24 / Goodwill—commendation.

Specimen 81 is a congratulatory letter. Note especially the last paragraph. In Figure 8.25 you can see another example of a letter congratulating a faculty person on his being appointed to an esteemed professional organization.

Dear Mr. Miller:

Word has just reached me concerning your appointment to the Social Policy Research and Action Committee.

On behalf of the City University, may I extend to you our sincerest congratulations and best wishes for continued success.

We, at the University, are indeed proud of your accomplishments.

Best regards.

Fig. 8.25 / Goodwill—commendation.

A letter of appreciation for a donation is exemplified in Specimen 82. Specimen 83 is, at first glance, a memorandum; but it is actually a brochure of appreciation to the staff of a medical clinic (it was posted on the bulletin board for the professional staff). Figure 8.26 is a letter of congratulations and appreciation.

Dear Bill:

I had known of your new responsibilities, but I don't believe I'd had the time to write congratulating you and at the same time expressing regret that our contacts must, of necessity, be fewer than they were. Your contributions to this company are significant. We continue to be the beneficiaries of these efforts even though you're taking on a new assignment.

With warmest personal regards, I am,

Fig. 8.26 / Goodwill—commendation.

Social relations, as used here, include greetings for holidays or special occasions, invitations, and condolences. Sometimes commendations may be combined with social relations in a given communication. Specimen 84 is an example. Note that the letter starts with an apparent holiday greeting, and then it announces a sale, along with an expression of appreciation for the customer's patronage.

A greeting for a special occasion (wedding anniversary) is seen in Specimen 85. Figure 8.27 is an invitation to a tea (special occasion). Note its informal mode as contrasted against the formality seen in Figure 8.28, which is an invitation to an open house for a professional organization. Professional codes and ethics dictate the more formal pattern.

Mrs. Jones, Mrs. Thompson and Miss Thomas cordially invite you to a tea at the Student Center

Friday, May 28
2:00-4:00 p.m.

R.S.V.P.
Student Center
357-3642

Fig. 8.27 / Goodwill—social relations.

The Partners and Staff of
Jones, Thompson, Thomas & Co.
Certified Public Accountants

Cordially invite you to an Open House

In our New Offices at

561 Main Street, Suite 400

R.S.V.P.—Miss Brown   Sunday, February 1
993-7158   2 to 4 p.m.

Fig. 8.28 / Goodwill—social relations.

Different types of condolences can be seen in Specimen 86, Figure 8.29, Figure 8.30, and Specimen 87. Specimen 86 exemplifies a letter of condolence to an employee who is ill; Figure 8.29 is an expression of sympathy concerning the death of an employee's wife. While this example is typed, many such expressions are written by hand.

Dear Bill:

It was shocking to hear of Mary's sudden death. We all knew and loved your wife, who was our kind and gracious hostess on so many happy occasions.

We hope this note will express the sorrow with which all of us here received the news. Please accept our heartfelt condolences.

Fig. 8.29 / Goodwill—social relations.

Figure 8.30 is a memorandum from the company president announcing a service in memory of a fellow employee.

A memorial service for Donald B. Thompson will be held on Tuesday, March 30, at 11:15 a.m. in Angel's Chapel. Mr. Thompson passed away suddenly on March 15.

In memory of Mr. Thompson, the Company will close down operations from 10:30 a.m. until 1:00 p.m. on March 30 so that employees who wish may attend the memorial service.

Fig. 8.30 / Goodwill—social relations.

A difference from the traditional American condolence can be seen in Specimen 87, a British company's announcement of the death of its managing director. Note the black border and the typographical handling to communicate the desired effect. Furthermore, this specimen is also giving inside information (which is discussed next) in that it is announcing the decedent's successor.

Inside information concerns organizational changes (internal and external), personal benefits (direct gains to the individual), and organizational benefits (indirect gains to the individual but intended for direct organizational gain). Organizational changes are evidenced in Specimen 88 and Figure 8.31. Specimen 88 is a memorandum concerned with an internal personnel change. Figure 8.31 is a brochure announcing changes in address and phone, as well as an addition to the staff to persons outside the organization.

THERE'S BEEN SOME *CHANGES* MADE

We've changed our office address! It's now 820 Main, Suite 200
We've changed our phone to: 833-9175
We've added to our staff!

    We are pleased to announce the appointment of Donald Thompson as Account Executive and Manager of our local office. Don is a graduate of City University. In addition to his agency experience in industrial and financial fields, he has worked as a film editor, copywriter, TV director and producer. He will play a key role in the expansion of our services.

Star-X Advertising, Inc.

Fig. 8.31 / Goodwill—inside information.

Personal benefits are exemplified in Figure 8.32, Specimen 89, and Figure 8.33. Figure 8.32 is a warning concerning the dangers of bears in a national park. Specimen 89 is an excerpt from a brochure on possible consequences from the misuse of drugs. Figure 8.33 is a simple form reminding the customer of the money saved from his having taken advantage of the special rate.

ENJOY THEM AT A DISTANCE

PARK BEARS AND OTHER ANIMALS ARE *DANGEROUS*

Don't encourage them to approach. Park regulations prohibit feeding or molesting animals. Stop cars in pullouts ONLY—not on roadway. Keep car windows closed when near bears.

THIS WARNING IS FOR YOUR PROTECTION

Fig. 8.32 / Goodwill—inside information.

Thank you for using our weekly special. You saved $_____. Be sure to watch for our money saving weekly special.

STAR-X CLEANERS & LAUNDRY

Fig. 8.33 / Goodwill—inside information.

Organizational benefits (which, you remember, are indirect gains to the individual but intended for direct organizational gain) can be seen in Specimen 90, a "Client Newsletter" from an accounting firm. While it details potential benefits to the individual, its obvious purpose is to get the customer into the accounting firm's office for consultation.

A summary of goodwill, the third of the personal predetermined purposes, can be seen in Figure 8.34.

Goodwill—Favorable

1. Commendation
2. Social relations
3. Inside information

Fig. 8.34 / Summary—goodwill.

Figure 8.35 summarizes the three personal predetermined purposes and the respective receiver roles.

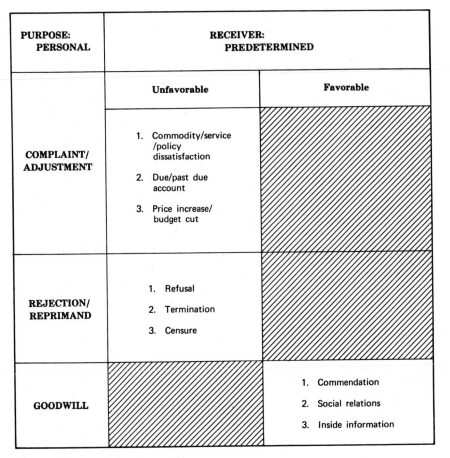

PURPOSE: PERSONAL	RECEIVER: PREDETERMINED	
	Unfavorable	Favorable
COMPLAINT/ ADJUSTMENT	1. Commodity/service /policy dissatisfaction 2. Due/past due account 3. Price increase/ budget cut	
REJECTION/ REPRIMAND	1. Refusal 2. Termination 3. Censure	
GOODWILL		1. Commendation 2. Social relations 3. Inside information

Fig. 8.35 / Summary—Chapter 8.

EXERCISES

exercise 1 Define each of the three predetermined personal purposes.

exercise 2 Using both unfavorable and favorable receiver perspectives, list specific purposes for each predetermined personal purpose.

exercise 3 Assuming a receiver perspective, examine each of the following figures: 8.3; 8.5; 8.12; 8.19; 8.31. In your evaluation, state (1) the purpose (e.g., goodwill); (2) the receiver perspective (e.g., favorable, commendation); (3)

where the document does or does not meet specific purpose and receiver perspective; and (4) the quality of clarity, correctness, and persuasiveness of each communication.

exercise 4 From the list of figures in exercise 3, rewrite one for each of the three predetermined personal purposes. In your rewrites, follow appropriate media guidelines, plus principles for clear, correct, persuasive communication.

exercise 5 Using instructions in exercise 3, evaluate one of Specimen 55, 76, or 90. After evaluation, rewrite your specimen choice following the pattern in exercise 4.

CASE PROBLEMS

1. Re: Specimen 22. You are Mr. Miller, and having reviewed Mr. Jones' letter of application, find that you have no job openings for one with his background. Furthermore, the poor quality of Jones' application letter causes you to want to discourage any further inquiry by him. Therefore, you need to tell him that you cannot grant him an interview.

Your Mission: Write a letter to Jones rejecting his letter of application and request for an interview. At the top of the letter, specify the exact specific purpose. Use an appropriate style and include necessary components; use the letter Communication Quality Control as a guide to check final product.

2. Re: Specimen 33. You are Mr. Miller and have read Mr. Jones' memo. Moreover, you have received three complaints from other departmental representatives who attended the meeting, all to the effect that the memo does not report correctly what went on. One also complained about the ambiguities and poor language usage in the document. While you cannot confirm whether the memo adequately reports what went on at the meeting, you do agree that the language of the memo is very poor.

Your Mission: Write a memo to Jones expressing concern about the alleged report discrepancy and also pointing out the poor language usage. Use a specific paragraph (or part) to illustrate to Jones the deficient use of language and why. (Note: refer to appropriate sections in Part IV as needed.) At the top of the memo, specify the exact specific purpose. Use an appropriate style and include necessary components; use the memorandum Communication Quality Control as a guide to check final product.

Chapter 9

TASK PURPOSES:
SITUATIONAL RECEIVER ROLES

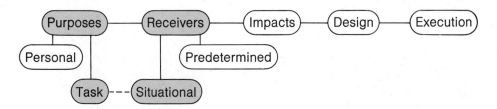

Your Learning Objectives:

1. To know the definition of task purposes.
2. To reinforce understanding of situational roles.
3. To know the three task situationally determined purposes.
4. To know the specific situational purposes for policy communications to unfavorable receivers.
5. To know the specific situational purposes for policy communications to favorable receivers.
6. To know the specific situational purposes for procedural communications to unfavorable receivers.
7. To know the specific situational purposes for procedural communications to favorable receivers.
8. To know the specific situational purposes for status communications to unfavorable receivers.
9. To know the specific situational purposes for status communications to favorable receivers.
10. To know how to identify and apply all situational purposes to specific task communications.

In Chapters 7 and 8, we treated personal purposes; Chapter 7 covered situationally determined receivers; and Chapter 8 was concerned with predetermined receiver roles. We are now ready to study task purposes, that is, those primarily oriented to the operations and jobs of the organization. Personal purposes are primarily geared to membership needs; task purposes are geared to the organization's needs, which are basically impersonal.

What are the most important task purposes? The most basic categories are:

1. Policy communications
2. Procedural communications
3. Status communications

Policy Communications

Policies are boundaries for managerial and organizational action. They may establish the firm's objectives, guidelines, or regulations, all of which give the direction for organizational activities, some very general, others more restrictive. You should remember that policies may be very broad (global), sometimes called "basic" policies, as well as more specific (subglobal), sometimes called "operational" policies, thereby restricting latitude. You should also remember that a policy—at any level—does allow latitude; therefore some policies are by nature ambiguous; others may be more specifically spelled out.

A basic policy permits broad organizational or managerial flexibility. Subglobal or operational policies permit less flexibility. In sum, a general statement of policy permits latitude; an operational policy is more restrictive.

Policy communications can be addressed to either unfavorable or favorable receivers dependent on the situation. The types for both unfavorable (neutral or unknown) and favorable (agreeable) receivers are three:

1. Constraints
2. Changes
3. Acceptance

Unfavorable Receivers

We shall start with those communications addressed to the unfavorable receiver (neutral or unknown).

Constraints may consist of objectives, guidelines, and regulations. As you can see, constraint is synonymous with policy. Let us start with policies typifying purpose or objective.

Remember that in our discussion of "organization" we include any collectivity —business, government, private, professional, social, and voluntary—in other words, any purposive administered group. (In this sense, the course you are taking at a university is an "organization.") An example of a voluntary organizational objective is seen in Figure 9.1. Note that the statements, while clear, are at the same time general.

Alcoholics Anonymous is a fellowship of men and women who share their experience, strength and hope with each other that they may solve their common problem and help others to recover from alcoholism. The only requirement for membership is a desire to stop drinking. There are no dues or fees for A.A. membership; we are self-supporting through our own contributions. A.A. is not allied with any sect, denomination, politics, organization or institution; does not wish to engage in any controversy; neither endorses nor opposes any causes.

Our primary purpose is to stay sober and help other alcoholics to achieve sobriety.

Fig. 9.1 / Policy—constraints.

The mission of a government organization (General Accounting Office) is stated in Figure 9.2, an excerpt from a recruiting brochure. While this is not the more formal statutory purpose, it is a translation of that for the layman.

WHO WE ARE The United States General Accounting Office is in the Legislative Branch of the Federal Government and is headed by the Comptroller General of the United States. We are responsible solely to the Congress and act in its behalf by examining and reporting on the operations of Federal departments and agencies. Although responsible to Congress, we are fully independent, nonpolitical and nonpartisan.

Fig. 9.2 / Policy communication—constraint.

Specimen 91 shows a partial statement of objectives of an academic accrediting association (American Association of Collegiate Schools of Business) for member schools. Note that the basic purpose (common body of knowledge) is itemized. This is a common way to communicate conceptual purposes. An even more structured and detailed policy is that in Specimen 92—a management guide for the superintendent of a production plant. Actually, this is a subglobal policy; in fact, it is a combination of positional objectives and guidelines for operations. Sections II and III are essentially guidelines, III being spelled out in eight items.

Other examples of guidelines can be viewed in Specimen 93 and Figure 9.3. Specimen 93 is an excerpt from an employee manual concerning conduct and appearance. You can see that it gives general guidelines to the employee. His judgment and that of his supervisor must obviously be exercised in interpreting what is said. An excerpt from a company policy manual is evidenced in Figure 9.3. It is a description of the general functions of the maintenance of a large manufacturing concern. Note again that judgment must be exercised in determining exactly how each operation and job is to be done.

The Maintenance Department's main job is to keep buildings, machines, and equipment in repair. A collateral job is to collect, segregate, and dispose of factory scrap.

As to buildings, the Maintenance Department performs cleaning, minor construction, electrical work, painting, installation of equipment, minor elevator repairs, roofing work, sprinkler maintenance, and boiler maintenance.

For machinery and equipment, the Maintenance Department handles minor repairs. Major repairs on machinery and equipment are performed by the Tool and Die Department. As a minor function, the Maintenance Department also makes special wooden boxes for the Shipping Department.

Fig. 9.3 / Policy communication—constraint.

Let us now turn to examples of policies in the form of regulations, which are often very restrictive. Indeed, some permit latitude only in that they allow a manager or operator to determine how the ends stated will be met (e.g., no smoking in this room). Figures 9.4 and 9.5 are regulations affecting employees. Figure 9.4 states the probationary policy for new company employees; Figure 9.5 gives a part of the policy on employee fringe benefits in a large production firm.

The probationary period for new company employees is three months. It is felt that in three months, most supervisors know whether or not the employee has passed the working test. A one step probationary salary increase may be given at the end of the three months' period.

Fig. 9.4 / Policy communication—constraints.

In order that fringe benefits remain in effect, employees on Military or Maternity leave of absence or Summer Vacation without pay must arrange for full payment of premiums to the Payroll Office.

Fig. 9.5 / Policy communication—constraints.

Changes include adjustments or modifications in existing policies or introduction of new policies. Whereas in discussing constraints, we were focusing on the statements of already existing policies (without reference to their introduction or formulation), here we shall deal with statements of existing policy revision or initiation of new ones. Most up-to-date organizations have policy handbooks or guides that are modified wholly or in part periodically or as special circumstances dictate. Let us now look at a few examples of changes addressed to unfavorable recipients.

A change in mailing policies of a university is seen in Figure 9.6. Why is it likely to be viewed unfavorably? Because it will result in departmental adjustments and dislocation, as well as requiring people to change their work habits, all of which are painful.

It is the intent of our Mail Services Department to process in the most expeditious manner all university connected communications submitted to the mail room for processing. In order to process the mail most efficiently, we are making these policy changes:

No material may be submitted for mailing which includes the following:

1. Solicitation of funds (excepting those originating in either the Department of Development or in Alumni Relations).

2. The endorsement or condemnation of political candidates or non-University groups or organizations.

3. Advertising or commercialism of functions not connected with the University.

4. Unstamped personal mailings of non-University connected material.

5. Student publications not authorized by the Dean of Student Life.

It is not the intent or responsibility of the Director of Mail Services to "censor" outgoing mail. He is, however, required to inquire as to the contents of third class bulk rate material and fourth class material, to insure that the contents being mailed meet the legal requirements of the postal department for such classifications.

Fig. 9.6 / Policy communication—change.

A change in library regulations can be seen in Figure 9.7. It is clear why this will be viewed unfavorably by faculty: their loan period is shortened so that students may have more access to library resources.

SUBJECT: Library Circulation Policies for Faculty

At its meeting on Tuesday, March 2, the Committee on Library Development approved the following changes in library circulation policies for faculty, effective beginning next term. The new policies permit students more access to library documents and apply to all libraries.

BOOKS, GOVERNMENT DOCUMENTS, AND MONOGRAPHS ON MICROFILM will be charged out for ONE TERM instead of for the academic year. A longer loan period may be requested at the time the book is checked out, if deemed necessary. Renewals may be made by telephone during the academic year; however, all books must be physically returned or renewed at the end of each Spring term.

NONCURRENT PERIODICALS (paper editions and microforms) may be checked out for ONE DAY instead of one week. A longer loan period may be requested at the time the periodical is checked out; however, since the availability of periodicals is critical, discrimination in the use of this privilege is urged. If periodicals are not returned promptly when due, the Libraries may have to further curtail their circulation.

Fig. 9.7 / Policy communication—change.

An obviously hostility-inducing document is seen in Specimen 94, a policy mandate from the Director of Research.

Acceptance is concerned with getting greater support of existing policy. Here there is no change in policy, merely communication designed to elicit more or better implementation of already established objectives, guidelines, or regulations. Frequently, employee handbooks have introductions from the president or other top official, which are intended to elicit support for all policies rather than a given one. In contrast, Figure 9.8 exemplifies communication to get support and cooperation of employees for a single policy (equal employment opportunity).

Whereas Figure 9.8 is concerned with adherence to a general goal, Figure 9.9 states a specific objective that must be achieved by the company in order to meet the equal opportunity policy. These two examples show the need to supplement a policy statement with one or more successive communications from time to time.

Favorable Receivers

We shall now examine the same three types (constraints, changes, and acceptance) as directed to favorable recipients.

Constraints, as you recall, include the *initial* objectives, guidelines, and regu-

Star-X Company and its subsidiaries have traditionally pursued a non-discriminatory policy in regard to equal employment opportunity.

Since April 5, 1961, the effective date of the first Presidential Executive Order relative to equal employment opportunity, and particularly since the enactment of the Civil Rights Act of 1964, we have emphasized and will continue to emphasize a policy to abide, without reservation, by both the spirit and the letter of all laws pertaining to equal employment practices.

All persons having any responsibility or duties relating to supervising, hiring, transferring, or promotion of personnel shall actively support a non-discriminatory policy which is free of any prejudice relating to race, color, religion, national origin, sex, or age.

Further, we urgently solicit the full cooperation of every employee in supporting this policy which, in brief offers equal opportunity for employment and advancement to all qualified applicants and employees.

Fig. 9.8 / Policy communication—acceptance.

SUBJECT: Affirmative Action Program

On July 30, the National Association of Manufacturers in cooperation with the U.S. Department of Labor's office of Federal Contract Compliance, the Equal Employment Opportunity Commission, and the Department of Justice sponsored a Video Teleconference on Equal Employment.

It almost goes without saying that an action program must establish goals and this was reiterated several times during the conference.

Our goal has to be to raise the total percentage and at the same time get more of these people into the more skilled positions. With this in mind our Staff Personnel Office is working with such agencies as the Bureau of Indian Affairs, the Urban League, the Concentrated Employment Programs of both the city and state to obtain qualified applicants for job openings in our company.

Fig. 9.9 / Policy communication—acceptance.

lations. Professional people are bound by codes of ethics. Indeed, their basic allegiance is frequently more to the professional organization of which they are members rather than to the administered organization by which they are employed. Therefore, Figure 9.10 exemplifies a code that will be favorably viewed by members of the professional organization.

CODE OF ETHICS

As a member of this Association, it is my responsibility:

To promote the advance of systems throughout management.

To maintain and improve sound business practices and foster high standards of professional conduct.

To cooperate with others in the interchange of knowledge and ideas for mutual professional benefit.

To hold in professional confidence any information gained of the business of a fellow member's company, and to refrain from using such information in an unethical manner.

To develop my abilities and improve my knowledge through constant study.

To maintain high personal standards of moral responsibility, character and business integrity.

To neither engage in, nor countenance, any exploitation of my membership, company or profession.

To refrain from using my membership in the Association, or the name of the Association, to promote the products or services of my company.

To uphold the standards of this Association.

Fig. 9.10 / Policy communication—constraints.

The last example of a favorable objective is seen in Figure 9.11. This is an excerpt from the bylaws of a professional organization, which again were formulated in part by members.

Section 2.   Objectives

The objectives of the Society are to advance the arts and sciences of technical communication by

(a) encouraging research,
(b) developing educational programs and establishing scholarships,
(c) stimulating the exchange of information by means of publications, meetings, and conferences,
(d) recognizing outstanding accomplishments, and
(e) cooperating with other societies and institutions in mutually beneficial projects.

Fig. 9.11 / Policy communication—constraints.

Guidelines directed to favorable readers are shown in Figure 9.12. Figure 9.12 is part of the same set of bylaws seen in Figure 9.11 except that here you see guidelines (powers and constraints). Note that these are more specific than the objectives set forth in the former.

Article II POWERS AND CONSTRAINTS

Section 1. Powers

The powers of the Society reside in its members. These powers are exercised on behalf of the membership by an elected Board of Directors.

Section 2. Constraints

The Society is nonprofit, nonsectarian, and nonpartisan. It cannot endorse or disparage a commercial enterprise, a political platform, or a candidate for public office.

Section 3. Use of Name

The Society name and insignia, singly or in combination, may be used only by persons authorized by the Board of Directors and only for Society purposes.

Fig. 9.12 / Policy communication—constraints.

Specimen 95 exemplifies objectives (purpose), guidelines (membership), and the last type of constraint, regulations (shares). Frequently, a given policy communication will include all three types.

Figure 9.13 is regulatory only. It will probably be favorably received in that it is a guarantee (warranty policy) on products purchased from the issuing organization.

WARRANTY POLICY

Star-X Corporation warrants each new Star-X product to be free from defects in material and workmanship under normal use and service for a period of 90 days after delivery to the ultimate user and will replace or repair the product, at our option, at no charge should it become defective and which our examination shall disclose to be defective and under warranty.

This warranty shall not apply to any Start-X product which has been subject to misuse, neglect, accident, incorrect wiring not of our own installation, or to use in violation of instructions furnished by us, nor extended to units which have been repaired or altered outside of our factory.

This warranty does not cover carrying cases, earphones, batteries, antennas, broken or cracked cabinets, or any other accessory used in connection with the product.

This warranty is in lieu of all other warranties expressed or implied and no representative or person is authorized to assume for us any other liability in connection with the sale of our products.

Sales receipt must accompany product to validate date of purchase.

Fig. 9.13 / Policy communication—constraints.

The last favorable regulatory constraint is exemplified in Specimen 96 which is a simplified table listing social security cash benefits.

Change is illustrated in Figure 9.14, a new policy that will be favorably received by company managers in that it presumably clarifies a previously ambiguous personnel policy.

NEW POLICY

At the last Divisional Managers' meeting, this new policy was adopted:

Employees sent to doctor for accident on job:

Will be paid for balance of day if Form SL3 states he is unable to work.

If sent back to work by doctor and goes home he will *not* be paid.

All subsequent visits to doctor must be on employee's *own* time.

Fig. 9.14 / Policy communication—change.

Introduction of a new policy on drug orders is shown in Specimen 97; it will be favorably received because it specifies exactly what is to be done while, at the same time, continuing the responsibility of the professional persons to make judgments. Figure 9.15 builds in a favorable response in that the changes were made as a result of polling organizational members.

After polling all membership about conducting meetings, your Board concluded that these changes were desired by most members:

1. Omitting trivial details and announcements.
2. Giving new and important professional information at most meetings.
3. Limiting meeting time to two hours.
4. Giving more opportunities for more members to participate in organizational activities.

Your Board will present a specific plan to implement these changes at our next monthly meeting.

Fig. 9.15 / Policy communication—change.

Acceptance (favorable) of existing policy is shown in Figure 9.16 and Specimen 98. Figure 9.16 is a reminder in the company house organ of workmen's compensation coverage for employees.

WORKMEN'S COMPENSATION COVERAGE

As an employee, you have certain rights and duties under the State laws concerning work-connected injuries. The details of the statutes are too lengthy and complex to cover here.

In brief, the Star-X Company is a self insuror complying with the provisions of the Workmen's Compensation and Occupational Disease Disability Laws. Read your Employee Handbook and ask your Supervisor about anything needing clarification.

Fig. 9.16 / Policy communication—acceptance.

Specimen 98 restates a company policy on the nonacceptance of gifts and gratuities from vendors or outsiders to company employees.

A summary of policy communications, the first of the task, situationally determined purposes, is shown in Figure 9.17.

POLICY COMMUNICATIONS

Unfavorable	Favorable
1. Constraints	1. Constraints
2. Changes	2. Changes
3. Acceptance	3. Acceptance

Fig. 9.17 / Summary—policy communications.

Procedural Communications

We have discussed policies, which you recall, are boundaries for managerial and organizational action. In contrast, a procedure gives the ways by which policies are to be carried out. Stated another way, policies establish goals or objectives; procedures tell how these goals or objectives are to be achieved. As with policies, procedures may be both general and specific. At higher managerial levels procedures may be fairly broad, giving latitude in their use; at worker level, they may be very detailed and exact, requiring strict adherence.

As with policy communications, procedures can be addressed to either unfavorable or favorable receivers. Categories for both unfavorable and favorable are:

1. Changes
2. Acceptance
3. Announcements

Unfavorable Receivers

Changes include introducing new, as well as modifying existing, procedures. As with policies, most modern companies have handbooks or guides that permit the insertion of new or revised procedural communications. Let us now consider examples of procedural changes addressed to unfavorable receivers.

Figure 9.18 introduces a general procedure (it admits options) of requiring identification for admission to company buildings.

SUBJECT: Employee Identification

No doubt you are already aware of additional security measures being taken in all Company buildings. You should also be aware that there may be occasions when it will be necessary to severely restrict access to these buildings. Therefore, it is essential that you possess either an official credential or your company identification card signed by Donald B. Thompson.

Fig. 9.18 / Procedural communication—change.

Another procedural introduction is seen in Specimen 99 ("suggestions" as procedures for handling patients by professional employees in a medical clinic). Procedures frequently are labeled "Instructions." An example of instructions to university applicants is seen in Figure 9.19. It is a "change" in that it is *new* to the applicant.

INSTRUCTIONS
1. Do not detach cards.
2. Please print or type all information.
3. Please supply *all* requested information.
4. Make checks payable to City University.
5. Return this form with your application for admission.

Please send check or money order, cash not accepted

Fig. 9.19 / Procedural communication—change.

A change in existing procedures is shown in Figure 9.20. This differs from

---

Due to changes in our bookkeeping procedures, professional charges and optical charges (including contact lenses) will be billed separately.

Statements will be sent at different times so that you may receive a separate statement for professional services and another for the optical charges.

Please make separate checks for each statement received.

Fig. 9.20 / Procedural communication—change.

the foregoing illustrations in that it refers generally to an internal procedural change (bookkeeping) that results in a specific external (customer) procedural change. A similar example is seen in Figure 9.21.

Dear Customer,

In the future our bills will not show specific days of service or day payments are received.

To eliminate much bookkeeping time, we will head the statement with the month and show only the total charges and credits for that month.

If there are any questions concerning this method or any specific statement, please feel free to call our office for an explanation.

Fig. 9.21 / Procedural communication—change.

Specimen 100 illustrates a common practice in that the procedure is actually labeled policy (Dangerous Weapon Policy). Note, however, the parenthetical "Supplement to Directive No. 10" indicates the *actual* policy (Directive No. 10); this memorandum is really a new procedural communication that imple ments the existing policy.

Acceptance is directed to gaining support for existing procedures. A familiar experience to students is the preparation of a term paper. Figure 9.22 sets forth procedures for preparation of such a document.

PREPARING YOUR RESEARCH PAPER—DEADLINE DECEMBER 1

In writing your paper, keep in mind the following points:

1. No categories should be omitted.
2. Remember that what is familiar to you may be unknown to many readers (including your instructor).
3. Use a minimum of three charts for the visual presentation of your ideas.
4. Type and double-space on plain white paper.
5. Length: minimum 15 pages; maximum 25 pages.
6. Follow proper and consistent footnote form.

Fig. 9.22 / Procedural communication—acceptance.

As a citizen of the United States, you have probably paid income taxes, al-though you may not have yet been required to pay quarterly estimated taxes. Figure 9.23 ("Reminder About Your Estimated Tax Payment") may help prepare you for this delightful experience.

Reminder About **YOUR ESTIMATED TAX PAYMENT**

Your next installment of estimated tax will soon be due. You will not receive a bill.

For calendar year taxpayers, due dates for estimated tax payments are April 15, June 15, September 15, and January 15. Fiscal year due dates are given in the instructions in your estimated tax forms package.

To help us identify your account, please use the payment voucher and self-addressed envelope from the tax package previously sent you. If you don't have them, send your payment and this notice to the Service Center address shown on the back of this notice. Please be sure to write your social security number on your check or money order.

The address on the back of this notice is the latest we have for you. If it is not correct, please change the address on your payment voucher, but if it is correct, do not change your voucher.

Note: If you are not required to make an estimated tax payment at this time, please disregard this reminder.

Thank you for your cooperation.

Fig. 9.23 / Procedural communication—acceptance.

Safety is all too often taken for granted in organizations; therefore communications to gain acceptance and to strengthen support are very common. Figure 9.24 exemplifies a procedural communication directed to this end.

A "sneaky" illustration using external regulations to get better acceptance of existing company procedures is shown in Specimen 101. The originator (Director of Company Mail Services) uses the rate increase to reaffirm and solicit acceptance of existing company mailing procedures.

Announcements as used here refer to procedures or instructions for meeting ad hoc situations or interim assignments. In Figure 9.25 you see assignments of employees to act as hosts for the company's open house for customers. The next Figure (9.26) is an announcement of a department head meeting with instructions for reporting departmental activities.

We have discussed three important types of procedural communications directed to unfavorable receivers, namely, change, acceptance, and announcements. We are now ready to deal with the same three types directed to favorable perspectives.

SUBJECT: Enforcement of Safety Policy

Your complete cooperation is needed to assure the safety and well-being of all visitors and employees. Be careful at all times and be alert to any hazardous or unsafe conditions. Report same to your supervisor at once. It is of the utmost importance to report the "Almost Accident" immediately. It is the responsibility of Supervisors and the Department Heads to establish the essential coordination required within the organization to obtain the efficiency that will result from the integration of all accident control activities into a plan. Internal procedures are your responsibility to insure the prompt reporting and correction, or removal from the service, of all malfunctioning equipment, broken furniture, inoperative lights, and the multitude of minor hazards which are created daily through normal use. All employees are enjoined to be particularly careful in their movements and actions to avoid injury. It is known that accident control can be achieved by a carefully planned program, carried out by well-trained supervisors and employees who constantly put in effect the resolution to promote and practice safety. Accident control, vigilantly practiced, means neater and cleaner departments and services, happier and healthier employees, and greater efficiency. It is hoped that all levels of management and employees will recognize their responsibilities and do everything within their power to contribute to the success of this highly important accident control program.

Fig. 9.24 / Procedural communication—acceptance.

SUBJECT: Open House for Customers

Following are the assignments for hosting the Open House on June 15.
Your duties are:
1. To greet guests
2. To mingle among guests and help them feel comfortable
3. To introduce guests to company officials

If you have any questions or conflicts as a result of this schedule, please let me know immediately.

1:00-3:00	3:00-5:00
C. Black	R. James
E. Browne	T. Swanson
A. Greene	W. Smith

Fig. 9.25 / Procedural communication—announcement.

SUBJECT: Report on Departmental Activities

A Departmental Head meeting will be held at 3:00 p.m., Monday, April 15, in the Conference Room of the Training Department.

Each of you will be given five minutes to report on your unit's activities in March using this format:

1. Accomplishments
2. Present projects
3. Employee turnover
4. Problems and plans

Fig. 9.26 / Procedural communication—announcement.

Favorable Receivers

Changes in procedures can be favorably received when the situation is right. Why would Figure 9.27 be viewed favorably? Because it sets forth possible benefits to an individual in the event he is arrested.

YOUR RIGHTS

1. To stop questioning insist upon a lawyer.
2. The arresting officer must adequately identify himself before you are required to give your name and address. (On campus you are required to give your I.D. number.)
3. The officer has no right to search without a warrant or probable cause. You are not required to allow search.
4. You have the right to communicate with a lawyer or bail bondsman. You have no right to make calls yourself.
5. You are not required to sign any documents.
6. You cannot be held without bail beyond the next court session.
7. Do not physically or verbally resist.

Fig. 9.27 / Procedural communication—change.

Likewise, Figure 9.28 shows the reader the precautions (benefits) he should take before embarking on a wallpapering project.

NOTICE: Safeguard your work. Take the following precautions.

1. Make sure this is the correct pattern.
2. See that each roll is the same shade of color.
3. Make note of the run number and specify it if additional material is needed.

Fig. 9.28 / Procedural communication—change.

The foregoing examples exemplify new procedures (that is, they are "new" to the recipients); Figure 9.29 and Specimen 102, illustrate changes in existing procedures as viewed by the readers. Figure 9.29 is a set of new procedures for making suggestions for company improvement.

NEW PROCEDURES FOR MAKING SUGGESTIONS

1. Submit the suggestion in writing on form provided.
2. Put the written suggestion in the suggestion box nearest to your office.
3. Write only one suggestion on a form.
4. Tips on writing your suggestion:
   Develop your idea fully; give all details
   Tell what your suggestion is about and what it will do for the company
   Give part numbers and names
   Make and submit sketches when helpful

Fig. 9.29 / Procedural communication—change.

Specimen 102 is a change in research lab procedures.

Acceptance is, as you remember, directed to gaining support for existing procedures. Figure 9.30 is a reminder to company employees on procedures for securing emergency medical treatment. It is likely to be favorably viewed, in this instance, as many requests had been made of the personnel office to supply the information in concise form for easy reference.

SUBJECT: Procedures for Emergency Medical Treatment

Quick service can be given if the employee will telephone the Medical Department for an appointment providing the illness or accident is such that immediate medical service is not necessary. When an emergency exists, immediate contact should be made with the Medical Department.

If you become ill and need the services of a physician after 5:00 p.m. on weekdays, or on Saturdays, Sundays and holidays—

Call 242-1157—Company operator will
obtain the physician
Physician will call ambulance when needed

Referrals to other physicians must have prior approval of the Medical Department.

Fig. 9.30 / Procedural communication—acceptance.

The brief safety checklist (Specimen 103) is a favorable procedural communication. The final example for gaining acceptance of procedures by favorable readers can be seen in Figure 9.31 ("Telephone Tips"). It is likely to be viewed favorably by the new employees who are anxious to acquaint themselves with the company's practices.

TELEPHONE TIPS

Answer Promptly. At the first ring if possible. Otherwise your caller may hang up and take his business elsewhere. Prompt answering helps build a reputation of efficiency for you and your Company.

Identify Yourself. Proper identification gets the conversation off to a good start. Identify the voice and personalize the call by using your name.

Answer with the name of the department and your name if it is a department telephone. For example, "Service Department, Brocker" or, "Credit Office, Miss Thomas."

If it is another person's telephone, answer with the name of the person's office and your name. For example, "Mr. Miller's office, Miss Thomas."

. . .

Fig. 9.31 / Procedural communication—acceptance.

Announcements, as you remember, are procedures or agenda to meet special situations. Figure 9.32 (planning procedures for the company's annual family picnic) is most likely to be favorably received.

SUBJECT: Administrative Staff Meeting

Our regular Administrative Staff Meeting will be held on Tuesday, November 17, at 3 p.m. We hope that this is a convenient time for you to attend. Rather than the normal Company business, we are going to plan the Company's Annual Family Picnic.

So that we can make the meeting fruitful and brief, please think of the following:

What is a good date? Where should it be held? What refreshments should the Company furnish? What activities and games should be included?

As a suggestion, please have someone in your department canvass your employees about their desires.

Fig. 9.32 / Procedural communication—announcement.

Figures 9.33 and 9.34 exemplify agenda for meetings. Figure 9.33 is a set agenda for a university faculty meeting. Why will it be favorably received? Reasons are twofold: the shortness of time ("3:00 to 4:00 p.m.") and the very few items to be covered (four). This gives the faculty assurance that the meeting will (hopefully) be brief and to the point. In Figure 9.34 you see a *preliminary agenda*. Why will this be viewed favorably? First, as a preliminary agenda, attendees are given a chance to respond to the tentative meeting coverage; second, the few items are again probable assurance that the session can be held within a short time.

SUBJECT: General Faculty Meeting

The next meeting of the General Faculty will be held on Tuesday, September 25, from 3:00 to 4:00 p.m. in the Faculty Center Auditorium.

Agenda
1. Approval of minutes of meetings of May 11 and May 15.
2. Election of two members to the Committee on Athletics.
3. Report of President of University.
4. New business.

Fig. 9.33 / Procedural communication—announcement.

Preliminary Agenda—Annual Meeting of Professional Council
June 5, 9:00 a.m.

Item #1 Report on Program Activities
  #2 Report of the Research and Development Committee
  #3 Report of the Resources Committee
  #4 Report on liaison with other professional organizations
  #5 New business and items from the floor
  #6 Adjournment (probably by noon)

Fig. 9.34 / Procedural communication—announcement.

A summary of procedural communications, the second of the task situationally determined purposes, is shown in Figure 9.35.

PROCEDURAL COMMUNICATIONS

Unfavorable	Favorable
1. Changes	1. Changes
2. Acceptance	2. Acceptance
3. Announcements	3. Announcements

Fig. 9.35 / Summary—procedural communications.

Status Communications

Let us now consider status communications, the last purpose within task-oriented perspectives. We have discussed policies (objectives or goals) and procedures (how to achieve objectives or goals). Status communications deal with *information directed to specialists* within or outside an organization. Status communications report past, present, or future happenings. They are, therefore, reports, but they communicate *specialized information.*

By *specialized*, we, of course, refer to information to the traditional *specialist*, including accountant, financier, producer, marketer, statistician, educator, scientist, or civil servant. But beyond the traditional specialists, status communications are also directed to any collection of people with homogeneous interests or purposes (e.g., nonbusiness groups such as social clubs, fraternities, churches, or ethnic identities; and, business-related collections such as managers, union members, or skilled employees). In other words, status communications generally arise from and are directed to specialists of comparable backgrounds, competencies, or interests. This unique objective distinguishes status information from other purposes.

From what we say, you will recognize that *status communications* are actually *reports*. However, they are *reports to specialists*. Some organizational reports go to other than specialists; these would not be classed as status communications. However, when they are addressed to specialists (thus classed as status communications) reports become both the medium (carrier) and the purpose (objective) of communication. This is the one organizational communication situation in which medium and purpose come together.

Status communications can go to either unfavorable or favorable receivers, categories for both of which are:

1. Descriptive
2. Evaluative

Unfavorable Receivers

Descriptive status communications are reportorial, that is, confined to the facts or data themselves. Since we discussed description in Chapter 4, "Reports," we present only a brief review here. Remember, in description, you do not go beyond that which has been observed or reported. For example, if you see three ducks with white feathers, yellow bills, and webbed feet, a proper descriptive statement is something similar to "I saw three ducks with white feathers, yellow bills, and webbed feet." It would be improper description to say "All ducks have white feathers, yellow bills, and webbed feet." This may seem an exaggerated illustration, but it is presented to make a point: any statement beyond the facts observed is not descriptive; it is evaluative. We shall be concerned with evaluative status communications later. Here, we shall examine examples of descriptive status communications for unfavorable receivers.

Figure 9.36 is a financial report relating to personal income and per capita

STATE PER CAPITA PERSONAL INCOME

Year	Amount State	Amount Nation	State % of Nation	National Ranking
19-7	$1,989	$2,048	97.1	16
19-8	2,101	2,064	101.8	16
19-9	2,182	2,163	100.9	16
19-0	2,283	2,217	102.9	14
19-1	2,357	2,268	103.9	11
19-2	2,440	2,368	103.0	12
19-3	2,464	2,449	100.6	17
19-4	2,566	2,566	100.0	19
19-5	2,710	2,746	98.7	20
19-6	2,919	2,978	98.0	22
19-7	3,135	3,159	99.2	20

PER CAPITA STATE AND LOCAL DEBT

	19-3 State	19-3 Nat'l Rank	19-5 State	19-5 Nat'l Rank	19-7 State	19-7 Nat'l Rank
State Avg.	$383.38	26	$486.24	17	$488.13	27
U.S. Avg.	463.65		513.43		579.15	

Note: The amounts in the tabulations may not add to the indicated totals because of rounding.

Fig. 9.36 / Status communication—descriptive.

state and local indebtedness as both affect the taxes of business and citizens. The relatively poor state rankings will be viewed unfavorably by taxpayer receivers.

In Specimen 104 you can see a descriptive document (minutes of a student-faculty council meeting). While it is descriptive in part, evaluative statements are interspersed throughout. In contrast, the minutes of the faculty meeting exemplified in Specimen 105 are, as they ought to be, descriptive. Specimen 104 will be viewed unfavorably because of the evaluative statements included; Specimen 105, the second set of minutes, although descriptive, will be viewed adversely because of the contentious ideas discussed at the meeting as indicated by the very close vote.

Often descriptive status communication can be given in tabular form. Figure 9.37 (reporting results of a study of business administration doctoral applicants for teaching positions) is such a document. Since it is part of a total report that shows that doctoral applicants for teaching positions far outnumber available slots, it will be unfavorably viewed by those seeking positions.

POTENTIAL DOCTORATE STUDENTS SEEKING POSITIONS

Institution	Accounting	Finance	Marketing	Management	Economics	Indus. Rel.	Insurance	Total
A	3	1		4	4	4		16
B	3	3	2					8
C	3	6	5					14
D			1	3		1		5
E	3	1	3	5	2		1	15
F	3	5	4	6	5			23
G		10	7	1	3			22
H								0
I	1	3	2	2		1		9
J	7	6	5	15	4			37
	23	35	29	36	18	6	1	148

Fig. 9.37 / Status communication—descriptive.

In Figure 9.38, you can see another type of descriptive status communication. Here, assumptions and procedures are set forth (described) for the reader. Although assumptions as such are evaluative, they are not here, because they are presented to describe the bases of the study itself. In addition, note the tabular listing of data following the description of assumptions and procedures. Such reports usually generate ill feelings on the part of the school involved; it considers this information private.

Graphs are also effective means of presenting descriptive status information. Figure 9.39 is a chart depicting the ups and downs of the value of shares in a mutual fund. It is quite clear why this document will be viewed unfavorably: note the downward plunge at the end.

You have no doubt read many college course descriptions. Figure 9.40 is a proposal for a new math course; this proposal was written so that it could be

RESULTS OF THE VALIDITY STUDY

Assumptions and Procedures

This study is based on the records of 103 students who had information available on all variables used in the study, including a first-year average based on at least 24 semester hours or the equivalent. These data were accumulated over several years and include students who entered at various times; exact information about year of entrance was not readily available. The group includes 73 full-time day students, 10 part-time day students, 3 full-time evening students, and 17 part-time evening students. Within the group, 79 students completed 24 hours in one year; 24 took two years to do it. The results are shown in Table 1 below.

Table 1

Predictor	Correlation Coefficient
Undergraduate Record Alone	.08
Test Total Alone	.09
Test Verbal Alone	.06
Test Quantitative Alone	.09

Fig. 9.38 / Status communication—descriptive.

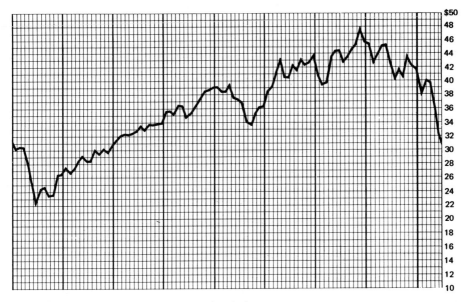

Fig. 9.39 / Status communication—descriptive.

Description of Course 85-101: Introduction to
Mathematical Models

This is a new freshman level course which develops the mathematics
necessary for quantitative models for study of the behavioral and social
sciences and in business.

Emphasis will be on developing mathematical models (see applications
below) and on techniques for solution of these models. Students will learn
to write computer programs and will use the computer extensively in
problem solving.

The mathematics topics covered include: probability and statistics, linear
equations and linear programming, difference equations and graph theory.

Applications include: population growth; learning models; economic models;
amortization; accounting and depreciation.

Text to be determined; there may be several reference books used rather
than a single text.

Instructor: Professor Donald B. Thompson

Fig. 9.40 / Status communication—descriptive.

considered by the faculty of the entire college. As you probably know, almost
any proposed new course is initially viewed negatively by most faculty.

Evaluative status communications are those that interpret, make judgments
about, draw conclusions from or that result in recommendations for action.
While frequently combined with descriptive information, they are inferential—
that is, they do go beyond the facts and observable data. Any decision making
or recommended action will always be evaluative. It is clear, therefore, that
this type of status communication is vital in managerial and organizational
activities. (As you no doubt recognize, we have just made an evaluative statement.)

By nature, evaluative status communications probably build in initial negative
reception. Why? Because they almost always report some deficiencies, discrepancies, problems, or needed corrections in an organization and its people.
You should therefore expect an unfavorable initial reader response to most of
the evaluative status documents you write. Therefore, we shall not point out
the reasons for the unfavorable reception for each of the nine examples that
follow: Figures 9.41, 9.42, and 9.43 and Specimens 106 through 111. Read each.
You will see why all invite beginning hostility or neutrality.

SUBJECT: A Computerized Registration System

Two overriding problems are apparent in studying any element of past registration systems:

(1) Faculty and Administrative staffs are prohibited from making effective decisions due to the lack of early and reliable information and analysis of need vs. class offerings.

(2) Early determination of need is further hindered by certain traditions which prohibit large numbers of students from making known those needs through early or advance registration.

Recommendations: The following systems general concepts should be adopted in design of the registration system to be employed.

(1) Maximum personal contact should be *available* for advising and assistance to students.

(2) *Requirements* for contact by individual students with separate offices and departments should be held to the minimum.

(3) Maximum flexibility should be maintained in changing schedules to meet need. The "Computer" need not demand a rigid fixed schedule. Greater flexibility and *exercise of judgment* are possible through computer manipulation of data seeking alternate solutions.

Fig. 9.41 / Status communication—evaluative.

STAR-X COMPANY

19—Results and Outlook for the Future

In the generally favorable climate during the past year, Star-X progressed significantly toward long range goals. For several years Star-X had been on a revenue plateau. The need for diversification was clear, and, Company management determined to move in this direction. New opportunities were sought out and new technologies were studied. From the range of new possibilities, we went into several new ventures. These included information systems, automation, and ecological studies and products.

The Company is succeeding. Gross revenues last year advanced nearly $250,000,000, much of the additional income coming from our diversification. We think that our future is bright.

Robert M. Jones, President

Fig. 9.42 / Status communication—evaluative.

THE YEAR'S SALES AND EARNINGS

Sales increased 5.4 percent but earnings decreased 10.8 percent. Why did this happen? Primarily our introduction of new products, together with lower sales in some of Star-X's major product lines, brought about this peculiar combination. We foresee a better profit picture for next year, which should result in increased earnings for the Company. Rest assured we shall do everything in our power to give the highest possible dividend to our shareholders.

Fig. 9.43 / Status communication—evaluative.

Favorable Receivers

Descriptive status communications are exemplified in 9.44 and 9.45 and Specimens 112 and 113. Figure 9.44 (enrollment data for a college) will be

SUBJECT: Autumn Enrollment Figures

Yesterday, you asked that I give you each semester's enrollment figures. I have just received some Autumn statistics which I pass on to you.

We had 18 special students, 505 freshmen, 437 sophomores, 403 juniors, and 362 seniors for a total enrollment of 1,725. In addition, we had 268 graduate students. This gives us a total student body of 1,993.

Of the 1,725 undergraduates, 1,565 were considered full-time students in that they carried 11.6 quarter hours or more. At the graduate level, 50% of the students were considered full-time. In addition, for what benefit the information may be to you, 69% of our undergraduates took all day classes and 3% took all evening classes, and the remaining 28% took a combined day and evening schedule.

Fig. 9.44 / Status communication—descriptive.

favorably received because the readers just the day before requested the information. The immediate response to their request will help to create a favorable impression. Figure 9.45 will be favorably received because it reduces very complex narrative information on computer systems to a clear graphic presentation that can be more easily understood by the systems specialists for whom intended.

Specimen 112 will be favorably received because it confirms prior oral agreements. Scientific and academic people expect clearly stated assumptions, cri-

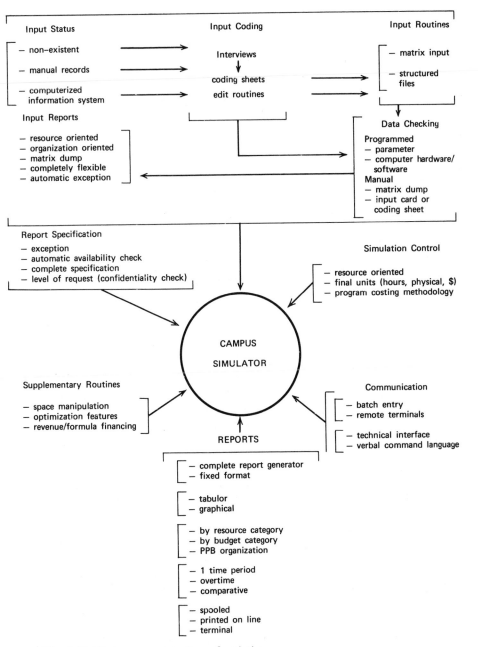

Fig. 9.45 / Status communication—descriptive.

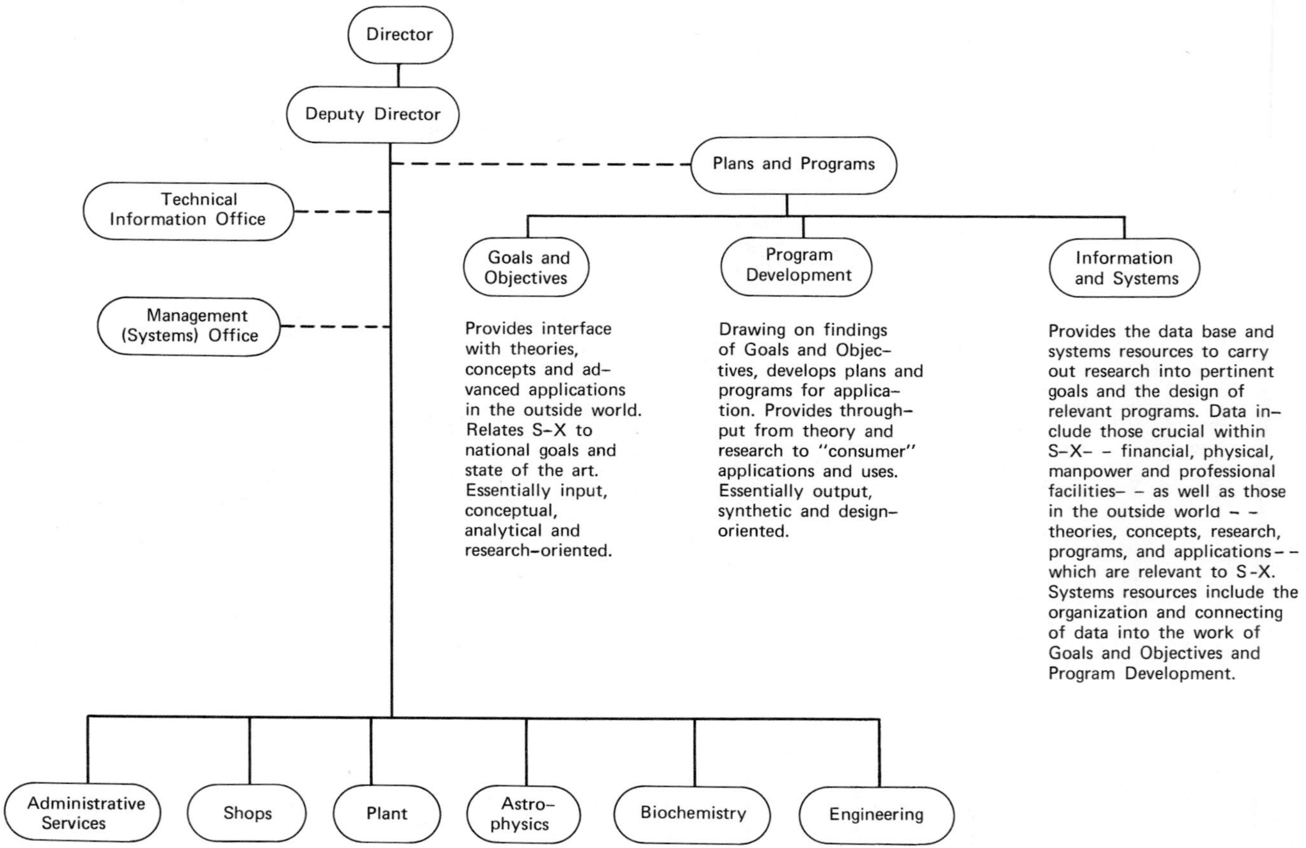

Fig. 9.46 / Status communication—evaluative.

teria, procedures, and definitions of terms; therefore, Specimen 113 will probably be favorably received because all these are explicitly done in that document.

Evaluative favorable status communications are relatively infrequent because specialists most often take an initial critical view. However, where ideas meet proper standards such as adequate description, proper reasoning, and logical conclusions, a favorable reception is often assured. A second likelihood for favorable view is when specialists have actively participated in decisions made. This builds in their commitment.

Figure 9.46 exemplifies participative decision making which, of course, is evaluative. In this instance, the analysis and redesign of the organization were done by the specialists directly affected. As a result, this organization chart (which they developed) is acceptable to them.

In Specimen 114, you can see a schedule of one year's anticipated income from membership dues of a professional society. The essential favorable appeal of this document is that the clear detailed exposition allows the members to examine critically the data and to see how the projected income can be realized.

Finally, Specimen 115 is a critique of a disaster drill held in a hospital. At the time issued, the Hospital Administrator said he was sure it would receive a good reception. Read it in light of the criteria for a favorable evaluative status communication. For example, are descriptive and evaluative dimensions clearly differentiated? Are descriptive terms used appropriately? Are evaluative terms used appropriately? Are criteria for the critique explicated? How helpful is the information given in the last two sentences? After answering these questions, do you agree with the Hospital Administrator's prediction of favorable response?

Figure 9.47 summarizes the third task-oriented situationally determined purposes, status communications.

STATUS COMMUNICATIONS	
Unfavorable	Favorable
1. Descriptive	1. Descriptive
2. Evaluative	2. Evaluative

Fig. 9.47 / Summary—status communications.

In Figure 9.48 you can see a summary of the three task situationally determined purposes and respective receiver roles.

Figure 9.49 summarizes all specific purposes (personal, situationally determined; personal, predetermined; and task, situationally determined), detailed in Chapters 7 to 9. It can be used as a comprehensive reference table to deter-

PURPOSE: TASK	RECEIVER: SITUATIONALLY DETERMINED	
	Unfavorable	Favorable
POLICY COMMUNICATIONS	1. Constraints 2. Changes 3. Acceptance	1. Constraints 2. Changes 3. Acceptance
PROCEDURAL COMMUNICATIONS	1. Changes 2. Acceptance 3. Announcements	1. Changes 2. Acceptance 3. Announcements
STATUS COMMUNICATIONS	1. Descriptive 2. Evaluative	1. Descriptive 2. Evaluative

Fig. 9.48 / Summary—Chapter 9.

mine where specific purposes relate to both unfavorable and favorable receiver roles.

You should now understand all specific purposes and related receiver roles so that you can quickly identify them for effective communication (whether sending or receiving). This background is key to communication control in that it gives you the "how to" for assessing planning for the communication task you confront.

EXERCISES

exercise 1 Define each of the three situational task purposes.

exercise 2 Using both unfavorable and favorable receiver perspectives, list specific purposes for each situational task purpose.

exercise 3 Assuming a receiver perspective, examine each of the following figures: 9.7, 9.13, 9.24, 9.27, 9.40, and 9.44. In your evaluation, state (1) the purpose (e.g., policy communication); (2) the receiver perspective (e.g., favorable, constraint); (3) where the document does or does not meet the specific purpose and receiver perspective; and (4) the quality of clarity, correctness, and persuasiveness of each communication.

exercise 4 From the list of figures in exercise 3, rewrite one for each of the three situational task purposes. In your rewrites, follow appropriate media guidelines, plus principles for clear, correct, and persuasive communication.

	PURPOSE	RECEIVER	
		Unfavorable	Favorable
PERSONAL SITUATIONALLY DETERMINED	ACKNOWLEDGMENT/ ACCEPTANCE	1. Receivers wrong 2. Apologies 3. Answers to inquiries	1. Receivers right 2. Apologies 3. Sender appreciation 4. Answers to inquiries 5. Assents to offers
	OFFERING	1. Applications 2. Quotations 3. Special inducements 4. Recommendations 5. Changes/ corrections 6. Transmittals	1. Quotations 2. Special inducements 3. Recommendations 4. Changes/ corrections 5. Transmittals
	SOLICITATION	1. Seeking information 2. Seeking contributions	1. Seeking information 2. Seeking contributions
PERSONAL PREDETERMINED	COMPLAINT/ ADJUSTMENT	1. Commodity/ service/policy dissatisfaction 2. Due/past due accounts 3. Price increase/ budget cuts	
	REJECTION/ REPRIMAND	1. Refusals 2. Terminations 3. Censures	
	GOODWILL		1. Commendations 2. Social relations 3. Inside information
TASK SITUATIONALLY DETERMINED	POLICY COMMUNICATIONS	1. Constraints 2. Changes 3. Acceptance	1. Constraints 2. Changes 3. Acceptance
	PROCEDURAL COMMUNICATIONS	1. Changes 2. Acceptance 3. Announcements	1. Changes 2. Acceptance 3. Announcements
	STATUS COMMUNICATIONS	1. Descriptive 2. Evaluative	1. Descriptive 2. Evaluative

Fig. 9.49 / Summary—purposes and receivers.

exercise 5 Using instructions in exercise 3, evaluate either Specimen 94 or 104. After evaluation, rewrite your specimen choice following the pattern in exercise 4.

CASE PROBLEMS

1. Re: Figure 9.6. You are Mr. Miller, a department chairman at City University. You have read this memorandum and disagree with the whole tenor and content of the new mailing policies. You feel that existing policies and procedures are adequate, that the new system will only create discord and inefficiency for the entire University. You want to persuade Jones, head of Mail Services Department, to study further the mailing problems. In any event, you do not want the announced system to go into effect without further discussion with faculty and administration of the University.

Your Mission: Write a memo to Jones expressing your feelings about the new mailing system and proposing further study by systems analysts, as well as discussion with faculty and administration before adopting a new system. At the top of the memo, specify the exact specific purposes and receiver roles. Use an appropriate style and include necessary components; use the memorandum Communication Quality Control as a guide to check final product.

2. Re: Figure 9.37. You are Dean Miller and have received this report on doctoral candidates from these ten institutions from which you draw many of your new instructors. You have vacancies in all seven departments; therefore, you want to get your share of the best candidates.

Your Mission: Write a memo to all department chairmen exhorting them to aggressively recruit from the limited number of candidates available. You want to convey a sense of immediacy and seriousness to all department chairmen so that they will go into action within the next two weeks. At the top of the memo, specify the exact specific purpose and receiver role. Use an appropriate style and include necessary components; use the memorandum Communication Quality Control as a guide to check final product.

Chapter 10

COMMUNICATION
IMPACTS AND DESIGNS

$$\text{(Purposes)} \!-\!\!-\!\!-\! \text{(Receivers)} \!-\!\!-\!\!-\! \text{(Impacts)} \!-\!\!-\!\!-\! \text{(Design)} \!-\!\!-\!\!-\! \text{(Execution)}$$

Your Learning Objectives:

1. To know specific receiver roles and conditions to overcome or control each.
2. To know initial receiver roles and needed impacts.
3. To know supportive and response receiver roles and needed impacts.
4. To know and to be able to use essential devices to achieve desired impacts.
5. To know how specific purposes relate to basic designs.
6. To know and to be able to use basic design sequences.
7. To know how to apply all the chapter's principles to typical communication situations.

We have discussed the nine essential written media with attendant specific purposes for both unfavorable and favorable receivers. We are now ready to move more into the "how to"—that is, ways to achieve these specific purposes.

In order to do this, we shall study: (1) specific receiver roles and related impacts, (2) devices to achieve desired impacts, (3) specific purposes related to basic designs, (4) basic design sequences, (5) applying basic design sequences, and (6) applications of principles to ten specimens.

You have been studying and applying many important communication concepts in preceding chapters. These principles have been largely narrated in detail for proper understanding and application. Starting with this chapter, we shall use more concise tabular presentation, along with specimen references for illustration. The tabular presentation will be supplemented with sufficient narrative explanation to permit proper comprehension of ideas. With your background of foregoing principles, you will find that these tables become succinct, ready references for your use in handling the new communication concepts discussed.

In the last section of the chapter we shall pull all principles together by applying them in the evaluation of ten selected specimens, followed by a checklist summary that you can use as a guide in your assessment, planning, and design for effective communication. To further strengthen and drive home principles, exercises at the end of the chapter will give you the opportunity to evaluate and rewrite certain specimens.

By applying what you have previously learned, together with studiously following this chapter's progression, you will have both high level understanding and skills in planning and producing effective organizational communication.

Specific Receiver Roles and Related Impacts

In preceding chapters, we have used general terms for receiver roles to encompass opposing, neutral, or unknown neutral attitudes, while favorable receiver outlooks referred to those in basic agreement with the sender and his message. We are now ready to analyze these roles in more depth. Furthermore, we are ready to relate roles to needed impacts. First we start with an in-depth analysis of roles.

Specific Receiver Roles

Let us now break unfavorable and favorable roles into even more useful classifications.

Specific *unfavorable* roles are *apathetic, sophisticated,* or *opposing.* Specific *favorable* roles are *credent* or *critical.* Rather than detailed textual exposition, Figure 10.1 presents these specific roles, together with definitions, conditions to overcome (unfavorable), or conditions to control (favorable) and specimen examples.

Initial Receiver Roles and Needed Impacts

Now that you understand the specific receiver roles, both unfavorable and favorable, let us examine the impacts required to handle each. It is essential to marshal your ideas so that they strike your receiver in the right way (make the right impact).

Let us start with *initial* roles, which could be any one of the five summarized in Figure 10.1. However, the conditions specified in Figure 10.1 actually dictate the starting role, not possible subsequent ones (which will be discussed later).

SPECIFIC RECEIVER ROLES

Role and Definition	Conditions	Spec. Ref.
UNFAVORABLE		
Apathetic: A "could care less" attitude; indifference; receiver is psychologically dead to communication (from Greek, *apatheia,* meaning "without feeling")	Prior deadly communications: past poor documents from specific sources or people (e.g., top management, personnel office)	29, 37
	Receiver saturation: inundation from given sources, people (e.g., "junk mail," report requests)	20, 21, 22, 36
	"Unimportant" subject: as perceived by reader (e.g., safety, management exhortations to do jobs better)	4, 30, 93
Sophisticated: A "wise-guy" outlook: an "unteachable" attitude; receiver assumes he knows as much or more than you can tell him (from Greek, *sophos,* meaning "wisdom")	Routines: ongoing activities of the organization (e.g., recommendations, application processing)	24, 25, 31, 32, 38
	Unrespected sources and people: those held in disdain by receiver (e.g., peer to peer, staff to line, nonexpert to expert, subordinate to superior)	23, 35, 101
	"So what's new!": receiver "knows" already (e.g., messages from same sources; message about same subject, communications among specialists)	26, 27, 28, 31, 92, 110
Opposing: A "hostile" attitude (overt or covert): an antagonistic outlook; receiver assumes that you are wrong and he is right (from Latin, *opponere,* meaning "to place against")	The "enemy": people, organizations, or sources who, prior to communication, "know" sender's hostile posture (e.g., staff recommendations for improvement, "efficiency" experts)	2, 5, 104, 105, 107, 108
	Potential or actual threats: assaults on ego, administrative coercion, legal demands (e.g., "slap on the wrist," demand for payment)	1, 56, 58, 60, 61, 62, 65, 66, 67, 68, 69, 71, 72, 74, 76, 79, 80, 99
	Hidden agenda: suspected ulterior motives (e.g., any communication with "free" gift, flattery, evasion)	59, 64, 72(1, 5)
	Possible dissatisfaction: "inequities" in policy or procedure (e.g., application turndown, dismissal)	3, 72(7), 73, 75, 77
	Resistance to change: hostility to any communication suggesting or dictating modification of personal or organizational activities (e.g., new policy, new procedure)	33, 34, 55, 57, 91, 94, 100, 106, 111

Fig. 10.1 / Specific receiver roles.

Fig. 10.1 (continued)

SPECIFIC RECEIVER ROLES

Role and Definition	Conditions	Spec. Ref.
	Resistance to giving resources: hostility to requests for voluntary gifts of time, money, men, or materials (e.g., charitable organizations, boss asking managers to assign personnel to special jobs)	48, 49, 63, 109
	Resistance to extra effort: hostility to being asked to perform "above and beyond the call of duty" (e.g., committee assignments; special questionnaires; special reports)	46, 47, 50, 54, 72(2, 3), 78, 99
FAVORABLE		
Credent: A "believing" outlook: receiver already accepts you and your message; he is already "saved" (from Latin, *credere,* meaning "to believe")	Personal benefits: actual or potential constructive outcomes for the individual (e.g., higher pay, savings, fringe benefits, better work conditions)	12, 13, 18, 39, 40, 44, 52, 90, 95, 96, 98
	Recognition needs: commendation for outstanding performance; congratulations on special occasions; to overcome failure feelings (e.g., praise for exceeding production quotas, anniversary greetings, constructive suggestions to do better job)	7, 8, 9, 10, 11, 81, 82, 83, 84, 85
	Assurance needs: expressions of support, condolence (e.g., death of official or employee, change of personnel or organizational structure)	86, 87, 88, 89
	Organizational objectives: new company goals, plans, policies (e.g., five-year marketing plan; expansion into new field; company diversification)	53, 102, 103
Critical: A "thinking" outlook: receiver is willing to accept ideas based on fact and sound reasoning; a scientific viewpoint (from Greek, *krinein,* meaning to judge or to discern) Note: as used here, critical is a constructive role— not the negative, carping or censorious sense in which the term is often used.	Consideration of vital issues: crucial problems, situations, conditions to be identified or analyzed or resolved (e.g., contracts, directives on new policies, solving "thorny" problems)	14, 15, 16, 19, 41, 42, 97, 112, 113, 114, 115
	Professional or specialist's communications: transactions between persons or units dealing with technical or specialized ideas or activities— assumes capacity and willingness to think critically (e.g., research reports, professional papers)	6, 17, 43, 45, 51

The *apathetic* role connotes psychological deadness or indifference to you or your message. Clearly, no communication can take place as long as this condition exists. Therefore, the needed impact is to awaken the receiver, in other words, *to get attention and sustain interest.* Attention refers to immediate receiver focus; interest refers to continuing attention throughout the communication. It is false to assume that once you get initial attention, the receiver automatically continues it. The burden is on you, the communicator, to sustain it. Needless to say, apathy is a very common initial role in both written and oral communication.

The *sophisticated* role refers to a "wise-guy" or "you can't tell me anything" attitude. Therefore, to overcome this intolerable condition, the needed impact is to make the receiver *see ideas in a new light.* As you will note under "Conditions" giving rise to this role (Figure 10.1), sophistication, too, is a common outlook, both initially and subsequently.

The *opposing* role means a hostile receiver attitude, whether overt or covert. Therefore, to overcome this antagonistic outlook, you must *lessen or eliminate hostility.* Clearly, you will confront opposition often in communication situations. As with sophistication, it can be present either initially or subsequently.

The *credent* role is a favorable perspective in that the receiver already "believes." Therefore, the desired impact is to *strengthen pre-existing belief.* This role can also exist initially or subsequently.

The *critical* role is a "thinking" attitude and ability, in other words, a perspective that examines ideas based on facts and sound reasoning. Therefore, the needed impact is to *rationalize ideas.* As with the credent, the critical also can be an initial or subsequent receiver role.

Subsequent Receiver Roles and Needed Impacts

Subsequent receiver roles are *supportive* and *response.* As will be seen when we discuss design, either may follow the initial role, and either may be the final role. In other words, one design sequence may be initial-supportive-response; the other may be initial-response-supportive. Let us first look at supportive roles.

Let us assume that you have overcome initial apathy (if not, your communication automatically fails). In other words, the reader is now awake, and focusing on your message from one of the other four perspectives (sophisticated, opposing, credent, or critical). Therefore you must now pursue the needed impact with the attendant role.

If the supportive role is *sophisticated* or *opposing,* you must pursue the same needed impacts given under initial role (respectively, to see ideas in a new light or to lessen or eliminate hostility).

With *credent* and *critical* roles, supportive impacts are a little different. In order to understand the difference, let us first discuss two different modes of persuasion: nonrational and rational. *Nonrational persuasion* refers to devices and appeals primarily directed to the psychological feelings or emotions (e.g., satisfying specific wants and needs; engendering dedication to organizational goals); in contrast, *rational persuasion* refers to devices and methods primarily directed to logical facts and reasoning (e.g., presenting reliable description and valid evaluation).

If the role is *credent*, the supportive impact should be *to strengthen belief* using *nonrational* devices (whether the role exists because you have already overcome an unfavorable role—apathy, sophistication, or opposition—or whether you are furthering an initial credent role).

If the role is *critical*, the supportive impact should be *to validate belief* using *rational* devices (whether the role exists once you have moved the receiver from any of the four initial roles—apathetic, sophisticated, opposing, or credent—or whether to continue control of an initial critical role). Bear in mind that a credent role, though potentially favorable, may not be desired in a given circumstance. If your receivers want or need to rationally consider ideas, the critical is the only favorable role (credence may mean "gullibility," which is antithetical to a rational purpose).

With response roles, it is assumed that you have overcome any unfavorable perspective (apathetic, sophisticated, opposing). In other words, the receiver is either credent or critical, whichever role is desired.

Again, with *credent* receivers the response impact is *to get intended belief*

INITIAL RECEIVER ROLE

Initial Role and Needed Impact
Apathetic: to get attention; sustain interest
Sophisticated: to see ideas in a new light
Opposing: to lessen or eliminate hostility
Credent: to strengthen pre-existing belief
Critical: to rationalize ideas

SUBSEQUENT RECEIVER ROLES

Supportive Role and Needed Impact	Response Role and Needed Impact
Sophisticated: to see ideas in a new light	Credent: to get intended belief or performance (nonrational)
Opposing: to lessen or eliminate hostility	Critical: to get intended belief or performance (rational)
Credent: to strengthen belief (nonrational)	
Critical: to validate belief (rational)	

Fig. 10.2 / Specific receiver roles and related impacts.

or performance using *nonrational* devices. With *critical* receivers the response impact is *to get intended belief or performance* using *rational* devices.

Note that response may be either belief or performance. Belief refers to instilling desired attitudes or tenets; performance refers to getting desired actions or behaviors.

Let us now look at specific receiver roles and related impacts in summary form; Figure 10.2 presents this information.

Devices to Achieve Desired Impacts

Now that you understand specific receiver roles (whether initial, supportive, or response), let us move to the devices through which you can attain needed impacts. Rather than a detailed exposition, we shall present these in a comprehensive, but very useful, table, Figure 10.3.

At first you may feel inundated by the mass of information presented in this figure. This is a natural, but misleading, reaction. You will soon discover that these are things you have been doing all your life. What we really present is a ready reference for classifying, analyzing, and using these tools. When you learn to consciously recognize and control the devices presented, you will then have the tactical "how to" skills to get the exact needed impact.

The devices are listed alphabetically, followed by a succinct definition. Moreover, appropriate specific roles are listed under initial, supportive, and response patterns. Within each specific role, under the three patterns, you will see either a check, numbered specimen reference, or a blank. If checked or a specimen reference listed, the device is generally appropriate to use with the indicated role in the given pattern. If blank, the device is normally inappropriate.

However, this table is not dogma; there are situations where items not checked may be properly used, and there are cases where items checked or referenced may be improper. Remember, your judgment must be exercised in the use of any device to achieve your purpose with any of the receiver roles. To help you make sound judgments for specific cases, we include a section "Special Applications and Cautions" presenting principles for selection and uses of appropriate devices.

DEVICE AND DEFINITION	INITIAL Apathetic	INITIAL Sophos.	INITIAL Opposing	INITIAL Credent	INITIAL Critical	SUPPORTIVE Sophos.	SUPPORTIVE Opposing	SUPPORTIVE Credent	SUPPORTIVE Critical	RESPONSE Credent	RESPONSE Critical	Special Applications and Cautions
1. Acting: as requested / Responding to a prior request	x	28:1.1 38:1.1	x	44:1.2 52:1.1	19:1 43:1			103:1.2		x		Use: as common ground introduction / Avoid: evasion or misinterpretation of receiver request
2. Acting: on another's behalf / Anticipating another's need	x	x	x	x	16:1,2 42:1				41:4			Use: as introductory or supporting device / Avoid: imputing wrong receiver wants or needs; avoid insincerity or overdoing
3. Advantages: organizational/ professional / Benefits (actual or potential) to the firm or profession	x	92	50:1	x	14:1	22:2,3 23:1.2; 3.1	x	7:1.3 10:2	14:3 51:3.1	30:2.1	31:5.1 32:2.2 42:3.3 45:1.4 111:3	Use: with receivers with sufficient organizational or professional dedication / Avoid: where dedication in doubt or cannot readily be built by other means (e.g., personal advantages)
4. Advantages: personal / Benefits (actual or potential) for the individual	37	x		39:1.1	x	92:2	x	18: (P.S.)	14:2	58:3 61:3 70:3.4 79:4	45:1.4	Use: in most any situation when properly handled / Avoid: imputing crassness or selfishness to receiver (may be more effective when accompanied by organizational/professional and social advantages)
5. Advantages: social / Benefits (actual or potential) for society (at large or some segment)		x	x	x	x	x	50:1.2;2	10:3	51:3.1	x	x	Use: when personal and organizational/professional advantages are satisfied and clearly related / Avoid: assuming that receivers will automatically respond favorably to even the highest social goals; (again, most receivers must see personal and probably org./prof. satisfactions in the given social advantages)

Fig. 10.3 / Devices to achieve desired impact.

Fig. 10.3 (continued)

DEVICE AND DEFINITION	Apathetic	INITIAL Sophos.	INITIAL Opposing	INITIAL Credent	INITIAL Critical	SUPPORTIVE Sophos.	SUPPORTIVE Opposing	SUPPORTIVE Credent	SUPPORTIVE Critical	RESPONSE Credent	RESPONSE Critical	Special Applications and Cautions
6. Asking for help. Requests for participation or guidance			46	x	51	x	47:1.4 50:3.2			x	x	Use: to get receiver attention and possible commitment. Avoid: appearance of "Mickey Mouse" antics; also be careful in situations where the device can boomerang (e.g., where an outcome contrary to one desired is possible)
7. "As you know..." Assuming the receiver's knowledge (whether or not he actually knows)—explicit or implicit		26 32 37		98:1.1	97:1.1 (implicit)	36:2.3	56:2.1-3					Use: especially effective for sophisticated or credent roles. Avoid: appearance of over-doing or insincerity (which can produce immediate opposition or apathy)
8. Candor: admission of wrongdoing. Acknowledging or apologizing for actual/possible error/failure		31	x	x	6:1			x			x	Use: very effective when actual or potential errors have been made or are probable (especially useful with opposing role); even more effective when accompanied by promise of future amends. Avoid: where dedication in for yourself ("methinks he doth protest too much"); also do not merely mouth apologies (you must appear to mean what you say)
9. Candor: basic assumptions and premises. Explicating starting points and ground rules		106:1.2 112:1			113:2.1							Use: very important in most critical communications and with some initial sophisticated roles. Avoid: unclear or unreasonable starting points

Fig. 10.3 (continued)

DEVICE AND DEFINITION	INITIAL					SUPPORTIVE				RESPONSE		Special Applications and Cautions
	Apathetic	Sophos.	Opposing	Credent	Critical	Sophos.	Opposing	Credent	Critical	Credent	Critical	
10. Candor: conclusions and implications Explicating reasonable outcome and consequences		x					109:9-12		113:8		x	Use: required for many critical communications Avoid: unclear or unreasonable outcomes
11. Candor: definition Explicating meaning of term		106:1.1	110		113:2.2-4	x	106:3	x	x			Use: essential in critical communications; may be useful with sophisticated and opposing roles to get receivers to see what you really mean Avoid: definition "mongering," which can lead to apathy or hostility
12. Candor: "laying it on the line" Explicating what is wrong			5 55			26:2	54:2.1 55:1.8, 2.1-2 56:3.1				24:3	Use: with opposing receivers when you want your viewpoint or position to be absolutely clear Avoid: unnecessary negativism or undue incitement of hostility (which only turns off the receiver)
13. Candor: open invitation to critique Asking for honest criticism							109:5				x	Use: very desirable with critical Avoid: mere appearance of openness; be prepared for genuinely critical responses
14. Candor: statement of gaps and weaknesses Explicating voids and deficiencies					x	x			115:5.1, 2,4		x	Use: highly important in critical communications; can be used with discretion for sophisticated role Avoid: unnecessary apology; undue detail beyond giving essential reasons

Fig. 10.3 (continued)

DEVICE AND DEFINITION	INITIAL					SUPPORTIVE				RESPONSE		Special Applications and Cautions
	Apathetic	Sophos.	Opposing	Credent	Critical	Sophos.	Opposing	Credent	Critical	Credent	Critical	
15. Candor: statement of issue Explicating the problem or basic idea to be considered			1:1 108:1.1-2	x	115:(heading)	x	111:2 57:2.1 67:3	x	97:1.3	x	x	Use: with all but apathetic roles; especially helpful in critical communications to clarify; useful with opposition to move to broader context Avoid: stating issue in un-acceptable terms for receiver role to which addressed
16. Candor: statement of procedures/methods Explicating how something was (or is to be) done					113:2		109:6-8		x		x	Use: necessary for many critical communications Avoid: intricate, lengthy details where not necessary (in other words, highlight the important)
17. Candor: statement of purpose Explicating objectives or goals		109:2			15:1.1	x	x		x			Use: essential to valid critical communications; may also be used with sophisticated role to shed a new light Avoid: including elements other than purpose (e.g., reasons, background); avoid unnecessary verbiage (state the purpose clearly and succinctly)
18. Challenge Throwing down the gauntlet or daring your receiver				x	x			x		x		Use: with credent or critical receivers initially; with credent receivers in conclusion Avoid: going beyond the ability or willingness to respond

Fig. 10.3 (continued)

DEVICE AND DEFINITION	INITIAL Apathetic	Sophos.	Opposing	Credent	Critical	SUPPORTIVE Sophos.	Opposing	Credent	Critical	RESPONSE Credent	Critical	Special Applications and Cautions
19. Commendation — Giving tribute or praise	x	x	54:1	11:1.1 85:1.2		x	1:5.2 47:2	9:4-5 81:2 85:3	51:3.3 115:5.7, 8	x		Use: initially—credent and opposing roles; backup—opposing, credent and critical — Avoid: overdoing or appearance of insincerity (which will produce antagonism)
20. Confirming documents — Communications recording prior agreements				21	14 15			44	15 16			Use: as followup to earlier communications for documentation — Avoid: making a "fetish" out of overcommunication on trivial or unimportant matters (which overloads communication channels)
21. Details: descriptive — Factual data, statistics, examples, illustrations	21 22:1	x	33:1	x	115:1-3	20:1.2	28:5.6.1	x	6:2 43:2.2	13:1.3 30:3,4	16:2 17 26:5 29	Use: essential in critical communications; helpful with noncritical roles using selected details — Avoid: overdoing or including "more than the receiver wants or needs to know"
22. Details: evaluative — Inferential facts, statistics, examples, illustrations				18:1.1	115:4	20:1.3, 4; 2	28:1.2; 2-4	x	43:2.3; 3	x		Use: to induce desired impact on receivers, especially credent and critical — Avoid: ditto descriptive plus mixing evaluative and descriptive details, especially with critical receivers (generally careful labeling of evaluative details is necessary in critical communications)

Fig. 10.3 (continued)

DEVICE AND DEFINITION	INITIAL Apathetic	INITIAL Sophos.	INITIAL Opposing	INITIAL Credent	INITIAL Critical	SUPPORTIVE Sophos.	SUPPORTIVE Opposing	SUPPORTIVE Credent	SUPPORTIVE Critical	RESPONSE Credent	RESPONSE Critical	Special Applications and Cautions
23. Details: heart interest Incidents with "happy" outcomes	x		49:1.1,2	x			x	9:2;3.2, 87		x		Use: another effective dramatic device when properly used Avoid: overdoing, Pollyanna or maudlin communication (all of which defeat your intended dramatic impact)
24. Details: heart rending Incidents with "tragic" outcomes			48:1-3	x			48:4	9:3.1		x		Use: another effective dramatic device when properly used Avoid: overdoing, Pollyanna or maudlin communication (all of which defeat your intended dramatic impact)
25. Details: inside Unknown or little known information	x	x		40:1 95:1		49:2	59:2 64:2.3-5; 4.2	39:2,3	52:2			Use: an effective dramatizing technique (lets receivers in on "what's going on") Avoid: confidential information, especially in writing (remember, you can be quoted)
26. Details: massing Piling on information for climactic effect							78:1.2-4	63:3.3		x		Use: very effective dramatic device for backup role especially with credent receivers Avoid: anticlimactic handling (must be appropriate and properly placed in the communication)

Fig. 10.3 (continued)

DEVICE AND DEFINITION	INITIAL					SUPPORTIVE				RESPONSE		Special Applications and Cautions
	Apathetic	Sophos.	Opposing	Credent	Critical	Sophos.	Opposing	Credent	Critical	Credent	Critical	
27. Expression: appreciation/ thanks — Statement of gratitude	x	x	3:1.1 67:1 (pro forma)	7:1.1 8:1.1		32:2.1	2:2.1 3:3 (pro forma)	10:4 (pro forma) 12:3.1 (pro forma) 52:2 (pro forma) 77:2.1	98:2.1	x	32:4 (pro forma)	Use: to communicate genuine gratitude to receiver. Avoid: pro forma statements or appearance of insincerity
28. Expression: concern — Statement of genuine interest for another			61:1.1 70: (special delivery) 70:2	12:1.2 (pro forma) 103:1.1			61:2.2-4 74:3.1 75:1.3	12:3.2 (pro forma) 18:2 (pro forma)		x		Use: especially applicable to express reassurance or a note of caution. Avoid: pro forma statements or appearance of insincerity
29. Expression: regret — Statement of condolence or sympathy			2:1.2,2	44:1.1 86:1.1 87:1								Use: to communicate compassion in situations of receiver grief or anxiety. Avoid: pro forma statements or appearance of insincerity
30. Familiar — Ideas already known by the receiver	x		x	11: (heading) 15:1.2,3			x	x	42:3.1	x		Use: to get receiver attention or common ground. Avoid: overdoing the obvious
31. Figurative language — Literary expressions (e.g., metaphor, understatement)	x	x	63:1.1-3	x		36:2.1, 2	x	77:2.2		x		Use: to breathe life into the commonplace; to get attention and dramatize ideas (could be used more frequently in organizations). Avoid: in most critical communications; avoid appearing "snobbish" by showing your "knowledge" or "cleverness"

238

Fig. 10.3 (continued)

DEVICE AND DEFINITION	INITIAL					SUPPORTIVE				RESPONSE		Special Applications and Cautions
	Apathetic	Sophos.	Opposing	Credent	Critical	Sophos.	Opposing	Credent	Critical	Credent	Critical	
32. Graphics Visual (as opposed to verbal) presentation of ideas	x	x	110	87		110	x	87	17 114	x	x	Use: to get attention; to show relations in condensed form; to dramatize; to clarify abstract concepts Avoid: sloppy or amateurish or ill-conceived visuals; avoid overcomplexity with relatively unsophisticated
33. Inevitable consequences The only possible outcome						x	64:3.2	63:4.2		x		Use: to point to logical outcomes, either adverse or beneficial Avoid: the "prophet of doom" or Pollyanna tone
34. Placing disagreement in broader context Moving specific opposition into larger universe of agreement			31:1.2 ‑77:1.2				70:2.3 79:2	63:3		x		Use: especially with opposing role to induce wider understanding and possible agreement Avoid: choosing an unacceptable "broader context": avoid beclouding or de-emphasizing the original more narrow disagreement
35. Provocative questions Interrogations to make readers think				x	41:1.3‑5	x		x	42:3 (1-5)	x		Use: to get attention; to focus on specific issues; to invite receiver participation Avoid: raising questions unrelated or trivial questions (which lead the receiver away from your main ideas); avoid questions inviting antagonism
36. Receiver participation Active or passive involvement of readers	x	x		x	41	x	57:2.4	53:2.2	114	61:4 89:2,3	17 23:3.2 45:1.4	Use: to get attention; to make reader feel he is a partner in the communication act; to create reader empathy Avoid: trivial or irrelevant in order to keep reader focus on your main ideas

239

Fig. 10.3 (continued)

DEVICE AND DEFINITION	INITIAL					SUPPORTIVE				RESPONSE		Special Applications and Cautions
	Apathetic	Sophos.	Opposing	Credent	Critical	Sophos.	Opposing	Credent	Critical	Credent	Critical	
37. Reluctance to act — Expressed displeasure to do the disagreeable			64:1.2				64:4.1	63:4.1				Use: especially applicable to opposing role to express sincere hesitance to do something harmful to the receiver — Avoid: insincerity and maudlin approach; appearing not to mean business if the receiver does not perform as he ought
38. Request: alternative — Offering an option			73:3			x	x			13:1.3 61:3 70:3,4	17 24:3	Use: when receiver may not be able to respond exactly as desired — Avoid: making the alternative the *emphatic* response
39. Request: direct — Involuntary and "dictated"				x				x		30:2-4 61:4 79:4	16:2 29:5 45:1.4	Use: when specific performance under given time, place, and circumstance is required and commensurate authority obtains to get it — Avoid: appearing dictatorial and coercive in communicating request
40. Request: implicit — "Unstated" desired action										77 89:2,3	31:2; 5.2 32:2.2	Use: when receivers are capable and willing to interpret as desired; when other devices carry the unstated request — Avoid: assuming too much capability or willingness to "get the message"
41. Request: open — Voluntary and "flexible"				x	41	x						Use: when specific performance is optional; when persuasion rather than authority is required — Avoid: mere descriptive devices (use appropriate persuasive techniques to insure desired action)

Fig. 10.3 (continued)

DEVICE AND DEFINITION	INITIAL					SUPPORTIVE			RESPONSE		Special Applications and Cautions
	Apathetic	Sophos.	Opposing	Credent	Critical	Sophos. Opposing	Credent	Critical	Credent	Critical	
42. Respected sources/ people Reference to authoritative origins	x	23:1.1 24:1.1	x	x	113:1	31:3-5	60:2.2 109:4 / 52:1.4 63:1.4 93:3.3	112:2.3; 4.1	x	x	Use: to authenticate and make ideas credible; for critical receivers, permits their checking your primary data or your interpretations Avoid: "name dropping" or condescension (which creates immediate antagonism or apathy)
43. Satire A caricature or lampooning		4		4		x	4				Use: to humorously take-off on some idea, person, or organization (permits your communicating the ridiculous without risk of undue antagonism) Avoid: sarcasm or poor taste which creates hostility
44. Saving face Giving the receiver a constructive way out			58:1 62:1			x	58:3.1				Use: to avoid ego assault of receiver when he is likely wrong Avoid: insincerity; letting him off the hook when he is in fact wrong
45. Shocking The startling; the macabre	61:1.1			89:1.4			x		x		Use: to get attention and dramatize ideas Avoid: overdoing or theatrics
46. Snob appeal Catering to in-group values or norms		x		x	45: (head-ing)	36:2.2	52:2.1 95: (11.3)	51:1.2			Use: with sophisticated or knowledgeable receivers or specific cultural groups holding common beliefs Avoid: condescension or overdoing
47. Support documents Supplementary communications (giving detail to primary written communications)		x		x	112:1	x	67:3.1 / 37:3.1 38:1.2 50:3.1	6:3.2 17	x	x	Use: especially for credent and critical roles; for credent groups to give face validity; for critical groups to give genuine validity Avoid: saturating the reader with unnecessary detail and documents

241

Special Note on Devices

In learning to recognize and use the devices, read through the list, noting definitions, special applications and cautions, and, if you wish further clarification, checking each against the specimen references indicated. Use the table as a reference. Do not try to memorize items all at once. As you work through the applications in Figures 10.6 through 10.15 and subsequent exercises in this chapter, you will become more and more familiar with each device and its proper uses.

Basic Design Sequences

Let us now see how the patterns (initial, supportive, and response) fit into two basic design sequences. The first design sequence is a *response* outcome; the second is a *supportive* outcome sequence.

The *response* outcome pattern follows this design sequence:

$$
\text{Give information} \rightarrow \text{Get} \nearrow \begin{array}{c} \text{conviction} \\ \text{(or)} \\ \text{reinforcement} \end{array} \searrow \atop \nearrow \text{Get right response.}
$$

As you can see, this sequence parallels the initial-supportive-response pattern discussed in the previous section. Giving information (the first step) can be for any one of the five initial receiver roles. However, information must be presented differently with certain roles. For apathetic, sophisticated, and credent roles, you should *dramatize information*; with opposing receivers, you should *make information acceptable*; with critical receivers, you should *validate information*.

In the supportive dimension (the second step) of the response outcome (the third step) design, the apathetic role no longer exists (since you have gained reader attention). Therefore, you deal with one of the four remaining, sophisticated, opposing, credent, or critical. The second design step is either *conviction* or *reinforcement*. *Conviction* is needed for the sophisticated, opposing, or critical roles (because you must instill belief). Conviction is obtained nonrationally with sophisticated or opposing receivers, but rational means must be used with the critical role. *Reinforcement* is called for with the credent role (because you must strengthen belief nonrationally).

To *get right response* (the last design step), you are concerned with only a *credent* or *critical* role (because you can get a desired response only when one of these exists). With credent receivers, the right response is to *get intended belief* or *performance* through *nonrational* means. With critical receivers, the right response is to *get intended belief or performance* through *rational* means.

The *supportive* outcome pattern follows this design sequence:

$$\text{Give information} \rightarrow \text{Get right response} \rightarrow \text{Get} \quad \begin{array}{l} \nearrow \text{ reinforcement} \\ \quad (\text{or}) \\ \searrow \text{ conviction} \end{array}$$

You will note that as in the first pattern, the supportive sequence starts with information and pursues the same modes in handling the five receiver roles. However, the second design phase is to *get* the *right response*, that is, to get intended belief (not performance) from either a credent (nonrational) or critical (rational) receiver. The last step is to get reinforcement or conviction, which parallels the supportive dimension. However, there is a basic difference in handling the supportive phase in this sequence, because only credent or critical receivers are involved. This follows because you are carrying over these two roles from the second step—get right response.

Specific Purposes Related to Basic Designs

How do you know whether to use the supportive or response outcome? We go right back to the basic PRIDE dimensions discussed in Chapters 7 through 9—specific purposes and receiver roles. In other words, our communication strategies and tactics all stem from what we want to do (purpose) and with whom we are trying to communicate (receiver). Only then can we make the proper decision concerning how we are to go about our task (make right impact) and how our ideas must be organized to achieve this impact (use proper design). In order to help you make proper design selection in relation to specific purposes and receivers, Figure 10.4 summarizes the nine specific purposes and receiver roles discussed in Chapters 7 through 9 in relation to appropriate design sequences for each. You can use this figure as a ready reference to determine whether your communication strategies and tactics are on target.

Applying Basic Design Sequences

In order to give you an easy to use, but comprehensive, guide in applying basic design sequences, we present a graphic summary (Figure 10.5) of how to use both the response and supportive outcomes. Once you have determined the proper design sequence (in light of your purpose and receiver) you can then readily follow each step for achieving the outcome intended.

SPECIFIC PURPOSE	DESIGN SEQUENCE
Acknowledgment/Acceptance (Unfavorable/Favorable)	(Supportive Outcome) Give Information
	↓
Goodwill (Favorable)	Get Right Response
	↓
Status Communications (Unfavorable/Favorable)	Get Reinforcement/Conviction

Offering (Unfavorable/Favorable)	(Response Outcome)
Solicitation (Unfavorable/Favorable)	Give Information
	↓
Complaint/Adjustment (Unfavorable)	Get Conviction/Reinforcement
	↓
Rejection/Reprimand (Unfavorable)	Get Right Response
Policy Communications (Unfavorable/Favorable)	
Procedural Communications (Unfavorable/Favorable)	

Fig. 10.4 / Specific purpose related to design sequence.

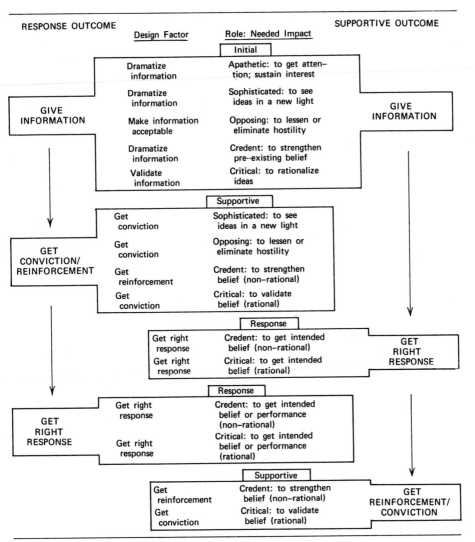

Fig. 10.5 / Applying basic design sequences.

Application of Principles to Ten Specimens

In order for you to get better "know-how" in using the principles discussed in this chapter, we present detailed analyses of ten representative specimens. Use these guides in interpreting analyses.

First, we identify what seems to be the writer's purpose and general receiver role addressed. Second, we identify the specific receiver roles and the probable conditions giving rise to them. Third, we specify the needed impacts and appropriate design factor sequence to control the specific receiver roles identified. Finally, we identify the devices actually used in the document (together with paragraph and sentence references). This is followed by an evaluation of the communication strategy and tactics using the foregoing criteria and findings, as well as principles of persuasiveness (Chapter 17).

If you carefully and thoughtfully study each specimen analysis, you will be able to rapidly and accurately size up the right and wrong uses of the principles discussed.

SPECIMEN NUMBER: 3

PURPOSE: Acknowledgment—unfavorable

Specific Receiver Role Pattern	Conditions	Needed Impacts	Design Factor Sequence	Reference Numbers and Devices Used
Initial: opposing	Possible dissatisfaction	To lessen or eliminate hostility	make information acceptable	1.1—Expression: appreciation 1.2—Candor: admission of wrongdoing
Response: opposing → credent	Potential constructive outcome	To get intended belief	get right response	2.1,2—Acting: on another's behalf
Supportive: credent	Potential constructive outcome	To strengthen belief	get reinforcement	3—Expression: appreciation

EVALUATION

Strategy and Tactics: Because receiver roles are controlled through effective use of devices, and following appropriate design sequence, this document accomplishes its purpose very well.

Persuasiveness: Generally, quite effective; the message is concise, to the point, and positive in tone.

Fig. 10.6 / Applications—Specimen 3.

247

SPECIMEN NUMBER: 10

PURPOSE: Acknowledgment—favorable

Specific Receiver Role Pattern	Conditions	Needed Impacts	Design Factor Sequence	Reference Numbers and Devices Used
Initial: credent	Recognition of needs: commendation	To strengthen pre-existing belief	dramatize information	1—Expression: thanks Detail: descriptive
Response: credent	Recognition of needs: commendation	To get intended belief	get right response	Implicit response growing out of paragraph 1
Supportive: credent	Recognition of needs: commendation	To (further) strengthen belief	get reinforcement	2,3—Advantages: organizational and social 4—Expression: thanks (*pro forma*)

EVALUATION

Strategy and Tactics: The initial paragraph gives a personal touch by thanking the receiver and noting specific time and place. His reaction is therefore likely favorable (belief), producing the right receiver response (implicit).

Paragraphs 2 and 3 are intended to further strengthen the favorable viewpoint toward the organization. However, the triteness of expressing the organizational and social goals creates probable incredibility. Thus the document, though beginning auspiciously, fails in the end.

Persuasiveness: Paragraphing—Paragraphs 2 and 3 could have been combined into one and better developed through use of selected descriptive and evaluative detail (e.g., What specific contributions were made to the success of the convention?). Tone—The third paragraph rings of patent insincerity ("motherhood, home, and country" platitudes) producing a very negative reader reaction from any perceptive reader. The *pro forma* ending, "Again, thank you so very much" is both trite and unnecessary.

Fig. 10.7 / Applications—Specimen 10.

SPECIMEN NUMBER: 20

PURPOSE: Offering—unfavorable

Specific Receiver Role Pattern	Conditions	Needed Impacts	Design Factor Sequence	Reference Numbers and Devices Used
Initial: apathetic	Receiver saturation	To get attention and sustain interest	dramatize information	None: no explicit attempt to get attention and sustain interest
Supportive: sophisticated	"So what's new"	To see in a new light	get conviction	1.1,1—Details: descriptive; 1.3,4; 2—Details: evaluative; 4.1—Support documents; 4.2—Expression: thanks (pro forma)
Response: credent	Organization objectives: applicant will be an asset to company	To get intended performance	get right response	3—Request: open

EVALUATION

Strategy and Tactics: No attempt is made to handle initial receiver apathy. Personnel directors or other employers get many, many application letters (receiver saturation). Therefore, conscious, well-executed devices must overcome an obvious indifference to this type of communication. Unless this is done, it is doubtful that the reader will go beyond the first or second sentence, resulting in communication failure.

Actually, the writer starts with the supportive segment. In most instances of this type (routine letters of application) the supportive role is sophistication. The devices used, details: descriptive and evaluative (1 and 2), really say nothing to make the sophisticated receiver see the writer in any "new light." Indeed, the commonplace statements probably induce immediate apathy. Note also that paragraph 4 is additionally supportive. This is really material that should be with the foregoing supportive ideas (the final paragraph is too late to sell yourself).

This is an open response (note that the writer even says "salary is open"). Furthermore, while he does suggest a personal interview, he almost guarantees that there will be none by prefacing the request with "if you believe my services can be effectively employed by your organization. . . ." Since he has given nothing to warrant such belief by the reader, he builds in failure.

Persuasiveness: Tone—The greatest weakness of the document is its negative tone. Red flags (1.4); the writer tells the reader that his firm needs help in the management of human resources. Whether true is beside the point. This immediately generates negative reaction. He compounds the felony in paragraph 2, in effect telling the reader that because of his educational background he has a *right* to a job. Writer-centeredness: The red flags above are writer-centered. Indeed, the entire letter is writer-centered. There is really nothing emphasizing the reader and organization needs or wants. In other words, the document fails as persuasive communication. If an interview is granted, it will be in spite of, not because of this letter.

Fig. 10.8 / Applications—Specimen 20.

249

SPECIMEN NUMBER: 36

PURPOSE: Offering—unfavorable

Specific Receiver Role Pattern	Conditions	Needed Impacts	Design Factor Sequence	Reference Numbers and Devices Used
Initial: apathetic	Receiver saturation	To get attention and sustain interest	dramatize information	1—Figurative language (a quote and a metaphor)
Supportive: sophisticated	"So what's new"	To see in a new light	get conviction	2.1, 2—Figurative language 2.2—Snob appeal 2.3—As you know 3—Details: evaluative: supporting document 3.2; 4—Advantages: personal
Response: credent	Personal benefits	To get intended performance	get right response	5—Request: open

EVALUATION

Strategy and Tactics: Essentially, this is a superior offering to an initially unfavorable (apathetic) receiver. Apathy is overcome through dramatic appeal. The supportive element (sophisticated receiver) is controlled effectively through the devices used. Personal benefits are communicated clearly, without crassness or overdoing. The open request in the last paragraph flows naturally, but directly, from the foregoing.

Persuasiveness: Even though obviously a mass distribution form letter, it is a highly persuasive document. Paragraphing, format, message clarity, and tone are well done. And note the reader-centeredness (as opposed to the writer-centeredness of Specimen 23) of the entire letter.

Fig. 10.9 / Applications—Specimen 36.

SPECIMEN NUMBER: 49

PURPOSE: Solicitation—unfavorable

Specific Receiver Role Pattern	Conditions	Needed Impacts	Design Factor Sequence	Reference Numbers and Devices Used
Initial: opposing	Resistance to giving resources: time	To lessen or eliminate hostility	make information acceptable	1.1—Respected sources 1.1,2—Heart interest
Supportive: sophisticated	"So what's new" Communication between specialists	To see information in a new light	get conviction	2 (1-3)—Details: inside
Response: critical	Professional or specialists communications; Consideration of vital issues	To get intended performance (through rational means)	get right response	3—Request: open (inviting the doctor's participation and support)

EVALUATION

Strategy and Tactics: This is a highly effective handling of a difficult role pattern (opposing-sophisticated-critical). The opposing role is overcome quickly by reference to a reputable organization (American Cancer Society) and communicating the assistance and help available to the reader-physician. Sophistication is overcome by pointing out the new and professionally helpful qualifications of the volunteers. Criticality is controlled by open candor: statement of issue, purpose of the project, procedures and methods to be followed, and an open invitation for reader participation.

Persuasiveness: Documents to meet this role pattern must be "soft-sell" at the outset and validate descriptively at the end. The format of this document meets these two criteria. Moreover, the entire communication is reader-centered, leaving the choice of whether to use the service with the physician (a must with this type of intraprofessional solicitation).

Fig. 10.10/Applications—Specimen 49.

251

SPECIMEN NUMBER: 58

PURPOSE: Adjustment

Specific Receiver Role Pattern	Conditions	Needed Impacts	Design Factor Sequence	Reference Numbers and Devices Used
Initial: opposing	Actual ego assault; legal demand	To lessen or eliminate hostility	make information acceptable	1—Saving face
Supportive: credent	Recognition need	To strengthen belief (nonrational)	get reinforcement	3.1—Saving face, 4—Expression: thanks (*pro forma*)
Response: credent	Personal benefits	To get intended performance	get right response	2—Request: direct, 3.1—Request: open, 3.2—Advantages: personal

EVALUATION

Strategy and Tactics: A common receiver sequence (opposing-credent-credent) for a letter of collection, this communication fails in achieving its purpose. Why? First, in handling the opposition, the writer's intent was no doubt worthy, that is, to try to save the reader's ego (saving face). The attempt probably boomeranged because of the way the idea was expressed (which is analyzed under persuasion). Supportive ideas are included in paragraph 3. The writer starts with another face-saving device but then shifts to an open request by offering the reader an option other than payment of the account. A *pro forma* expression of thanks concludes the letter—another supportive attempt. The only allusion to the primary purpose of the document (to get payment of the overdue account) is the one short sentence in paragraph 2. While stated clearly, its design sequence is improper (and emphasizes the reprimand more than anything else).

Persuasiveness: Let's look at two glaring deficiencies: emphasis and tone. While normally considered under paragraphing, let us view it here in relation to the letter's basic purpose. The communication begins by moving directly to a reminder of the reader's failure to pay the account (paragraphs 1 and 2). It then shifts to letting the reader "off the hook" by offering an option (which he can easily seize upon), which does not accomplish the primary mission. Additionally, the option is placed last (a more emphatic position in the document). The ending, *pro forma* "thank you for your cooperation," reinforces the option to avoid payment. Moreover, it is a platitude that detracts from, rather than adds to, persuasion. The primary red flag is the introductory statement that borders on sarcasm. This is likely to increase antagonism rather than overcome the reader's initial opposition. For this reason, the document probably will fail at this point alone.

The glaring deficiency in tone is the letter's communication of insincerity. While no doubt intended to be reader-centered, the sarcasm and emphasis on wrong purpose create a question concerning the seriousness (genuine sincerity) of the sender.

Fig. 10.11 / Applications—Specimen 58.

SPECIMEN NUMBER: 69

PURPOSE: Rejection

Specific Receiver Role Pattern	Conditions	Needed Impacts	Design Factor Sequence	Reference Numbers and Devices Used
Initial: opposing	Ego assault; Possible dissatisfaction: inequities	To lessen or eliminate hostility	make information acceptable	1—Expression: thanks (*pro forma*)
Supportive: opposing	Ego assault; Possible dissatisfaction: inequities	To lessen or eliminate hostility	get conviction	2.1—Candor: statement of issue 2.2—Inevitable consequences
Response: credent	Assurance needs	To get intended belief	get right response	3.1—Expression: thanks (*pro forma*) 3.2—Expression: concern (*pro forma*)

EVALUATION

Strategy and Tactics: Rejections automatically build in hostility. No one wants to be turned down, especially for an important situation such as this one. Unfortunately, however, turndowns must be made in certain cases. Let us look at the letter in this light. The initial opposition is handled by a *pro forma* "thank you for your recent inquiry . . ." This is not overcoming any opposition, but merely acknowledging the receipt of the reader's letter. In all probability, this unnecessary statement increases rather than decreases hostility. Since opposition prevails, the next device, candor: statement of issue, is a possible proper device. However, the initial qualifying word, "normally," is an admission that exceptions can be made. And, followed as it is with the terse inevitable consequences, " . . . we cannot admit you . . ." certainly does not overcome hostility. It cannot other than inflame the applicant all the more. The concluding *pro forma* expressions of thanks and concern are only more fuel on the fire. Since the student is still hostile, his hostility is only heightened. The intended right response is to get sufficient belief on the part of the applicant so that he will not pursue the matter further. However, the last "if we can be of further service, please let us know" leaves the door open for further communications from him.

Persuasiveness: The document unfortunately is a classic example of many university letters to applicants. Like most, it is poor. Particularly deficient is tone: specifically, red flags, insincerity, and writer-centeredness. Red flags are the *pro forma* introduction and conclusion, the "normally" that tells the applicant that he is possibly being given inequitable treatment, and the abrupt (almost haughty) inevitable consequences of his not measuring up to the policy, resulting in his being turned down. Insincerity is communicated from the foregoing plus the patent form letter that a student receives. Clearly, this letter is used for all turndowns and gives the message that the receiver is being treated as just another number rather than as a unique individual. The whole document is university not applicant centered. The *pro forma* expression of concern really emphasizes this deficiency all the more.

Fig. 10.12 / Applications—Specimen 69.

253

SPECIMEN NUMBER: 98

PURPOSE: Policy—favorable

Specific Receiver Role Pattern	Conditions	Needed Impacts	Design Factor Sequence	Reference Numbers and Devices Used
Initial: credent	Potential personal benefits	To strengthen pre-existing belief	Dramatize information	1.1—"As you know"
Supportive: critical	Consideration of vital issues	To validate belief (rational)	Get conviction	1.2—Advantages: organizational 2—Expression: appreciation advantages: personal (*pro forma*)
Response: critical	Consideration of vital issues	To get intended performance	Get right response	1.2 (last part)—Request: direct

EVALUATION

Strategy and Tactics: The initial credent role calls for strengthening receiver belief. This is done with the "as you know" device concerning the policy prohibiting supplier gifts to employees. The supportive dimension involves a critical receiver role. Here the letter uses advantages: organizational, expression: appreciation, and advantages: personal. These are not generally appropriate to control a critical viewpoint (they are more useful in non-critical situations). Since paragraph 2 is directed to credent receivers (not critical), it (or pertinent elements of it) should be included in handling the initial credent role. A clear, candid statement of the issue together with pertinent supporting descriptive detail would be a better device to control the supportive role—critical. The direct request is broken up in that the reader must relate the policy (1.1) to the direct request in the latter part of 1.2. More important, the request is improperly placed in terms of proper design. It should be the concluding element, perhaps accompanied by pertinent descriptive reasons.

Persuasiveness: Actually the tone of the document rings of sincerity and reader-centeredness. Emphasis is a glaring deficiency. The letter deals too much with good wishes for the holiday season rather than focusing on getting conformance to the company policy. Message clarity is adversely affected because of the undue emphasis plus the fact that ideas do not follow one another properly. The lack of clear explication of the direct request—namely, that suppliers are not to make gifts to employees—can result in lack of desired reader performance, whether deliberate or not.

Fig. 10.13 / Applications—Specimen 98.

SPECIMEN NUMBER: 103

PURPOSE: Procedure—favorable

Specific Receiver Role Pattern	Conditions	Needed Impacts	Design Factor Sequence	Reference Numbers and Devices Used
Initial: credent	Organizational objectives	To strengthen pre-existing belief	dramatize information	1.1—"As you know"; expression: concern
Supportive: credent	Organizational objectives	To strengthen belief (nonrational)	get reinforcement	1.2—Acting: on another's behalf
Response: critical	Consideration of vital issues	To get intended performance	get right response	1.2 (last part)—Request: open Items (1-4)—Candor: statement of procedures

EVALUATION

Strategy and Tactics: The receiver role pattern and the design sequence (dramatize information-get reinforcement-get right response) are both followed, using minimum wording. The credent roles are effectively handled by "as you know" and expression: concern (initial) and acting: on another's behalf (supportive). The critical role, however, is not adequately controlled. Why? Because items 1 through 4, the "procedures," are not spelled out sufficiently. Much more descriptive detail would be expected by critical receivers. The items are so ambiguous as to be worthless in the eyes of supervisors and department heads with critical outlooks. The document therefore fails at this crucial point. Furthermore, the response request ". . . which you may wish to post" leaves the door open for non-performance, certainly something that the writer does not want. This, together with the ambiguity of the procedural elements, guarantees communication failure.

Persuasiveness: Two factors stand out as deficiencies: the subject "Safety" is anathema in most organizations. It is therefore a red flag, and it could induce initial apathy, defeating communication effectiveness at the outset. The other weakness is the indifferent attitude conveyed in the document's wording and presentation. It almost expresses a "going through the motions" without any serious intent. In this respect, the memorandum rings of insincerity.

Fig. 10.14/Applications—Specimen 103.

SPECIMEN NUMBER: 111

PURPOSE: Status Communication—unfavorable

Specific Receiver Role Pattern	Conditions	Needed Impacts	Design Factor Sequence	Reference Numbers and Devices Used
Initial: opposing	Resistance to change	To lessen or eliminate hostility	make information acceptable	1—Candor: basic assumptions/premises
Response: critical	Consideration of vital issues: organizational problems	To get intended belief (rational)	get right response	2—Candor: statement of issue (in terms of reasons for job failure)
Supportive: critical	Consideration of vital issues: organizational problems	To validate belief (rational)	get conviction	3—Request: open (using advantages: organizational)

EVALUATION

Strategy and Tactics: Basic assumptions/premises are generally not appropriate for an opposing role: too clear explication of starting points invites rather than overcomes hostility. A better device would have been setting forth specific organizational advantages (e.g., criteria for successful operation). Furthermore, the "problem" referred to in 3.1 is not included, which will produce only greater antagonism from potentially critical receivers. Actually, the "problem" exists—whatever it is). Following the appropriate design, this paragraph should be last and attempt to convince the critical receiver by pointing out exactly how each of the four items, when corrected, would solve Star-X communications' "problems." Paragraph three should be the second paragraph. If the proper device had been used in the first paragraph, opposition would have been overcome and a critical role induced. Furthermore, more important descriptive details are needed to validate the ideas presented.

Persuasiveness: While introductory sentences are clear, the development of each paragraph is inadequate with respect to sufficiency of detail and unity. While the format does follow the traditional problem-analysis-solution sequence, it is not related to the initial (opposing) or desired response (critical) role, and thus is not adequate. The message would be clearer had captions and typographical cues been used. Positive rather than negative statements (red flags) in paragraph 2 would have made the tone more convincing.

Fig. 10.15 / Applications—Specimen 111.

256

PURPOSE and RECEIVER	IMPACT	DESIGN

ACKNOWLEDGMENT/
  ACCEPTANCE
—unfavorable/favorable—
  (personal: determined)
	Initial
	Apathetic: to get attention;
	  sustain interest
	Sophisticated: to see ideas in a
	  new light
	Opposing: to lessen or eliminate
	  hostility
		Give Information

GOODWILL
—favorable—
  (personal: predetermined)
	Credent: to strengthen pre-
	  existing belief
	Critical: to rationalize ideas	

STATUS
  COMMUNICATIONS
—unfavorable/favorable—
  (task: determined)
	Response
	Credent: to get intended belief
	  (nonrational)
	Critical: to get intended belief
	  (rational)
		Get Right Response

	Supportive
	Credent: to strengthen belief
	  (nonrational)
	Critical: to validate belief
	  (rational)
		Get Reinforcement/
		  Conviction

OFFERING
—unfavorable/favorable—
  (personal: determined)
	Initial
	Apathetic: to get attention;
	  sustain interest
	Sophisticated: to see ideas in a
	  new light	

SOLICITATION
—unfavorable/favorable—
  (personal: determined)
	Opposing: to lessen or eliminate
	  hostility
	Credent: to strengthen pre-
	  existing belief
	Critical: to rationalize ideas
		Give Information

COMPLAINT/
  ADJUSTMENT
—unfavorable—
  (personal: predetermined)
	Supportive
	Sophisticated: to see ideas in
	  a new light	

REJECTION/REPRIMAND
—unfavorable—
  (personal: predetermined)
	Opposing: to lessen or
	  eliminate hostility
	Credent: to strengthen belief
	  (nonrational)
		Get Conviction/
		  Reinforcement

POLICY
  COMMUNICATIONS
—unfavorable/favorable—
  (task: determined)
	Critical: to validate belief
	  (rational)	

PROCEDURAL
  COMMUNICATIONS
—unfavorable/favorable—
  (task: determined)
	Response
	Credent: to get intended belief
	  or performance (non-
	  rational)
	Critical: to get intended belief
	  or performance (rational)
		Get Right Response

Fig. 10.16 / Summary—How to use purpose and receiver related to impact and design principles.

Summary: How to Use Purpose, Receiver, Impact, and Design Principles

Let us now turn to a way by which you can put into action the first four PRIDE elements. First, in order to pull together essentials of what we have discussed, we present a tabular summary of purpose and receiver related to impact and design concepts and principles (Figure 10.16). With this figure as background, you will then be ready to understand and use the checklist in Figure 10.17 for effective application of the first four steps of the PRIDE sequence.

CHECKLIST USING PURPOSE, RECEIVER, IMPACT, AND DESIGN PRINCIPLES

	Reference
1. Know specific communication purpose and general receiver role.	Fig. 9.49
2. Identify the exact receiver role.	Fig. 10.1
3. Determine subsequent receiver roles and related impacts.	Fig. 10.2
4. Select proper devices to achieve needed impacts.	Fig. 10.3
5. Relate specific purpose to appropriate design sequence.	Fig. 10.4
6. Apply basic design sequence.	Fig. 10.5

Fig. 10.17/ Checklist: using purpose, receiver, and design principles.

If you properly apply the six yardsticks in Figure 10.17, you will have completed the essential planning of your communication, which gives you a sound basis for execution, the final step in the PRIDE sequence (Chapter 11).

EXERCISES

exercise 1   List and define each of the five specific receiver roles.

exercise 2   (a) List initial receiver roles and related needed impacts;
(b) List supportive receiver roles and related needed impacts;
(c) List response receiver roles and related needed impacts.

exercise 3   In schematic form present (a) the response outcome design sequence; likewise, (b) set forth the supportive outcome design sequence.

exercise 4 (a) List the three purposes applicable to the supportive outcome design sequence;
  (b) List the six purposes applicable to the response outcome design sequence.

exercise 5 Review Figures 10.8 and 10.11. Then rewrite Specimens 20 and 58, using the proper specific receiver role pattern, conditions, needed impacts, and design factor sequences. You may also wish to consider suggestions under "Evaluation." In your rewrites, deliberately use different devices from those used by the writer. Attach a separate sheet to each letter, specifying all devices you use. Give specific references for each device, following the pattern under "Reference Numbers and Devices Used."

exercise 6 Using the same dimensions given for "Application of Principles" (Figures 10.6–10.15), analyze and rewrite either Specimen 79 or 99. Attach a separate analytical sheet in which all items (except "Evaluation") are completed.

CASE PROBLEMS

1. Re: Specimen 36. You are Mr. Jones and you are quite impressed with the letter sent to you by Mr. Miller, Director of the Literary Society. You want to commend him for his excellent communication in the document.

Your Mission: Write a letter to Mr. Miller complimenting him on three outstanding communication qualities and why each is outstanding. (Review the analysis of the specimen, Figure 10.9, as well as all principles presented in this chapter.) As in Exercise 6, attach a separate analytical sheet in which all items (except "Evaluation") are treated.

2. Re: Specimen 41. You are a member of the Community Action Club and have read the questionnaire letter sent by Jones. You consider it inappropriate to question members in this manner; you also consider the document as very poor communication. You want Jones to know your feelings.

Your Mission: Write a memorandum expressing your feelings to Jones. As above, attach a separate analytical sheet in which all items (except "Evaluation") are completed.

Chapter 11

COMMUNICATION EXECUTION

Your Learning Objectives:

1. To know the nature and importance of communication execution.
2. To know essentials of letter execution.
3. To know essentials of memorandum execution.
4. To know essentials of report execution.
5. To know basic media missions.
6. To know basic media formats.
7. To know media mission—media format relationships.
8. To know essentials of execution to achieve specific purposes.
9. To be able to execute communications to achieve specific purposes.
10. To get an integrated view of the total PRIDE sequence for effective communication.

We come now to the final PRIDE element: execution, the "payoff" step in communication. All the preceding PRIDE components go into the *planning* of documents, but execution is the carrying out of all that goes into the planning, the culmination of your communication decision making. It is clear that even the best planning can be for naught if equally competent communications execution is not accomplished. Therefore, this topic is a most important one.

Specifically, execution refers to the right selection and handling of the medium (or media) to be used in achieving your desired communication result. By media we mean, of course, the nine types of documents discussed in Chapters 2 through 6: letters, memoranda, reports, proposals, agreements, directives, manuals, forms, and brochures. In discussing each medium we did touch generally on execution. However, since you have studied the purpose, receiver, impact and design facets, you can now see that there is more to the subject of execution than has been said before. Let us, therefore, view communication execution in a different, and even more valuable, perspective.

This discussion will be presented in three parts: (1) execution: letters, memoranda, and reports; (2) execution: media missions related to media formats; and (3) execution: purposes related to media.

Execution: Letters, Memoranda, and Reports

Because they are the most commonly used media, we shall deal with these three in depth. Furthermore, all are individually oriented—that is, addressed to specific persons or positions inside or outside the organization. Therefore, it is important that you know the proper means of executing each.

Using specimens, our discussion will focus on (1) right and wrong execution and (2) handling of messages. In analyzing media use, we shall note whether proper or improper and why. In analyzing message handling, we shall draw on all previous PRIDE principles. From this presentation you will gain even deeper insights and greater skills in analysis and presentation of letters, memoranda, and reports.

Letters

Remember that a letter is a written medium that (1) is personally addressed, (2) can meet a broad spectrum of purposes, and (3) can be used both within and outside the organization. Stated another way, a letter has personalism, potential to attain a variety of objectives, and possibilities for internal and external communication.

Chapter 2 presented four types of letters: nonroutine; routine—prepared parts; routine—complete; and mass distribution. Nonroutine letters are individually written to meet unique, special, or important situations. Routine—prepared parts letters are individually written but are those composed of "canned" paragraphs or sections put together to handle frequent anticipated situations. Routine—complete letters are prepared as units to handle common important anticipated situations. They may be already produced and ready for filling in names, dates, and the like; or they may be composed, kept in a manual or file, then typed or reproduced as the anticipated situation arises. Mass distribution letters are prepared for dissemination to broad segments or groups (rather than to individuals as such). Generally mass distribution letters meet a specific purpose at a given time (e.g., a year-end sale).

For ease of your understanding the proper selection and uses of letter media, as well as your gaining deeper understanding of the handling of messages, we shall present three tables (Figures 11.1, 11.2, and 11.3) analyzing the first three types: nonroutine, routine—prepared parts, and routine—complete. Only letters with an essential letter *media mission* will be analyzed in these figures. Media missions will be discussed in the next section.

	NONROUTINE LETTERS
	Evaluation
Specimen 5 Medium: Improper Handling: Improper	The basic question is whether the letter should be written at all. Why? While not explicit, the writer really wants a lower than 9% interest rate. The letter defeats this purpose in two ways: (1) it confirms *in writing* his agreement to the 9% rate; (2) the negative tone of the letter (a diatribe) may well cause the bank to turn down the loan altogether.
Specimen 7 Medium: Proper Handling: Proper	This letter has a positive, sincere ring. While not required, the letter creates goodwill for the writer and gives the reader a commendation for his handling of the writer's inquiry. The reader will probably remember this writer (applicant) in the event of a later job opening (either with his organization or some other).
Specimen 8 Medium: Proper Handling: Improper	While this *pro forma* thank you letter is executed using the proper medium, it may be better not sent because it communicates negatively. Why? Close reading shows this not to be a commendation or sincere appreciation to the reader but an implicit commendation of the writer himself. Note especially the writer-centered last sentence.
Specimen 13 Medium: Proper Handling: Fair	The international cablegram communicates what is needed in this case: a sense of importance, a sense of urgency, and a clear request for postponing an answer. While a trans-Atlantic telephone call could have been made, it would have been far more costly and probably no more effective.
Specimen 18 Medium: Proper Handling: Improper	The medium is proper because it is confirming a prior oral commitment. But the letter's poor organization and lack of proper emphasis reflect adversely on the writer. Specifically, the P.S. could have been included in the first paragraph (following sentence 2). The *pro forma* expression of concern rings of insincerity and should be omitted.
Specimen 47 Medium: Proper Handling: Improper	Three wrongs stand out: (1) an initial opposing receiver role (resistance to extra effort) is neither recognized nor overcome; (2) the design of the entire document is not appropriate—it should focus on a response (not a supportive) outcome; (3) insincerity is accentuated by the last paragraph, which is an attempt at commendation, but which will no doubt be interpreted as an afterthought "buttering up" of the reader.

Fig. 11.1 / Execution—nonroutine letters.

Fig. 11.1 (continued)

NONROUTINE LETTERS	
	Evaluation
Specimen 54 Medium: Proper Handling: Fair	The letter is well done in that the writer recognizes and attempts to overcome initial receiver opposition through commendation. However, the letter is addressed impersonally. Would not it be more persuasive if the Zone Manager were addressed by name? The basic design (give information—get conviction—get right response) is followed until paragraph 4. The "right response" is to get either a refund of money or another case of tuna, not just a reply from the Zone Manager. Paragraph 4 should be omitted. The credibility of the writer may be questioned from a seemingly trivial oversight. Note sentence 3.2 ("his" rather than "this"). The reader may well suspect that a person who is this careless in his writing may be equally careless in his statement of facts.
Specimen 56 Medium: Proper Handling: Proper	This is a clear, candid "laying it on the line" communication. In addition to using proper devices and design, the letter attempts to secure additional leverage for the right response by sending a copy of the letter to the reader's boss.
Specimen 71 Medium: Improper Handling: Improper	This document should never have been written. It is a personal vendetta that will only inflame the reader rather than produce any constructive outcome. Even more important, the writer represents his organization, and this document can only tarnish the organization's image. Remember also that the writer has now put *his feelings on paper*. If such feelings must be communicated, informal oral means (e.g., "off the record" conversation) should be used.
Specimen 81 Medium: Proper Handling: Proper	The medium and handling are very well done. The design to give information—get reinforcement (through expression of thanks and commendation) and get right response (implicit, keep up the good work), is concise but very persuasive. The tone of the whole message rings of reader-centeredness and writer sincerity.
Specimen 82 Medium: Proper Handling: Fair	The basic deficiency of this letter is that the devices of appreciation and commendation are "overdone" creating an impression of insincerity. The insincerity is further emphasized with the parting paragraph that is a *pro forma* ending.

	ROUTINE—PREPARED PARTS
	Evaluation
Specimen 2 Medium: Improper Handling: Improper	Rather than routine—prepared parts this should be a nonroutine letter that deals with the specific complaint of the reader (e.g., what expense, what repairs, what circumstances?). The letter as written is obviously intended to handle any complaint and a perceptive reader senses this immediately (creating antagonism). Sentence 1.1 emphasizes the company's mishandling in that it shows a month's delay in replying (to which it admits). This merely reinforces initial hostility. No reason is given for the delay, but an abrupt change of thought to expression of concern without any transition is presented. Following this, a further "delay" is the method for handling the complaint (which further reinforces hostility). The second paragraph is a *pro forma* expression of appreciation and restatement of promising to check into the complaint. The letter would be better without this paragraph, since it is completely company-centered and gives no additional important information. A very important "red flag" to the reader is the failure to include the District Manager's name and the lack of any evidence showing that the complaint letter was indeed forwarded to him (e.g., "cc:" notation). In sum, the letter creates more incredibility than credibility, therefore more hostility than belief.
Specimen 60 Medium: Improper Handling: Improper	This is a classic example of using inapplicable prepared parts. To illustrate, would not these paragraphs fit the following different situations: paragraph 1—overdrawn *checking* account; paragraph 2—opening a *new* savings account; paragraph 3—overdrawn *checking* account; paragraph 4—any letter (*pro forma*) ending. Moreover, note the amount overdrawn (47¢). How much does it cost to write and process a letter like this? Furthermore, what is the psychological cost in terms of receiver alienation? Would not a telephone call be better? And, assuming a significant amount overdrawn, would not a nonroutine letter directed to the specific situation be called for?

Fig. 11.2 / Execution—routine—prepared parts.

Fig. 11.2 (continued)

ROUTINE—PREPARED PARTS

	Evaluation
Specimen 67 Medium: Proper Handling: Improper	Routine—prepared parts is appropriate for frequent recurring situations such as a job turndown. However, the handling is deficient in at least two fundamental respects: (1) the letter's tone is insincere and, in paragraph 2, almost negative; (2) the writer's purpose is obviously to discourage further communication or contact on the part of the reader. But, paragraph 4 invites further activity. Note also the inconsistency of messages in paragraphs 4 and 5, an obvious use of inapplicable part (or parts).
Specimen 85 Medium: Proper Handling: Improper	A well-done routine—prepared parts letter is a useful way to convey congratulations or commendations to customers. The handling, however, is deficient in two respects. First, the greeting should have been addressed to both Mr. and Mrs. Miller. Second, paragraph 2 conveys a crassness (almost a "payoff") by offering the gift because Mr. Miller has done business with the writer's firm. This destroys the intended sincerity of the message, resulting in reader alienation rather than greater credence.
Specimen 86 Medium: Improper Handling: Improper	As used here, this medium does more harm than good. A "get-well" card would probably be much better. Why? Because a well done card will be reader-centered, which is in complete contrast to this letter. Note the writer's impersonality as reflected in paragraph 1 (e.g., he *admits* his secretary called). Paragraph 2 is even more offensive in that the writer emphasizes organization advantages to the exclusion of personal advantages for the reader's recovery. In sum, this is a "canned" writer-centered letter.

	ROUTINE—COMPLETE
Specimen 9 **Medium:** Improper **Handling:** Improper	The cost of acknowledging a $5.00 gift with a personally typed letter outweighs all benefits. A preprinted fill-in form (e.g., card of acknowledgment) would meet the purpose and save money. The entire letter is overdone ringing of insincerity (e.g., ". . . your generous donation of $5.00 . . .").
Specimen 10 **Medium:** Proper **Handling:** Improper	A routine—complete letter is proper for thanking several persons who contributed their services to a project such as this. However, the intended gratitude is overshadowed by two major factors: (1) the left column (listing of ten officers' names and addresses) bespeaks "advertising" of professionals; (2) although the letter states, "This is to sincerely thank you . . ." the entire document rings of insincerity. Only organizational advantages are emphasized, and even these are platitudes that only alienate a thoughtful reader.
Specimen 12 **Medium:** Improper **Handling:** Improper	A well-designed form would better handle a routine inquiry like this. In addition to eliminating a poor impression created by an obvious routine—complete (form) letter, costs would be less and processing more rapid and efficient. The real message is that other materials are being sent under separate cover; that the applicant should fill out the form as directed; and send the completed form and evaluation fee to the Office of Admissions and Records. All the rest of the letter is *pro forma* "garbage."
Specimen 58 **Medium:** Improper **Handling:** Improper	If an initial attempt to collect, a well-designed form (e.g., second or third notice) would serve much better to keep an appropriate official and impersonal tone. If after several collection attempts, then a personal nonroutine letter is essential to handle the uniqueness and seriousness of the situation. Remember, a preprinted, routine—complete letter broadcasts loudly that the firm has many delinquent accounts. (Handling: see Figure 10.23 for an in-depth analysis.)
Specimen 61 **Medium:** Improper **Handling:** Improper	The use of a routine—complete letter for purposes similar to this is all right. However, the patent attempt to create the impression of a handwritten letter (mass produced) is an affront. Therefore, the adverse appearance makes the medium improper. In terms of content and design, a close examination of the use of devices and design sequence shows this to be a basically effective letter. Deficiencies are that it is

Fig. 11.3 / Execution: routine—complete.

Fig. 11.3 (continued)

ROUTINE—COMPLETE

Specimen 61 (continued)	not individually addressed, typed, and signed, together with an authenticating title of the sender. This is a case where a well written and produced routine—complete letter could be very effective—if it *appears* to the receiver to be a *nonroutine* communication.
Specimen 62 **Medium:** Improper **Handling:** Improper	For reasons given in the analysis of Specimen 12, a form would be more appropriate. However, if it judged that a letter is to be used, then that letter should be *selling* the former member. This document is an admixture of insult, begging, and poor pointing out of possible personal and organizational benefits. As a document from a professional organization, it is an affront to the reader and will probably reinforce his decision not to rejoin the organization. Incidentally, look at the misspelling in 2.1, and the incoherent paragraphing in 3.
Specimen 68 **Medium:** Proper **Handling:** Improper	A routine—complete letter is appropriate for this type of recurring situation (job turndown). However, the handling needs improvement. The letter is addressed to a professional applicant, who expects professional level communication. This document is an obvious "get off my back" answer that will only incense a perceptive reader. Note the *pro forma* initial and ending paragraphs. Note also that in showing *pro forma* concern in paragraph 2 (in order to make the reader feel good while being "brushed off"), the writer in the last sentence leaves the door open for further inquiries (e.g., ". . . at present" may give false hope that some future opening is available).
Specimen 73 **Medium:** Proper **Handling:** Improper	On the surface, the design sequence is appropriate (the right response—"don't call us, we'll call you"—being implicit. However, a close examination shows the letter as full of unnecessary detail and creating an impression of evasion. Moreover, it is generally writer-centered and condescending.

Memoranda

Remember that memoranda are basically in-house letters. While a few may go outside the organization, they are exceptions. Therefore, memoranda have two of the same characteristics as letters: (1) personally oriented and (2) meet a variety of purposes.

In Chapter 3, memoranda were analyzed in two ways: (1) from whom sent and (2) to whom written. In order to simplify and make our analysis more effective, Figure 11.4 is presented from each receiver perspective (name, position, department, population designations) in relation to appropriate sender designations. Specimen examples are given for each receiver/sender relationship.

RECEIVER (to)	SENDER (from)	SPEC. REF.
Name(s)	Name(s)	11, 42, 52, 69, 74
Position(s)	Name(s)	97
	Position(s)	23, 33, 46, 57, 65, 66, 103
	Department(s)	1, 45, 101
Department(s)	Name(s)	
	Position(s)	80, 100
	Department(s)	30
Population	Name(s)	4, 41
	Position(s)	40, 79, 83, 88, 99, 102, 112
	Department(s)	35, 37
	Special groups	53

Fig. 11.4 / Receiver/sender relationships of specimen memoranda.

Figure 11.4 presents specimen references following the conventional memorandum format. We do this in order to emphasize good and poor execution of receiver/sender designations. As with letters, however, when we discuss media missions, you will see that many documents using a memorandum format actually perform other functions. This will be discussed in the next section.

Figure 11.5 presents executions of selected receiver/sender designations, together with analysis of subject statement in relation to message. (You may wish to review Chapter 2 or appropriate sections of memoranda principles.)

Reports

As you recall, reports communicate one, two, or all of (1) what has happened; (2) what is happening; and (3) what will or should happen. In other words, reports convey the state or condition of past, present, or future events, relations, objects, persons, or things.

SPEC. REF.	RECEIVER*	SENDER*	SUBJECT STATEMENT
	Name(s)	Name(s)	
11	Proper (informal note)	Proper (informal note)	Not precise: suggest change—Appreciation: Your Book "Effective . . . Ideas"
42	Improper (position needed)	Improper (position needed)	Not exact: suggest change—Staffing: Planning and Scheduling Position
	Position(s)	Name(s)	
97	Proper except "Administration" position should be designated (e.g., Director of Administration)	Proper (important position is implicit: hospital director)	Not complete: suggest change—New Policy: Questionable Drug Orders
	Position(s)	Position(s)	
23	Proper (adequately identified)	Proper (adequately identified)	Proper: adequately covers essential message
33	Improper (several vice presidents: needs specific position in formal memo)	Improper (only partial identification of department—Systems and Procedures)	Completely inadequate: suggest change—Recommendations: Integrating Company Computer Facilities and Relocating Accounting Responsibility
	Position	Department	
1	Proper (adequately identified)	Proper (adequately identified)	Proper: language intended not to further antagonize a hostile reader but at same time to cover the essential message
45	Proper (adequately identified)	Improper (needs identity of specific originating department)	None stated: suggest—Capability of GAO to Analyze Audit Defense Expenditures: GAO Philosophy and Objectives
	Department(s)	Position(s)	
80	Improper (needs specific name)	Improper (needs specific name)	Not adequate, precise, nor complete: suggest change—Procedure for Gathering Information from Dean of Students Offices
100	Proper (adequately identified)	Proper (adequately identified)	Mis-stated: suggest change—New Dangerous Weapon Policy and Procedures (Supplement to Directive No. 10) More a procedural statement than a policy; the policy is really related to the parenthetical directive

Fig. 11.5 / Execution—memoranda receiver/sender designations and subject statements.

Fig. 11.5 (continued)

SPEC. REF.	RECEIVER*	SENDER*	SUBJECT STATEMENT
	Department(s)	Department(s)	
30	Improper (should be to all department heads)	Improper (needs official name, e.g., Safety Department)	Not complete: suggest change —Attendance for Fire Safety Film Showings
	Population	Name(s)	
4	Proper (in-group)	Proper (in-group)	Omitted: informal and satirical; subject unnecessary
41	Proper (in-group)	Improper (needs position designation)	Not complete: suggest change —Improving Community Action Club Activities
	Population	Position(s)	
40	Proper (adequately identified)	Proper (adequately identified)	Omitted: suggest adding— Employee Benefits: Favored Tax Shelter Program Attention getting (personal benefits) as well as descriptive
79	Proper (adequately identified)	Proper (adequately identified)	Not complete: suggest change —Need for Proper Attire and Appearance Emphasizes the reasons for the directive calling for proper attire and appearance (organizational objectives) thereby making it more acceptable to employees
	Population	Department(s)	
35	Proper (adequately identified)	Proper (adequately identified)	Not exact: suggest change— Proper Examination Schedule: *Spring Booklet* Emphasizes the right response
37	Proper (adequately identified)	Proper (adequately identified)	Omitted: proper in this instance because it follows letter format
	Population	Special Groups	
53	Proper (implicit)	Proper (adequately identified)	Omitted: proper as document is a formal invitation

* Note: When either position or department is designated as receiver or sender and a name is included in specimen, the emphasis is on the position or department. In most cases, the name is secondary identification.

Furthermore, you remember that reports can also be classified from a thinking perspective, that is, whether descriptive, or evaluative, or both. You may wish to review Chapter 4 (or appropriate sections of it) to renew your understanding of report principles.

While reports can be viewed as either short, expository documents or as complex/technical communications, we shall focus on the first. Why? Because the more brief expository one is the more common document in modern organizations. Since the complex technical report is more applicable to specific disciplines or professional groups and cannot be treated apart from the discipline or speciality, we shall not concern ourselves with it beyond what was said in Chapter 4.

For convenience, we present report execution in four tables. Figures 11.6, 11.7, and 11.8 exemplify time perspectives and general types of reports. Figure

SPECIFIC TYPE	SPEC. REF.	
Background/Explanations	106	(Assumptions and Basic Problems)
	109	**(Why The Review Was Made)**
	111	(paragraph 2)
	113	(paragraphs 1-3)
Observations	104	
	105	
	110	**(Symptoms)**
	115	(paragraphs 1-4)

Fig. 11.6/Execution of reports—past perspectives.

SPECIFIC TYPE	SPEC. REF.	
Findings/Conclusions	89	
	108	(last paragraph)
	109	(from "Findings and Conclusions" through statistical table)
	115	
Problem Identification	106	
	110	**(PROBLEM)**
	111	(paragraph 2)
Definition	113	(paragraphs 4-8)
Resource (e.g., sales, personnel, financial, product status)	88	

Fig. 11.7/Execution of reports—present perspectives.

SPECIFIC TYPE	SPEC. REF.
Recommendations/Solutions	111 (paragraph 3)
	112 (paragraph 3, items 1-4)
Forecasts	109 (last four paragraphs)

Fig. 11.8 / Execution of reports—future perspectives.

Specimen 88

Clarity of purpose   Not clear: the subject "Personnel Changes" is misleading; the implicit purpose is to announce the departure of one person and to name his replacement. Beyond this should be a very important purpose: to give assurance to receivers and to gain support for the replacement. This purpose was evidently ignored.

Receiver perspective   Improper: should be opposing to credent role; no explicit devices used to handle either.

Format   No clear format: a shifting from departing person to replacement back to departing person then to replacement is confusing.

Description/Evaluation Differentiation   Paragraphs 1 and 2, descriptive; paragraphs 3 and 4, evaluative (which seems to have dictated the basic format, rather than the real purpose and receiver perspectives).

Specimen 106

Clarity of purpose   Clear: implicitly to point out the importance of communication responsibility and to give an operational definition of it.

Receiver perspective   Proper: addressed to critical role; basic devices: statement of assumptions and statement of definition.

Format   Appropriate and clear: "Assumptions and Basic Problems" to "An Operational Definition of Communication Responsibility" pattern; headings and enumerative devices cue reader to essential ideas.

Description/Evaluation Differentiation   Implicit but not explicit (e.g., paragraph 1 essentially evaluative; paragraph 2 both evaluative and descriptive).

Specimen 110

Clarity of purpose   Unclear: not stated

Receiver perspective   Proper: addressed to critical role; basic devices: statement of symptoms with clear relation to underlying problems.

Format   Appropriate and clear: "Symptoms" to "Problems" pattern; headings and graphic cues alert reader to relations between specific symptoms and important problems.

Description/Evaluation Differentiation   Explicit differentiation between symptoms (descriptive) and problems (evaluative).

Fig. 11.9 / Execution—reports.

Fig. 11.9   (continued)

Specimen 112
Clarity of purpose   Partially clear: subject "Information Related to Seminar" not exact; should be "Report: Dr. Miller's Comments, May 24 Meeting"
Receiver perspective   Proper: credent role.
Format   Not appropriate: for a favorable status communication (credent) design should be give information—get right response—get reinforcement rather than that represented in the memorandum (give information—get conviction—get right response).
Description/Evaluation Differentiation   Although not explicit, paragraph 1 is essentially evaluative; paragraphs 2 and 3 are essentially descriptive.

Specimen 115
Clarity of purpose   Partially clear: implicitly to review disaster drill activities and to recommend needed improvements.
Receiver perspective   Improper: should be a critical perspective, but apparently addressed to credent role; starts with descriptive detail then moves abruptly to rudimentary evaluative detail; the "Critique of Said Drill" section is an admixture of gaps and weaknesses, recommendations (explicit and implicit) and commendation.
Format   Appropriate but not clear: implicitly description of drill activities to "Critique . . ." pattern; however, the first needed heading is not given.
Description/Evaluation Differentiation   Paragraphs 1 and 2 are essentially descriptive; the rest of the report mixes description and evaluation.

11.6 will treat reports or excerpts therefrom dealing with a past perspective; Figures 11.7 and 11.8, respectively, give present and future perspectives in the same light. In Figure 11.9, we will then analyze selected total specimens using clarity of purpose, receiver perspective, format and description/evaluation differentiation. In analysis and evaluation, we shall not question the need for the report, nor will we concern ourselves with its accuracy or validity, for these are matters that obviously must be judged in a given organization and speciality context.

Execution: Media Missions Related to Media Formats

We now move to a fundamentally different way to view media. While all the principles presented up to this point give you very useful methods and tools to make definite improvements in your personal and your organization's communication, the concepts and relationships presented in this section give an integrated understanding that can give you optimal control *to get the best communication products and execution.* In order to achieve the understanding of this integrated approach, it will be necessary for you to take a more rigorous view of communication media. You have already noted our several references to the intermixing of certain media with others (e.g., a *proposal* following *letter* format; a *directive* following *memorandum* format). Furthermore, as stated in the previous section, mass distribution letters were referred to as "brochures."

Let us now define "media missions" and "media formats," then relate these two terms to what we have previously called media.

A *media mission* is the *basic objective* or thrust *of the communication document; media format* is the *presentation pattern* of the media mission. For example, the media mission may be a proposal; it may be presented through one of several modes (media formats). Among others, it could be a letter mode; it could be a memorandum style; it could be a brochure pattern. Another example: your media mission may be a directive, which could be carried in letter, memorandum, or manual form.

Media missions are restricted to six: letters, memoranda, reports, proposals, agreements, and directives. Media formats are also limited to six: letters, memoranda, reports, manuals, forms, and brochures. Note that all three individually oriented "media" appear as both media missions and media formats. Further, the three legally oriented "media" appear as media missions. In other words, a proposal, agreement, or directive is a legitimate communication mission, but not a communication format. Finally, the three organizationally oriented "media" (manuals, forms, brochures) are media formats, not media missions.

In order to make media mission and media format relationships more clear, we have put all specimens into their proper categories in Figure 11.10. Let us explain our classification rationale. Note that the six media missions are on the horizontal scale and the six media formats are listed vertically. We start with the media mission as the base for classification—that is, the first question is, "What is the *document* itself supposed to do?" We then look at its format (or formats) to determine how the media mission is accomplished. You will note that we indicate multiple formats for some documents by a parenthetical letter following the specimen number. Moreover, a parenthetical notation preceding the specimen number refers to either an excerpt (e) or a supportive (s) document. The key in Figure 11.10 details what each symbol means. To get real understanding, take time to study this chart; examine some actual specimens. You will grasp the relationships after looking over a few representative examples.

Examples: Purposes Related to Media

Let us now look at some representative samples to see where media and purposes do and do not properly fit together.

Key: (B) brochure (e) excerpt
(F) form (s) supportive
(L) letter
(Ma) manual
(Me) memorandum

MEDIA MISSION

MEDIA FORMAT	Letter	Memorandum	Report	Proposal	Agreement	Directive
Letter	2, 5, 7, 8, 9, 10, 12, 13, 18, 47, 54, 56, 58, 60, 61, 62, 67, 68, 69, 71, 73, 81, 82, 85, 86		20, 22, 24, s26, 28, s31, s32, s38, s43, 44, 70		15, 16, 19, 76	75
Memorandum	1, 4, 11, 35, 46, 52, 78		88, 112	23, 30, 33, 42, 57, 80	74	65, 66, 79, 94, 97, 99, 100Ma, 102, 103
Report			104, 105, 106, e108, e109, 110, 111, 114, 115	e34, 107		
Manual						e91, e92, e93, e95
Form	72				e14, 17	
Brochure	3, 48, 49, 50, 51, 63, 64, 77, 87, 90	37L, 53, 83, 101	e89, e113	6L, s21, s25, s27, 29, 36L, 39L, 40Me, 41F,Me, 45Me, 55, 59, 84L		e96, 98L

Fig. 11.10 / Specimens—media mission and format.

Fig. 11.11 / Media for execution.

		INDIVIDUAL Mission and Format				LEGAL			ORGANIZATIONAL Format		
Category	Situation/Format	Letter	Memo	Report	Proposal	Agreement	Mission	Directive	Manual	Form	Brochure
Personal / Situation Determined	Acknowledgment/Acceptance (1-19)	X	X				X			X	X
	Offering (20-45)	X	X			X			X	X	X
	Solicitation (46-53)	X	X							X	X
Personal / Predetermined	Complaint/Adjustment (54-66)	X	X			X		X	X	X	X
	Rejection/Reprimand (67-80)	X	X			X	X	X	X	X	X
	Goodwill (81-90)	X	X	X							X
Task / Situation Determined	Policy Communications (91-98)	X	X				X	X	X		X
	Procedural Communications (99-103)	X	X			X	X	X	X	X	X
	Status Communications (104-115)	X	X	X						X	X

Specimen 17 Purpose: Acknowledgment/Acceptance/This is a "Registration or Information Request" which, if completed in the top section and returned with payment (or promise to pay), becomes an agreement. On the other hand, if any of the first three boxes at the bottom is checked, the form serves as a letter (purpose: solicitation or transmittal). The admixture of several purposes and different media messages (agreement or letter) weaken what ought to be the primary end: to get the person to register (an agreement). By adding the peripheral informational items, the basic objective can very easily be lost in the maze. This example points out clearly the need for knowing your basic media mission in relation to the intended specific communication purpose and media format so that the document will be properly executed.

Specimen 21 Purpose: Offering/This resume is a supportive document for the specific proposal (letter of application, Specimen 20). As noted in Figure 11.10, resumes are classed as brochures (media format). Specimen 21 is appropriate with respect to the specific communication purpose (offering), the media mission (proposal—supportive), and media format (brochure).

Specimen 34 Purpose: Offering/This is an excerpt (recommendations section) from a more lengthy report. The excerpt itself is a proposal (media mission) included in a report (media format). Since it was addressed to critical receivers (upper managers), the document reflects appropriate choice of media mission and media format to achieve the intended purpose (offering).

Specimen 83 Purpose: Goodwill/This is addressed to all of a population (all employees) and, in this instance, posted on several bulletin boards in the firm. Under these conditions, it is a memorandum (media mission) and because of its public exposure (on company bulletin boards where anyone—employees and the public—could read it) it is a brochure (media format). This document can be criticized on several counts. First, what was accomplished in issuing it in the first place? It is addressed to all employees (and to the world) about a confidential matter (between the credit manager and the customer). Second, even if circulated as a memo, what is the impact on receivers? Will they not perceive it as a "Self-Praise" memo written by and for the credit manager? Third, if praise is to be given, are not other media missions and formats more appropriate? For example, could this have been more appropriately discussed in a staff meeting and, if desired, included in the minutes? Or, could it have been put in the company newsletter? In either case, the customer's name should not be disclosed "for the record."

Specimens 81, 85, and 86 Purpose: Goodwill/Specimen 81 reflects very good choice to meet the intended purpose. It is a letter (media mission) as a letter (media format). A nonroutine letter of this type is proper for a special occasion (congratulating a professor on a new publication). On the other hand, Specimens 85 and 86 could be more effective using a different type of letter or a more appropriate media format. Close examination shows both to be routine —complete letters. As written, Specimen 85 comes through as· an "offering" purpose (gift for further business) and as a "proposal" media mission, which defeats the intended goodwill purpose. Specimen 86 comes through as a "policy" purpose (return to work) and as a "directive" media mission because organizational advantages, not personal advantages, are emphasized. Better alternatives could be either (1) to write both as nonroutine letters (directed to the specific circumstances and emphasizing personal receiver benefits) or (2) to send a congratulatory card (Specimen 85) or get well card (86). These cards as brochures (media format) would serve the media mission (letter) and far better meet the intended purpose of both (goodwill).

Specimen 98   Purpose: Policy Communication/This is a brochure (media format—mass distribution letter) to persons outside the organization. It is a directive (media mission) to remind receivers of an existing company policy. In paragraph 1, the media mission and media format are compatible with the purpose. However, one may question whether the holiday greetings in paragraph 2 are appropriate in light of the serious intent of this directive.

Specimen 101   Purpose: Procedural Communication/This is written as a memorandum (media mission) and since it goes to all of a population (mass distribution) its media format is a brochure. Unfortunately, the document will probably fail because it does not have any real organizational power. Why? The sender, as head of the Mail Service, has no genuine leverage with other units in the organization. Therefore, he must, as he says, offer only "suggestions." Had the document been issued as a directive (media mission) over the signature of the appropriate executive, then the procedural purpose would be more likely achieved.

Specimen 107   Purpose: Status Communication/Even cursory examination shows this purported report to be no more than a self-seeking proposal to extend the powers of the writer. Apart from the abysmal presentation itself, the document should have been written for what it is, a proposal. Or, looked at another way, it should have been either a report and written accordingly, or a proposal, and labeled and written accordingly. Unfortunately, this sort of "mislabeling" is a common unconscious or deliberate practice in many organizations. It can lead an unperceptive reader "down the primrose path." To interpret and act upon a putative report that is, in fact, a proposal can cause untold adverse consequences in an organization.

Summary: PRIDE Sequence

We have now completed the presentation of the five PRIDE components. Figure 11.12 summarizes and gives you a graphic perspective of the entire sequence. You can use this figure as a comprehensive, ready reference in communication analysis, decision making, and execution.

Practical Applications of the PRIDE Method

You have now studied in-depth principles for communication planning (summarized as a checklist in Figure 10.17) and for execution (presented in this chapter). What are some practical applications of the method? In what specific ways can you use the PRIDE decision making sequence for more effective writing products? Here are five practical possibilities (doubtless you can think of more).

1. The "natural" focus: That is, write the document "off the top of the head" without conscious attempt to apply any PRIDE yardsticks. Then check against PRIDE principles, revising as needed.
2. Purpose and receiver focus: That is, consciously identify your specific purpose and general (or exact) receiver. Write the document, check against other PRIDE yardsticks, then rewrite as needed.
3. Message focus: That is, consciously write to communicate your essential idea or ideas. Then check against the total sequence, revising for more effective communication.
4. Receiver focus: That is, try to put yourself in your reader's shoes and write accordingly. Check against all steps, then revise for greater effectiveness.
5. Conscious PRIDE focus: That is, start by deliberately following the sequence step-by-step; let the first draft "cool"; then review against all PRIDE guidelines (as many times as needed) to get the exact product required.

The fifth method is especially appropriate for crucial personal or organizational communications, whether you are a sender or a receiver. As a sender, it gives you the skills and know-how to get the exact results you want; as a receiver, it gives you skills and know-how for rapid and accurate evaluation. Moreover, if you use the sequence properly and often enough, you will become so "programmed" that PRIDE becomes your automatic response to any communication situation. As you can see, this brings you full circle back to the "natural" focus (the first one), but it becomes your habitual way to achieve far better results than the typical "off the top of the head" focus.

PURPOSE and RECEIVER	IMPACT	DESIGN	EXECUTION	
	Initial			
	Apathetic: to get attention; sustain interest			
	Sophisticated: to see ideas in a new light			
	Opposing: to lessen or eliminate hostility			
	Credent: to strengthen pre-existing belief			
	Critical: to rationalize ideas			
ACKNOWLEDGMENT/ACCEPTANCE —unfavorable/favorable— (personal: determined)		Give Information	Letter Memorandum Agreement Form Brochure	ACKNOWLEDGMENT/ACCEPTANCE
GOODWILL —favorable— (personal: predetermined)	Response	Get Right Response	Letter Memorandum Report Brochure	GOODWILL
	Credent: to get intended belief (nonrational)			
	Critical: to get intended belief (rational)			
STATUS COMMUNICATIONS —unfavorable/favorable— (task: determined)	Supportive	Get Reinforcement/Conviction	Letter Memorandum Report Form Brochure	STATUS COMMUNICATIONS
	Credent: to strengthen belief (nonrational)			
	Critical: to validate belief (rational)			
	Initial			
	Apathetic: to get attention; sustain interest			
	Sophisticated: to see ideas in a new light			
	Opposing: to lessen or eliminate hostility			
	Credent: to strengthen pre-existing belief			
	Critical: to rationalize ideas			
OFFERING —unfavorable— (personal: determined)		Give Information	Letter Memorandum Proposal Manual (excerpt) Form Brochure	OFFERING
SOLICITATION —unfavorable/favorable— (personal: determined)	Supportive		Letter Memorandum Form Brochure	SOLICITATION
	Sophisticated: to see ideas in a new light			
	Opposing: to lessen or eliminate hostility			
	Credent: to strengthen belief			
	Critical: to validate belief (rational)			
COMPLAINT/ADJUSTMENT —unfavorable— (personal: predetermined)	Response	Get Conviction/Reinforcement	Letter Memorandum Proposal Directive Manual (excerpt) Form Brochure	COMPLAINT/ADJUSTMENT
REJECTION/REPRIMAND —unfavorable— (personal: predetermined)	Credent: to get intended belief or performance (nonrational)		Letter Memorandum Proposal Agreement Directive Manual (excerpt) Form Brochure	REJECTION/REPRIMAND
POLICY COMMUNICATIONS —unfavorable/favorable— (task: determined)	Critical: to get intended belief or performance (rational)	Get Right Response	Letter Memorandum Directive Manual Brochure	POLICY COMMUNICATIONS
PROCEDURAL COMMUNICATIONS —unfavorable/favorable— (task: determined)			Letter Memorandum Proposal Agreement (supportive) Directive Manual Form Brochure	PROCEDURAL COMMUNICATIONS

Fig. 11.12 / Summary—PRIDE.

EXERCISES

exercise 1 List the three major attributes of a letter.

exercise 2 Give the missions of nonroutine, routine—prepared parts, and routine—complete letters.

exercise 3 Rewrite Specimen 60 (analyzed in Figure 11.2 as a routine—prepared parts letter) as a nonroutine letter. Assume a $50.00 amount overdrawn, caused by a bank cashier's computational error at the time the account was closed. Attach a separate sheet analyzing your rewrite according to the dimensions given in Figure 10.6 (excluding evaluation and persuasiveness).

exercise 4 Rewrite Specimen 33 (a memorandum partially analyzed in Figure 11.5). Attach a separate sheet analyzing your revision, using the dimensions given in Figure 10.6 (excluding evaluation and persuasiveness).

exercise 5 Rewrite Specimen 107 (entitled "Report" when in fact, a proposal) as an actual report. In revision, (a) use an acceptable report format (if necessary, review Chapter 4); (b) eliminate all unnecessary information; and (c) use all appropriate elements of clarity, correctness, and persuasiveness. Attach an analytical sheet as in exercise 4.

exercise 6 Distinguish media missions from media formats, giving a real or hypothetical example to illustrate the difference.

exercise 7 List the six media missions.

exercise 8 List the six media formats.

exercise 9 Rewrite Specimen 24 (a letter of application) and Specimen 25 (the accompanying vita) to achieve the most persuasive impact. Attach an analytical sheet (for the letter) similar to that in previous exercises.

exercise 10 (a) What two media missions can be used with any purpose?
(b) What one media format can be used with any purpose?

CASE PROBLEM

You are President of Star-X Manufacturing Company, which will institute a four-day work week for its 1000 employees on August 31. Employees will work 37 hours (Monday through Thursday) and be paid for 40 hours (which represents a 7½% hourly wage increase). The plant will be closed 50 more days in the work year. In weeks where the holiday falls on Monday, the work week will be Tuesday through Friday. Employees will receive 40 hours pay plus holiday pay if the holiday is a scheduled one. The Shipping and Receiving Dock (previously open Monday through Friday, 7:00 a.m.-4:00 p.m.) will now be open to receive and ship goods as follows: Monday through Wednesday—7:00 a.m. to 5:00 p.m.; Thursday—7:00 a.m. to 4:00 p.m.; Friday—emergency delivery only. (Emergency items means only those goods required to insure continued plant operation.)

Your Missions: Write appropriate documents to (1) employees, (2) vendors and (3) customers. Select appropriate data from the above for each receiver segment's communication. Attach analytical sheets for all documents using the pattern specified for cases in Chapter 10.

Part III

Related Communication Resources

(Oral Communication)—(Automating Communication)—(Using Right Resources)

Having thoroughly covered the most important traditional written media and PRIDE applications to them, we are ready to study complementary organizational communications resources: oral communications, automation of written communications, and finally, the proper uses of all (written, oral, automated).

Chapter 12, "Oral Communications: Speaking and Listening," covers the three significant forms of spoken discourse (presentation, person-to-person, conference) plus principles and guides for effective listening to the three types.

Chapter 13, "Automating Written Communications," treats the four important types of mechanisms (automatic typewriter, data processing, printing, reprography), together with their possible applications to conventional written media.

Chapter 14, "Using the Right Communications Resources," presents guidelines for selection of the communication resource (written, oral, automated), to best achieve your purpose in given circumstances.

Part III completes the book's textual materials. (The last two parts are reference materials: Part IV is concerned with fundamentals of language usage; Part V contains the 115 written specimens that are used for illustration and practice.)

Chapter 12

ORAL COMMUNICATIONS:
SPEAKING AND LISTENING

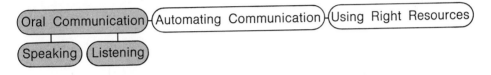

Your Learning Objectives:

1. To know the nature and importance of oral communications in organizational activities.
2. To know the most important modes of organizational oral communications.
3. To know essentials of and to be able to plan, execute, and evaluate oral presentations.
4. To know essentials of and to be able to plan, execute, and evaluate person-to-person communications.
5. To know essentials of and to be able to plan, execute, and evaluate conference communications.
6. To know the nature and importance of listening in organizational activities.
7. To know PRIDE applications to effective listening.
8. To know essentials of and to be able to listen effectively to oral presentations.
9. To know essentials of and to be able to listen effectively to person-to-person communications.
10. To know essentials of and to be able to listen effectively to conference communications.

Chapters 1 through 11 have been concerned with PRIDE for important organizational written documents. And, since written communication is this book's primary focus, we rightly give most attention to it.

However, as you probably know, oral communications—both speaking and listening—play a vital role in the modern organization's activities. Indeed, in terms of both magnitude and importance, speaking and listening far outweigh written communications in handling day-to-day problem solving, decision making, supervision, and operations. Therefore, it is mandatory that you get sufficient understanding of important organizational oral communications in order to be able to know when and how to use them efficiently and effectively.

Space limitations permit only a highlighting of speaking and listening, but we shall optimize our presentation by building on the PRIDE sequence used in our discussion of written communications, for most of the same principles apply.

Our discussion will first treat the three most important oral communication media, after which we shall present principles and guides for effective listening. Specifically, the discussion sequence is: (1) oral presentations, (2) person-to-person communication, (3) conference communication, and (4) listening: principles and guides.

Oral Presentations

Often called "public speaking," this medium is essentially monologue in that one person conveys ideas to a small or large group of listeners. Often several people at a given meeting may give a succession of presentations (sometimes called "symposium"). In any event, the basic attribute of oral presentations is that of a "one-to-many" relationship. While most commonly the person and audience are in the same room (therefore directly confronting one another), presentations to a group also include electronic hookups (e.g., radio, television) where the speaker and audience may be apart. The essential difference between oral and written presentation is in execution: the *person is the communication carrier* in oral presentations. In writing, a piece (or pieces) of paper carries the message, but human beings must do this in speaking. Certainly written as well as audio-visual means may be used to help your oral presentation, but the primary burden is on you as a person.

What this means is that you must have the requisite *personal presentation capability* to convey ideas clearly, correctly, and cogently. Effective execution of oral presentation requires: (1) proper attitudes and outlooks; (2) personal oral presentation competence; (3) adequate execution procedures; and (4) presentation critique.

Proper Attitudes and Outlooks

In this respect, you need to recognize some basic things that can make or break you in speaking to a group.

First, *objectivity* is necessary, that is, an ability to view yourself and your presentation with proper detachment, to see both in proper perspective. This is necessary if you are to know yourself, the oral communication situation you confront, and what needs to be done to succeed. It is vital also if you are to strengthen your communication assets and to eliminate liabilities. While there is no easy way to attain it, you can (1) repeatedly remind yourself of the need for objectivity; (2) get feedback from critically oriented persons with whom you communicate; and, using the principles in this book, (3) chart a deliberate course to develop the required objectivity.

Second, *idea and receiver commitment* is necessary for an effective oral presentation. Are your ideas really important? And can they have real importance for your group? Will it make a real difference if your listeners properly comprehend and respond to your ideas (or if they misunderstand with attendant wrong responses)? Answers to questions like these are good clues to your presentation and listener commitment. If not present, you may fail, because the degree of constructive commitment is tied directly to the degree of success in oral presentations to groups.

Third, *constructive confidence* is a must in successful oral presentations. This does not mean an artificial "Pollyanna" outlook—a "sweetness and light" view of yourself and the world.

It means a confidence that springs from objectivity and commitment, plus seeing yourself as a worthy and competent speaker. Do you feel that you have something important to say? Do you know what you are talking about? Are you thoroughly prepared? Have you brought together all essential ideas? Have you planned for contingencies?

If your answer is "yes" to these questions, you should have the needed confidence for successful execution of your oral presentation. To the extent you cannot give affirmative answers, confidence will be lacking.

Personal Oral Presentation Competence

You have seen that your confidence is largely based on your oral presentation proficiency, which includes several dimensions.

First, *communication planning* (which has been discussed in the PRIDE sequence) refers to knowing your specific purpose, knowing your receivers, knowing required impacts, and selecting the right design sequence.

Second, *verbal, vocal, and physical execution* refers to your ability to use language, the voice, the body, and other graphic and visual aids presenting ideas to a group. (Remember that principles of visual communication were given in Chapter 4, many of which apply equally to oral communication.) All these are output factors, that is, all are involved in the presentation delivery. Therefore, it is clear that, as with written communications, even the best planning may be futile if you do not effectively execute (or carry out) your oral presentation.

These questions will help pinpoint items that affect your execution in communicating to a group. Do you *use words correctly* (appropriate grammar, diction, and terminology)? Do you *pronounce words correctly* (that is, within situationally acceptable limits)? Do you *speak distinctly* (acceptable articulation and enunciation)? Do you use *directness in phrasing ideas* (rather than garbled and rambling syntax)? Is your speaking characterized by *clarity and simplicity* (rather than fogginess and unnecessary jargon)? Do you use a *sufficient variety* of *words, phrases,* and *terms* (rather than the deadly repeating of the same "noises" over and over again)? Do you observe *propriety of speech* (or do you offend by unnecessarily "vulgar" or "out-of-place" communication)? Do you effectively use *eye contact, facial expression, posture, gestures,* and *proper appearance?* Where appropriate, do you supplement your words with graphic or visual aids or other external devices?

These are the kinds of questions you should carefully ponder. If you are unable to answer them accurately right off, try this: (1) record your next presentation (or even informal conversation) and play it back. This can be very revealing (if not sometimes shocking); (2) ask a group of constructively critical people with whom you communicate often to fill out the critique sheet (Figures 12.1 and 12.2) at the end of this section. Compare theirs with your own analysis. You may be surprised at the consensus of outsiders' (and at the deviations from your own) judgments. Normally you should assume that the outsiders' evaluations are valid, and you should be guided accordingly in shaping up your verbal, vocal, and physical communication.

Communication sensitivity means your ability to recognize and handle receiver feelings and roles as well as their informational needs—that is, your capacity to speak to important psychological and logical demands of the listener. This is a dimension that pervades all of oral presentation planning and execution.

We have discussed two basic dimensions affecting you as a presentation medium: (1) your attitudes and outlooks and (2) your personal oral presentation competence. Let us summarize by putting each in a separate analysis form (Figures 12.1 and 12.2).

Adequate Execution Procedures

This refers to possession and proper use of techniques and methods for delivery of your message to your listeners. Let us draw on what you already know about the PRIDE sequence and to apply those principles for executing oral presentations. Essentially this involves: (1) presentation size-up; (2) presentation out-

FACTOR	EVALUATION					Needed Improvement (Specify)
	Poor	Fair	Good	Excellent	Superior	
Objectivity						
Idea/Receiver Commitment						
Constructive Confidence						

Fig. 12.1 / Evaluation of personal attitudes and outlooks.

FACTOR	EVALUATION					Needed Improvement (Specify)
	Poor	Fair	Good	Excellent	Superior	
Communication Planning						
Verbal/Vocal/ Visual/Physical Communication						
Communication Sensitivity						

Fig. 12.2 / Evaluation of personal oral presentation competence.

line; (3) presentation delivery; and (4) presentation critique. We shall give a brief discussion of each facet, together with a graphic figure for use at each stage.

Presentation size-up refers to assessment of the presentation situation you confront: your *specific purpose*; the *essential message* you want to convey; the *receiver roles* you confront; the *needed impacts* to handle each listener role; and the *design* and devices you plan to use to get the desired impacts. Figure 12.3 puts these elements into worksheet form, which you can use for presentation size-up.

Presentation outline grows out of size-up and refers to putting your ideas on paper, as well as the accompanying devices you plan to use with all dimensions: introduction, essential content (both basic and supporting ideas), and conclusion. Figure 12.4 offers a practical way to go about this phase.

Presentation delivery is the actual carrying out—the real payoff point—in oral presentation. A whole book could be written about this stage, but we shall condense the most useful general principles into the table in Figure 12.5.

	INITIAL	SUPPORTIVE	RESPONSE
SPECIFIC PURPOSE:			
ESSENTIAL MESSAGE: (summarize)			

RECEIVER ROLES:
 Apathetic, Sophisticated,
   Opposing, Credent,
   Critical
	↓	↓	↓

IMPACTS:
 Get attention/interest
 Gain new insight
 Lessen/eliminate hostility
 Get/strengthen/validate
   beliefs
 Get intended belief/
   performance
	↓	↓	↓

DEVICES (including visual aids)	1. 2. 3.*	1. 2. 3.*	1. 2. 3.*

* Extend as necessary.

Fig. 12.3 / Presentation size-up.

Presentation Critique

This refers to getting feedback on oral presentation effectiveness. No presentation, however well prepared and executed, will be "perfect." The communicator knows he can always improve his performance, so he deliberately solicits realistic comments and reactions from listeners. Obviously, the more competent the listener-communicator, the better will be his critique. However, even the relatively untutored listener critic can give you some valuable information for your improvement. The "Presentation Critique Checklist" (Figure 12.6) can be used as a comprehensive, but easy-to-complete instrument to get candid listener evaluations of your presentation.

In using this form you need not ask all auditors to complete it (unless it is a small group of highly competent critics). Rather, a sample of five to ten competent people is normally sufficient to tell you where you did well and where you need to do better in future presentations. Superior communicators have generally become so by deliberately following a procedure similar to the one suggested here.

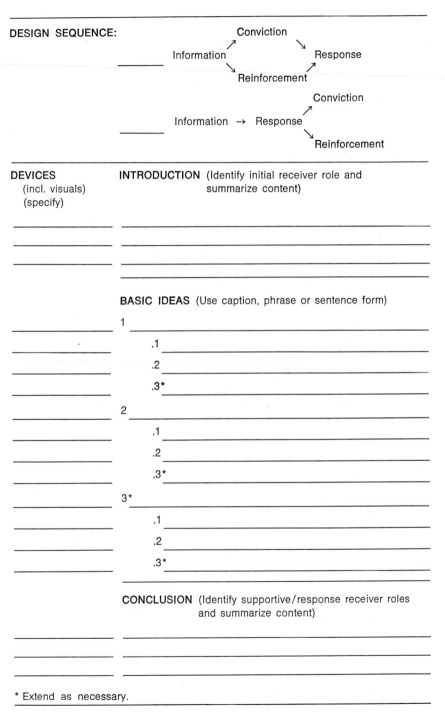

DESIGN SEQUENCE:

Conviction

Information ↗ ↘ Response

↘ Reinforcement ↗

Conviction

Information → Response ↗

↘ Reinforcement

DEVICES
(incl. visuals)
(specify)

INTRODUCTION (Identify initial receiver role and
summarize content)

BASIC IDEAS (Use caption, phrase or sentence form)

1

.1

.2

.3*

2

.1

.2

.3*

3*

.1

.2

.3*

CONCLUSION (Identify supportive/response receiver roles
and summarize content)

* Extend as necessary.

Fig. 12.4 / Presentation outline.

INTRODUCTION	POSSIBLE PURPOSES: To get attention; to handle initial listener role; to lead into basic ideas
Principle	**Remarks**
1. Have notes/aids accessible	Place notes for ease of use so that you can follow without losing your place; have audiovisuals ready to go and convenient to use.
2. Be brief	Come to the point as soon as conditions permit; avoid "long windedness."
3. Use only relevant ideas/devices	Include only those ideas and devices that directly contribute to handling the initial receiver role and to your purpose and essential message. Especially avoid unnecessary jokes, stories, and other "obvious" devices.
4. Create the right atmosphere and start	Some guides to a constructive tone and setting are: (1) Avoid apology (e.g., "I haven't had much time to prepare. . . ." or "I know very little about this subject. . . .") (2) Avoid holding an apathetic, sophisticated, or opposing *presenter role*; you should take either a credent or critical outlook as appropriate. (3) Talk *with* your listeners—not *to* them; avoid "preaching" or "lecturing"—even if the subject is serious. (4) Assume a confident manner. Start positively and strongly; this gives you added confidence and produces greater audience confidence in you. (5) Have a "message starter." Even if memorized, *know* your initial remarks. This is a very steadying influence to get you going in the right direction and in the right way.

BASIC IDEAS	POSSIBLE PURPOSES: To sustain interest; to get receiver understanding of message; to move listeners to either credent or critical role.
Principle	**Remarks**
1. Keep contact with audience	Look primarily at specific persons in the group—not at your notes or visuals; actually see persons (eye contact)—do not merely stare into space, keep your head down, or move distractingly. Moreover, watch listeners for signs of apathy or misunderstanding, adjusting your delivery and message as needed.

Fig. 12.5 / Presentation delivery principles.

Fig. 12.5 (continued)

2. Use proper physical communication	Use appropriate gestures and body movements to keep audience attention and to emphasize ideas; avoid distracting motions or actions (hand in pocket, jingling keys, fidgety handling of pointer, pacing back and forth, habitual facial grimaces).
3. Use notes and other aids to supplement ideas	Use your notes as guides to idea development—not as devices that inhibit audience contact and adequate physical communication. Time your presentation of audiovisuals and supplements with the related idea or ideas; do not show before or after, but simultaneously with the point or points they reinforce.
4. Use sufficient listener cues	Use adequate connectives, summaries, variety in delivery rate, volume, and pitch to keep attention and to help auditors follow your ideas. If necessary, reinforce by restatement, illustration, graphic aids, and the like.
5. Talk to listeners' interests and viewpoint	Use appropriate devices to communicate to auditors' wants, needs, beliefs. Set a positive tone; use specific and clear language (to the receiver); take the "you"—rather than "I"—approach.

CONCLUSION POSSIBLE PURPOSES: To assure ending credent or critical listener role; to give note of finality; to summarize basic ideas; to emphasize special ideas; to give implications; to get right response.

Principle	Remarks
1. Conclude as soon as appropriate	End the presentation as quickly as possible; avoid unneeded lengthy, wearisome discussion.
2. Conclude with finality	Avoid ending in the middle of an idea or leaving ideas "up in the air" or just "winding down;" complete your essential message with a positive ending.
3. Use concluding cues	Use ending transitions and connectives (e.g., "To summarize," "To conclude," "In closing," "My final point. . . .") to alert receivers that you are ending. *Caution:* then end!
4. Conclude on a positive note	End on a constructive note. Even in serious cases end by offering hope and a way to overcome obstacles. Moreover, avoid "Thank you" in concluding. This is merely a *pro forma* "I don't have anything else to say" statement. (And should not listeners really thank you if your presentation has accomplished its mission—which is to give receivers something of value?)

293

PRESENTATION CRITIQUE CHECKLIST

	Supe-rior	Excel-lent	Good	Fair	Poor	Specify Needed Improvement
MESSAGE						
Did the *introduction* get attention?						
Were *basic ideas* clear and cogent?						
Were *ideas adequately developed?*						
Was the *conclusion proper?*						
Was the *essential message* clear?						
RECEIVER INFLUENCE						
Did the presentor *address* himself to *you as a person?*						
Did he *address* himself at *your level of understanding?*						
Did he take *your viewpoint?*						
Did he appear to be *sincere, warm, open?*						
Were you *convinced* at the presentation's end?						
LANGUAGE/VOICE/PHYSICAL COMMUNICATION						
Were language, diction, grammar *correct?*						
Were language, diction, grammar *cogent?*						
Was there proper vocal *volume, tone,* and *variety?*						
Were *gestures* appropriate?						
Was *audience contact* sufficient?						
PRESENTATION AIDS AND FACILITIES						
Were *audiovisuals* well prepared and handled?						
Were *written handouts* well prepared and handled?						
Was the *room properly set up* for the presentation?						
Was *equipment* well handled?						
Were *physical distractions* well handled?						

Note to Critic: Complete this sheet as candidly and constructively as possible. Remember, the presenter will use your evaluations to improve his presentation, so he wants your realistic evaluation of his performance.

Fig. 12.6 / Presentation critique checklist.

Person-to-Person Communication

Sometimes called "face-to-face speaking," this medium is a "dialogue" between one person and another person. Rather than the unilateral, preset pattern of oral presentations, person-to-person speaking is interactive and fluid. However, even though flexible, effective person-to-person communication is deliberately planned and executed, a topic that we shall treat in detail a little later.

What are common examples of person-to-person speaking? Job interviews, boss-to-subordinate communications, telephone conversations, fact-finding interviews, and teacher-student consultations are everyday illustrations. Indeed, you can see that it is one of the most frequently used and one of the most important organizational oral media.

The background principles presented under oral presentations concerning proper attitudes and presentation competence apply in kind to person-to-person situations; therefore we shall go directly to execution procedures, using the same analytical dimensions except that the fourth is follow-up (rather than critique).

Person-to-Person Size-up

Once more you should essentially follow the PRIDE sequence of identifying specific purpose, receiver roles, the needed impacts, and the design and devices required for success. Figure 12.7 is an eight-step guide to size-up.

Person-to-Person Outline

Figure 12.8 presents a self-explanatory useful graphic scheme for outlining your discussion.

Person-to-Person Discussion

As with oral presentation, we present this part concisely in tabular form (Figure 12.9).

Follow-up Activities

This dimension is in part a critique of effectiveness in that success or failure is gauged by whether you get the results or outcomes you sought (e.g., the participant does what he is asked, or an accurate confirming document is received, or the problem discussed is resolved). Figure 12.10 is a simple format for this most important phase.

296

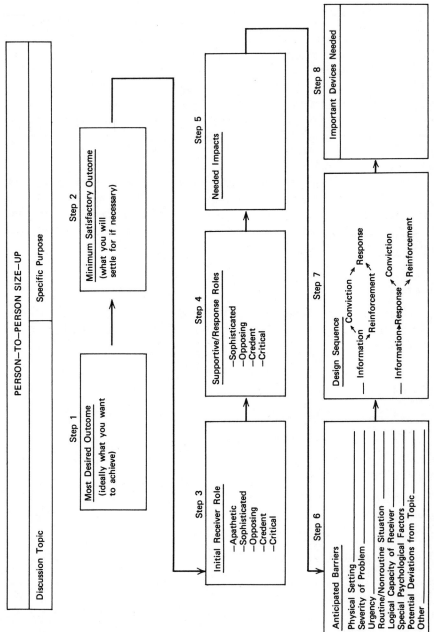

Fig. 12.7 / Person-to-person size-up.

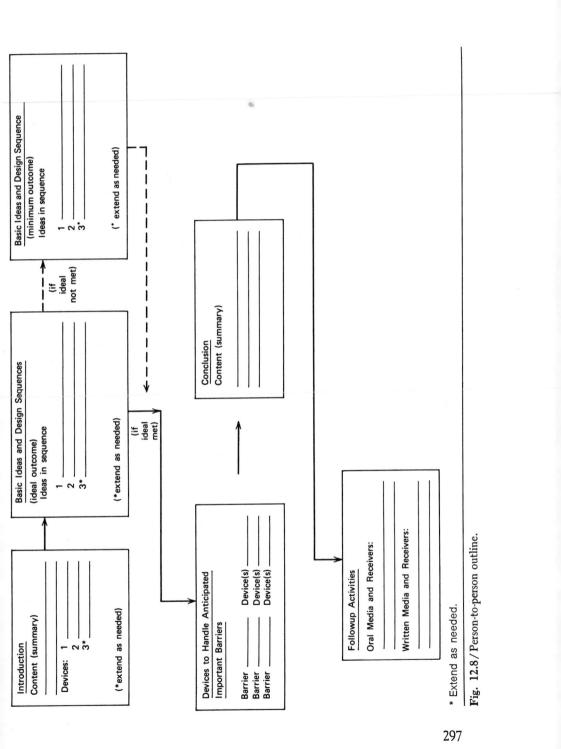

* Extend as needed.

Fig. 12.8 / Person-to-person outline.

297

INTRODUCTION   POSSIBLE PURPOSES: To handle initial receiver role; to set proper atmosphere; to lead to basic ideas/problem/situation.

Principle   **Remarks**

1. Introduce self properly — Observe appropriate social amenities, whether informal or formal (e.g., shaking hands, "Good morning," "Please sit down").

2. Create right atmosphere and start to handle initial receiver role — Establish proper tone (serious or friendly; formal or informal); then, using proper devices, move to topic of discussion

3. Be attuned to receiver readiness and progress — Observe that the other person is with you—logically and psychologically; if not use needed devices to bring along (e.g., provocative questions, receiver participation, statement of issue).

4. Eliminate unneeded "breeze" — Avoid the trite, commonplace (e.g., discussions of weather, world conditions) and nonessential ideas.

BASIC IDEAS   POSSIBLE PURPOSES: To handle supportive/response receiver roles; to get and give information; to clarify and handle receiver attitudes/feelings; to answer objections; to get support and agreement; to make forward progress.

1. Give/get information for mutual understanding — Involve the other person; get his ideas and feedback to assure understanding; use examples and illustrations to clarify; get him to talk and raise questions; observe both receiver visual cues (e.g., facial expressions, restlessness) and verbal expressions to know whether he understands you and whether he knows your understanding of him.

2. Clarify/handle receiver attitudes/feelings — Observe cues (visual and verbal) of disagreement/agreement (e.g., scowl, smile, silence, involvement); handle negative and positive outlooks with proper devices; if negative, focus on problems or issues rather than personalities; use proper devices to overcome apathy/sophistication/opposition.

Fig. 12.9 / Person-to-person discussion principles.

298

Fig. 12.9 (continued)

BASIC IDEAS (continued)

3. Overcome objections — Use proper devices for overcoming sophistication/opposition or controlling criticality; answer objection as quickly as possible, then return to main ideas; do not evade objection (although postponement may be proper if objection is to be answered later); if possible, put objection into broader context—making it unimportant or showing to favor receiver after answering; turn objection into "sale" by assuming it to be the only barrier to getting right response.

4. Get support/ agreement — Focus on advantages: personal/organizational/social; use common interests/beliefs to show that "you are with him;" use receiver participation for commitment; build on receiver ideas; use "request for help" device where proper.

5. Make forward progress — Use summaries; make transitions from idea to idea; handle digressions by returning to point (without alienating receiver); point out need to meet specific deadlines; "postpone" tangential or irrelevent ideas; first get agreement on the easiest points, then move to the more difficult; involve the receiver (e.g., ask him to summarize, or to tell you where you are and where you need yet to go); get assent on points of agreement (and disagreement).

CONCLUSION

POSSIBLE PURPOSES: To end on the right psychological note; to know what has been achieved; to know what needs yet to be done.

1. End on right note — Conclude constructively (even if disagreement persists); point out mutual benefits of discussion.

2. Know where you stand — Summarize essential points; restate points of agreement/disagreement; get receiver assent to both of preceding.

3. Know what needs to be done — Clarify follow-up activities (e.g., further meetings, confirmation in writing, operational actions to be taken).

4. End at right point and time — If possible conclude on points of agreement (rather than disagreement); conclude within time constraints; if further meeting required, set for later date.

299

FOLLOW-UP ACTIVITIES—PERSON-TO-PERSON COMMUNICATION

Specific action(s) to be taken:

1. _____

2. _____

3.* _____

Specific departments and people for each action

Action	Department(s)	Person(s)
1. _____	_____	_____
2. _____	_____	_____
3.* _____	_____	_____

Deadlines for Actions   Follow-up Communications Needed

Action 1 _____   Oral _____   Written _____

                          _____   _____

Action 2 _____   Oral _____   Written _____

                          _____   _____

Action 3* _____ Oral _____   Written _____

                          _____   _____

* Extend as necessary.

Fig. 12.10 / Follow-up activities—person-to-person communication.

Conference Communication

Among others, this medium may be called a "committee meeting," "staff meeting," or merely "conference on. . . ." As used here, conference communication refers to small-group (normally from five to twenty-five participants) interaction for some specific organizational or task purpose (whether explicit or implicit).

When properly used and when competent participants (both leader and member) are involved, it can be one of the most fruitful of oral media. When (as is so commonly the case) improperly employed or when incompetent people participate, disaster can follow. Again, conference communication is a subject unto itself, so only highlights will be presented.

Generally conferences will be directed primarily to task purpose missions (policy communications, procedural communications, and status communications). Personal purposes (situational or predetermined) may enter into the discussion, but they are subordinate.

Most of the principles discussed under Person-to-Person Communication (Figure 12.9) are equally applicable to conferences; therefore we shall not repeat those ideas here. Rather, we shall enumerate additional items unique to the conference medium. Our discussion follows this sequence: size-up, planning, discussion principles, and follow-up.

Conference Size-up

Figure 12.11 presents a practical scheme for assessing the situation either as a leader or member of the conference. If you are the leader, assume that perspective in completing items (that is, analyze the conference mission and membership). If you are a member, take that view. (that is, analyze the conference mission, peer members, and the leader).

Conference Planning

Although the leader and member play somewhat different roles in conference planning, the same basic components obtain for each. Figure 12.12 presents a scheme for planning preconference activity and discussion. Unique leader functions in each step are preceded by (L), otherwise the operation applies to both.

Conference Discussion Principles

Although the leader and member are part of the same conference team, their roles differ in discussion. Therefore we shall present a table specifying both leader and member activities and responsibilities for essential conference functions (Figure 12.13).

Follow-up Activities

Since person-to-person and conference follow-up are basically the same, you may, therefore, use Figure 12.10 as your guide in assuring proper post-conference activities.

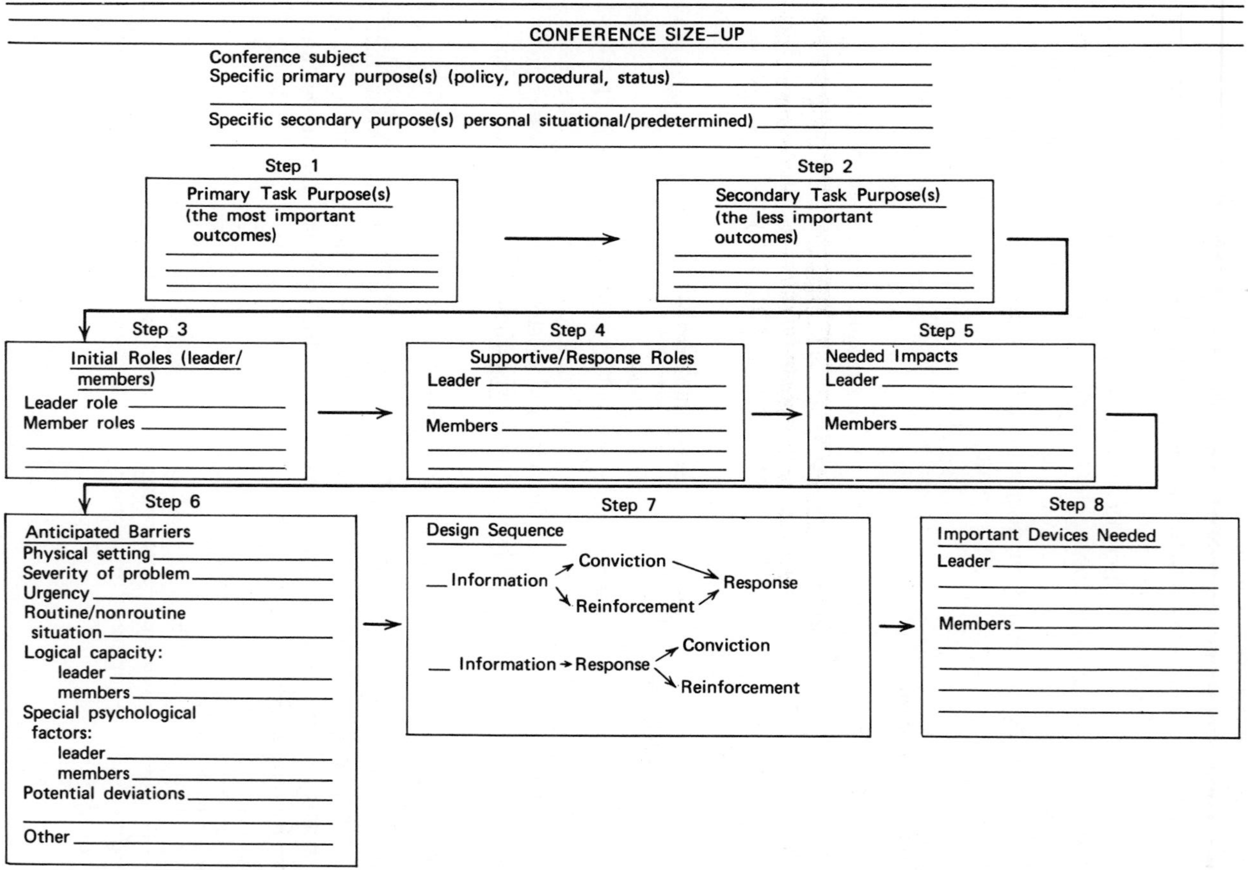

CONFERENCE SIZE-UP

Conference subject _____
Specific primary purpose(s) (policy, procedural, status) _____
_____
Specific secondary purpose(s) personal situational/predetermined _____
_____

Step 1

Primary Task Purpose(s)
(the most important outcomes)
_____
_____
_____

Step 2

Secondary Task Purpose(s)
(the less important outcomes)
_____
_____
_____

Step 3

Initial Roles (leader/members)
Leader role _____
Member roles _____

Step 4

Supportive/Response Roles
Leader _____
Members _____

Step 5

Needed Impacts
Leader _____
Members _____

Step 6

Anticipated Barriers
Physical setting _____
Severity of problem _____
Urgency _____
Routine/nonroutine situation _____
Logical capacity:
  leader _____
  members _____
Special psychological factors:
  leader _____
  members _____
Potential deviations _____

Other _____

Step 7

Design Sequence
_____ Information → Conviction → Response → Reinforcement
_____ Information → Response → Conviction → Reinforcement

Step 8

Important Devices Needed
Leader _____
Members _____

Fig. 12.11 / Conference size-up.

302

Preconference Activity	Conference Discussion
(L) Agenda (preparation/needed distribution)	(L) Introduction
Agenda items_____	Content (summary)_____
_____	_____
_____	_____
_____	Handling initial roles_____
Distribution _____	_____
(persons/ _____	_____
units) _____	Basic Ideas (original agenda or modification)
(L) Initial Purpose Statement	Item 1_____
Primary_____	
_____	Item 2_____
Secondary_____	Item 3*_____
_____	Handling anticipated supportive/response roles
(L) Distribution: Agenda/Purposes	
Initial medium_____	_____
Follow-up medium_____	_____
Checking Understanding of Agenda and Purpose	(L) Conclusion
Leader medium_____	Content (summary)_____
Member medium_____	_____
	_____
(L) Arranging facilities/physical setting	Handling anticipated supportive/response roles_____
Needed equipment_____	_____
Needed room/seating_____	_____
	* Extend as needed.

Fig. 12.12/Conference planning.

CONFERENCE DISCUSSION PRINCIPLES

INTRODUCTION

Function	Leader Responsibilities and Activities	Member Responsibilities and Activities
1. Clarify and get agreement on purposes	State succinctly; give reasons/background; determine member understanding/agreement; get group consensus	Raise relevant questions of leader and other members; use examples, illustrations to determine if purpose clearly understood; state any disagreement and why; help leader get understanding and agreement
2. Determine discussion sequence and procedures (e.g., formal or informal handling; recording minutes or making summary notes; use of resource members, e.g., experts, "umpire" to point out digressions/disagreements)	State suggested approach or ask group to set; modify agenda/procedures as needed; get positive group response to original/modified version	If appropriate, suggest a "better" approach; raise questions concerning the what, why and how of leader or other member suggestions; ask other members for suggestions; if approach "wrong," candidly state reasons; if time allows, ask for group reconsideration or postponement pending better sequence/procedures
3. Set right discussion atmosphere	Move members from unfavorable to favorable role (normally critical); create open, candid communication situation; help members see conference importance (e.g., using personal/organizational/social advantages); "warm" the group to conference purpose and significance (e.g., pointing out adverse/beneficial consequences of success/failure)	Help leader create open, candid, constructive atmosphere; clarify conference significance through questions, examples, involvement of other members; help get "silent opposition" out into the open; use appropriate devices to get constructive, dynamic interaction of members (e.g., "devil's advocate," provocative questions, asking other members for reactions); help leader move dissident or obstructive members to constructive role

Fig. 12.13 / Conference discussion principles.

Fig. 12.13 (continued)

BASIC IDEAS

Note: All principles given for person-to-person "Basic Idea" discussion apply (Figure 12.9). These are for both leader and member use in effective conference discussion. Only additional conference principles are given here.

Function	Leader Responsibilities and Activities	Member Responsibilities and Activities
1. Keep group focus on conference purpose/ problem	Use written or oral aids (agenda, flipchart, blackboard, tape recorder playback); use summaries of progress; reiterate purpose/ problem; point out "digressions;" suggest "breaks" or different activities to handle group breakdowns or deviations; ask members to help monitor anticipated problems (e.g., membership hostility; losing sight of problem; needless delays; giving insufficient consideration to specific ideas; jumping to wrong conclusions; overriding certain member views; lack of total membership participation)	Assist leader and group in ways suggested by assuming and carrying out responsibilities and actions that keep the conference purpose and problem oriented; listen carefully and speak out when you can make a constructive contribution
2. Help group progress toward its goals	All above apply, plus: if possible, get group understanding and agreement to each major point (e.g., "As I understand it, we are saying. . . . Is this correct?"). If total agreement not possible, get majority view or make note of points of disagreement for possible later consideration. Observe and listen for "unsaid" misunderstandings or disagreement (e.g., uninvolved members; "silent or sullen" members; carping or sarcastic comments); use appropriate devices to handle apathy/sophistication/ opposition/"gullible" credence	Help leader and group by assisting the leader in carrying out functions listed; ask for summaries at salient points; ask for clarification of important ideas; make notes on ideas covered, points of agreement/disagreement; help group maintain constructive and critical role (without alienating members)

305

Fig. 12.13 (continued)

BASIC IDEAS (continued)

Function	Leader Responsibilities and Activities	Member Responsibilities and Activities
3. Help group balance task and member needs	Use all devices under "Help group progress toward its goals," plus: try to maximize total member participation; try to understand the "what and why" of member disagreement/opposition; solicit member suggestions for resolving differences; if necessary, "blow the whistle" on members blocking group progress; or use other members to call a halt to obstructional acts; remember that both logical and psychological needs must be met in conference discussion; use appropriate devices for anticipating and handling receiver role needs	Help leader and group by assisting the leader in carrying out functions listed; all responsibilities and activities are essentially the same as the leader
CONCLUSION	Note: the four functions (principles) listed for person-to-person "Conclusions" apply equally to conferences (that is, (1) End on right note; (2) Know where you stand; (3) Know what needs to be done; (4) End at right point and time). And the "Remarks" apply to both the leader and members. Therefore, use the "Conclusions" section, Figure 12.9, for guidance in effective conference closings.	

Listening: Principles and Guides

Now that we have looked at an organization's three primary oral *transmission* media (oral presentations, person-to-person communication, and conference communications), let us turn to the *reception* part: listening. When you speak, your listener is the receiver; when you listen to others, you are the receiver. In most organizations, people spend more time in listening than in any other communication activity.

Unfortunately, most "listening" is not really *reception* of *ideas,* but rather mere bounding sound waves off the ear drums of those to whom we address our speaking. All too frequently the "noises" we make (or those made to us) never penetrate the cortex so that accurate meaning and proper interpretations result. Listening, then, transcends hearing (sensing sound waves); it involves both sensing and thinking.

Again, we can only highlight some principles and guides to improve listening. We shall do this by, first, discussing PRIDE applied to listening; then we shall present checklists that you can use with each of the three oral media.

PRIDE Applied to Listening

As you probably already see, the PRIDE sequence is just as applicable to listening as it is to writing and speaking. Let us, therefore, use it as the basis for discussion and application.

Purpose is fundamental to effective listening. If you are to make a worthwhile attempt to receive ideas, you need a clear, conscious objective for reception. A good listener knows initially what he ought to get from a presentation (or person-to-person or conference communication); furthermore he is able to change his original purpose if developments dictate. Any of the purposes presented for written communications can be related to listening. For example, let us assume the speaker is quoting (offering) a product for a lower price; your listener purpose could well be seeking information (solicitation) to assure that the facts are accurate and that the item will be satisfactory, and if so, could lead to your assenting to the offer (acceptance). Or assume that the production manager is giving an oral report on production output and costs (status communication), your purpose may be the same as his in that you are listening to determine whether accurate description and proper evaluation are made. If well done, your purpose may shift to acknowledgment (receiver is right). Thus you can see the interplay and dynamics of purposes in effective listening.

Receiver roles are directly applicable to effective listening. The three "negative" roles—apathetic, sophisticated, opposing—are clearly detrimental to listening. If apathetic, you will probably not even hear—much less listen to—what a speaker is saying. If sophisticated, your "wise guy" outlook will probably cause you to dismiss much of what he says as "obvious"—without your really knowing what the sender is trying to get across. If opposing (even though "right"), you can easily miss all or most of the sender's message, or some part of value. If you really listen, you might even find that you are in greater agreement than you originally thought. And even if in disagreement, you may know the "enemy" position much more clearly, as well as gain reinforcement for your original views.

Only one of a credent or critical role is proper for listening in serious organizational communication. Apart from blind gullibility, the credent role is proper when you are seeking deeper insights about something in which you already believe. For example, if you assume that your firm is putting out the best product on the market, the credent role is appropriate if you listen to a speaker expound some "inside detail" plan about making the product even better.

The critical role is more often the proper perspective of any person occupying a responsible position in the firm. Remember, "critical" means a thinking, rational outlook. In assuming it, the listener is still persuadable, but he will be persuaded on the basis of facts and sound reasoning—a rational approach.

What does this mean to you as a listener? For one thing, you should try to start with either a credent or critical role (as appropriate). Second, you should shift your role (from credent to critical or vice versa) as the situation dictates. If the speaker has thoroughly convinced you, the critical listener, that he knows what he is talking about (factually and inferentially), then it may be all right to take a credent stance. On the other hand, in another instance, you may start with a credent perspective, but you may find it necessary to move to a critical posture because the speaker seems to be "off base" or going beyond what you can reasonably accept.

Avoid, if possible, slipping into an apathetic, sophisticated, or opposing listener. You may well be justified in many cases, but rarely will there be any constructive outcome for you. If you are to hear the boss's monotonous remarks, required in a meeting, you can still learn something—even if only how to avoid duplicating his miserable performance. Furthermore, the boss will expect you to know and follow what he has said. Woe unto you if you do not!

If, on the other hand, you are in a situation that you can control, proper application of the critical role tells you when to cut off the communication as well as what is needed to assure proper understanding by your receivers.

Impact is certainly an important dimension in listening. What devices is the speaker using on you? Are they appropriate? Are they well executed? Do they contribute constructively to message impact? Competent and willing listeners know every technique the speaker uses; and they know whether the devices and techniques are appropriate or inappropriate, whether well executed or poorly handled. Contrary to popular opinion, knowing what the speaker is doing to achieve a certain impact does not detract from message assimilation for competent and willing receivers. A good artist knows the techniques and materials that have gone into a fine painting by a fellow artist, and he appreciates the painting all the more because of it. Furthermore, he invariably understands better than the untutored viewer what the other artist was trying to accomplish. The same principle holds true in listening: the accomplished listener knows good oral communication when he hears it, and he knows why it is effective. But he still gets the message. What about the incompetent or unwilling listener? He will invariably completely miss the essential ideas of even the best speaker.

Design is basic to effective reception of oral communication. Knowing the speaker's organization of basic and subordinate ideas and knowing the role sequence employed are necessary to follow the speaker's ideas and to be able to remember them when he has finished. We have discussed this in detail with respect to writing. You can see that the principles can be translated directly to oral communications.

Execution refers to medium use to achieve purpose. As in writing, a speaker must choose the right medium to achieve his oral communication objective. The boss who uses an oral presentation to a large group to reprimand a single listener has probably exercised poor judgment. A private person-to-person dialogue would be more appropriate for most cases of this sort. Or let us assume that the same boss wants to "set his subordinate supervisors straight" because they are not enforcing the "no smoking" rule on the factory floor. He then calls a "conference to discuss" the issue. In all probability, he will not get the results he wants. Why? The boss really wants *understanding* and *enforcement* of a directive (rule)—not a discussion of its merits. This is a proper place for an oral presentation—not a conference. Of course, questions from supervisor-listeners are in order—but they are questions for clarification—not for evaluation of the directive.

When, as a listener, you know which media are appropriate to achieve specific purposes, you know whether to expect right results—both from the speaker's perspective and from yours as listener.

Listener Checklist Guides

We now present checklists that put all PRIDE principles into practical guides for use with each oral medium. Figure 12.14 is for oral presentations; Figure 12.15 is for person-to-person communications; and Figure 12.16 is for conference communications. Use of these instruments can markedly sharpen your listening. After sufficient practice, good listening will be a habit; it will be one of your most valuable tools in managerial and organizational communications.

LISTENING: PRESENTATIONS

Speaker _____

Specific subject _____

Essential idea _____

_____

PRESENTATION OUTLINE

Introduction _____

_____

_____

_____

Presentation Evaluation

Purpose
What was it? _____
Was it proper? _____ Why or why not? _____

Receiver Roles
Which initial role was addressed? _____
Which subsequent role(s) was addressed? _____

Were roles properly handled? _____ Why or why not? _____

Impact and Design
Impact: Were devices properly used? _____
Why or why not? _____
Design: Was the right outcome sequence used? _____
Why or why not? _____
Execution
Was handling of purpose, receiver roles, impacts, and design
proper for situation? _____
Why or why not? _____

Devices used _____

Fig. 12.14/Listening—presentations.

Fig. 12.14 (continued)

Basic ideas

1 _____

.1 _____

.2 _____

.3* _____

2 _____

.1 _____

.2 _____

.3* _____

3* _____

.1 _____

.2 _____

.3* _____

Conclusion _____

_____

_____

* Extend as necessary.

Language/Voice/Physical Communication

Were there grammatical errors? _____

Were there mispronunciations? _____

Were words well chosen? _____

Was the speech easily heard? _____

Was the voice forceful? _____

Were words spoken distinctly? _____

Was posture easy and natural? _____

Were gestures and movement effective? _____

Was speaker poised and at ease? _____

Was eye contact satisfactory? _____

Presentation Aids

What aids were used? _____

Were aids properly used? _____ Why or why not? _____

General Evaluation

____ Superior; ____ Excellent; ____ Good; ____ Fair; ____ Poor

Listener name _____

LISTENING: PERSON-TO-PERSON

Person-to-Person Communication

Name —————

Specific subject(s) discussed —————

Purpose
What was it? —————
Was it proper? ————— Why or why not? —————

Receiver Roles
Which initial role was addressed? —————
Which subsequent role(s) was addressed? —————

Were roles properly handled? ————— Why or why not? —————

Impact and Design
Impact: Were devices properly used? —————
Why or why not? —————
Design: Was the right outcome sequence used? —————
Why or why not? —————
Execution
Was handling of purpose, receiver roles, impacts, and design
proper for situation? —————
Why or why not? —————

Discussion Outline

Devices used

Introduction —————
—————
—————
—————

Fig. 12.15 / Listening—person-to-person communication.

Fig. 12.15 (continued)

Basic ideas

1 _____

  .1 _____

  .2 _____

  .3* _____

2 _____

  .1 _____

  .2 _____

  .3* _____

3* _____

  .1 _____

  .2 _____

  .3* _____

Conclusion _____

_____

_____

* Extend as necessary.

Language/Voice/Physical Communication

Were there grammatical errors? _____

Were there mispronunciations? _____

Were words well chosen? _____

Was the manner conversational? _____ Direct? _____

Was the voice pleasant? _____ Easily heard? _____

Was spoken expression effective? _____

Was posture easy and natural? _____

Were gestures and movement appropriate? _____

Was speaker poised and at ease? _____

Were distracting mannerisms avoided? _____

Person-to-Person Discussion Principles

Were they properly followed? _____ Why or why not? _____

General Evaluation

____ Superior; ____ Excellent; ____ Good; ____ Fair; ____ Poor

Listener name _____

LISTENING: CONFERENCE

Conference

Purpose

What was it? ——————————————— Was it proper? ————— Why or why
not?

Receiver Roles

	By:	Leader	Member 1	Member 2	Member 3*
Which initial role was addressed?					
Which subsequent role(s) was addressed?					
Were roles properly handled?					
Why or why not?					

Impact and Design

Impact: Were devices properly used? ....
Why or why not? ....

Design: Was the right outcome sequence
used? ....
Why or why not? ....

Group ——————

Leader ——————

Member 1 ——————

Member 2 ——————

Member 3* ——————

Summary of Discussion

Devices
used

Introduction ——————
——————
——————

Fig. 12.16 / Listening—conference.

Fig. 12.16 (continued)

Basic ideas

1 _____

(1)_____

(2)_____

(3)*_____

2 _____

(1)_____

(2)_____

(3)*_____

3*_____

(1)_____

(2)_____

(3)*_____

Conclusions _____

_____

_____

* Extend as necessary

Execution

Was handling of purpose, receiver roles,
impacts, and design proper for situation?
Why or why not? ....

**Language/Voice/Physical
Communication**

Were there grammatical errors? ....
Were there mispronunciations? ....
Were words well chosen? ....
Was posture easy and natural? ....
Was voice easily heard? ....
Were gestures and movement appropriate?
Was speaker poised and at ease? ......

Conference Discussion Principles

Specify participant strengths and weaknesses in use of principles

Strengths
Weaknesses

General Evaluation

Rate each participant as appropriate:
Superior; Excellent; Good; Fair; Poor. ....
Listener name _____

315

EXERCISES

exercise 1 Define oral presentation and give two examples of its use.

exercise 2 Define person-to-person communication and give two examples of its use.

exercise 3 Define conference communication and give two examples of its use.

exercise 4 List and discuss the four qualities required for execution of effective oral presentations.

exercise 5 (a) Using the worksheets in Figures 12.3 and 12.4, size up and plan an oral presentation to your class on some topic related to communication in organizations. When presented, use the form "Listening: Presentations" (Figure 12.14) for feedback on effectiveness.
  (b) When completed forms are returned to you, write a report on your needs for improvement and what appear to be areas of needed improvement of your listeners.

exercise 6 Using the worksheets in Figures 12.7 and 12.8, size up and outline a person-to-person communication situation. Select an important activity related to any one of the purposes presented in Chapters 7 through 9 (e.g., offering: job application interview; complaining: hostile customer). When presented, use the form, "Listening: Person-to-Person" (Figure 12.15) for feedback on your and your listeners' effectiveness.

exercise 7 Using the worksheets in Figures 12.11 and 12.12, size up and outline a conference, taking either a leader or member role. Select an important activity related to any of the purposes presented in Chapters 7 through 9 (e.g., policy: formulation of a new one for recruitment of employees; procedure: how the new recruitment policy is to be implemented). When presented, use the form, "Listening: Conference" (Figure 12.16), for feedback on your and your listeners' effectiveness.

exercise 8 Discuss the PRIDE sequence in relation to effective listening.

exercise 9 Listen to an oral presentation (e.g., a class lecture, a public presentation, a television speech). Use Figure 12.14 for the critique. Then write a report analyzing important strengths and weaknesses, and how the latter could be improved.

exercise 10 Listen to a person-to-person dialogue or a conference communication. Use either Figure 12.15 or 12.16 (as appropriate) for the critique. Then write a report analyzing strengths and weaknesses, and how the latter could be improved.

Chapter 13

AUTOMATING WRITTEN COMMUNICATIONS

Oral Communication — Automating Communication — Using Right Resources

Automatic Typewriter — Data Processing — Printing — Reprography

Your Learning Objectives:

1. To know the nature of automation for written communications.
2. To know four important automation mechanisms applicable to organizational written communications.
3. To know the nature of automatic typewriters.
4. To know automatic typewriter applications to written communications.
5. To know the nature of data processing.
6. To know data processing applications to written communications.
7. To know the nature of printing.
8. To know printing applications to written communications.
9. To know the nature of reprography.
10. To know reprographic applications to written communications.

We now come to a very important resource: automating written communications. While certain oral communications can also be automated, it is such a complex and sophisticated subject that we shall exclude it from our discussion. Our focus in this chapter is on useful, practical mechanisms for automating the written communication media previously presented.

In examining potential for automation, we shall consider *only* the *final written product*—not all the preparatory steps (many of which could also be automated). Taking this view permits our looking at automation as related to media missions and media formats (discussed in Chapter 11). Moreover, we shall essentially focus on the *routine, mass distribution* communications—not the nonroutine, one-of-a-kind writing. For example, we shall not discuss nonroutine letters, but rather the routine types—prepared parts, complete, and mass distribution.

Automation Mechanisms and Final Written Product

What are the four essential automating mechanisms for processing final written output? They are: (1) automatic typewriter, (2) data processing, (3) printing, and (4) reprography. Bear in mind that we are talking about automation potential of the final written product using any of the four, whether the capability (machines and manpower) is inside or outside the firm. Even many large organizations use outside service bureaus for automatic typewriter and data processing output. And commercial concerns are commonly used for printing and certain types of reprography.

With these restrictions in mind, let us now consider primary uses of each of the four automation mechanisms for written media.

Automatic Typewriter

This equipment is essentially an electrically operated typewriter complex using a tape for "storage" of messages. Final products appear as would a "custom-typed" communication, thus enhancing its appeal to the reader. At the same time, this processing greatly reduces costs per unit. While many firms may use automatic typewriting for preparation of nonroutine correspondence, focus here is on its two basic uses for routine, mass distribution written products: *routine letters* and *supportive documents for proposals*.

Routine—prepared parts letters are readily adaptable to automatic typewriter processing. Certain paragraphs or sections can be stored and retrieved in any configuration desired. For example, inquiries can be answered by having prepared replies to anticipated questions. The letter is then "composed" by calling for, say, paragraphs 1, 7, 15, and 19. Generally the receiver's name and address are typed manually (either from a prepared list or from previously addressed envelopes).

Routine—complete and mass distribution letters are even more simple for automatic typewriter processing. The name and address (if used) are typed manually, then the machine takes over to complete the message. Thus, even better economies for these two types can be made in unit costs over the routine —prepared parts.

Supportive documents for proposals (often called "boiler plate") can be very economically done, while at the same time getting a finished product that looks custom made. Boiler plate supporting documents for proposals are really brochure media format in that they are standardized elaborating and backup information to make the proposal proper more persuasive. If done with an automatic typewriter, this supporting material can appear as an original and unique supplement to the body of the proposal. However, as you no doubt surmise, preparation of such boiler plate content must be done with utmost competence and care if it is to achieve its intended effect—that of originality and complete relevance to a given proposal. It means continuing scrutiny and necessary updating in order to keep boiler plate statements current and pertinent.

Data Processing

This includes a great range from the relatively simple billing or business machine to the most sophisticated, complex computer facility. We shall not get into a detailed study of data processing (another subject unto itself). Rather, we shall discuss its applications to two media: letters and reports.

Data processing can be efficiently and effectively used with certain routine letters and special mass distribution correspondence. The routine "letter" types to which data processing is most applicable are items such as invoices and statements. As you recall, these are actually routine "letters" in their primary media mission. A preprinted form is used for fill in of the needed information, which can be done very rapidly and accurately by the computer. Any routines such as these accounting operations constitute closed systems, any of which lend themselves to computerization. Where feasible and proper, data processing should be considered for similar routine letters.

Data processing of mass distribution letters is exemplified by letters of solicitation in which the type is exactly like that of the computer printout. The receiver's name, address, and salient internal personal allusions (e.g., Mr. Jones or Miss Thomas) are inserted at specific points in the body of the routine letter. Names and addresses (which may be already stored for other purposes) are used as appropriate. This use of computers is becoming more widespread, promising to revolutionize mass distribution letter production. For large batches, output is very economical, and some studies indicate that these letters get better responses than traditional finished products.

Data processing equipment is especially applicable to reports (the most common use in organizations). Both nonroutine and routine report outputs can be efficiently and effectively produced. Unfortunately, however, because some managers think of it as a kind of "Delphic oracle" and because it is "the thing to do," data inundation is the order of the day in many organizations.

To digress, let us point out the distinction between "data" and "information." Data are "bits" or discrete, symbolic units; "information" is shaped data—that is, bits put into meaningful form *for the receiver*. If the data-information distinction were more often clearly drawn, and if reports were then produced only in relation to real organizational and managerial needs—that is, made truly informative—there would be fewer, but far more significant report outputs from data processing centers.

Nonroutine reports—special requests—can be readily and efficiently produced by data processing. For example, if the comptroller wants to know the exact budget status of a department or for the entire organization at a given time, he can get a quick and accurate printout—sometimes immediately. Random access also permits the inquirer to retrieve specific information (e.g., sales to specific customer segments, costs of sales per unit, or costs of sales trends). Data processing of nonroutine reports is a great automation tool, providing that the tool is used with competence and prudence. However, if used as an end in itself or as some managerial "toy," it can lead to financial catastrophe or create untold organizational havoc.

Routine reports are those required periodically for specific information purposes. A monthly bank statement, a semiannual personnel inventory, a weekly inventory assessment are examples. In an academic context, you are no doubt familiar with class registration cards, printouts of class lists, and university admission counts, all products of data processing. Obviously data processing lends itself admirably to the output of routine report documents. Once more, however, as with the nonroutine—*information needs* must be served—not mere data output—if data processing automation is to be used for legitimate and constructive results in organizational reporting.

Printing

Our definition of printing is broad, including any letter press, offset, or mimeograph machine output ("mimeograph" includes all the spirit duplicators). Seen in this perspective, printing is one of the most common and useful automation mechanisms. It is applicable to a variety of written media: complete routine and mass distribution letters and memoranda; nonroutine and routine reports; proposals and supporting documents; routine agreements; and "universal" directives. Furthermore, printing also is applicable to three media formats not mentioned in preceding automation mechanisms: manuals, forms, and brochures.

Routine—complete letters and memoranda may be offset produced, after which names and addresses are filled in. A quality offset production, together with competent and careful typing can result in a document that appears custom written (except to the eye of a professional). For mass distribution letters any of press, offset, or mimeograph processes can do the job. Here you must select in terms of receiver expectations, the importance of the situation, the quantity needed, the time allowed, and costs—unit and total. In many cases, tradeoffs are required. For example, in sending out a large number of letters of solicitation, costs could be significantly lower if mimeographed, but sales returns may be sufficiently higher to justify the more costly offset printing.

Reports—both nonroutine and routine—must be viewed similarly to mass distribution letters and memoranda. Importance of the situation should be one of the most crucial bases for choice. Why? Because the appearance of the finished product communicates something of its importance in the mind of the receiver. The same report information produced by spirit duplicator may appear as just more "information pollution" to most readers, while, if quality produced by either offset or letter press, the impact may make all the difference between getting reader attention and response or having it thrown in the waste basket as "junk."

Proposals and supporting materials also can be produced by any of the three processes. In most cases, the importance of the situation and receiver expectations should dictate which method to use. If you are going after a possible $1,000,000 contract, and if you are bidding against stiff competition, you cannot afford a "penny-wise and pound-foolish" output. Even though significantly more costly, you may decide on an expensive three-color letter press product in order to serve situational importance and receiver expectations. On the other hand, a simple internal suggestion (proposal) to peers or subordinates may require the least expensive and most easily processed mimeograph output.

Sometimes the proposal proper and supporting materials are printed using different processes (e.g., the proposal may be mimeograph, the boiler plate letter press). This process difference may be acceptable in certain situations. But if the difference in output appearance is so great as to cause reader doubt or apprehension about the credibility of the proposal, the competence of originators, or the integrity of the organization, it is self-defeating. Printing production methods should be such that the total product—proposal and supporting materials—create a consistent and cogent appearance.

Routine agreements are preprinted "forms" for recurring situations (e.g., a publisher's contract with an author; purchase agreements), which are then filled in by typewriter or other appropriate mechanism. Once more, situational importance and receiver expectations should probably override monetary costs in determining which printing process to use.

"Universal" directives are those for distribution to all (or most) members of the firm. At first you may think that costs should be the primary factor to consider in production. More reflection may show this not to be true. A "junky" appearance of the directive communicates junkiness of content. Most enlightened organizational managers recognize that company directives must be made just as attractive as documents going outside the organization. It may cost more to produce an offset or letter press directive, but the job performance generated by the more attractive product can far outweigh the relatively trivial production cost difference. At the same time, too "slick" an output can possibly cause employee resentment because of a perceived waste of organizational resources. With directives, receiver expectations are probably the most important yardstick to determine the printing production process.

As stated before, printing is also the primary automation mechanism for producing manuals, forms, and brochures. Granted that these are media formats (rather than media missions), they are mass produced, organizationally oriented documents as final products. In selecting printing process—letter press, offset, or mimeograph—all the variables mentioned before (user expectations, importance, quantity, time, and costs) must be carefully scrutinized to determine the optimal means. Again, user expectations are more important than generally thought. However, realistically, monetary costs must be carefully considered in production, because dollar amounts are generally significant in these large-quantity (and sometimes voluminous) documents.

Reprography

This refers to the many types of *copier machines*, one of the most versatile and valuable automation mechanisms for written communications. Its universality of application, rapidity, ease of use, and availability make for wide employment. However, the last factor—availability—can be detrimental to an organization. Why? Because equipment can be *too available*, inviting overuse or misuse, with attendant excessive monetary and psychological costs. If overused, dollar costs to the firm can be increased tremendously; if misused (e.g., habitual copying and distributing of any items—even inconsequential ones), psychological costs can be heightened by creating undue receiver apathy, sophistication, or opposition. This means that proper management and surveillance of reprographic machine use is a must if costs—monetary and psychological—are to be kept under control.

As stated, reprographic automation can be used with any written media. However, some of the more appropriate applications follow:

Nonroutine letters: can be used in lieu of carbon copies.

Mass distribution letters: original can be copied; important variables to be considered are quality of product and costs.

Memoranda: can be used with restricted or limited distribution (e.g., rather than printing or making ten carbon copies).

Reports (nonroutine and routine): variables are the same as for mass distribution letters and memoranda.

Proposals (body and boiler plate): receiver expectations and importance are

	MEDIA MISSION									
	Letters and Memoranda		Reports		Proposals		Agreements		Directives	
MECHANISM	Routine	Mass Distr.	Non-routine	Routine	Proper	Supp. Document	Non-routine	Routine	Re-stricted	Uni-versal
Automatic typewriter	x	x				x				
Printing	x	x	x	x	x	x		x		x
Reprography		x	x	x	x	x	x	x	x	x
Data processing	x	x	x	x						

→

PRIMARY MEDIA FORMATS
Manuals
Forms
Brochures

Fig. 13.1 / Media and automated mechanisms.

primary, but costs must also be considered. Monetary costs can be especially deceptive in proposals. The major cost of a lengthy document is in set up (or composition). But this may be outweighed by the volume (or number) in aggregate costs. For example, five copies of a 100-page proposal may cost .05 per page if reproduced on a reprographic machine. In other words, 100 copies of a five-page proposal would cost $25.00. For offset printing, a nominal cost may be $2.50 per page (minimum charge for 100 copies—or less—of one page). This results in a total cost of $250.00 (100 × $2.50). In other words, in this many-page, small-volume instance, the proposal can be reproduced on a copier for one-tenth the dollar costs of offset ($25.00 vs. $250.00). In contrast, if 100 copies of the 100-page proposal are needed, the costs would be as follows: reprography—$500 (100 × 100 × .05); offset—$250 (100 × $2.50). This points out the importance of calculating your costs in each case.

Of course, dollar costs must be weighed against rapidity of production— the printing production probably taking a longer time—and the quality of output against situational importance and receiver expectations.

Agreements (nonroutine and routine): can be used for copies of original to customer and other involved units and people.

Directives: can be used for copies to "outsiders"; also useful in production of certain restricted types (e.g., confidential matters such as impending price changes to meet competition).

Summary: Automating Written Communications

Figure 13.1 presents in tabular form highlights of automation mechanism applications to primary media missions and to the three media formats discussed.

EXERCISES

exercise 1 Discuss the basic media applications for automatic typewriters.

exercise 2 Discuss the basic media applications for data processing equipment.

exercise 3 Discuss the basic media applications of printing.

exercise 4 Discuss the basic media applications of reprography.

exercise 5 Gather one example of an effective and one example of an ineffective communication prepared by automatic typewriter. Write a report assessing strengths and weaknesses of each document, together with suggestions for improvement.

exercise 6 Gather one example of an effective and one example of an ineffective communication prepared by data processing equipment. Write a report assessing strengths and weaknesses of each document, together with suggestions for improvement.

exercise 7 Gather one example of an effective and one example of an ineffective communication prepared by printing equipment. Write a report assessing strengths and weaknesses of each document, together with suggestions for improvement.

exercise 8 Gather one example of an effective and one example of an ineffective communication prepared by reprographic equipment. Write a report assessing strengths and weaknesses of each document, together with suggestions for improvement.

exercise 9 Visit an organization to learn of its use of any of the four automation mechanisms. Collect representative examples of media used in the organization. Write a report on the effectiveness of use and possible improvements in automation applications. (For this exercise, you may wish to review the interview suggestions presented in Chapter 1.)

exercise 10 Assess the use of one of the automation mechanisms used by your college or university (for either the entire institution or for some unit). Write a report on the effectiveness of use and possible better applications. Attach examples of media products of the automation mechanism evaluated.

Chapter 14

USING THE RIGHT
COMMUNICATIONS RESOURCES

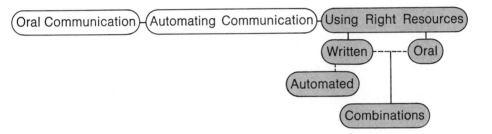

Your Learning Objectives:

1. To recognize the importance of choosing the right communication resource (or combinations) to achieve an intended objective.
2. To know the essential qualities of writing.
3. To know potential qualities of writing for managerial and organizational uses.
4. To know when to use written communications.
5. To know the essential qualities of speaking.
6. To know potential qualities of speaking for managerial and organizational uses.
7. To know when to use oral communications.
8. To know when to use combinations of oral and written communications.
9. To know guidelines for determining feasibility of automating organizational communications.
10. To get an integrated perspective for looking at and choosing from the organization's total communications resources.

We have now covered three major organizational communication resource areas: written, oral, and automated. And while the major emphasis of the book has been on organizational written communications, we have also highlighted oral and automated types, because these two play important and unique roles in modern organizations.

In order to understand what each is and how it functions, we have treated the three areas independently. But how do you make a choice among the three resource types? Which one (or ones) is most efficient and effective to do the job? In this chapter our purpose is to give general guidelines for use in choosing whether to use written, oral, or automated communications (or combinations) to do the best job.

Our discussion follows this format: (1) when to use written communications; (2) when to use oral communications; (3) when to use combinations of oral and written communications; and (4) when to use automated communications.

When to Use Written Communications

Essential and Potential Qualities of Writing

In order to know better when to use written communication, let us first look at its *essential* qualities. Viewed generally, writing is "frozen," recorded symbolization of ideas. Stated another way, writing is static and permanent communication.

More specifically, writing has the following *potential* qualities for managerial and organizational uses: (1) binding time and extending space; (2) storage and retrieval; (3) objectivity; (4) idea reliability and validity; (5) impersonality.

Binding Time and Extending Space/Writing permits the communicator to be vicariously represented by symbols on the printed page, which allows his ideas to be conveyed across temporal and spatial boundaries without his physical presence. Writing is a very important potential for idea interchange in other than face-to-face situations.

Storage and Retrieval/Since it is recorded, writing permits storage and retrieval for immediate and for future decision making. Whether automated or manual, this potential for reserving of and referral to recorded symbols makes writing vital for review of the past and present, as well as for prediction of future events.

Objectivity/Writing is "out there"—outside the human cranium (externalized). As such it has potential for objectivity beyond that of "in the head" (internalized) oral communication. And while it can be "wrong" (or misrepresent), because the same symbols are open to scrutiny by more than one person, there is greater likelihood that writing can be made more exact, more rigorous, and more reality-centered than the spoken mode.

Idea Reliability and Validity/Growing out of its objectivity, written communication permits receivers to react to and interpret the same symbols, producing two important consequences: (1) since the writer knows he is committing himself on paper, he is more likely to exercise greater thought and care in his idea output. Thus, idea reliability and validity can be enhanced; also (2) the receivers of the written message can check the writer's output for reliability and validity, feeding back to the writer (and interchanging with other receivers) their reactions and responses. This interplay and cross-checking can result in a much more reliable and valid idea product than unilateral communication.

Impersonality

While it can be "personalized," writing, as contrasted to oral communication, is more impersonal and dispassionate. Its "frozen," recorded, and external attributes make for possible detachment and separateness. Whereas a person's speaking is difficult to delineate from himself, his writing can be examined as something apart.

When to Use Writing

Its essential general and specific potential qualities give rise to some very important managerial and organizational uses.

1. When You Need to Extend Yourself in Time and Space/If you need to convey ideas bridging time and distance, written communications offer one of your most useful vehicles (e.g., directives to company branches throughout the world; "to the file" communications for a record of certain transactions).

2. When you Need Idea Storage and Retrieval/If you or your organization need records of transactions and ready access to these records, a communications storage and retrieval system (manual or automated) is required. And while most firms may have inadequate systems (either overdone or underdone), no viable organization can survive without some storage and retrieval mechanism for its written communications.

3. When Objectivity and Authentication Are Needed/Objectivity is required for considering crucial organizational issues or problems so that right managerial decisions can be made; objectivity and authentication are required in certain company documents, especially the legally oriented: proposals, agreements, and directives. Reports and other status communications also frequently require written objectivity and authentication. Organizational forms are essentially designed to achieve optimal objectivity (standardization) and convenient authentication (both department and person). And certainly most letters and memoranda require authentication and for-the-record objectivity.

4. When Idea Verification Is Needed/As you have seen, writing is better than oral communication for *idea focus*. Its external, time-binding, and objective qualities permit scrutiny and penetrating thought not possible in most oral communication modes. When verification of ideas is vital, writing is the best ultimate communication vehicle (even if supplemented by one or more of the important oral media).

5. When the Nonpersonal Is Paramount/When rational needs are preeminent (e.g., making vital managerial decisions, solving significant organizational problems, researching troublesome internal or external issues), writing should probably be the emphatic communication means. Its potential for objectivity, detachment, precision, and openness to plural scrutiny build in its advantages for removing personal biases and for focusing on the real-world situation you confront. This is why perceptive managers want their subordinates to write up those proposed "hot ideas." In the dispassionate and rigorous exercise of putting the utopian suggestion on paper, it can "cool" the writer's passions, and, once written, it allows the manager to view the idea in its cold reality so that the proposal can be more easily seen for its true worth.

6. When Written Communication Is More Acceptable/Some persons (especially in professional and scientific circles) insist on writing as the only acceptable way to communicate ideas for worthy consideration. And in modern organizations, more and more managers are of this rational school of thought, building in a bias in favor of written communication. Once more, we are not saying that such people communicate only through writing. They, too, use the whole spectrum of oral and automated media, but for consideration of vital ideas writing is the expected mode.

7. When Written Supplements Are Needed/In many instances, oral or automated communications need to be complemented by written documents. For example a conference is frequently a combination of oral and written media: an agenda (written) is prepared and distributed; the conference discussion (oral) is held, after which a summary or minutes (written) is produced and distributed. Or a computer printout of monthly sales (automated) is distributed to key managers; it is accompanied by an explanatory memorandum (written) from the marketing manager. Or, a presentation (oral) may be made to highlight a proposal, accompanied by a voluminous written supporting document that spells out items in full detail. Countless other combinations could be cited.

Summary: When to Use Written Communications

Figure 14.1 summarizes conditions calling for written communications.

1. For extension in time/space
2. For idea storage/retrieval
3. For objectivity/authentication
4. For idea verification
5. For nonpersonal emphasis
6. For situations where writing more acceptable
7. For supplementing oral/automated types

Fig. 14.1 / Summary—when to use written communications.

When to Use Oral Communications

Essential and Potential Qualities of Speaking

As contrasted to the basic nature of writing, spoken communication is essentially more fluid and ephemeral, that is, moving and momentary. While oral communications can be recorded (e.g., tape—audio—or visual), most organizational speaking is interactive and immediate, requiring instant message intelligibility. In writing the reader can control the situation by gaining understanding at his own rate and by his own method (even rereading as needed). In speaking, however, the speaker (or speakers) control the listener in that the receiver must comprehend ideas simultaneous with utterance and accumulate all into a total message. Of course, dialogue is possible in oral communications (e.g., question-answer session after a presentation; person-to-person interaction; conference), something not part of most written communication situations. This dialogic quality is a great potential strength in that understanding can be checked and reinforced through both verbal and physical symbolic interchange.

Specifically, speaking has the following potential qualities for managerial and organizational activities: (1) handling sensitive or confidential matters, (2) transmitting personalism, (3) creating open atmosphere, (4) handling non-rigorous information, (5) handling rapid communication, (6) assuring maximum understanding, and (7) meeting social needs.

Handling Sensitive or Confidential Matters/Because it is "human" and unrecorded, speaking is capable of handling "ticklish" or confidential communications. In spoken communications your chances for getting feedback (visual, aural, verbal) are enhanced, thus permitting proper adaptation in sensitive cases; and its transitory nature makes speaking much more acceptable and easy for confidential situations.

Transmitting Personalism/Speech is the communication mode for the feelings, for conveying the qualities of warmth and spontaneity. Writing is more often idea-centered. Oral communication is more commonly addressed to both feelings and ideas.

Creating an Open Atmosphere/Spoken communication permits openness through candor and exploration. It permits free interchange to handle the unforeseen.

Handling Nonrigorous Information/By nature less exact and more momentary than the written mode, oral communication is generally adapted to conveying and receiving nonrigorous information (which constitutes most information sending and receiving situations in modern organizations).

Handling Rapid Communications/Generally spoken communication is the primary mode when time is short, when important deadlines must be met, when crucial information is needed immediately.

Assuring Maximum Understanding/When crucial matters require that all parties have full understanding, oral communication is often the best way to be sure that such understanding takes place. In addition to using oral means to get attention and sustain interest, checks and feedback are possible in oral communication to get assurance of comprehension.

Meeting Social Needs/Because of its potential for confidentiality, personalism, openness, fluidity, rapidity and general "human" orientation, oral communication satisfies important social needs such as collective cohesion and a sense of belonging.

When to Communicate Orally

Its basic and specific attributes make oral communication applicable to significant situations for managers and organizations.

1. When Sensitive or Confidential Matters Need Discussion/People are less likely to be defensive and more likely to be receptive in sensitive cases (e.g., a reprimand or rejection) when proper oral communication is used (rather than written). Moreover, it may be imprudent to record "privileged information."

2. When Ideas Need to Be Candidly and Forthrightly Aired/Properly handled, oral communication permits delving, bouncing ideas back and forth, soliciting feelings and reactions—all of which may be necessary to get ideas and attitudes out into the open (e.g., determining how people really feel about a procedural change—by "listening between the lines," as well as to what is said).

3. When Strengthening Positive Feelings Is Needed/Its potential for "humaneness" makes speaking powerful in reinforcing preexisting feelings and attitudes. Properly handled, oral communication is a manager's most important tool in renewing and deepening member dedication to job and organizational goals. Furthermore, its potential for getting and holding attention helps assure success.

4. When Information Needs to Be Transferred Quickly/When new decisions, emergencies, or unanticipated situations require rapid dissemination, oral communication can be used to "get the word" to intended receivers. A long distance telephone call will give a key manager new vital information immediately; a letter may take several days. Of course, certain electronic written communications (e.g., cablegram, telegram) may serve just as well as spoken communication in some instances (e.g., a night letter that will be transmitted at the start of the next working day).

5. When Vital Issues Demand Full Understanding/While writing is more exact and rigorous, it does not necessarily assure adequate receiver understanding. Why? Because there is no face-to-face confrontation that permits both sender and receiver to know whether messages are comprehended as they ought to be. In certain cases (e.g., assuring that all specifications of a new product are clearly understood by key production people), more than mere verbal exposition is needed: questions and answers for clarification; demonstration; examples and the like help to assure that all parties know—and know that they know.

6. When Personal Influence Is Needed/Writing has power for official authentication; however, speaking is more likely to communicate greater personal influence. This, of course, assumes that the communicator has prior positive influence or respect (or can adroitly use oral communication to gain it).

7. When Group Needs Must Be Met/Oral communication is generally the proper mode for creating improved group cohesion and belonging. While writing, too, can help (e.g., a letter of commendation for a department's outstanding work), well-aimed and well-executed speaking is even more effective in most situations of this sort.

Sometimes, of course, both oral and written communications can be combined for predictably better results (e.g., a "pep talk" by the production manager on the merits of a new procedure for employees, accompanied by written handouts describing the new operation).

Summary: When to Use Oral Communications

Figure 14.2 summarizes circumstances appropriate to managerial and organizational uses of oral communication.

1. For sensitive/confidential matters
2. For candid discussion
3. For strengthening positive feelings
4. For quick information transfer
5. For assurance of full understanding
6. For exercising personal influence
7. For meeting group needs

Fig. 14.2 / Summary—when to use oral communications.

When to Use Combinations
of Oral and Written Communication

You have seen that in certain instances writing and speaking complement one another. Let us now examine typical situations where you may profit from using the two together.

1. When "Carry Home" Needs Exist/For example, if you want your receivers to take away some specific ideas from your oral presentation (for further thought or as a reminder of requested action), combining your spoken message with a written handout may be a very effective way to accomplish your intended purpose. Or you may hand out a detailed document on a five-year capital investment plan, after which you give oral highlights as to how you want your receivers to use the written material. These are just two examples of the many, many other "carry home" possibilities.

2. When Exploration Is Needed/When you do not know final answers (perhaps not even the problem or problems), and when you are seeking help in exploring an "open" situation, oral-written combinations can be very helpful. For example, you could telephone (or write a memo) to your staff stating symptoms or evidence of some unidentified basic problem. You could then ask each person to write up his analysis and bring it to the next staff conference. At the conference, the idea write-ups are then pooled, discussed, and interpreted by participants; the discussion is followed by writing a final document reflecting the consensus of the staff. The final written communication may result in several specific actions (including the generation of other communications, both oral and written). This is merely one example of the multitude of possibilities in using oral-written combinations for exploratory organizational situations.

3. When Involvement Is Needed/This situation is related to 2, but the primary need is to get organizational or audience members to participate actively. You may desire participation for psychological reasons (e.g., to build member esteem or to get more member commitment) or for the pragmatic purpose of exploiting all possible idea resources. Examples of oral-written combinations to get involvement include: (1) use of written case analyses of situations for conference discussion; (2) an oral presentation highlighting the organization's financial plight, followed by a comprehensive written financial report handout, after which listener comments and suggestions are solicited for possible solutions to the troubles communicated; (3) circulation of representative letters of complaint, after which a conference is held to identify clearly the problems represented, as well as possible ways to overcome them.

Again, the plethora of possibilities beyond these three examples of using oral-written combinations to meet involvement needs is obvious.

4. When Communicating Abstract or "Unimportant" Ideas/Abstract ideas are general or conceptual (to listeners or readers); unimportant ideas are those seen by receivers as "nonrelevant" or remote to their concerns and interests. If either (or both) condition exists, combinations of oral and written communications may help to achieve the needed impact (get attention and sustain interest) to produce proper receiver belief or response.

5. When Optimal Understanding Is Needed/Optimal understanding refers to gaining the highest receiver comprehension commensurate with costs. As an example, it is ideal to get 100% understanding by all employees of a new directive, but costs to get this level may be prohibitive. Therefore you may decide on a 75% level of understanding as an acceptable tradeoff between costs and understanding. Frequently a combination of oral and written communications (often a complex, planned total organizational communications program) is necessary for optimization.

6. When Both Understanding and Right Reaction Are Needed/This goes beyond 5 in that you want both adequate receiver comprehension and belief/response. As an example, you want your receivers to understand the new directive at 75% comprehension and you want at least 75% conformance to it. Writing, as the vehicle of clarity, can be directed to getting the 75% understanding; speaking, as the vehicle of feelings and beliefs, can be used in gaining the desired conformance.

7. When Follow-up Is Needed/As an example, after an oral presentation you may want to know whether plans or actions are actually carried out. To get feedback you may ask for special written progress reports. Or a memorandum directive may be distributed, after which you hold person-to-person or conference discussions to assure right understanding and conformance. You can see that oral-written combinations can play vital roles in follow-up.

Summary: When to Use Oral-Written Combinations

Figure 14.3 summarizes the use of oral-written combinations.

1. When "carry home" needs exist
2. When exploration is needed
3. When involvement is needed
4. When communicating abstract/"unimportant" ideas
5. When optimal understanding is needed
6. When both understanding and reaction are needed
7. When follow-up is needed

Fig. 14.3 / Summary—when to use oral-written combinations.

When to Use Automated Written Communications

Remember that as we use the term, "automated written communications" includes the use of automatic typewriters, data processing equipment, printing, and reprography.

Automated communications are generally feasible when the following conditions obtain: exact controllable routines exist; controllable standardization is possible; mass processing and distribution are possible; economics can be optimized; data are available and accessible; resources are available; users are competent and receptive. Let us discuss each of these contingencies.

1. Exact Controllable Routines Exist/Automation of communications is possible when operations can be rigorously specified and controlled. For example, let us consider the company payroll accounting system. A computer can calculate salaries rapidly and accurately and print checks for company employees. Properly programmed and updated, computerized payroll systems for even medium-sized firms are much more efficient and effective than the manual.

2. Controllable Standardization Is Possible/Here controllable routines may not exist (or exist only in part). But if through combinations, revisions, or new procedures, a standardized operation (or set of operations) can be constructed to handle actual or anticipated routines, automated communication may be appropriate. Remember that in such cases you are *predicting* that things will fall together properly to give you a workable automated system for handling the newly born routine or routines. Rarely will the prediction be completely right on the first try (or several early tries) at automation. Be prepared for "debugging"—even discarding—what you may think is a "perfect" mechanized system.

3. Mass Processing and Distribution Are Needed/"Mass" is of course relative; it may mean 1000 direct mail letters using automatic typewriter production for one firm; it may mean reprographic production of 25 personnel inventory reports for another company. The basic questions to be asked are, "Do we have enough important documents to justify the resource allocation (money, men, machines) necessary for automation?" And, "Will we save enough and/or get sufficient beneficial returns (monetary, job, psychological) to justify automated processing?"

4. Economics Can Be Optimized/While of course closely related to number 3, this feasibility guideline refers to more systematic, long-range planning for automated communications. Whereas number 3 primarily embraces possible automating in terms of immediate or special needs, economic optimization means to systematically study ways to mechanize manual operations or to improve automation of already mechanized communications. Planning generally encompasses a specified time frame (e.g., six months, a year, two years, five years). Organizations frequently use systems analysts (internal or external) to study and recommend ways and means of implementing plans.

5. Data Are Available and Reliable/This guideline means that a source (or sources) of input data exists (or could feasibly be brought into being) and that such inputs are predictably sufficiently accurate for the purpose intended. No automated communications system will be any better than input data availability and reliability.

6. Resources Are Available/Obviously this refers to adequacy of money, man-power, and machinery to support and implement plans for automated communications. Incidentally, many, many organizations have suffered grievously from not planning for and getting adequate resources before launching ambitious mechanized communications programs. (Some indeed have gone bankrupt.) An intelligent approach generally means to start modestly on the most obvious and important needs, then, using a well-formulated plan, to develop stage by stage the budget, facilities, people, and machines to automate appropriate company communications.

7. Users Are Competent and Receptive/This last (and perhaps most important) index is too often ignored or merely given lip service, either of which invites failure in an automated communications system. If, for example, company computer specialists have designed the most sophisticated system and have acquired the most up-to-date elaborate machines, but have not consulted with the users of the automated communications output to determine problems (as these consumers view them), odds are high that another utopian computer system is doomed. Furthermore, unless computer specialists deliberately help users to achieve competence in interpreting and processing automated communications, nothing but a waste of money and increase of user hostility can result. Users can sabotage the most marvelous mechanized communications systems in more ways than the typical computer specialist would ever dream. Even if all six preceding indices are met, but this one is not, extreme caution is in order. Before wasting resources and creating organizational havoc, it would be wise to know that worthy, workable plans exist or that right actions are being taken to assure user competence and acceptance of any projected automated communications system in the company.

Summary: When to Use Automated Communications

Figure 14.4 summarizes guides that you can use to judge feasibility for automating organizational communications.

---

1. When exact controllable routines exist
2. When controllable standardization is possible
3. When mass processing and distribution are desired
4. When economic optimization is possible
5. When data are available and reliable
6. When resources are available
7. When users are competent and receptive

Fig. 14.4 / When to use automated communications.

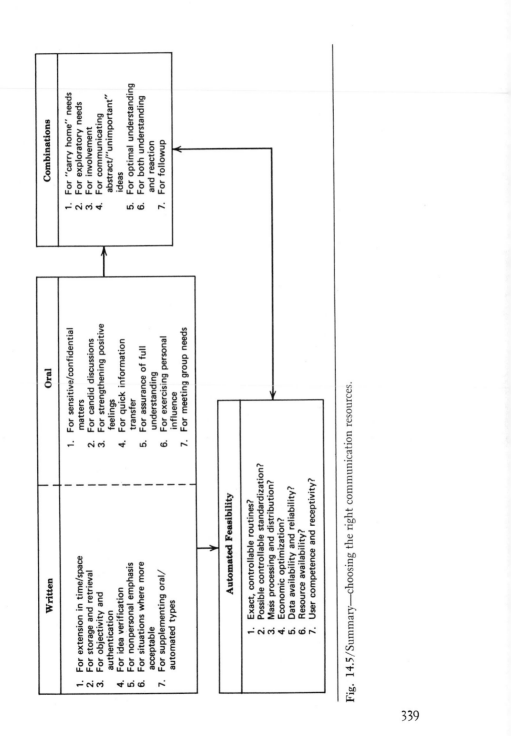

Written

1. For extension in time/space
2. For storage and retrieval
3. For objectivity and authentication
4. For idea verification
5. For nonpersonal emphasis
6. For situations where more acceptable
7. For supplementing oral/automated types

Oral

1. For sensitive/confidential matters
2. For candid discussions
3. For strengthening positive feelings
4. For quick information transfer
5. For assurance of full understanding
6. For exercising personal influence
7. For meeting group needs

Combinations

1. For "carry home" needs
2. For exploratory needs
3. For involvement
4. For communicating abstract/"unimportant" ideas
5. For optimal understanding
6. For both understanding and reaction
7. For followup

Automated Feasibility

1. Exact, controllable routines?
2. Possible controllable standardization?
3. Mass processing and distribution?
4. Economic optimization?
5. Data availability and reliability?
6. Resource availability?
7. User competence and receptivity?

Fig. 14.5/Summary—choosing the right communication resources.

Summary: Using the Right Communications Resources

Figure 14.5 summarizes our discussion schematically by listing general checkpoints for choice of the right communication resources (or combination) for best results.

EXERCISES

exercise 1 Discuss the five essential qualities of writing.

exercise 2 Give the seven important managerial and organizational uses of writing.

exercise 3 Discuss the seven important managerial and organizational uses of oral communication.

exercise 4 Discuss the seven important combinations of oral and written communication for organizational and managerial users.

exercise 5 Discuss the seven criteria for determining feasibility for automating communications.

exercise 6 Visit an organization to learn of its uses of written, oral, automated, and combinations of communications. Make notes and gather examples of applications.
   (a) Write a report on the efficiency and effectiveness in the uses of the organization's communications.
   (b) Give an oral presentation reporting on one of the above organizational uses (written, oral, automated, combinations). *Note:* Use appropriate supporting materials: for *written and automated*—display selected examples of effective and ineffective communications. For *oral*—play an audio recording (e.g., tape or cassette) of a person-to-person dialogue, conference, or oral presentation. For *combinations* (e.g., oral/written; oral/automated)—present examples of both.

Part IV

Reference Materials: Effective Language in Organizations

Rationale

This section is included for those who need review of fundamental language principles and mechanics. All of us at times may forget some of the simple language elements that we have learned (perhaps better stated, to which we have been exposed). Thus, this part is for: (1) diagnosis/improvement and (2) use as a reference section.

For diagnosis and improvement, by doing the exercises in each dimension, you can know where you have certain patterns of language weakness. Or you may already suspect deficiencies in certain areas (e.g., from past experience; from instructor criticisms of term papers). In either instance, you may use pertinent principles and exercises for strengthening your language proficiency where needed.

For reference purposes, the section can be a ready source to handle some of the more common and thorny language problems you confront in everyday organizational writing.

General Coverage

We have included only those elements that we have found to be the most frequent causes of writing troubles for people who work in administered organizations. By no means have we attempted to cover the whole of writing; rather we have focused on specific parts that seem to make the greatest difference between language usage failure or success.

Therefore, should you find that you need to overcome writing deficiencies not covered here, use additional sources for help: good books on writing; basic writing courses; counsel and advice from your instructor (or, if working, your supervisor or peers). The bibliography at the end of Part V gives selected books for guidance.

Specific Coverage

Part IV includes three chapters: Chapter 15, "Clarity"; Chapter 16, "Correctness"; and Chapter 17, "Persuasiveness." Beyond the dimensions presented in the previous fourteen chapters, we set forth those important elements of clarity, correctness, and persuasiveness, which seem to help most organizational members and college students in improving their writing.

Our approach is a combination of succinct explanation or exposition of each element, followed by practice exercises for skill improvement. Scoring keys are at the ends of Chapters 15 and 16.

Chapter 15

CLARITY

Clarity refers to *understandability* (or clearness) *of ideas to the receiver* of the communication. Whether or not the thoughts are clear to you, the sender, is of secondary importance. Stated another way, your basic question to test the clarity of your written communication is, "Does the writing convey to the reader what I intend—nothing more, nothing less?"

We have found that three factors commonly affect clarity in most organizational written communications: (1) precision, (2) wording, and (3) conciseness.

Precision

As used here, precision refers to *exactness*. Stated negatively, it is reasonable avoidance of ambiguity and vagueness. To be sure, some thoughts can properly be expressed generally, but the writer who wishes to achieve clarity puts his ideas as precisely as needed to get his intended message to the reader.

In examining an idea for precision, remember an important point: as with clarity in general, precision is relative to the reader. Furthermore, different degrees of precision are needed, depending on the circumstance. Thus, proper precision is a *judgment* as to whether what is written does convey an idea with sufficient exactitude. Normally, the more specific the wording (e.g., number, time, place, method), the more precise the idea. The following exercises are designed to help you develop such judgment.

EXERCISES: Precision

In the following sentences judge whether the italicized word or phrase is sufficiently precise. If so, check "sufficiently precise" as the correct answer. If not, check which of the other two choices is more precise. (Answers are given at the end of this chapter.)

      1   **2**

Please *contact* your office *soon.*

1 ☐ sufficiently precise   2 ☐ sufficiently precise
   ☐ telephone   ☐ this week
   ☐ communicate with   ☐ before noon tomorrow

      3   **4**

The boss was *undoubtedly* enthusiastic about your *recent* proposal.

3 ☐ sufficiently precise   4 ☐ sufficiently precise
   ☐ fairly   ☐ last
   ☐ somewhat   ☐ February 14th Star-X

      5   **6**   **7**

Include a *couple of* advertisements, *several* alternatives, and *not too many* examples in your proposal.

5 ☐ sufficiently precise 6 ☐ sufficiently precise 7 ☐ sufficiently precise
   ☐ two   ☐ a couple of   ☐ no more than four
   ☐ few   ☐ three   ☐ limited

      8   **9**

Star-X will *evaluate* your proposal *as time permits.*

8 ☐ sufficiently precise   9 ☐ sufficiently precise
   ☐ consider   ☐ within the next month
   ☐ examine   ☐ February 15 or 16

      10

The education officer and *concerned* division chief will select trainees for the programs.

10 ☐ sufficiently precise
    ☐ appropriate
    ☐ responsible

      11

I have referred your memo to *the one* in the Personnel Office who handles such recommendations.

11 ☐ sufficiently precise
    ☐ Don
    ☐ Donald Thompson

                    12   **13**
Your *correspondence* of *February 15* was helpful.

12 ☐ sufficiently precise   13 ☐ sufficiently precise
    ☐ memorandum   ☐ Tuesday
    ☐ communication   ☐ last week

                         14   **15**
We will meet *at the usual place just before lunch*.

14 ☐ sufficiently precise   15 ☐ sufficiently precise
    ☐ downstairs   ☐ about noon
    ☐ at the cafeteria entrance   ☐ at 11:45 a.m.

                                           16
Terminating employees are to follow *revised company regulations*.

16 ☐ sufficiently precise
    ☐ regulations issued earlier this year
    ☐ regulations dated January 5, 19___

                                     17
Mail should be routed *according to company policy*.

17 ☐ sufficiently precise
    ☐ according to Procedure Manual, Section 5.12
    ☐ as has been the policy for many years

    18   **19**   **20**
July 23rd, Mr. Miller will *fly* to Dallas, Texas, on American Airlines, *Flight 211*.

18 ☐ sufficiently precise   19 ☐ sufficiently precise   20 ☐ sufficiently precise
    ☐ Tuesday   ☐ go   ☐ at 10:25
    ☐ Next week   ☐ travel   ☐ in the morning

Wording

This refers to *proper use of common symbols*. We are concerned here with frequent word confusions in organizational written communications, whether caused by misspelling, word misuse, or word confusion because of similar sound.

Following is an alphabetical list of the most frequent confusions of commonly used words. This list is followed by fifty practice sentences to test your word usage and to help you learn to use correctly those you may confuse. First, review the list, concentrating on those words you may sometimes misuse or about which you feel in doubt, then complete the exercise sentences. Check your answers against the scoring key.

1. **accept**: taken when offered
   except: leave out
2. **accelerate**: speed
   exhilarate: enliven
3. **accent**: emphasis
   ascent: climb
   assent: agree
4. **access**: availability
   excess: too much
5. **adapt**: adjust
   adept: skillful
   adopt: take as one's own
6. **addition**: act of adding
   edition: printing of a book
7. **adverse**: unfavorable
   averse: disinclined
8. **advice**: counsel given
   advise: give counsel
9. **affect**: influence
   effect: outcome or result
10. **aisle**: a narrow passage
    isle: an island
11. **alleviate**: temporary easing of a basic misery
    relieve: reduction of misery
12. **all ready**: wholly ready
    already: prior to a specific time
13. **all right**: all correct
    alright: *incorrect*
14. **all together**: in a group
    altogether: entirely
15. **all ways**: all methods
    always: forever
16. **allay**: lessen
    alley: narrow lane
    ally: friend
17. **altar**: center of worship
    alter: change

18. **allusion**: indirect reference
    illusion: false impression
19. **among**: applies to more than two things
    between: applies to two things
20. **amount**: lump sum
    number: countable objects
21. **angel**: heavenly being
    angle: geometric figure
22. **annual**: yearly
    annul: cancel
23. **assistance**: act of assisting
    assistants: plural of assistant
24. **appraise**: set a value
    apprise: inform
25. **bail**: security for a prisoner's release
    bale: a large bundle
26. **bare**: naked, to uncover
    bear: carry, endure
27. **baring**: making bare
    barring: obstructing
    bearing: carrying
28. **beside**: near, close to
    besides: in addition to
29. **born**: brought into being
    borne: carried
30. **both**: two considered jointly
    each: one of two or more considered separately
31. **breath**: intake of air
    breathe: to inhale/exhale
32. **cannon**: large gun
    canon: law, code
33. **canvas**: cloth
    canvass: solicit
34. **capital**: sum invested; chief city
    capitol: statehouse building

35. **censure:** condemn
    criticize: judge (favorably or un-favorably)
36. **cession:** giving up
    session: gathering, meeting
37. **character:** a person's real moral nature
    reputation: the character imputed to a person
38. **climactic:** pertains to climax
    climatic: pertains to climate
39. **choose:** select
    chose: have selected
40. **cite:** quote
    sight: view
    site: place for specific use
41. **coarse:** rough
    course: prescribed plan
42. **common:** shared by two or more individuals or things
    mutual: interchanged; reciprocal
43. **complement:** complete a deficiency
    compliment: praise
44. **conscience:** inner moral sense
    conscious: aware
45. **corespondent:** joint respondent in a divorce suit
    correspondents: those who write communications
    correspondence: communication in writing
46. **council:** an assembly; advisory group
    counsel: to advise; an advisor
47. **currant:** a dried berry
    current: flow; of the hour
48. **dairy:** pertains to milk products
    diary: autobiography, journal
49. **desert:** barren country
    dessert: food

50. **deference:** respect
    difference: unlikeness
51. **decent:** respectable
    descent: downward slope or movement
    dissent: disagreement
52. **device:** scheme (noun); appliance
    devise: scheme (verb)
53. **differ from:** persons, things, and differ from one another
    differ with: persons differ in opinion with one another
54. **disinterested:** impartial
    uninterested: without interest
55. **dual:** expressing equivalent of 2
    duel: combat between two persons
56. **emigrate:** move out
    immigrate: come in
57. **eminent:** important
    imminent: about to happen
58. **erred:** made a mistake
    errored: *incorrect*
59. **expand:** spread out
    expend: use up
60. **explicit:** expressed
    implicit: not expressed
61. **faint:** pass out
    feint: a pretense
62. **fair:** light color; reasonable; carnival
    fare: set price for journey
63. **feat:** well done
    feet: plural of foot
64. **fewer:** smaller number
    less: smaller amount
65. **formally:** according to set rules
    formerly: in past time
66. **forth:** forward
    fourth: follows third

67. **foul:** offensive
    fowl: poultry
68. **granite:** rock
    granted: permitted
69. **grate:** stove part
    great: large
70. **hanged:** pertains to people
    hung: pertains to objects
71. **healthful:** conducive to health
    healthy: having good health
72. **hear:** sense sound
    here: at a given place
73. **heard:** perceived sound
    herd: collection of cattle
74. **holey:** an opening
    holy: sacred
    wholly: entire
75. **imply:** to include; to mean
    infer: to deduce; to draw a conclusion from
76. **ingenious:** proceeding from genius
    ingenuous: frank; open
77. **instance:** an example
    instants: periods of time
78. **its:** belonging to a thing
    it's: contraction of it is or it has
79. **judicial:** pertaining to courts of law
    judicious: discreet, prudent
80. **later:** after
    latter: second of two items
81. **lay:** put or place
    lie: put oneself down, be in a reclining position
82. **lead:** a metal; to guide
    led: past tense of to lead
83. **loan:** to lend
    lone: single
84. **loose:** to free
    lose: to suffer loss of
    loss: act of losing

85. **many:** refers to number
    much: refers to quantity
86. **maybe:** perhaps
    may be: can be
87. **miner:** one who works in a mine
    minor: under legal age; unimportant
88. **moral:** good, just, ethical
    morale: spirit
89. **ours:** belonging to us
    our's: *incorrect*
90. **pair:** two of a kind
    pare: to peel
    pear: fruit
91. **passed:** gone by
    past: before
92. **patience:** forbearance
    patients: plural of patient
93. **peer:** an equal; to look narrowly
    pier: dock
94. **pedal:** lever moved by foot
    peddle: sell
    petal: part of a flower
95. **persecute:** oppress
    prosecute: bring charges in court
96. **personal:** private
    personnel: staff
97. **plain:** simple; a prairie
    plane: flat surface; tool
98. **planed:** smoothed out
    planned: arranged
99. **pole:** long stick
    poll: vote
100. **poor:** deprived; needy
    pore: opening
    pour: cause to flow
101. **precede:** go before
    proceed: advance
102. **precedence:** priorities
    precedents: authoritative examples

103. **presence:** state of being present
presents: gifts
104. **principal:** the head; most important; sum of money
principle: a rule or truth
105. **prophecy:** foretelling (noun)
prophesy: foretelling (verb)
106. **quiet:** still
quit: give up
quite: completely
107. **rain:** water from clouds
reign: rule of a monarch
rein: part of a harness
108. **respectably:** estimably, properly
respectfully: with deference or respect
respectively: in the order mentioned
109. **role:** part
roll: bread; turning
110. **root:** part of a plant
route: a way traveled
111. **scene:** a view; part of a play
seen: past tense of see
112. **shone:** past tense of shine
shown: past tense of show
113. **sole:** all alone
soul: spirit of man
114. **sometime:** occasionally
some time: amount of time
115. **stake:** a wager
steak: slice of beef
116. **stationary:** not moving
stationery: writing paper
117. **statue:** sculptured likeness
stature: height
statute: a law
118. **steal:** take another's property
steel: metal made from iron
119. **straight:** not crooked
strait: waterway

120. **suspect:** *verb or noun*
suspicion: *noun*
121. **tear:** water from eyes; rip apart
tier: row
122. **their:** belonging to them
there: in that place
they're: contraction of they are
123. **therefor:** to that end; for that thing
therefore: for that reason
124. **thorough:** complete
threw: past tense of throw
through: into and beyond
125. **to:** toward
too: also
two: number
126. **track:** an imprint; on a roadway
tract: area of land; a treatise
127. **vain:** proud
vane: device on steeple showing wind direction
vein: blood vessel
128. **waist:** middle of the body
waste: useless loss
129. **wait:** hold in time
weight: measurement
130. **ware:** something to sell
wear: to have on
131. **wary:** cautious
weary: tired
132. **waive:** give up
wave: swell of water
133. **weather:** state of climate
whether: a choice
134. **whose:** possessive of who (not of which)
who's: contraction of who is or who has
135. **your:** possessive of you
you're: contraction of you are
136. **yours:** possessive of your
your's: *incorrect*

EXERCISES: Wording

1. Robert Jones is a better manager (than, then) Bill Miller.
2. (Their, There, They're) is a better way to handle (their, there, they're) situation.
3. (To, Too, Two) expedite the case, the group (to, too, two) was required to make (to, too, two) decisions.
4. Mr. Jones must go to Pittsburgh in spite of the (weather, whether).
5. The court (erred, errored) in (its, it's) decision.
6. The manager (lead, led) the conference with skill.
7. Robert Miller (emigrated, immigrated) to the United States as an (emigrant, immigrant) from Great Britain.
8. Bob Jones (preceded, proceeded) to give instructions to participants (preceding, proceeding) the conference.
9. The manager will not return to his office for (some time, sometime).
10. Bob's (advice, advise) to Bill was to (canvas, canvass) the employees before making a decision.
11. Bob Jones is an (eminent, imminent) attorney and (adapt, adept, adopt) at handling cases involving administrative agencies.
12. They may (loose, lose, loss) many sales because of (loose, lose, loss) handling of orders, resulting in a (loose, lose, loss) of profit.
13. The supervisor was given easy (access, excess) to the files.
14. A new (addition, edition) to the library is Professor Miller's latest (addition, edition) of his marketing text.
15. (Capital, Capitol) gains in the state have decreased since Governor Jones invoked a ban on industry in the state (capital, capitol).
16. The manager (complemented, complimented) Mr. Thompson on his handling of an (all ready, already) difficult situation.
17. The (principal, principle) speaker at the seminar discussed (principals, principles) of management.
18. From (passed, past) experience, the manager recognized that he must carefully (choose, chose) new employees.
19. The group (passed, past) a resolution commending the members of the finance (council, counsel) for the (access, excess) funds in the treasury.
20. Robert Jones was (all ways, always) under the (allusion, illusion) that someone was trying to get his job.
21. The supervisor attempted to (allay, alley, ally) his manager's fears.
22. The (altar, alter) of the church had been placed at a right (angel, angle) to the organ.
23. The sales manager (appraised, apprised) his employees to (accept, except) the new situation.
24. The (accent, ascent, assent) of the entire board was needed before the (cession, session) could be held.

25. He asked for (assistance, assistants) in getting up the stairs.
26. The judge set (bail, bale) at the (bare, bear) minimum allowed by law.
27. The expense was to be (born, borne) by the company (baring, barring, bearing) unforeseen complications.
28. Today's high smog index makes it difficult to (breath, breathe).
29. Bob was not (conscience, conscious) of the (affect, effect) of his actions.
30. Dr. Jones felt that his (patience, patients) ought to have more (patience, patients).
31. The actor played (dual, duel) (roles, rolls) in the opening (scene, seen).
32. The cattlemen (heard, herd) that heavy snows were expected.
33. The car salesman ranked (forth, fourth) in total sales.
34. His use of (foul, fowl) language was (holey, holy, wholly) unacceptable.
35. There were two (aisles, isles) in the main auditorium.
36. Our (desert, dessert) was (currant, current) pie.
37. Judge Jones reprimanded the attorney for allowing the use of (hearsay, heresy) evidence.
38. The report on company (moral, morale) was (respectfully, respectively) submitted.
39. (Personal, Personnel) turnover within the company was (accessive, excessive).
40. In some sport car rallies there is a prescribed (root, route) while in others, driving is limited to a (track, tract).
41. He was (adverse, averse) to continuing on the project.
42. The sun (shone, shown) through the window.
43. He (suspected, suspicioned) someone might be following him.
44. The (cite, sight, site) chosen for the plant (may be, maybe) changed.
45. (Who's, Whose) book have you been using?
46. The owner had to obtain a (quiet, quit, quite) title before he could (sale, sail, sell) his home.
47. The manager tried to (lessen, lesson) pressure on his employees.
48. The fisherman caught (many, much) perch from the (peer, pier).
49. Please order sufficient (stationary, stationery) to meet anticipated needs.
50. (Wait, Weight) (hear, here) until I finish my (dairy, diary) entry for today.

Conciseness

Conciseness refers to *brevity consistent with clarity*. Good writers use the right words and the right number of words to clearly convey their meaning. While some writers use too few words, the more frequent fault is excessive wording. We, therefore, focus on the latter.

Overwording produces verbal debris, which the reader must mentally eliminate in order to grasp essential meaning. Excess verbiage may come from *redundancy* (the unnecessary repetition of an idea: e.g., "the month of March" for "March"); *weakened verbs* (e.g., "give an indication of" for "indicate"); *unneeded prepositions and adverbs* (e.g., "face up to" for "face"); *unneeded pronoun openers* (e.g., unneeded "There are . . . ," "It is . . . ," and "The fact that . . ." beginnings and internal phrasings: "There are three causes for the company's poor sales. These are . . ." rather than, "Three causes of poor company sales are . . ."); *hedging* (avoidance of a positive statement; unnecessary caution: e.g., "I *think that* Miss Thompson's record *appears* to demonstrate that she *seems* able to do the job." All italicized words are "hedging." A more positive and clear statement is, "Miss Thompson's record demonstrates her ability to do the job." Or if caution is needed, "I think that Miss Thompson's record . . ."); or *filler phrases* (e.g., "It is interesting that . . . ," "It may be said that . . .").

We present an alphabetical list of expressions together with suggestions for improvement.

CONCISENESS: WORDY EXPRESSIONS AND IMPROVEMENTS

REDUNDANCY

Wordy expression	Improvement
1. adequate enough	use one or the other
2. any and all	use **any** or **all**
3. as a general rule	use **as a rule, generally,** or **usually**
4. at the present time	omit or use **now**
5. by return mail	omit or, if needed, use a specific date
6. by the use of	use **by** (sufficient in most cases)
7. enclosed herewith	use **enclosed**
8. few in number	use **few**
9. if and when	use **if** or **when**
10. in the course of	use **in** or **during** as appropriate
11. in the range of (eight to ten thousand)	omit: the numbers indicate range
12. merge together	use **merge**
13. necessary requisite	use **requisite**
14. reason is because	use **because** or **reason is that**
15. still continue	use **continue**

WEAKENED VERBS

16. achieve verification   use **verify**
17. analyses were made   use **analyze**
18. carry out experiments   use **experiment**
19. come to a decision   use **decide**
20. is found to be   use proper form of **be**
21. give an indication of   use **indicate**
22. make an examination of   use **examine**
23. make a study of   use **study**
24. present a report   use **report**
25. take into consideration   use **consider**

UNNEEDED PREPOSITIONS/ADVERBS

26. as to whether   use **whether**
27. enter into   use **enter**
28. in between   use **between**
29. off of   omit **of**
30. outside of; inside of   omit **of**
31. plan on   omit **on**
32. repeat again   omit **again**
33. still remain   use **remain**
34. succeed in doing   use **do**
35. up to this time   use **before** or **previously**

UNNEEDED PRONOUN OPENERS

36. There are seven reasons why the company cannot increase production. They are . . . .   The company cannot increase production for seven reasons: . . . .
37. This is a vital part of our program and it should be done.   This vital part of our program should be done.
38. It would be appreciated if you would return these applications to me soon.   Please return the applications soon.
39. It is possible that we may not get the proposal.   We may not get the proposal.
40. The fact that he did poorly on the exam caused his frustration.   His poor examination performance caused his frustration.

HEDGING

41. In my judgment I think this ap-   I think this is a good proposal.
    pears to be a good proposal.
42. It appeared that the applicant   The applicant seemed nervous.
    was possibly nervous.
43. It seems possible that the em-   The employee may quit his job.
    ployee appears likely to quit his
    job.
44. In my opinion, I believe that a   I think a recession is likely.
    recession is likely.
45. We may perhaps take a possible   We may take a pay cut.
    pay cut.

FILLER PHRASES

(italicized phrases are fillers)

46. *It is interesting to note that* Mr.   Mr. Miller left the city yesterday.
    Miller left the city yesterday.
47. *You will be interested to know*   William Miller made the highest
    that William Miller made the   score.
    highest score.
48. Mr. Miller *is the type of executive*   Mr. Miller is always punctual.
    who is always punctual.
49. *With respect to* late employees,   We must punish late employees.
    we must punish them.
50. *In the field of* economics, one   One studies many abstract principles
    studies many abstract principles.   in economics.

EXERCISES: Conciseness

All sentences in this exercise contain unnecessary wording. Write each more concisely by eliminating unneeded wording or phrasing, and if necessary, recast the sentence for more clarity. Check your answers with the scoring key.

1. The production workers' output is adequate enough.
2. At the present time the company's sales exceed all of last year's.
3. We shall overcome low employee morale by the use of a better work incentive plan.
4. Management projects lower production costs in the range of $50,000 to $75,000.

5. Good planning is a necessary requisite to tight inventory control.
6. Customers still continue to complain about the latest price increase.
7. Management will achieve verification of production costs by December 1.
8. Sales analyses were made to determine causes of lower profits.
9. We must come to a decision immediately, or we lose an opportunity to enter a new market.
10. Results of the recent cost-cutting program were found to be disappointing.
11. Better management gives an indication of the effects of last year's training program.
12. Let us make an examination of our personnel selection methods.
13. The Systems Department will make a study of the use of computers in the Accounting Department.
14. Top management will present a report to employees.
15. We must take into consideration all possible factors before deciding.
16. I do not know as to whether William Miller will go.
17. Let us enter into discussion of possible merger.
18. We shall plan on repeating again the sales conference.
19. Verna Thomas succeeded in doing a difficult task.
20. There are two reasons why we cannot continue: . . . .
21. It would be appreciated if you would return the form by January 15.
22. The fact that he succeeded in his new assignment pleased his boss.
23. It appeared that the new supervisor was pessimistic.
24. You will be very interested to know that the company plans to diversify.
25. In the field of statistics, you find some valuable business applications.

Key: EXERCISES

Precision 1. telephone; 2. before noon tomorrow; 3. sufficiently precise; 4. February 14th Star-X; 5. two; 6. three; 7. no more than four; 8. sufficiently precise; 9. February 15 or 16; 10. responsible; 11. Donald Thompson; 12. memorandum; 13. sufficiently precise; 14. at the cafeteria entrance; 15. at 11:45 a.m.; 16. regulations dated January 5, 19___; 17. according to Procedure Manual, Section 5.12; 18. sufficiently precise; 19. sufficiently precise; 20. sufficiently precise.

Wording 1. than; 2. There, their; 3. To, too, two; 4. weather; 5. erred, its; 6. led; 7. immigrated, emigrant; 8. proceeded, preceding; 9. some time; 10. advice, canvass; 11. eminent, adept; 12. lose, loose, loss; 13. access; 14. addition, edition; 15. capital, capital; 16. complimented, already; 17. principal, principles; 18. past, choose; 19. passed, council, excess; 20. always, illusion; 21. allay; 22. altar, angle; 23. apprised, accept; 24. assent, session; 25. assistance; 26. bail, bare; 27. borne, barring; 28. breathe; 29. conscious, effect; 30. patients, patience; 31. dual, roles, scene; **32.** heard; **33.** fourth; **34.** foul, wholly; **35.** aisles; **36.** dessert, currant; **37.** hearsay; **38.** morale, respectfully; **39.** personnel, excessive; **40.** route, track; **41.** averse; **42.** shone; **43.** suspected; **44.** site, may be; **45.** whose; **46.** quit, sale; **47.** lessen; **48.** many, pier; **49.** stationery; **50.** wait, here, diary.

Conciseness **1.** The production workers' output is adequate. **2.** The company's sales exceed all of last year's. **3.** We shall overcome low employee morale by a better work incentive plan. **4.** Management projects lower production costs of $50,000 to $75,000. **5.** Good planning is a requisite to tight inventory control. **6.** Customers continue to complain about the latest price increase. **7.** Management will verify production costs by December 1. **8.** Sales were analyzed to determine causes of lower profits. **9.** We must decide immediately, or we lose an opportunity to enter a new market. **10.** Results of the recent cost-cutting program were disappointing. **11.** Better management indicates the effects of last year's training program. **12.** Let us examine our personnel selection methods. **13.** The Systems Department will study the use of computers in the Accounting Department. **14.** Top management will report to employees. **15.** We must consider all possible factors before deciding. **16.** I do not know whether William Miller will go. **17.** Let us discuss a possible merger. **18.** We shall plan on repeating the sales conference. **19.** Verna Thomas did a difficult task. **20.** We cannot continue for two reasons: . . . . **21.** Please return the forms by January 15. **22.** His success in his new assignment pleased his boss. **23.** The new supervisor seemed pessimistic. **24.** The company plans to diversify. **25.** In statistics you find some valuable business applications. Or: You find some valuable business applications in statistics.

Chapter 16

CORRECTNESS

As used here *correctness* refers to *proper use of traditional mechanics of grammar.* You may feel that you already know this subject. Unfortunately, if known, not all students nor all organizational writers rightly practice correctness. All you need do is examine a representative sample of term papers (for students) or of written documents (of an organization) to see the appalling number of gross violations.

As with clarity, this chapter will cover only those elements and principles most commonly affecting the quality of student and organizational writing. Once more, if you need work in other aspects, consult other books or take remedial writing courses or talk with your instructor. Essentials covered are: (1) punctuation, (2) spelling, and (3) capitalization.

Again, we follow the same format of first presenting principles and examples of each element, succeeded by practice exercises. A scoring key is at the chapter end.

Punctuation

Essentially punctuation may be viewed as (1) word-related, (2) internal, (3) ending, (4) incidental/explanatory/emphatic, and (5) source-related.

Word-related

The two important devices are hyphen and apostrophe. The most common principles and examples are presented in Figure 16.1.

Internal

Three common internal punctuations are the comma, the semicolon, and the colon. Figure 16.2 presents important principles and examples.

Ending

Closure devices include the period, the question mark, and the exclamation point. Figure 16.3 sets forth common principles and examples.

HYPHEN: indicates connections between words;
indicates word divisions

Most Common Principles	Examples
1. To indicate compound words	pre-exist; re-create
2. To indicate adjectives formed of two or more words	out-of-date; full-bodied
3. To indicate compound numerals between twenty-one and ninety-nine	thirty-seven; forty-four
4. To indicate fractions used as adjectives	*one-fourth* inch; *one-half* mile
5. To indicate syllable division at end of line	mile- [end of line] stone; pre- [end of line] sent
6. To indicate suspensive effect	a one- or five-dollar bill; a single- or double-sized bed

APOSTROPHE: indicates possession or omission of letters
(sometimes numbers)

Most Common Principles	Examples
1. To indicate singular possessive: add apostrophe before *s*	boy's arm; student's book
2. To indicate plural possessive: if not formed by *s*, add apostrophe and *s*	women's clothing; children's toys
3. To indicate possessive plural of nouns ending in *s*, add apostrophe	boys' arms; students' books
4. To indicate omission of letters/ numbers	won't; Class of '64

Fig. 16.1 / Word-related punctuation.

COMMA: indicates the smallest degree of separation;
indicates thought unfinished, that following
words closely relate to preceding

Most Common Principles	Examples
1. To separate words, phrases, clauses in sentence	The student had money, good looks, and a pleasing personality. The father wanted the best for his wife, for his son, for his daughter.
2. To separate independent clauses joined by a co-ordinating conjunction (e.g., *and, or*)	We shall study hard, and we shall study effectively. The student must change his ways, or he will fail the course.
3. To separate introductory phrases and clauses	To earn his tuition, the student worked during the holiday season. When he finally received his passing grade, the student wept with joy.
4. To separate expressions that if omitted do not change essential meaning of the sentence (non-restrictive words, phrases, clauses)	Mr. Miller, we know that we can trust you. We shall send Mr. Miller, our sales representative, to clear up the account.

SEMICOLON: indicates greater degree of separation
than comma

Most Common Principles	Examples
1. To separate independent clauses when coordinating conjunction implied (e.g., *and, but*)	The student's official dismissal came; he had anticipated it.
2. To separate items when a comma creates unclearness	Here are important company figures: 13,500 employees; $6,000,000 annual sales; and $725,000 net profit.
3. To separate series elements when one or more prior elements are broken up by commas	Mr. Miller had served the company in Dallas, Texas; New York, N.Y.; and Chicago.

COLON: indicates emphasis, that something important
is to follow.

Most Common Principles	Examples
1. To point forward or introduce something important (including a series)	Three causes of low morale are apparent: poor supervision, low pay, and lack of communication.
2. To follow the salutation of a formal letter	Dear Mr. Miller:
3. To introduce a lengthy quotation	Mr. William stated this opinion: "This is no easy problem, and it has no easy solution. It will require. . . ."

Fig. 16.2 / Internal punctuation.

PERIOD: indicates completion of a thought;
also used after abbreviations

Most Common Principles	Examples
1. To show end of a statement sentence	Mr. Miller will go next week.
2. To show end of an imperative sentence	Leave now. Go tomorrow.
3. To show abbreviation	Mr.; Mrs.; Denver, Colo.; New York, N.Y.

QUESTION MARK: to indicate completeness of an interrogative thought

Most Common Principles	Examples
To show the end of a question.	Will you go with me?
Note: Do not use question mark in an "imperative" question	Will you please answer this letter immediately.

EXCLAMATION POINT: to indicate emphatic thought or strong feeling

Most Common Principles	Examples
1. To show emphatic thought	It was quite a shock to fail the course after making straight A's in all examinations!
2. To emphasize an imperative	Go to blazes!

Fig. 16.3 / Ending punctuation.

Incidental/Explanatory/Emphatic

These refer respectively to punctuation devices that point to nonessential, elaborating, and important ideas. These include parentheses (or brackets), dash, and underline (or italics). Figure 16.4 presents principles and examples.

PARENTHESES (or brackets): to indicate explanatory materials; to indicate incidental ideas

Most Common Principles	Examples
1. To indicate explanatory or incidental materials	Mr. William Miller (who has twelve years experience in accounting) thinks our payroll system is out-of-date. You have already studied clarity in written communications (see Chapter 15).
2. To indicate numerical accuracy following the written amount	The company has seven thousand (7000) employees.
3. To indicate enumeration	We plan to improve sales by (1) increasing advertising, (2) making more face-to-face visits to customer plants, and (3) getting salesmen to believe more in their products.

DASH: indicates abrupt change of thought; indicates explanatory material

Most Common Principles	Examples
1. To indicate abrupt change of thought	We know—or perhaps we should know—what will happen.
2. To indicate explanatory material	Costs—monetary and psychological—must be reduced if the firm is to remain competitive.

UNDERLINE (or italics): to indicate emphasis

Most Common Principles	Examples
1. To indicate essential words or phrases	Communication refers to the four elements of speaking, writing, listening, and reading.
2. To indicate emphasis of certain words or phrases	Contrary to opinion, communication is not simple.

Fig. 16.4 / Incidental/explanatory/emphatic punctuation.

Source-related

Three punctuation devices are included in this grouping: quotation marks, ellipsis dots, and underlines. Figure 16.5 gives principles and examples.

QUOTATION MARKS: to indicate verbatim quotes; to indicate unusual use	
Most Common Principles	**Examples**
1. To indicate verbatim quotes *Note:* use single quotation marks for quotes within quotes (e.g., "I told them 'No' when asked about contract renewal.")	Mr. Miller said, "I'll do the job, no matter what the costs."
2. To indicate unusual use of word or phrase	It was "definition mongering" of the worst sort.

ELLIPSIS DOTS: to indicate omissions from quotes	
Basic Principles	**Examples**
1. Use three dots to indicate internal omissions	"The communication . . . was . . . clear, but . . . not persuasive."
2. Use four dots to indicate ellipsis at the end of a sentence	"Persuasion is a mighty force in a democratic society. . . ."

UNDERLINES (italics): to indicate source titles	
Most Common Principles	**Examples**
1. To indicate names of books, newspapers, brochures, manuals *Note:* Sometimes quotation marks are used rather than underlines (especially in newspaper writing)	Effective Communication of Ideas The New York Times Star-X Administrative Manual
2. To indicate names of works of art; names of ships, airplanes, submarines	The Nightwatch The submarine, Nautilus
3. To indicate foreign words or phrases not fully anglicized	The manager has real savoir faire
4. To indicate Latin-derived symbols common to footnotes and bibliographies	ibid., op. cit., loc. cit. *Note:* underlining footnote symbols is the traditional view; more "liberal" authorities say that these items are not underlined.

Fig. 16.5 / Source-related punctuation.

EXERCISES: Punctuation

In the following sentences you are to check "correct" if the appropriate punctuation is used; if not, check the alternate option.

      1   **2** **3**
We shall re-create last years sales-plan.

1 ☐ correct   2 ☐ correct   3 ☐ correct
   ☐ recreate   ☐ year's   ☐ sales plan

                 4   **5**
We must bring all our employees' skills up to date.

4 ☐ correct   5 ☐ correct
   ☐ employee's   ☐ up-to-date

   6   **7**   **8**
One-hundred men and twenty-five women attended the meeting, held last week.

6 ☐ correct   7 ☐ correct   8 ☐ correct
   ☐ One hundred   ☐ twenty five   ☐ no comma needed

     9   **10**
About one third of our quota has been met which is very gratifying.

9 ☐ correct   10 ☐ correct
   ☐ one-third   ☐ comma needed

               11   **12**
The manager instructed us to use the two or three wheeled cart for carrying packages.

11 ☐ correct   12 ☐ correct
    ☐ two-   ☐ three-wheeled

13 **14**   **15**   **16**
"Bill," said the manager, take the invoice to the controller.

13 ☐ correct   14 ☐ correct   15 ☐ correct   16 ☐ correct
   ☐ no quota-   ☐ no quota-   ☐ quotation   ☐ quotation
      tion mark   tion mark   mark   mark
      needed   needed   needed   needed

17   18
A managers pay was increased twenty five percent.

17 ☐ correct   18 ☐ correct
   ☐ manager's   ☐ twenty-five

19   20
Womens' pay is lower than men's.

19 ☐ correct   20 ☐ correct
   ☐ Women's   ☐ mens'

21
All students' classes were cancelled.

21 ☐ correct
   ☐ student's

22   23   24
Dont underestimate the Class of 76.

22 ☐ correct   23 ☐ correct   24 ☐ correct
   ☐ Don't   ☐ Class'   ☐ '76

25   26   27 28
The teacher had, a good background, friendliness, and, excellent classroom presentation.

25 ☐ correct   26 ☐ correct   27 ☐ correct   28 ☐ correct
   ☐ no comma   ☐ no comma   ☐ no comma   ☐ no comma
      needed   needed   needed   needed

29
We must increase sales, or we cannot pay the same dividend as last year.

29 ☐ correct
   ☐ no comma needed

30
Assuming you get to the meeting on time we should finish by 10:00.

30 ☐ correct
   ☐ comma needed

31   32
Mr. Miller, whom you may know will attend the meeting.

31 ☐ correct   32 ☐ correct
   ☐ no comma needed   ☐ comma needed

33

Company sales decreased sixty-seven percent; this was more than had been expected.

33 ☐ correct
☐ no semicolon needed

             34   **35**

The annual report brought out this information sales of $1,500,000; net profits

     36   **37**

of $152,000; return on investment; of 8 percent.

34 ☐ correct   35 ☐ correct   36 ☐ correct   37 ☐ correct
    ☐ colon   ☐ no semi-   ☐ no semi-   ☐ no semi-
       needed   colon   colon   colon
                  needed   needed   needed

      38   **39**   **40**

Mr. Miller, traveled to Jonesboro, Arkansas; Wichita, Kansas, and Omaha, Nebraska.

38 ☐ correct   39 ☐ correct   40 ☐ correct
    ☐ no comma   ☐ no semi-colon   ☐ substitute
      needed   needed   semicolon

         41   **42** **43**

We need three things: better working conditions better pay better communication.

41 ☐ correct   42 ☐ correct   43 ☐ correct
    ☐ no colon   ☐ comma   ☐ comma
      needed   needed   needed

      44

Leave now?

44 ☐ correct
    ☐ substitute period

          45

Are you going with Mr. Miller.

45 ☐ correct
    ☐ substitute question mark

46
Angrily, he shouted, "No!"

46 ☐ correct
   ☐ period needed

47
Will you please answer immediately.

47 ☐ correct
   ☐ substitute question mark

        48   **49**   **50**
You can find the instructions (for writing letters) in your manual (see pages
  51
15–16).

48 ☐ correct	49 ☐ correct	50 ☐ correct	51 ☐ correct
☐ parenthesis not needed	☐ parenthesis not needed	☐ parenthesis not needed	☐ parenthesis not needed

    52   **53**
The company knows—or it ought to know—how many production workers will
  54
be needed?

52 ☐ correct	53 ☐ correct	54 ☐ correct
☐ dash not needed	☐ dash not needed	☐ substitute period

      55   **56**
The last trip by the three managers was a real "boondoggle."

55 ☐ correct	56 ☐ correct
☐ quotation mark not needed	☐ quotation mark not needed

   57   **58**   **59**
"The letter . . . . was . . . . abrupt . . ."

57 ☐ correct	58 ☐ correct	59 ☐ correct
☐ . . .	☐ . . .	☐ . . . .

  60
Ibid.

60 ☐ correct
   ☐ underline

Spelling

Most writers are plagued by some spelling problems. The English language, arising as it has from multiple sources and having evolved over a period of more than two thousand years, is a spelling conglomeration. Therefore, everyone at some time or other is bothered in the spelling of English words (both American and British).

However, no element of writing is more open to attack or criticism. While some words can be spelled in more than one way, "absolutes" exist for readers to use to censure spelling. And while there is no real relation between spelling proficiency and intelligence, popular opinion associates the two. Thus, the poor speller is viewed by most people as lacking in intellect. For no other reason, then, you should do all in your power to sharpen your spelling proficiency.

Even more important, a misspelled word can mislead or confuse the reader (e.g., *forth* for *fourth*; *then* for *than*), resulting in wrong understanding or performance. At best it can result in tarnishing your image with a perceptive reader (including your boss or teacher).

We shall take a pragmatic approach in helping to improve spelling. Whether from poor concentration, poor phonetic background, or poor understanding of all the many rules, we are going to help you attack your spelling problems directly. First, we shall present several principles which, if understood and applied, can correct many misspellings. Second, we shall present an alphabetical listing of words commonly misspelled by student and organizational writers. Third, we set forth a listing of words in order of misspelling frequency. This list comes from an examination of more than 5,000,000 words from college of business student term papers and essay exams over a period of two years. In addition to the listing in order of frequency of misspelling (most frequent first), we also include the most common ways the word is misspelled. Fourth, we then have an exercise section that includes common misspellings.

You should first read and understand the principles, after which look over the two lists for words that may give you trouble. Go over them until you get each into your nervous system. Then do the exercises as a check on your proficiency. If words other than the ones you predicted are shown to be problems, review these until you can spell all correctly.

There may be words (beyond the two lists) which you habitually misspell. Keep track of them from your term papers, essay exams, and other written feedback. Using these suggestions, along with constant and consistent efforts to spot and correct misspellings, can pay off in significant improvement. A final note: keep a dictionary handy for checking doubtful instances.

Figure 16.6 presents important spelling principles and examples. Bear in mind, there are exceptions to all, so be alert for deviations.

PRINCIPLES	EXAMPLES
1. **Nouns/verbs** ending in *y* preceded by *consonant:* **Nouns:** plural formed by dropping *y*, adding *ies* *Verbs:* same principle for forming present tense, third person	lobby—lobbies mercy—mercies carry—carries modify—modifies
2. **Nouns/verbs** ending in *y* preceded by *vowel:* **Nouns:** plural formed by adding *s* **Verbs:** same principle for forming present tense, third person	attorney—attorneys joy—joys journey—journeys obey—obeys
3. Final silent *e retained:* when suffix begins with consonant	abate—abatement excite—excitement hate—hateful
4. Final silent *e dropped:* when suffix begins with *vowel*	believe—believable guide—guidance shape—shaping
5. *ie/ei* spellings: with long *e,* use *i* before *e,* except after *c*	achieve; believe; receive; conceive. *Note these exceptions:* either, neither, seize, leisure, weird

6. Doubling final consonant: one syllable/accent on last syllable: if a single consonant preceded by single vowel, *double final consonant*	One syllable:
	  clap—clapped; hop—hopped
	 Accent on last syllable:
	  control—controlling
	  patrol—patrolled

7. Final *l: one syllable words:* spelled with two *l's; more than one syllable words:* spelled with one *l*	fill, doll, still, bill, bell, until, compel, conceal, repel, reveal

8. cede/ceed/sede endings: almost all end in *cede* (note exceptions opposite)	accede, concede, intercede, precede
	 Exceptions
	  ceed endings: exceed, proceed, succeed
	  sede ending: supersede

Fig. 16.6 / Basic spelling principles.

abridgment	caliber	desirable
accede	canceled	determinable
accessible	cancellation	determine
accessory	cannot	develop*
accommodate	capable	development
accumulate	casualty	diagramed
achieve	certain	diagrammatic
acoustic	chancellor	dialed
acquire	changeable	dilettante
adequate	characterize	discernible
admirable	chlorophyll	disenfranchize
admissible	cigarette	dispatch
advertise	coconut	dissatisfied
adviser	coerce	distill
affect	collapsible	distributor
aging	collateral	divisible
airplane	collectible	do
align	colossal	does
all right	combustible	dossier
aluminum	comfortable	dreamed
ambassador	commitment	dueled
amount	committee	dullness
analyze	communicable	durable
answerable	companies	
apologize	compare	ecstasy
appall	comparison	edible
apparent	compatible	effect
aquatic	competitive	efficient
aqueduct	comprehensible	eligible
argument	compromise	embarrass
ascendance	connoisseur	emphasize
assassinate	consensus	employee
audible	consummate	enameled
	contemptible	encase
bargain	controvertible	enclose
battalion	convertible	endorsement
begin	conveyor	enforcement
believable	corollary	enroll
beneficent	corruptible	enterprise
benefit	credible	entrench
benefited*	criticize	entrepreneur
bloc		equaled
breakable	decision	exceed
burned	deductible	existence
business	defensible	exhaustible
	definite	exhibitor
caffeine	deplorable	exorbitant

* First spelling in *Webster's Third New International Dictionary.*

Fig. 16.7/ Words commonly misspelled.

Fig. 16.7 (continued)

fallible	inoculate	misspell
fantasy	inquire	moccasin
feasible	insistence	modeled
fiber	install	modeler
flammable	instill	mold
flexible	insure	molt
fluctuate	intelligible	monopolize
fluorescent	interceptor	movable
focused	interfere	
forbade	interpret	nearby
forcible	iridescent	necessary
forecast		negligible
foregone	jeopardize	neighbor
foresee	judgment*	
forgettable		occur
forswear	kerosene	occurrence
fulfill	knowledgeable	offense
furor		omelet
	labeled	oneself
gasoline	lacquer	ostensible
gaiety	led	
gauge	legible	paid
generalize	leveled	paneled
glamorous	libeled	paraffin
glamour	license	paralleled
good-by	likable	parceled
gray	liquefy	particular
grievance	liter	partisan
grievous	livable	pastime
guarantee	lose	peaceable
	losing	peddler
hemorrhage		penciled
heterogeneous	madam	perform
homogeneity	manageable	personnel
hypocrisy	maneuver	perishable
	manikin	permissible
idiosyncrasy	marketable	plaque
idyll*	marshal	plausible
impaneled	marshaled	plow
impel	marveled	possible
imperceptible	marvelous	practice
imperiled	meager	precede
impostor	meant	preceding
improvise	medieval	prepare
indispensable	merchandise	prerogative
innocuous	mileage	principal
innovation	milieu	principle
innuendo	millennium	privilege

Fig. 16.7 (continued)

proceed
proffer
programmatic
promissory
propellent
psychology

quantity
quarreled
questionnaire
queue

rarefy*
rarity
ratable
rattan
raveled
receive
recognize
recommend
reconnaissance
reconnoiter
refer
referable
referring
regard (in . . . to)
reinforce
reliable
relieve
renaissance
reorganize
reparable
repellent
reprehensible
respectable
responsible
rivaled

sacrilegious
salable
satellite
savable
savior
savor
secede
seize
sensible
separate

shellacking
siege
similar
siphon
skeptic
skillful
smolder
soliloquy
sources
stenciled
stratagem
stubbornness
stupefy
substantial
subtlety
succeed
successful
suggestible
supersede
supervise
surprise
surreptitious
surveillance
susceptible
synonymous

taboo
tactitician
tangible
tattoo
taxied
technique
than
then
their
therefore
there
theater
threshold
through
throughout
tie
tied
to
today
too
totaled
trafficking

tranquilizer
transatlantic
transferable
transferred
transship
traveled
tying
typify

understandable
until
usable

vacillate
vicissitude
villain
visible
vying

washable
whereas
whether
whisky
willful
withhold
without
woolen
workable

X ray

Correct Spelling	Misspellings: root word and permutations
affect	effect
cannot	can not; canot; cann't
separate	seperate; seporation; sepreation; separetly
occur	occure; occurr; occour; accure
definite	definate; deffinate; definitly
receive	recieved; receaved
existence	existance; exsistance
effect	affect
their	thier; there
lose (losing)	lossing; loose; loss; loseing; loosing
perform	preformed; preformance; peaform
then	than
through	thorough; thru
analyze	analyse; annulyze; anualize; analize
refer-referring	refered; referal; refering; refference
preceding	preceeding; proceed
companies	companys
efficient	effecient; effeciency; efficientcy
development	developement
fluctuate	fluxuate; flucuation; fluctation
commitment	committment
necessary	necessiary; neccessary; neccesary
until	untill
too	to; two
than	then
paid	payed
forecast	forcast
therefore	therefor; there for
determine	determing; deturmine; determain; determins
principal	principle
psychology	psycology; psycological
adequate	adquate; adequatly
personnel	personal
argument	arguement
bargain	bargan; bargin
begin	begaining; bigin; beginer
certain	certian; certon; certianly
desirable	desireability; disirable; desireable
(in) regard (to)	regards
without	with out; with-out
benefit	benifit; benefite
compare	compair; comparred; comperable
competitive	competative; competetive; competive
interpret	interpet; enterpret; interprete
prepare	prepair; preperation
privilege	priviledge; provlege

Fig. 16.8 / Spelling errors in order of frequency.

Fig. 16.8 (continued)

Correct Spelling	Misspellings: root word and permutations
successful	sucess; sucessful; sucessfull
to	too
throughout	through out
amount	amont; ammount
apparent	apparant; appearent; aparently
business	businees; bussiness; buseness; buisness
fulfill	fullfill; filful; fullfil; fulilling
principle	principal
quantity	quanity
there	their
whether	wheather; weather; weither; wether
do (does)	due; dose
led	lead
particular	particilar; particularily; perticularly
comparison	comparason; compareson; compair
decision	decesion; descision; dicision; decions
interfere	interfer; interfear
questionnaire	questionairre; questionaire
recommend	recommed; recomend; recomended
substantial	substancial; substansial; substancially
guarantee	garantee; guarentee; gurantee
prerogative	perogative
whereas	where as
achieve	acheive; acheivement; acheving
collateral	colateral; collaterial; collatural; coladeral
entrepreneur	entreprenaur; entreprenuer; intreprenues
enterprise	enterprize; interprise
grievance	grievence; greviance
meant	ment
permissible	permissable
similar	similiar; similer
sources	sourses; souces

EXERCISES: Spelling

1. The student's grade average was (affected, effected) by the failing mark.
2. (Separation, seperation) of accounting from finance is an artifact.
3. Procedures should be (definate, definite) and clear for (receivers, recievers).
4. Rather than the company's "profit (performance, preformance)," it would be more proper to call it a "(lose, loss)" operation.
5. Let us (analize, analyze) the sales figures of other (companies, companys).
6. (Developement, Development) of an (adaquate, adequate) sales plan requires total organization (commitment, committment).

7. The invoice will not be (paid, payed) (until, untill) it is corrected and returned (to, too) us.

8. A study of (psychology, psycology) will help us determine which (principals, principles) can be used (sucessfully, successfully) in an incentive plan.

9. Managerial (judgement, judgment) is always (neccesary, necessary) in selection of (personal, personnel).

10. Clear specifications are (desirable, desireable) in (buseness, business) contacts.

11. (Compair, Compare) your (interpetation, interpretation) of instructions with mine.

12. The students complained that (their, there, they're) was (to, too) much (interferance, interference) and (to, too) little freedom.

13. (Wheather, Whether) to satisfy a customer with quality or (quanity, quantity) can be a dilemma.

14. In (particilar, particular), sharp (comparason, comparison) of quality is needed before making a (decesion, decision) to buy.

15. To (acheive, achieve) increased sales, we shall make (garantees, guarantees) (similar, similiar) to those (offered, offerred) by our (competators, competitors).

16. The manager (can not, cannot) dictate employee (moral, morale).

17. (A, An) catastrophe can (occur, occure) if an organization does not control its expenses.

18. (Their, There, They're) company's very (existance, existence) is jeopardized.

19. Rather (than, then) going (thorough, through) the production manager, a complaint should be (refered, referred) directly to the sales department.

20. An (analisis, analysis) should be made of production (effeciency, efficiency) using data from the five (preceeding, preceding) years.

21. Good planning (necessarily, neccesarily) requires consideration of (fluctations, fluctuations) in prices and market conditions.

22. (Therefore, Therefor), we think this is a poor (forcast, forecast).

23. After (their, there, they're) (arguement, argument), the two men made a satisfactory (bargain, bargin).

24. With (regard, regards) to fringe benefits, this (companies, company's) compensation is (competative, competitive).

25. (Prepair, Prepare) for (priviledged, privileged) motions in formal meetings.

26. (Through out, Throughout) it was (apparant, apparent) that the (amont, amount) in question was (negligable, negligible).

27. (Do, Due) you want to be (lead, led) or to be a leader?

28. Answers to the (questionairre, questionnaire) will (determain, determine) our (recomendations, recommendations).

29. In a free (enterprise, enterprize) system, it is (permissable, permissible) to (adapt, adept, adopt) to changing market conditions.
30. The complaint was (refered, referred) to the individual (responsable, responsible) for the error.

Capitalization

The last element of correctness, capitalization, is less exact than spelling. Different authorities hold some differing views about this subject. While we give some of the more important and common principles, you should remember that specific organizations and situational practices may dictate changes. We cover capitalization under five headings: (1) order in sentences, (2) salutations/ closings, (3) names, (4) titles, and (5) proper adjectives/governmental designations. Following are principles and exceptions, together with examples of use.

CAPITALIZATION

Sentences

First word or one-word sentences:
   I'll go to Dallas tomorrow.
   Oh! What? Yes.

With a quoted sentence:
   He said, "I'll go by plane to Dallas tomorrow."
   He said, "I'll go by plane. . . ."

Do Not Use Capitals

When first word(s) of quotation omitted:
He said ". . . to Dallas tomorrow."

Pronoun *I* is always capitalized:
   I do not know whether I will go with you.

Letter Salutations/Complimentary Closings

Salutations—initial word and nouns:
   Dear Mr. Miller
   Dear Employee

Do Not Use Capitals

When "dear" is not initial word:
   My *dear* Mr. Miller

Complimentary closings—initial word only:
   Very truly yours
   Sincerely yours

Names

Individuals:
    Robert Jones
    William Miller

Geographic location/region/thing:
    Bronx Zoo, Mississippi River, West Coast, Middle Atlantic, Far East

Commercial/governmental/political/voluntary:
    Department of Agriculture
    General Accounting Office
    Democratic Party
    Sears Roebuck and Company
    American Cancer Society

Trade/product:
    Polaroid, London Fog, Kodacolor, Mobil

Courses/classes:
    Principles of Accounting
    Business Statistics

Time unit:
    Sunday, Monday; January, February; Fourth of July, Thanksgiving Day

Do Not Use Capitals

When person uses lower case (e.g., deBoer, vonBergen)

When not using official name: zoo in the Bronx; river in Mississippi
When refers to point on compass: north of Denver

If used generically: a course in principles of accounting; a class in statistics

When season or time of day: fall, winter, spring; two-thirty, noon, midnight

Titles

Personal—professional/civic/military/
religious/family preceding personal
names:

Dr. William Miller; Mayor William
Miller; General William Miller;
Reverend William Miller; Uncle
William

Position—when used as a substitute for
or following the name of person occupying the position:

The group was addressed by the
Dean.

The employees were addressed by
William Miller, Chairman of the
Board.

Publications (e.g., books, journals, articles, works of art) initial and all principal words in titles:

The New York Times (newspaper)
Effective Communication of Ideas
(book)
"The Age of Reason" (article)
"The Nightwatch" (work of art)

Do Not Use Capitals

When a position title is used generically: A dean has many different
duties.

When beginning "the" is not part of
the title: the *Newsweek*

Proper Adjectives and Governmental Designations

Proper adjectives:

English language, Persian rug,
Judeo-Christian ethic

Governmental designations:

a Federal judge, our Nation's flag,
State Government pensions

EXERCISES: Capitalization

In the following sentences, determine whether each numbered item should be capitalized. If not correct, check "capitalize" as the right answer.

1   **2**
he will be in college next january.

1 ☐ correct   2 ☐ correct
  ☐ capitalize   ☐ capitalize

3   **4**   **5**   **6**
"yes," said James, "i'll be in New york next wednesday.

3 ☐ correct   4 ☐ correct   5 ☐ correct   6 ☐ correct
  ☐ capitalize   ☐ capitalize   ☐ capitalize   ☐ capitalize

7
Mr. William Miller

8
Widespot, Texakana

7 ☐ correct   8 ☐ correct
  ☐ capitalize   ☐ capitalize

9
My dear Mr. Miller:
  Thank you for your kind note.

                  10
                  sincerely yours

9 ☐ correct   10 ☐ correct
  ☐ capitalize   ☐ capitalize

         11   **12**
John was going to the museum in chicago.

11 ☐ correct   12 ☐ correct
   ☐ capitalize   ☐ capitalize

     13   **14**   **15**
The republican party is the party of private property.

13 ☐ correct   14 ☐ correct   15 ☐ correct
   ☐ capitalize   ☐ capitalize   ☐ capitalize

   16   **17**

The river was in missouri.

16 ☐ correct   17 ☐ correct
    ☐ capitalize   ☐ capitalize

         18 **19**

Chicago is located on lake michigan.

18 ☐ correct   19 ☐ correct
    ☐ capitalize   ☐ capitalize

        20   **21**

The Red cross performs many acts of mercy for our nation.

20 ☐ correct   21 ☐ correct
    ☐ capitalize   ☐ capitalize

         22   **23**

He took a course in statistics in a university.

22 ☐ correct   23 ☐ correct
    ☐ capitalize   ☐ capitalize

       24   **25**

John took principles of Management, B61-160, at city University.

24 ☐ correct   25 ☐ correct
    ☐ capitalize   ☐ capitalize

       26   **27**

He had a polaroid camera, which he purchased at sears Roebuck.

26 ☐ correct   27 ☐ correct
    ☐ capitalize   ☐ capitalize

      28 **29**   **30**

The federal judge used the English language superbly.

28 ☐ correct   29 ☐ correct   30 ☐ correct
    ☐ capitalize   ☐ capitalize   ☐ capitalize

     31   **32**

The fourth of July is a national holiday every summer.

31 ☐ correct   32 ☐ correct
    ☐ capitalize   ☐ capitalize

| 33 | 34 |

At noon we will honor the French ambassador.

33 ☐ correct   34 ☐ correct
☐ capitalize   ☐ capitalize

| 35 |

He always buys gasoline at a texaco station.

35 ☐ correct
☐ capitalize

Key: EXERCISES

Punctuation 1. correct; 2. year's; 3. sales plan; 4. correct; 5. up-to-date; 6. One hundred; 7. correct; 8. no comma needed; 9. one-third; 10. comma needed; 11. two; 12. three-wheeled; 13. correct; 14. correct; 15. quotation mark needed; 16. quotation mark needed; 17. manager's; 18. twenty-five; 19. Women's; 20. correct; 21. correct; 22. Don't; 23. correct; 24. '76; 25. no comma needed; 26. correct; 27. correct; 28. no comma needed; 29. correct; 30. comma needed; 31. correct; 32. comma needed; 33. correct; 34. colon needed; 35. correct; 36. correct; 37. no semicolon needed; 38. no comma needed; 39. correct; 40. substitute semicolon; 41. correct; 42. comma needed; 43. comma needed; 44. substitute period; 45. substitute question mark; 46. correct; 47. correct; 48. parenthesis not needed; 49. parenthesis not needed; 50. correct; 51. correct; 52. correct; 53. correct; 54. substitute period; 55. correct; 56. correct; 57. 3 dots; 58. 3 dots; 59. 4 dots; 60. underline.

Spelling 1. affected; 2. separation; 3. definite, receivers; 4. performance, loss; 5. analyze, companies; 6. Development, adequate, commitment; 7. paid, until, to; 8. psychology, principles, successfully; 9. judgment, necessary, personnel; 10. desirable, business; 11. Compare, interpretation; 12. there, too, interference, too; 13. Whether, quantity; 14. particular, comparison, decision; 15. achieve, guarantees, similar, offered, competitors; 16. cannot, morale; 17. A, occur; 18. Their, existence; 19. than, through, referred; 20. analysis, efficiency, preceding; 21. necessarily, fluctuations; 22. Therefore, forecast; 23. their, argument, bargain; 24. regard, company's, competitive; 25. Prepare, privileged; 26. Throughout, apparent, amount, negligible; 27. Do, led; 28. questionnaire, determine, recommendations; 29. enterprise, permissible, adapt; 30. referred, responsible.

Capitalization

1. capitalize; 2. capitalize; 3. capitalize; 4. capitalize; 5. capitalize; 6. capitalize; 7. correct; 8. correct; 9. correct; 10. capitalize; 11. correct; 12. capitalize; 13. capitalize; 14. capitalize; 15. correct; 16. correct; 17. capitalize; 18. capitalize; 19. capitalize; 20. capitalize; 21. capitalize; 22. correct; 23. correct; 24. capitalize; 25. capitalize; 26. capitalize; 27. capitalize; 28. capitalize; 29. correct; 30. correct; 31. capitalize; 32. correct; 33. correct; 34. capitalize; 35. capitalize.

Chapter 17

PRINCIPLES OF
PERSUASIVE WRITING

Since Chapters 15 and 16 respectively cover elements of clarity and correctness, we assume your mastery of these dimensions.

Our focus here is on four salient features which, from our experience, need most improvement in everyday organizational writing. These are certainly not exhaustive, but when properly used, these four go far to produce effective written communication: paragraphing, format, message clarity, and tone.

Rather than getting into elaborate detail, we shall highlight crucial aspects. In order to maximize your understanding, we shall give a brief discussion of principles, followed by tabular summaries, which include specimen examples. These tables are ready, useful references in your own communication assessments and rewrites.

Paragraphing

In organizational prose writing, a good paragraph meets these criteria: (1) unity of idea, (2) adequate development, (3) communicative coherence, (4) sufficient emphasis, and (5) proper length.

Unity of idea means that the paragraph communicates *one* thought. Often, this central idea will be stated in a single sentence, called the "topic sentence." A topic sentence is most often explicit; however, sometimes because writers think that an idea is so "obvious," a topic sentence is only implicit. In order to achieve optimal unity in most organizational writing, it is probably best to make the topic sentence explicit. In other words, you should not leave the reader in doubt as to what you intend.

Where, in the paragraph, should the topic sentence appear? Actually, it could appear anywhere. Frequently, it begins or ends the paragraph; sometimes it is placed in the middle. You should place a topic sentence where it will most effectively unify ideas for the reader.

To reinforce unity, a topic sentence should be accompanied by directly supporting ideas. Digressions and tangential points hamper unity. Any "debris" or any point not directly related to the topic sentence is a hindrance. In sum, you should test paragraphs for unity with these two questions: (1) Is there a clear topic sentence? (2) Do all ideas directly relate to the topic sentence? Figure 17.1 exemplifies explicit and implicit topic sentences from specimens. It also shows examples of idea relations to topic sentences.

PARAGRAPHING: UNITY OF IDEA			
	Topic Sentence		Related Ideas
Spec. Ref.	Location	Type	Clarity
63:1.2,3	middle	implicit	clear
63:2.1	beginning	explicit	clear
90:1.3	end	explicit	clear
90:2.1	beginning	explicit	clear
79:1.1-4	entire paragraph	implicit	clear
	Relation to Topic Sentence and Comments		
63:1 and 2	O.K.		
90:1	O.K.		
90:2.2	O.K.		
90:3.1	Improper placement: actually relates to topic sentence 2.1 and should be final sentence in paragraph 2.		

Fig. 17.1 / Paragraphing—unity of idea.

Adequate development refers to the support or elaboration of the paragraph's central theme. In other words, good paragraph development may validate, clarify, or vivify the basic idea. Some of the more useful methods of paragraph development are: analogy; cause-effect (or effect-cause); comparison/contrast; definition; essential elements; examples; figurative language; question-answer; quotations; restatement; slogans; verbal and statistical details. Figure 17.2 gives examples of different types as used in certain specimens.

Coherence literally means "sticking together," in other words, that ideas in the paragraph are properly related through transitions. If a paragraph is unified and adequately developed, you can then supply proper transitions for communicative coherence. Some of the more useful types of transitions are antecedent references, connective cues, and parallel constructions. Figure 17.3 sets forth principles for antecedents, together with examples from specimens; Figure 17.4 presents principles and examples of connective cues; Figure 17.5 gives principles and examples of parallelism.

Emphasis grows out of paragraph unity, development, and coherence. It directs reader attention to that which you want him to understand and retain. In other words, proper emphasis puts important ideas into the foreground (and places peripheral ideas into the background) for the reader.

PARAGRAPHING: ADEQUATE DEVELOPMENT

Methods	Spec. Ref.
analogy	63:1-3, 36:2.1,2
cause-effect	70:2, 98:1
comparison/contrast	54:1,2, 63:1
definition	113:2,4,5
effect-cause	99:1 (effect—complaint; possible causes— 8 suggestions)
	110
essential elements	95
examples	39:3.2, 48 (hypothetical), 96
figurative language	36:1, 63:1.1-3
question-answer	41:1.3-5, 63:1, 111:2
quotations	36:1, 63:1.4
restatement	61:1, 84:2
slogans	59 (at end), 99:2 (8)
verbal and statistical details	78:1.1-3, 79:2, 95:3-4

Fig. 17.2 / Paragraphing—adequate development.

PARAGRAPHING: COHERENCE—ANTECEDENT REFERENCES

Pronouns and demonstrative adjectives are used to refer to antecedents in preceding sentences to connect ideas to achieve coherence. Common pronouns: you, he, she, it, they, I, we, our, each, either; common demonstrative adjectives: this, that, these, those.

Principles	Spec. Ref.	Comments
1. Use consistently (e.g., singular with singular; plural with plural).	64:1-5	Consistent use of "we" throughout refers to company; but note inconsistent shift to "I" in last sentence followed by "our."
2. Make antecedent completely clear.	65:2.2	"This" refers to "premise check" (2.1); "additional question" (3.1) followed by "that question." In 3.2, "it" refers to "equipment." In 4.2, the antecedent of "this" is not clear.
3. Use pronoun or demonstrative adjective in reasonable proximity to antecedent.	87:1.1 87:2.1	"We" and "our" (for the company); "he" and "his" (for Mr. Bloom).
4. Repeat antecedent (e.g., name, place) as necessary for reader understanding.	87:2.1	"Company" (repeated).

Fig. 17.3 / Paragraphing—coherence—antecedent references.

PARAGRAPHING: COHERENCE—CONNECTIVE CUES

These are generally conjunctions and transitional words or phrases which connect sentence elements and also relate sentences to other sentences. Categories of some of the frequently used connective cues are: purpose, time, addition, priority, comparison/contrast, exemplification, intensification/repetition, result, cause/reason, and summary.

Categories	Spec. Ref.
purpose: it is (not) the purpose, for this purpose, toward this objective, to attain this goal	89:2.1
time: in the past, today, tomorrow, after, at this time, now, recently, immediately, meanwhile, subsequently, before	28:2.1, 31:5.3, 44:2.2, 79:4.1
addition: first, second, third . . . , next, one other, and, again, also, furthermore, moreover, last, finally	74:2.4
priority: most of all, most important, of great signifi-cance, highly important, above all, of secondary importance, least important, of equal importance, insignificant, better, worse	77:3.4, 93:2.1
comparison/contrast: but, however, in comparison, in contrast, on the other hand, on the contrary, likewise, nevertheless, still, whereas	5:3, 43:3.2, 113:7.1
exemplification: for example, for instance, case in point, in particular, to exemplify, consider . . . , to illustrate	41:3.2, 64:2.3,4, 80:2.1
intensification/repetition: as stated, as . . . said, remember, bear in mind, in fact, in other words, obviously, of course, that is, clearly, certainly	36:2.2, 39:4
result: so, thus, as you can see, therefore, consequently, accordingly	1:3.1, 46:3
cause/reason: for this reason, because, due to	40:1.2, 60:3.1
summary (often implicit): in summary, in brief, in sum, it all adds up to, all . . . means that	33:5.1

Fig. 17.4 / Paragraphing—coherence—connective cues.

Useful techniques to achieve emphasis are: sentence placement, sentence contrast, and proportion. Figure 17.6 presents principles and specimen examples of these three techniques.

Paragraph *length* should be viewed from the logical, psychological, and media perspectives. Some organizational subject matter falls easily into logical units that dictate paragraph lengths. Other materials require a variety of long, average, and short paragraphs to meet inherent logical demands.

A psychological perspective concerns your reader. Sophisticated, critical read-ers may be capable of assimilating ideas presented in lengthy, complex para-graphs. On the other hand, short, simple paragraphs may be necessary to communicate thoughts to receivers with little or no background.

PARAGRAPHING: COHERENCE—PARALLEL CONSTRUCTION

This is the use of similar sequential sentence patterns. Generally, each sentence follows the same word order, voice, and mode. Properly used, other transitional forms may not be needed within a given paragraph. In organizational communication, parallel construction is especially applicable to policy and procedural documents.

Spec. Ref.	Type of Document	Comments
91 (a-e)	policy	clear and effective
92 (III)	policy	with exception of item 1, is clear and effective; item 1 too detailed in relation to items 2, 3, and 4
94	procedure called policy	mislabeled "policy" when actually procedural; statements 1 through 6 are not parallel in style
106:3	report	items 1 through 8 concise, clear action-centered parallel statements

---

Fig. 17.5 / Paragraphing—coherence—parallel construction.

PARAGRAPHING: EMPHASIS

---

sentence placement: Generally, beginning and ending sentences are primary emphasis points in a paragraph, the ending commonly the more emphatic of the two. Spec. 1:2.1, beginning; Spec. 1:5.2, ending; Spec. 2:1.3 ending; 2:2.2, ending; 5:2.1, beginning; 108:1.1, beginning.

sentence contrast: This is concerned with sentence length and type. Contrast is achieved by placing sentences of different length or type in proximity. Sentence contrast is attention getting, giving life to your writing.

Spec. Ref.	Type	Length	Comments
41:1.1	complex	long	
.2	complex	long	effective contrast
.3	question	short	
.4	question	medium	
.5	question	long	
47:1	simple	short	"jerky" pattern; ineffective contrast
57:2.1	simple	medium	
.2	question/ complex	long	effective contrast
.3	compound	long	
.4	simple	short	
.5	simple	short	

proportion: This deals with the magnitude of detail given to an idea in a paragraph. Generally, the more lengthy and detailed treatment emphasizes an idea over one given less length and detail. Spec. 5:2—size of paragraph corresponds to emphasis desired by writer; Spec. 6—all paragraphs are approximately the same length, giving insufficient emphasis to the last paragraph, which is the most important; Spec. 31—emphasis lost in that writer does not give more detail in a single paragraph and less detail to peripheral points in another short paragraph.

Fig. 17.6 / Paragraphing—emphasis.

The medium also is an important determinant of paragraph length. For example, technical reports frequently contain lengthy, involved paragraphs. On the other hand, many company brochures (e.g., house organs), are written in a journalistic style (frequently one sentence paragraphs). Letters and memoranda may employ paragraphs that are lengthy, short, or a mixture of both, depending on the subject matter and the receivers to which addressed.

Since principles of paragraph length are self-evident, we will not present a figure to exemplify them. A summary of paragraph essentials is shown in Figure 17.7.

PARAGRAPHING		
Unity of Idea:	Clear topic sentence Ideas directly relate	

Adequate Development:	Methods
	  analogy
	  cause-effect
	  comparison/
	   . contrast
	  definition
	  effect-cause
	  essential
	   elements
	  examples
	  figurative
	   language
		question-
		  answer
		quotations
		restatement
		slogans
		verbal and
		  statistical
		  details

Coherence:	Antecedent references
	Connective cues
	  purpose
	  time
	  addition
	  priority
	  comparison/
	   contrast
	Parallel construction
		exemplification
		intensification/
		  repetition
		result
		cause/reason
		summary

Emphasis:	Sentence placement Sentence contrast Sentence proportion	
Length:	Logical perspective Psychological perspective Media perspective	

Fig. 17.7 / Paragraphing.

Format

This refers to the idea pattern or organization of the communication as a whole. Whereas we have discussed individual paragraph development (admittedly format for that compositional unit), we are here concerned with the structure of ideas in an entire letter, memorandum, report, brochure, and the like.

As you remember, we have discussed format in relation to specific media (e.g., letters, memoranda, reports, proposals). Here we shall be concerned with traditional formats cutting across any type of written communication. Depending on circumstances, these sequences may be used singly, or combined with another in a given document.

Following are six of the more common, useful formats for organizational communications: (1) time sequence, (2) space sequence, (3) essential elements, (4) problem-analysis-solution, (5) order of importance, (6) statement-elaboration-restatement.

Bear in mind that these are commonly used conventional logically oriented patterns of organization. They have definite utility, but they also have limitations. Figure 17.8 sets forth the six conventional patterns together with specimen references.

FORMAT

Traditional Format and Definition	Spec. Ref.
time sequence: chronological pattern—most common, past, present, future (e.g., company growth, development); first, second, third, . . . (e.g., procedures), or variations	23 (present, past, future) 115 (past)
space sequence: pattern—locational (e.g., department or building)	
essential elements: important logical divisions of a topic (e.g., job description)	29, 101
problem-analysis-solution: 1. statement of the trouble; 2. why it exists; 3. how to solve it (e.g., recommendation report)	33, 70, 79, 111
order of importance: ascending or descending sequence (e.g., "an important idea is . . . , even more important is . . . , but the most important is.")	92 (most important implicit III.1; less important, 2-4, descending order) 93 (explicit [1,2] and implicit [3-5] ascending order) 100 (implicit, ascending order) 107 (p. 3 "conclusions")
statement-elaboration-restatement: 1. clarification of issue; 2. details of what, when, where, why; 3. reassertion of issue	24, 28, 64

Fig. 17.8 / Format (traditional).

Message Clarity

This dimension is self-defining in that it refers to clearness of the essential idea (or ideas) in the document. It goes without saying that unless your basic message can be clearly perceived by the reader, the communication fails. Unfortunately, this factor is too often ignored in writing organizational documents.

Certainly, proper paragraphing and format enter into message clarity. Beyond these, the following can strengthen this factor: (1) subject and prefatory materials, (2) compositional devices, and (3) typographical devices. All three are illustrated in Figure 17.9.

MESSAGE CLARITY			
Spec. Ref.	Materials: Subject/Prefatory	Devices: Compositional	Devices: Typographical
6	heading as salutation	block design	capitals; exclamation point for attention and emphasis
25	name of document, person, title	section headings; indentations	capitals; underlining
89	repetition of heading	indentation; footnotes	heading in color (not shown); contrasting type faces and sizes
92	I. Function— overview of job	enumeration; section headings; indentations	capitals; underlining
96	title and introductory sentence	section headings; indentation; columnar captions; parenthetical explanation	headings in color (not shown); contrasting type faces and sizes
97	subject heading and introductory paragraph	block indentation	

Fig. 17.9 / Message clarity.

Tone

Tone refers to the writer's attitude *as perceived by* the *reader* of the document. It can be viewed as either positive or negative, and, if the message is to have maximum impact, tone should be positive. The following characteristics are crucial to positive tone: (1) avoidance of red flags, (2) avoidance of overfamiliarity, (3) avoidance of insincerity, (4) avoidance of writer-centeredness. Using specimen references, Figure 17.10 presents illustrations of negative and positive tone.

TONE

Spec. Ref.	Avoidance of Red Flags	Avoidance of Overfamiliarity	Avoidance of Insincerity	Avoidance of Writer-centeredness
40	adequate: no mention of IRS (red flag) in heading	adequate: good blending of formal mode while pointing out reader benefits	adequate: gives basic benefits but leaves decision to reader	adequate: organization is depicted as medium to help the reader; reader perspective
48	poor: obvious mass distribution solicitation	poor: informality and maudlin details create air of condescension—"soap opera"	poor: overdone in heart-rending and begging theme	poor: reader benefits incidental; writer-perspective
58	poor: obvious mass distribution dun (address and salutation fill-in)	poor: overdoing of "buddy-buddy" through inappropriate "humor"	poor: "humorous" introduction appears sarcastic to most readers	poor: attempt to make "goodwill" in last part obliterates basic issue (collection of past due account)
65	poor: heading "Audit" generally creates reader hostility	adequate: formality creates impersonality	poor: last sentence in memo only allusion to reader cooperation	poor: entire document writer-centered (management perspective)
66	poor: heading "Budget Reduction" creates reader defensiveness	adequate: formality creates impersonality	poor: last sentence in first paragraph is patent insincerity	poor: entire document writer-centered (management perspective)
74	poor: heading "Job Termination" could cause unnecessary reader hostility; if changed to "Confirmation of Job Termination" would probably be lessened or eliminated	adequate: personal touch with formality	adequate: facts stated clearly along with sincere expression of goodwill	adequate: combination of company requirements and receiver perspective
78	poor: negative evaluative heading immediate red flag to receiver	poor: reader is being personally blamed for breakdown	poor: overdone in a piling on of discrepancies and rubbing the reader's nose in them	poor: personal attack overshadows the real issue; emphatic writer perspective

Fig. 17.10/Tone.

Summary: Principles of Persuasive Writing

Figure 17.11 summarizes the dimensions of persuasive writing.

PRINCIPLES OF PERSUASIVE WRITING	
Paragraphing	Unity of Idea
	Adequate Development
	Coherence
	Emphasis
	Length
Format	Time Sequence
	Space Sequence
	Essential Elements
	Problem-Analysis-Solution
	Order of Importance
	Statement-Elaboration-Restatement
Message Clarity	Subject and Prefatory Materials
	Compositional Devices
	Typographical Devices
Tone	Avoidance of Red Flags
	Avoidance of Overfamiliarity
	Avoidance of Insincerity
	Avoidance of Writer-centeredness

Fig. 17.11 / Summary—principles of persuasive writing.

EXERCISES

exercise 1 List and define the five paragraphing elements discussed in this chapter.

exercise 2 List the six format types, giving an example of each.

exercise 3 List the three elements of message clarity.

exercise 4 List the four elements of positive tone.

Part V

Reference Materials: Specimens

Specimen/1

MEMORANDUM

TO   W.S. Miller, Dean of Students   DATE October 12, 19--

FROM   R.M. Jones, Systems and Procedures Department

SUBJECT   Reports of Mr. Thompson and Miss Thomas

I wish to clarify the issues you raise respecting the reports by
Mr. Thompson and Miss Thomas.

No one in this department has any knowledge of the report
of Mr. Thompson. However, Dr. Theodore Browne in the Management
Department did give me Miss Thomas' report to do with it as I
wished. I read through it and then gave it to the department
involved with the comment that it might be of interest.

As you can see, I merely acted as a communication link when I
received the report from Dr. Browne. Our Department had no
official or unofficial part in the study to which you refer.

The Systems and Procedures Department never assigns anyone
outside this Department to examine University procedures. Any
official studies are always conducted by full-time Department
personnel who are given the complete sanction and cooperation
of the unit involved.

I am sorry for any misunderstanding that has arisen. I have
fully enjoyed working with you and your staff. I know that I
speak for the entire Department in wishing to continue this kind
of relationship.

RMJ:ti
cc: Dr. Theodore Browne

LETTERHEAD

Reference:

March 13, 19--   18-038-1824

Mr. William S. Miller
1200 Central Avenue
Spencer, Transylvania 54321

Dear Mr. Miller:

    Please excuse our delay in answering your letter of
February 14th. We were very sorry to hear the expense
and repair work suffered on your automobile. In order
that we might check into this matter more thoroughly, we
are taking the opportunity of sending your letter to our
District Office.

    Please be assured that we appreciate your patronage
of our products and services and want you to be satisfied
with the services we offer. Your complaint will be
checked into and we thank you for bringing this to our
attention.

Yours very truly,

Robert M. Jones
Senior Creditman

RMJ:ti

Specimen/3

THANK YOU . . .

Item(s):

LADIES GARMENT BAG, DELUXE

_____

_____

_____

. . . for your recent order for
Star-X merchandise. Unfortunately,
due to heavy demand, some of the
merchandise is temporarily out of
stock.

Rather than delay your entire order,
we are shipping those items which
are available now. The balance of
your order, which is listed on the
left, will be shipped shortly.

We at Star-X look forward to the
pleasure of serving you again very
soon.

Specimen/4

MEMORANDUM

March 30, 19--

TO: Budget Study Committee

FROM: Robert M. Jones, Chairman

An extremely important item has come up which calls for
immediate attention (my secretary Cindy doesn't fully
agree with the urgency of the matter)!

Don Thompson has sent me a maroon, Arrow Nausau, Ban-lon,
100% nylon Perma-Iron, large size polo shirt. I picked
this up near one of the chaise -ounges at the motel thinking
it belonged to Don. I put it in his room before leaving.
He has now kindly returned it to me thinking it was mine.

Either I am now a thief or it belongs to one of you. Please
let me know immediately if it does belong to you. It is
important that I know so that I can be relieved of the
tremendous guilt feelings I now have at being a thief.
If I hear from more than one of you, I will cut the shirt
up and send you each a part.

I eagerly await your attention to this matter.

LETTERHEAD

September 13, 19--

Mr. William Miller
Loan Officer, Spencer Bank
1200 Central Avenue
Spencer, Transylvania 54321

Dear Mr. Miller:

I stopped by the bank this morning, but you were out
of your office. I am sure your secretary gave you my
signed note for the $10,000 loan.

Frankly, I'm deeply disappointed to have to pay a 9%
interest rate. While I can understand the risk you
feel the bank is taking because of the small amount
of collateral I can offer, I feel that you have completely
disregarded my credit record for the last 10 years. I
have always paid my bills, and I have always repaid past
loans to all financial institutions, including yours.

However, since I seem to have no alternative, and since
I need the money immediately, I have reluctantly signed
the note.

Sincerely,

Robert Jones

RJ/ti

LETTERHEAD

September 15, 19--

Mr. William S. Miller
1200 Central Avenue
Spencer, Transylvania   54321

SEMINARS IN UNIVERSITY ADMINISTRATIVE SYSTEMS

We apologize! We did not anticipate the large number
of people who are interested in learning more about
the planning and budgeting problems of colleges and
universities. We have been unable to accommodate all
applicants in the originally scheduled seminars.

Eight administrative seminars were held including
planning a budgeting system and a management information
system. These seminars covered three different situations:
a university, a health sciences educationcomplex, and a
small college.

In order to satisfy the requests of those who were unable
to be accommodated in our original series, we have added
two more administrative seminars to be held in October
and December. These are described in the enclosed
brochures. We hope that you will find these dates
convenient and be able to attend one of these sessions.

ROBERT M. JONES - DIRECTOR

ti
Enclosures: 2

Dear Mr. Miller:

A note of thanks for your courteous reply to my request
about job possibilities with your firm. I'm sorry you
have no current openings into which I could fit. But
a little courtesy goes a long way towards better
business, even if neither one of us profits directly.

Sincerely,

Robert Jones

Specimen/8

LETTERHEAD

August 6, 19--

Dear Mr. Miller:

Thank you for your letter of July 2.
I have received the copy of your book, and
I appreciate your having sent it to me.
I am glad to hear that you found my ideas
helpful.

Sincerely yours,

Robert M. Jones

Mr. William S. Miller
1200 Central Avenue
Spencer, Transylvania   54321

LETTERHEAD

March 19--

Dear Mr. Miller:

I wish to thank you and acknowledge your generous donation of $5.00. Your kindness is deeply appreciated.

It is your assistance that enables us to go about our daily tasks, and to extend a hand of love and friendship to the young and the old. All of this is included in the material help you have given to us.

We read about people who are indifferent to the sufferings of others, people who do not care. YOU CARE. Your concern marks the difference between hope and despair for these people.

Each day we offer prayers for the needs and intentions of our benefactors. We are pleased to include you as a friend.

May God bless you always.

                              Sincerely yours,

                              Reverend Robert M. Jones

LETTERHEAD

October 10, 19--

19---19-- OFFICERS

Professor William S. Miller
City University
400 College Street
University Park, Nohio 98765

Dear Professor Miller:

    This is to sincerely thank you for your kind help and assistance at the Annual Convention of the Public Accountants Society of Nohio held on September 26 and 27.

    Your appearance before our group contributed greatly toward the success of the convention.

    It is hoped that our members will reciprocate the favor by being better accountants and of greater service to the community in which we live.

    Again, thank you so very much.

        Cordially yours,

        PUBLIC ACCOUNTANTS SOCIETY OF NOHIO

        Robert M. Jones
        President

RMJ:ti

Specimen/11

INTRAOFFICE TRANSMITTAL SLIP

TO   Dr. William Miller   DATE March 23, 19--

FROM   Bob Jones

SUBJECT   Book on "Effective Communication of Ideas"

      Enjoyed your book and found it to be a clear analysis of the processes, normally taken for granted, of getting ideas across. I think I will be more conscious of "how" to hit the targets in the future.

Specimen/12

April 14, 19--

Mr. William S. Miller
1200 Central Avenue
Spencer, Transylvania   54321

Dear Mr. Miller:

Thank you for your recent inquiry concerning the University. We are sending you additional material under separate cover and welcome the opportunity to answer any questions you may have after you have studied this material.

To apply for admission to the University, please fill out the application form, according to the instructions enclosed. Forward this completed form, along with a check or money order for the required evaluation fee, to the Office of Admissions and Records.

Thank you again for your interest in the University. If we can be of any further service, please let us know.

Sincerely,

Robert M. Jones
Director
Office of Admissions
 and Records

RMJ:3

Specimen/13

W   U   TELEGRAM
WESTERN UNION

1000A CDT JUL 24 7 KA 137
K CDU080 AZ DWU 539 28/27 PD INTL FR CD KOEBENHAVN
VIA WUI 24 2153

COLLEGE OF BUSINESS
    ADMINISTRATION CITY UNIVERSITY UNIV PRK
W. A. MILLER
    MR THOMPSEN ON HOLIDAY CANT FIND HIM PLEASE WAIT
FOR ANSWER UNTIL MONDAY 27
    JOHANSEN   MORGANISATIONEN
    27.

Specimen/14

. . .

I hereby offer to purchase the automobile above described, at the above price. The price quoted is for immediate delivery, but if for a new car on which the price should be changed by the manufacturer before I have taken delivery, then this offer shall be construed as if the changed price was originally inserted herein. If this offer is accepted by the dealer, then the delivery is subject to strikes, fires, floods or any other cause beyond the dealer's control.

The undersigned warrants that the used car offered in trade is free and clear of all encumbrances and taxes, and will furnish clear title at time of delivery.

It is agreed that this car if purchased by me is subject to provisions of the Manufacturer's Warranty if any, and that it is the only warranty, either expressed or implied, made under this order, or otherwise. No warranty or guarantee of any kind is given on used or second hand cars or trucks, unless given in writing.

. . .

OFFEROR'S SIGNATURE _____

Specimen/15

LETTERHEAD

17 November 19--

Mr. William Miller
Gourmet Catering
1200 Central
Spencer, Transylvania

Dear Bill,

This letter will simply document our recent conversations
regarding the dinner, Gourmet Catering, will cater at the
Seminar Center, on Wednesday, 18 November. The menu remains
the same as stated in Mrs. Thomas' letter of 10 September
in which you have confirmed to us. You have also confirmed
that the following will be served as hors d"'Oeuvres
with cocktails at 6:00 p.m.:

       Fresh Tahitian Shrimp with Pineapple Sauce
       Crab Cakes
       Turkey Rubins

The cost of this mean will be $7.50 plus 10% tip or a total
charge of $8.25. You will be providing the mix, for the
cocktails, however we will have the liquor available for you
upon your arrival. Following the dinner I have instructed
you to send the bill to me.

I have given you a guarantee of 30 people, however as I
explained there will be no more than 27 or 28 people in
attendance. If you have any questions regarding these
arrangements, please contact me.

Sincerely

Robert M. Jones
Assistant Director

RMJ:ti

cc: Mrs. Verna Thomas
    Mr. Donald B. Thompson

Specimen/16

30 Juli 19--.

Mr. Prof. Miller.

We thank you for your letter of 15 Juli asking
for a room. We have for you reserved:
    1 double room with shower and toilet.
    Arrival: 13 Sept. after 12:00 AM.
    Departure: 18 Sept. before 10:00 AM.
    Price: Kr. 57.50 incl. taxes and service.

Deposit: 24 hours before Arrival we must have 10 Dollars.

Yours very sincerely,

R. Johansen

Mimersgade 11-13
1100 KBH. N.

Specimen/17

Registration or Information Request

Please register me in the administrative/technical seminar

on the following date:
(please indicate a first and second choice)

☐ March 17   ☐ July 14

☐ April 14   ☐ August 18

☐ May 12   ☐ October 27

☐ June 16   ☐ December 1

_____
Name

_____
Position

_____
Organization

_____
Address

_____
City   Province or state   Zip Code

☐ I would like more information

☐ Please send me information on
hotel accommodations

☐ Other people from my organization
will be attending seminars and information
concerning them has been attached

☐ Payment enclosed

☐ Bill my organization

☐ Bill me

LETTERHEAD

July 23, 19--

Mr. William S. Miller
1200 Central Avenue
Spencer, Transylvania   54321

Dear Bill:

I enjoyed talking to you today and was delighted
to hear that you plan to visit us on August 12.
Pursuant to our conversation, I will expect you
sometime in the vicinity of 1:30 pm.

If I can be of any further assistance do not
hesitate to contact me.

Cordially,

Robert M. Jones
Division Manager

RMJ:ti

P.S. I hope to have an approximation both on the
Thompson and Thomas matters for you when you
arrive here in town on August 12.

LETTERHEAD

January 29, 19--

Star-X Ltd.
Box 123
Spencer, Transylvania 54321

Attention: Mr. W. S. Miller

Subject: In-House Audit

Reference: Yellowrock Plant of America United
            Petroleum Corporation Near Wolf Creek

Gentlemen:

In accordance with your letter of January 22, we agree
to an audit of our books by American United after
January 31.

We request that you advise the name of the person who
will be handling this audit.

                    Yours very truly,

                    GOLDEN EQUIPMENT LTD.

                    Robert M. Jones

RMJ/ti

LETTERHEAD

April 12, 19--
300 South Main Street
Widespot, Texakana 24680

Star-X Apparel Corporation
1200 Central Avenue
Spencer, Transylvania 54321

Attention: Mr. W. S. Miller

Gentlemen:

In June of this year, I will be awarded the degree
of Bachelor of Science in Business Administration from
the School of Business at City University. During the
past two years I have worked part-time as a bookkeeper
with a small retail clothing store. This has given me
much insight as to how a business works. In addition, I
have learned much in the management of human resources,
which I am sure will be of great value to your firm.

This is why I am applying to your company. I think
my background in quantitative methods, management, system
analysis, and communication qualify me for a position
in your firm.

Salary is open. If you believe my services can be
effectively employed by your organization, I would
appreciate the opportunity of a personal interview.

Enclosed you will find a detailed personal data
sheet. Thank you for your time and consideration.

Sincerely yours,

Robert M. Jones

RESUME

Robert M. Jones   December, 19--

Personal	Married 5'11" 170 Pounds 24 Years Old
Professional Objective	Eventual managerial position with a dynamic and creative, public-minded organization
Education	A.B., 19--, City University (Spencer) Major: Philosophy Minor: Biology and Chemistry Graduation with "Honors in Liberal Arts and Sciences"; Dean's List numerous quarters; Eligible for Omega Beta Pi Honorary Fraternity.
	M.B.A., February, 19--, State University Graduate School of Business Administration All core business courses. Field of Concentration: Quantitative Methods and Computers. Dean's Honor List.
Work Experience	Math and Science Teacher. Instructed sixth and seventh grade youngsters in Texakana.
Summer Work	Earned one-third of total college expenses. (Earned 100% of graduate expenses.) Miscellaneous summer employment: Star-X Tractor operator, Summer, 19--. H.M. Moush Co.--Router, Sumer, 19-- Forest Preserve District of Spencer County-- Golf Starter, Summers 19-- and 19--. Spencer County Assessor's Office--Clerical Assistant--Summer, 19--
Interests	Wife, a graduate of City University, is an Art Instructor. No children. Enjoy traveling. Recently toured the Southwest. Interested in politics, painting, music, and active sports. Enjoy entertaining.
References	References will be furnished upon request.

411

LETTERHEAD

May 2, 19--

Mr. William S. Miller
1200 Central Avenue
Spencer, Transylvania 54321

Dear Mr. Miller:

Let me introduce myself. My name is Robert M. Jones. I live at 300 South Main. My telephone number is 899-7676. I am single, a U.S. citizen, and I was born August 9, 19--. I am 6' tall and weigh 185.

I am finishing my bachelor's degree in business administration this June. I majored in management and minored in industrial psychology. This background, together with my ambition to succeed in business, in my opinion, qualifies me for a management position in your firm. Incidentally, even though my father is an Air Force officer, I have no aspirations for a military career.

My avocational interests are tennis, golf, swimming, and mountain climbing. You can see, therefore, that my background and interests are certainly compatible with what your company needs to carry on its essential functions.

I would like a personal interview at your convenience. You may communicate with me at the above address.

Sincerely,

Robert M. Jones

Specimen/23

To William S. Miller, Personnel Director   **DATE**   March 15, 19--

FROM Robert M. Jones, Project Leader, Engineering Division

SUBJECT Application for Manager of Research

My supervisor, Donald B. Thompson, has informed me that the above position is open as of May 1st. I think I am completely qualified to do this job successfully and in the best interests of the Company.

As you will see in my personnel record, I held a comparable position with the Allright Engineering Company before coming here two years ago. I managed that department with success, increasing revenues from $50,000 to $175,000 per year in the three years I was in the position. As you well know, I was forced to move West because of my wife's health.

While I thoroughly enjoy my present position, I feel that I can best serve the company in the position of Manager of Research. Would you carefully examine my personnel record, then let me come in for a talk with you?

CC: Donald B. Thompson

LETTERHEAD

AIR MAIL

Dean William S. Miller
School of Business
City University
University Park, Transylvania 54321

Dear Dean Miller:

Dr. Donald Thompson, a mutual friend, has told me that you are looking for a full professor to teach management sciences for the coming academic year. I am very much interested in this position. The enclosed vita highlights my qualifications.

Please give me details concerning (1) salary; (2) teaching load; (3) courses to be taught; (4) tenure policies; (5) writing and research facilities; and (6) compensatory benefits.

I would be delighted to visit your School and to talk with you, providing, of course, that you pay my travel expenses. I am looking forward to hearing from you.

Sincerely,

Robert M. Jones, Ph.D.

Encl: Vita

VITA

Robert M. Jones, Ph.D.

Professor of Management
College of Business Administration,
State University

DEGREES: A.B., M.A., Harvard University; Ph.D., Stanford

PUBLICATIONS:
Books: fourteen (14); most recent: Management Theory
in Twentieth Century; Communicating for Effective
Management.

HONORS AND AWARDS:

Phi Beta Kappa   Dictionary of American
Who's Who in the East   Scholars

PROFESSIONAL MEMBERSHIPS AND OFFICES:

John Smith Publishing Company, Management Series,
Consulting Editor
Management Consultants, Inc.,President
Academy of Management
Eastern Academy of Management
Delta Sigma Pi
International Business Education Association

CONSULTATION AND RESEARCH:

Fifteen years' experience with over 200 hundred business,
governmental, and professional organizations, including:

American Society of Training Directors
Martin Marietta Corporation
U.S. Civil Service Commission
U.S. Department of Health, Education and Welfare
United Air Lines
Shell Petroleum Company
Asbjørn Habberstad, Oslo
British Board of Trade, London
Special study of management roles in Western
European government and business (West Germany,
Great Britain, Austria, Denmark, France).

LETTERHEAD

April 22, 19--

Mr. William S. Miller
Assistant Dean, Graduate College
School of Business
City University
University Park, Nohio 98765

Dear Dean Miller:

At present either you or one of your associates are evaluating my application for admission to City University School of Business.

I am writing this letter to give a more complete picture of myself because I feel that the application seemed to be based almost entirely on my undergraduate record. I feel that my experiences of the past three years have also been an influential and important part of my record.

Since my graduation in 19-- with a B.A. in Social Sciences, I have been teaching 7th and 9th grade Social Studies in a culturally deprived area. This social studies curriculum involves American history in the 7th grade and government and economics in the 9th grade. My experience in teaching this 9th grade curriculum, plus my thoughts for the future have drawn me toward my decision to apply to your division of the University.

Frankly, I feel that I want a career in business rather than in education. My three years of teaching has brought me this realization. That is why I am applying to your school. A graduate degree in business will complement my undergraduate Bachelor's degree and better enable me to prepare myself for a career in business, whether it be in advertising or marketing.

I would like to interview you about my application. I am going to be in your city on August 15. May I see you at 10:00 a.m. on that date?

Thank you very much for your time and consideration.

Sincerely yours,

LETTERHEAD

CONTRACT MAINTENANCE DIVISION

Contract maintenance services by Star-X include project
management, planning, scheduling, providing necessary manpower
and other functions related to maintenance or operational programs.
These services may be applied to a continuous or short term program to meet your specific requirements.

The most up-to-date methods of data processing and critical path
planning are employed to assist with administration, planning and
cost accounting. They assure our customers of complete current
information on work progress and financial status.

The procurement of materials and supplies required in connection
with any contract, is the function of our Procurement Department.
Through experience gained in purchasing materials for many and
varied industries, this group has developed a high degree of
competence and accumulated a wealth of resource material. These
services also include expediting of deliveries and complete
material control.

Through the efforts of a well qualified and experienced safety
group, Star-X has developed a safety program encompassing all
company operations. This program, in close coordination with our
Insurance Company Safety and Claims Department, as well as
Individual State Industrial Commissions, has resulted in an
excellent Safety Record.   . . .

LETTERHEAD

March 15, 19--

Mr. William S. Miller
Star-X Engineering Consultants
1200 Central Avenue
Spencer, Transylvania 54321

Dear Mr. Miller:

You have asked for a quote on a training course in modern
management for your top executives. We can give you all
training materials and equipment for our course for a very
reasonable figure.

Today, the transition from hourly worker to supervision--
and from supervision to management--can be accomplished
far more effectively because we have developed a pretested
program that helps supervisors and managers become effective
members of the management team without using the trial and
error methods of the past.

Our Program centers around practical, self-development,
self-evaluating materials that cover all of the vital areas
of supervision and management. They also include valuable
information in everyday business economics, in public
affairs and politics, and in how to handle critical conference
and inter-personal situations.

The program is easy to use, and is presented in an exciting,
educational format. It will make a real impact on everyone
whose job performance is related to his management knowledge
and attitudes.

This comprehensive program is available in motion picture
film and/or video tape for companies that prefer to hold
their own supervisory or management discussion conferences.
All are described in the enclosed brochures.

Our price for all materials and equipment to train one
hundred people is $18,000. I am sure you can see that this
is a very low cost for upgrading your executives' competence.
I look forward to hearing from you.

Sincerely yours,

Robert M. Jones
Director

RMJ: ti
Encl: 2

LETTERHEAD

DEPARTMENT OF MANAGEMENT SERVICES

Examination Number	Title	Monthly Salary Range
1026/74:1294	ASSISTANT DIRECTOR	$1572-$2037

DUTIES:

Under the direction of the Executive Director, assists in planning, directing, and administering the functions of the Department of Management Services; acts for the Executive Director in assigned areas of responsibility; assists in budget development and adminis- stration; represents the departments in meetings and conferences, with delegated authority to speak and act for the department. Administers the Division of Central Services and related areas or divisions to provide services to the various state agencies. Establishes standards and specifications; coordinates services with other divisions and departments; supervises the writing of instructions and information manuals for all services; prepares and executes budgets of the area assigned; assists in planning a cost accounting and billing system for all activities and implements and maintains the system.

REQUIREMENTS:

Graduation from college with a Bachelor and Masters degree in public or business administration, or a closely related field. Six years of progressively responsible professional and administrative experience in the fields of private business or government, includ- ing the planning and supervision of the work of others. Experience in financial and operational planning is desirable. Additional professional or administrative experience at the State PAT VI level (major division chiefs or deputy directors at beginning salary of $1328) or its equivalent in private business may be substituted for the graduate degree requirement.

EXAMINATION:

Written qualifying examination and an oral examination weighted 100%.

APPLY WITH:

Personnel Office, Room 5516, by June 15.

DATE RELEASED: May 15, 19--.   POST THRU: June 15, 19--

LETTERHEAD

TO: All Departments

From: Safety

Subject: Fire Safety

    The Company has received a series of film strips and records pertaining to Fire Safety.

    In an effort to have maximum attendance, it is desired that all Department Heads regulate the work schedules of the employees to enable them to view one (1) of the six (6) periods scheduled. The entire program will last approximately one (1) hour.

The film strips to be shown are as follows:

Fire Safety Procedures.	20 Min
Fire Hazards.	20 Min
Fire Extinguisher Equipment.	20 Min

Schedule:

When: 1 May, 19--   Where: Room 442
                                        Building C
Times: 10:00 AM
          2:00 PM
          7:00 PM
          8:30 PM
          3:00 AM
          4:30 AM

                                          Robert M. Jones
                                          Safety Officer

Specimen/31

March 13, 19--

PERSONAL

Vice-President William S. Miller
City University
University Park, Nohio 98765

Dear Bill:

Especially since nothing as yet has materialized -- I
regret to report -- where John is concerned, I apologize
for having imposed on you quite some time ago in the hope
and expectation that he might again be qualified to return
to City University. However, we see signs of greater
maturity producing results that we were unable to force.

My real purpose in writing you is to ask how I might learn
of the status of an applicant for the University's post
graduate Business School, Mr. Donald Thompson, who is a
graduate of Country Club Prep and presently a senior at
South State College or University -- I'm not sure which.

An inquiry about his admission has come from his father,
Jim Thompson, past president and board chairman and still a
director of Wells Mills, Inc., and who is a neighbor of ours
here in Hacienda Estates.

The Thompsons are outstanding people by any measurement and
very good friends of ours since acquiring our place near his
five years ago; they were close friends of Martha Brown and
of course remain so with Verna whose winter residence is
also nearby. I gather also that Jim has a daughter at the
University and also a neice or a nephew. Both of the latter
students are reported doing well and liking their experience.

While of course I have not met Don, judging by all indicators
he should make a worthy graduate student. I will call you
next week when I expect to spend most of that week in town.
Meanwhile, I thought you might like to know this much about
this applicant. Again, thanking you for your courtesies,

                              Sincerely,

421

LETTERHEAD

March 3, 19--

Star-X Manufacturing
1200 Central Avenue
Spencer, Transylvania 54321

                        Attention: Employment Office Director

Gentlemen:

        I am writing on behalf of Donald B. Thompson who
has recently applied to your company as a management trainee.
This man will graduate from South State University in June
(B.A. Degree).

        Any assistance you can give Don will be personally
appreciated by me. He has my unqualified recommendation and
I sincerely feel will justify this trust should his
application be favorably considered.

        He is academically qualified, as you will note
from his record. On the personal side I want you to know
he is personable, responsible and knowledgeable. He has
been a leader in many of his undergraduate activities and
I sincerely feel would be an asset to your company.

        Please advise me when a decision has been made
and accept my deep appreciation for your assistance
in this matter.

        With warm personal regards and every good wish,
I am,

                        Sincerely yours,

                        Robert M. Jones, M.C.

RMJ:TI

Copy to Donald B. Thompson

Specimen/33

To: William S. Miller,
Vice President

From: R. M. Jones,
Director, Systems

Subject: Recommendations - Decisions required from higher authority.

Joint and individual concern having been expressed regarding timeliness of status reporting of accounting and budget matters to those having management interest and control, a meeting was held October 31. Representatives from involved departments were in attendance at the meeting held on that date.

As it was obvious from the onset that all situations which gave rise either to lack of current timeliness of reporting or progress in further management reporting aims had been laundered in detail on a number of such occasions, two recommendations were made by this author which were to the heart of the problems of not only the budget reports, but also all other sub-systems to a total management informations systems. Neither was totally new, however neither had been discussed with such broad representation present not with apparant general agreement as to the need for some action and authoritative decision.

The recommendations are as follows:

1. That all computer facilities of this Company be brought under the Computer Division with one and only one director of the division. That this unit shall be responsive to and serve the needs for data processing and computing for both administrative reporting and research efforts. That this unit shall be organizational so placed that it is not responsible to one department or area of use, but rather in a position to be equally responsive to all Company needs.

2. That the total accounting responsibility and activities of the Company be placed with the Office of Accounts and that all reporting units will be responsible to him.

It was the opinion of the group that these recommendations be placed before the proper authorities and that each of the attendees would endorse these recommendations as stated above with or without qualifications by attached memo.

Specimen/34

RECOMMENDATIONS

COMMUNICATION RESPONSIBILITY

1. At both regional and divisional levels, there should be clear, operational, and comprehensive policies specifying the importance of and establishing guidelines for communication responsibility at all levels and for all personnel. Administrative heads should reinforce the seriousness with which these policies are to be viewed, once they are formulated, approved and released.

2. Once policies are formulated, requirements for communication responsibility should be set forth for each position and for each organizational sub-unit. These should embrace the communication procedures, operations, and performance levels required for ensuring communication responsibility. Each person should be thoroughly indoctrinated in the specific requirements involved in his carrying out his job with requisite communication responsibility.

3. Monitoring and correction of communication responsibility should be systematically carried out, based on the stated policies and requirements. Communication responsibility should be included in all performance appraisals and appropriate "quality increase" procedures. Graphs, profiles, or logs can be used as bases for review of communication responsibility with personnel. Supervisory personnel should be held directly responsible for the communication responsibility of those directly under them. They should be given adequate orientation and training to carry out effectively these functions of monitoring and correction. While these procedures should emphasize the constructive approach of counseling and training to improve communication responsibility, repeated and flagrant cases of communication irresponsibility should bring forthright administrative action, including replacement if necessary. Bad examples must not be allowed to act as negative models for other personnel, nor to attenuate the importance of communication responsibility.

Specimen/35

CITY UNIVERSITY
MEMORANDUM

To   All Faculty Members   Date March 1, 19--

From   Robert M. Jones, Registrar

Subject   Final Exam Schedule - Spring Semester

Please follow the final examination schedule printed in the schedule of classes book for the spring semester. The examination schedule for the entire year was printed in the autumn schedule of classes book. There is a discrepancy the exam schedule for the spring semester as listed in the fall schedule book and the one listed in the spring schedule book. Please follow the examination schedule found in the spring schedule book.

Specimen/36

Dear Reader,

Above the door of the workshop of Aldus, the great fifteenth century printer, a sign proclaimed a warning to visitors. 'Whoever you are who wish to see Aldus, be brief: and when business is finished go away; unless indeed you are able and willing to assist him as Hercules did Atlas in his need: and even then remember that whoever gains here a footing must work hard and with perseverance.'

Aldus, whose device is reproduced in the introduction to the enclosed prospectus, was deeply concerned with both the text of his books and with their appearance. So indeed is The Literary Society, and it is just this attention to the text - that it should be both readable and accurate - and to the appearance - that it should be individual, attractive and a complement to the text - that makes membership of the Society so rewarding for lovers of fine books. If you are already a member you will know this for yourself, if not I would like to introduce you to a unique collection of fine editions.

Membership is simple and not expensive, and you will find both the Society and all the available publications fully described in the prospectus. Pages 5 and 6 give details of the Society's free presentation volume, a handsomely produced and lavishly illustrated ninth century account of the life of Charlemagne.

An increasing number of members in the USA and Canada are finding that their personal relationship direct with London is both rewarding and efficient, and it is worth pointing out that you will not be charged for post and packing.

Naturally I look forward to welcoming you to membership in the near future.

Yours sincerely,

Director

TI

LETTERHEAD

As an employee . . .

you probably already know about the Company's Home Protection policies, designed especially to meet the life insurance needs of employees covered by the Company's retirement plans.

This is term insurance which provides its largest amount of protection initially, reducing by schedule to recognize decreasing insurance needs. It can provide important additional coverage at moderate outlay for you, while your annuity accumulations are increasing, children are growing up, etc.

The enclosed leaflet gives the details. You can apply by completing the application form (also enclosed) and mailing it in the return envelope. We look forward to hearing from you.

Sincerely,

Robert M. Jones
Personnel Director

Encs.

300 South Main Street
Widespot, Texakana   24680
August 1, 19--

Dr. William S. Miller
City University
College of Business Administration
Office of the Dean
University Park, Nohio 98765

Dear Dr. Miller:

I am enclosing all the necessary items for admission to
the University. Also sent under separate cover was a
letter of recommendation from Dr. Donald Thompson of
Progressive Oil Company.

In evaluating my records, I would like to point out the
fact that I was working full time at Progressive Oil
Company and carrying twelve semester hours during my last
two years at South State University. I am positive
that I would be a successful candidate for the Masters
degree at City University.

                         Sincerely,

                         Robert M. Jones

RMJ/ti
Enclosures
CC: Donald B. Thompson

LETTERHEAD

Dear Customer:

How about <u>100 Gallons of Gas FREE?</u> It's yours, if you
finance <u>your next new car DIRECT</u> at First National in
Spencer. Doesn't have to be right now...any time before
December 31!

Here's all you do. Shop around, select the car you want,
determine the amount you wish to finance. Then, drop in
and see us or call us at First National's Instalment Loan
Department. We're here from 9 to 5 every weekday, ' til
7 p.m. Fridays.

When your loan is completed, the First National gives you
a check made out to the Seller. And another check, for
100 gallons of gas. Probably takes you 3,000 miles in a
Compact, 1,500 miles in a larger car. It's just that
easy, that's all there is to it.

Remember, you must come in or call First National to
arrange your car loan, and we ask that you present this
letter, (it'll speed things up).

Thank you for doing your banking with us.

                                        Sincerely,

                                        Robert M. Jones
                                        Vice President

RMJ:ti

Specimen/40

TO: All Employees of City Memorial Hospital

Our hospital has been approved by the Internal Revenue
Service as a non-profit organization. For this reason, we
are able to offer each of you a favored tax shelter program,
which you are eligible for and entitled to by law.

This program will save you tax dollars and help you accumulate
money for the future.

A representative of one of the companies authorized to fund
this money by the Internal Revenue Service will be here to
set up appointments on an individual basis to explain your
rights and benefits.

We wish to assure you that there is no obligation whatever
on your part; however, the time spent in getting the full
details of the program will be of the utmost importance
to you.

Yours very truly.

Robert M. Jones
Administrator

PLACE: Personnel Office

TIME: June 5 - 9 A.M. to 12 Midnight

MEMORANDUM

TO   CAC Members   DATE May 29, 19--

FROM   R.M. Jones

SUBJECT   Community Action Club Activities

It seems that at least some members of Community Action believe, without being very explicit about it, that this organization should somehow have more impact on the community than it does. On the other hand there is a rather widespread recognition that in some ways (again not made very explicit) the Club is a bit of an anachronism. Does the Club have little impact? If so is this because what it represents is out of step with the times? Or is a widespread but incorrect belief that it is not very relevant to the times the reason why it has little impact?

Whatever the answers to questions like these, it is apparent that CAC receives very little support from its membership. A recent compilation indicates that there are 97 members. Yet only six members attended the last meeting at which officers were nominated (and one of these attending -- yours truly -- was 20 minutes late!). This is typical (in all respects).

So what? Well, I wonder what this means that you, the members, are thinking about the Club. In particular how would you answer the following?

1. By virtue of having joined

    (a) did you then feel that you had some responsibility to help maintain the Club?
    (b) do you now feel that you have some responsibility to help maintain the Club (make it flourish)?

2. If your answer to 1(b) is "Yes", where does your obligation lie? (check all that are appropriate)

    (a) to not bad-mouth the Club
    (b) to answer and return questionnaires like this one
    (c) to participate in the recruitment of new members
    (d) to do some important work, such as serving on the membership committee, serving as an officer, etc.
    (e) to develop programs that will better impress the values of the Club on the community at large and further the Club's objectives

Specimen/41 (continued)

3. Is it that although you believe CAC to be a worthy enterprise, there are other worthy enterprises (more worthy enterprises) that impose such demands on your time that none but 2(a) above can apply to you?

    If yes to this, is it really, really true?

4. What should CAC be doing?

    (a) nothing
    (b) inducting new members
    (c) other things, as follows

5. What should CAC do to more surely earn your interest and support?

    If you will return your answers to these questions to me, I'll try to make some use of what you say.

431

Specimen/42

INTEROFFICE CORRESPONDENCE

January 16, 19--

TO: W. S. Miller

FROM: R. M. Jones   SUBJECT

                            Planning and Scheduling

In accordance with our recent conversation, our project
management staff has been reviewed to determine if there is
a man available for assignment to the planning and scheduling
group.

A review of the current project management staff indicates
that we have in the past month lost three people. The only
possibilities that I can see within the staff for a permanent
assignment as a planning and scheduling person would be
Donald Thompson. I will discuss this possibility with him
in the next few days.

Actually, you can see that we are not horribly overstaffed
anymore. Our best approach is to do something we talked about
and that is to pursue the hiring of a planner and scheduler
from outside the company. It is my understanding that we
are endeavoring to grow, and if such is the case, this is
one way to promote a growth situation.

                                    R. M. Jones

RMJti

432

Specimen/43

December 31, 19--

Professor W.S. Miller
Chairman, General Business
City University
University Park, Nohio 98765

Dear Professor Miller:

You have asked that I write a letter evaluating Donald Thompson's credentials as a college teacher.

I recommend Mr. Thompson very highly as a teacher. I have had opportunity to observe him both as a graduate student (about six years ago) and since then as a member of our faculty. I know Don to be an excellent teacher, both very knowledgeable in his subject matter (behaviorial and quantitative management) and deeply dedicated to his students.

Frankly, I dislike the prospect of his leaving us. But Donald Thompson is too good a man to be held because he is valuable to a given institution. I predict he will go far in his academic career, and, again, I strongly recommend him to you.

Sincerely yours,

Robert M. Jones
Department Chairman

RMJ:ti

Specimen/44

LETTERHEAD

September 10, 19--

Mr. William S. Miller
1200 Central Avenue
Spencer, Transylvania   54321

Dear Mr. Miller:

Many thanks for your kind letter and I regret that it
will not be possible for you to go ahead and proceed
with your plans for the Executive Seminar at this time.
I have cancelled all tentative arrangements that had
been made on your behalf for May.

As your plans become more firm for the rescheduled dates
for the Seminar, November 15 through 18, we look forward
to working with you on specific details. Meanwhile, if
you find you are in the area, please don't hesitate to
stop in.

Very truly yours,

Robert M. Jones
Conference Director

RMJ/i

Specimen/45

UNITED STATES GENERAL ACCOUNTING OFFICE

To each GAO staff member, GS-13 and above:

The booklet "Capability of GAO to Analyze
and Audit Defense Expenditures" is being used
in our training programs to show staff members
the current philosophy and objectives of GAO.
Many GS-13's and above have not taken a training
course since the booklet was issued. We believe
that you should have access to the current
philosophy and objectives of GAO so we are
distributing these booklets now instead of waiting
until you participate in a training program. The
entire booklet is well worth your time to read
but we suggest you especially read pp. 13, 21,
and 27-34.

Specimen/46

MEMORANDUM

To   All Department Heads   DATE   June 11, 19--

FROM   Robert M. Jones, Director of Personnel

SUBJECT   Procedures Manual

We are in the process of developing a new procedures manual for secretaries and other interested personnel and your help is requested.

Each Department who has practices or procedures universally used are requested to send such practices or procedures, clearly defined, to the Personnel Office.

Our target date in January for the completion of this manual, therefore, your expediting this information to us will be appreciated.

Specimen/47

LETTERHEAD

Dear Dr. Miller:

I graduated from City University with a MBA this past August. I am now living and working in Texakana. My firm desires that I attend State University graduate school to study their program concerning Information Systems and Computers (MBIS). To obtain admission to this Masters program, I need a recommendation from the Dean of my previous graduate school. I would greatly appreciate your attention on this matter. The recommendation should go to:

> Dean of Graduate Studies
> School of Business Administration
> State College
> Parksville, Texakana   24678

I would like to take this opportunity to say that I enjoyed the program and the people that made up the Business School at City University. I think the MBA at City University is a worthwhile degree.

> Thank You

> R. Montgomery Jones, Jr.

Specimen/48

LETTERHEAD

I WOULD LIKE TO INTRODUCE YOU TO JILL AND JACK . . .

Jill and Jack are twins. Brown eyes. Blond. Together
they are about as big as a minute. Ask them how old they
are and they'll say, "three and a half."

Ask them what they want for Christmas, and Jill will say,
"a red coat with big buttons." Jack will answer, "a baseball."

Their eyes sparkle at the thought of Christmas, but on
Christmas morning this sparkle will turn to tears unless
someone helps.

Their mother is confined to bed at home recovering from
a serious operation. Their father has been gone for over
three years. Neighbors have been generous in helping care
for the children, but mother is frightened at the thought
of Christmas without enough money to provide a happy day
for the twins.

Every Christmas Charity Incorporated takes children like
these into their hearts because their need is so great.
Jill and Jack are typical of the many other children and
families who so urgently need our help.

Please help. Share the strength of your love with Jill
and Jack this Christmas. Join with us and give as generously
as you can. When you do, your Christmas will be brighter.
All that you put into the lives of others will come back into
your own.

Robert M. Jones   Donald B. Thompson
Christmas Chairman   President

THANK YOU for your support of Charity Incorporated through
your Community Fund. This annual CHRISTMAS solicitation
however, is NOT a part of the activites supported by the
Community Fund.

Specimen/49

October 31, 19--

Dear Doctor:

With the assistance, guidance and approval of the local unit
of the American Cancer Society, an additional volunteer
patient visiting service is now available. The Civic
Mastectomy Association, A Reach to Recovery project, is
now screening and training volunteers to visit post-
operative mastectomy patients. The volunteers will have
the following qualifications:

1. All women have themselves undergone mastectomies.

2. All women have been approved by their physician
    and/or surgeon as being emotionally and physically
    equipped to do voluntary work.

3. All women have undergone further screening and
    training by the visiting committee of the Civic
    Mastectomy Association.

Visiting service will be provided only upon the request
of the patient's physician. Primarily the purpose is to
give the patient confidence and understanding and by
example prove that normal living can and should be continued.
Kits will be presented to the patient containing these items:

1. A handbook of suggestions and exercises as prepared
    by the Reach to Recover Program of the National
    American Cancer Society.

2. Exercise aids to be used in conjunction with the
    handbook (with approval of patient's physician).

3. A temporary prosthesis along with information as
    to types, cost, and availability of breast forms.

Requests for volunteers should be made to Miss Verna Thomas
of the local unit of the American Cancer Society, phone
888-4867. We hope that this service will be of assistance
to your patients and solicit your support to ensure a
successful visiting program.

Sincerely,

Robert M. Jones, M.D.
Medical Advisor

437

LETTERHEAD

October 16, 19--

Dr. William S. Miller
Professor of Statistics
City University
University Park, Nohio 98765

Dear Dr. Miller:

For several years it has become increasingly evident that
the computer technology field requires more adequate
foundations in coherent theory and valid scientific
methodology. We feel that one way to obtain a more
rigorous understanding of the field is through the creation
of a scholarly journal directed toward this goal.

For several reasons we feel that the best way to obtain
funds to help launch the journal is to go directly to
the business community. When we do thi, however, we
would like to be able to show that there exists academic
support for such a journal.

A copy of the proposal that will be sent to the business
community is enclosed for your perusal. We would like
to list your name as one of the academic endorsers of
this project. If you feel the project has merit and
agree with it in principle, we would appreciate hearing
from you. A card is enclosed for this purpose.

Thank you for your time and consideration.

Sincerely yours,

Robert M. Jones, Director
Journal Feasibility Project

Enclosure

Specimen/51

October 20, 19--

Star-X Company
W. S. Miller, Sys. Anal
1200 Central Avenue
Spencer, Trans   54321

Dear Mr. Miller:

We would appreciate your comments and opinion on current
trends in management, systems and data handling problems,
especially on trends in your own organization. We are
writing only to a selected number of executives and would
especially like to know your opinions and in what ways your
operations have been improved in the following areas:

> In what ways have you made cost-savings in your data
> processing operations? What systems, methods or
> equipment have contributed most to this increased
> efficiency?

> As new and more sophisticated information and data
> handling systems become available, what is your Company
> doing to make sure that top management becomes informed
> as to capabilities, advantages and disadvantages?

> Do you personally favor greater participation by
> business firms in actively attempting to solve
> community social problems? How?

Costs are rising so rapidly that executives in every
industry urgently need improved systems and cost cutting
methods. Should you have suggestions that may help
management -- based on your own company's experience, or
your own personal background -- do please write at length.
Your comments and suggestions will be extremely helpful
in planning articles and an editorial balance more
consistent with your current needs.

Many thanks for an early reply.

Cordially,

Robert M. Jones
Assistant to the Publisher

RMJ/ti

439

Specimen/52

TO   Mr. Miller

                                    DATE June 3, 19--

FROM   Robert M. Jones

Pursuant to your suggestions at our last staff meeting, we have asked the Civil Defense to offer a twelve-hour course in shelter management. This course is designed specifically for hospital-based operations and I wonder if you would be kind enough to designate one of your housekeeping persons to attend this meeting, along with one or two other persons from the Hospital. We expect the course to be offered sometime in July; however, I have no further details on it at this moment. They strongly suggest that the Hospital include a Housekeeping representative and a Dietary representative. Please let me know as soon as you have arrived at a conclusion on this.

Thank you!

Specimen/53

AN INVITATION

To inaugurate a year devoted to planning a new library building for City University, the Faculty Committee on Library Development is sponsoring an exhibit on New and Recently Completed Academic Library Buildings. The exhibit will be held in the second floor lounge and corridors of the Student Center from 8:00 a.m. to 10:00 p.m. daily from Monday, October 6, until Friday, October 10.

All members of the University community are especially invited to view this exhibit. A form will be provided requesting your reactions to the models, plans, and drawings displayed. We hope that you will respond so that we may take your ideas and reactions into account in the planning effort that we shall be conducting this year for the new library building at City University.

                                      Faculty Committee on
                                      Library Development

                                      Robert M. Jones, Chairman

300 South Main Street
Widespot, Texakana 24680
February 15, 19--

Star-X Foods
1200 Central Avenue
Spencer, Transylvania 54321

                    Attention: Zone Manager
Gentlemen:

I have dealt with your grocery chain for nearly 25 years,
and I have always received good service, courteous attention,
and quality commensurate with price.

This is why I am very disturbed that the one time I bought
an item (a case of tuna) with which I was dissatisfied,
I have been rebuffed. All cans in the case were "swellheads."
When I tried to return the case to the store from which I
bought it, the manager, Mr. Donald Thompson, refused to
either refund my money or exchange the tuna. He said that
since I had no register receipt he could not do anything for
me.

It seems incredible to me that a firm with the reputation
for fair dealing which Star-X has could take an attitude
like this. I am asking that you see that his matter be
taken care of.

I will be awaiting your reply.

                    Sincerely,

                    Robert M. Jones

Woodstock Nation was found on the idea of communal living as
the dormitories and the union are based on communal feeding and
living. This causes us to seriously question the validity of
keeping these structures open while the Woodstock Community is
being forced to close down. The denial of our physical structures
is a denial of our original ideas, as an open University community.
We still wish to implement the ideas put forth in the Woodstock
Statement. We are against war, violence, and racism. We have
no intention of destroying, only creating -- we want to be
non-violent. We are interested in the proposals that have been
made for a variation of the physical structures we originally had,
but regardless of the decisions of President Thompson, Woodstock
Nation must survive. We wish to do what is stated in the Woodstock White Paper but will not do so unless the above demands
are considered.

We the people of Woodstock Nation West view the recent actions
of both police and President Thompson as a mockery of those
rights which are specifically granted us as members of this country
and this University community. The destruction of the physical
structures and the arrest of several members of it was a
politically repressive act, just as the arrest of liberal thinkers
across the country is an attempt to squelch dissention.

Specimen/56

March 18, 19--

Mr. William S. Miller
Service Manager
Star-X Auto Sales and Repairs
Spencer, Transylvania 54321

Dear Mr. Miller:

    I am writing you to express my complete dissatisfaction
with the "service" your shop rendered in trying to repair
my car. This is the third time in the last two weeks that
I have left the car for a full day for you to fix the
transmission. The first time, I was assured that the trouble
had been corrected. I drove only 175 miles and the same
trouble (a very noisy condition) recurred.

    I then returned the car a second time and when I picked
it up, you told me that the trouble had, to quote you, "been
absolutely fixed." I did drive it 225 miles that time before
the whole transmission went to pieces. As you know, I had
to have Jake's Towing Service bring the car to your shop
where it now sits.

    Frankly, I am sick and tired of your slick talk. I want
my car repaired. If you do not fix the car as it should
be this time, I am going directly to the Star-X Zone Manager.
In fact, you will note I am sending him a carbon copy of this
letter.

Sincerely,

Robert M. Jones

CC: Mr. Donald B. Thompson
       Zone Manager, Star-X Motors

Specimen/57

TO   W.S. Miller, Personnel Director   DATE   May 15, 19--

FROM   R.M. Jones, Production Manager

    I know that existing policy gives you primary responsibility for hiring production workers for the assembly line. And it is not my intention to try to change this basic policy.

    However, I am concerned that my production supervisors are not consulted sufficiently about new hires. Wouldn't it be better for all concerned if after your department screens an applicant, he would then be referred to the production supervisor involved for his appraisal and recommendation? I realize this may take more time and effort on the part of all of us, but I think we would get better new employees and more commitment on the part of the production supervisors. I'd be glad to discuss this policy problem with you. I think it is one that we may want to change for the company's good.

Specimen/58

LETTERHEAD

July 24, 19--

Mr. William S. Miller
1200 Central Avenue
Spencer, Transylvania   54321

Dear Mr. Miller:

    When you opened this letter, it reminded you of a good intention, something you forgot to do.

    It was to send us a check.

    We are sure this account was simply overlooked; however, if there is some other reason for non-payment, please let us know. Simply jot a note on the bottom of this letter and use the envelope enclosed for your convenience.

    Thank you for your cooperation.

                Sincerely,

                STAR-X HOTEL, INC.

                Robert M. Jones
                Credit Manager

Enclosure

Specimen/59

LETTERHEAD

A FRIENDLY SUGGESTION ABOUT INCOME TAXES:

Payment of your account before December 31 may entitle you to a deduction.

Medical expenses are deductible in the amount exceeding 3% of adjusted gross income.

BEST WISHES FOR A HAPPY HOLIDAY SEASON

Specimen/60

LETTERHEAD

April 27, 19--

William S. Miller
1200 Central Avenue
Spencer, Transylvania 54321

RE: Savings Acct. #046360
Amt. Overdrawn - $.47
Date Overdrawn - 4/5/--

Dear Mr. Miller,

Your savings account with us, identified by the account number shown above, is overdrawn in the amount indicated on the date shown.

We encourage thrift among our depositors, and we are most interested in retaining your account indefinitely. We are, of course, members of the Federal Deposit Insurance Corporation, and pay the highest rate permitted by law on your savings dollar.

For this reason, we are writing to ask that you deposit sufficient funds to cover the overdraft, and to make every effort to continue deposits on a regular basis in the future.

If I can be of service in this matter, please feel free to contact me.

Very truly yours,

R.M. Jones,
Asst. Vice President

RMJ:ti

445

Dear Customer,

I was shocked when our Collection Manager informed me today he wanted to place your account with an attorney in your local county seat. Mr Thomas feels that you will not pay Star-X unless you are forced to do so by the County Courts.

In reviewing your case you appear to be sincere and honest people. That is why I have taken the time to send one final appeal to you. You must have some type of problem or else you would be paying. Court action will not help you, it will only be more costly and embarrassing for you.

I have seen many honest people go through the added expense of Court procedure when they could have been making smaller payments until such time as they were back on their feet, and able to resume regular monthly payments.

I can only hold your file out for one week. If you will cooperate by sending one monthly payment, along with a definite plan for paying the balance you will find me most considerate and helpful.

R.M.J:i

Sincerely,
Robert M. Jones.

LETTERHEAD

June 20, 19--

Dear Former Member:

Although we are certain it has been an over-sight, our records indicate that your membership in our Society has lapsed. We urge you to rejoin now.

The Society is attempting to meet the demands of the times trhough improved and expanded services. The recent developmental project is one example of this effort. Expanded programs in Information Sciences and in aiding the disadvantaged are all in progress.

The Society needs your support. Please do not under-estimate the importance of your contribution. A member-ship application form is enclosed.

We hope to welcome you back as a member of our Society soon.

Sincerely yours,

Robert M. Jones
Secretary

encls.

RMJ/ti

LETTERHEAD

April 25, 19--

Dear Parents:

A Van Gogh original, a Mercedes-Benz, an education at a private university or college. What do a painting, a car, and private higher education have in common? They're all expensive. As William F. May, Chairman of the Board and President, American Can Company, stated recently, for the average American, educating your children is getting to be like buying a home.

No university is more aware of the costs of higher education than City University. Increased operating costs and inflation, combined with expansion of our facilities, have catapulted our annual budget from $4 million to $27.9 million in the past 15 years.

The plight of City University is symptomatic of higher education in general. The past decade saw unprecedented growth in colleges and universities as they stretched their facilities -- and their budgets -- to meet the needs of increasing numbers of students. Let me cite just a few examples of this growth:

  --More than 300 new colleges and universities have been founded since 1945.

  -- Faculty salaries have doubled in the past 10 years.

  --The total expenditure for U.S. higher education this year is $20 billion, more than three times what it was 15 years ago.

To help meet expenses the University is forced to raise tuition $300 per year beginning next September. I know you will understand why we have found it necessary to do this. Rest assured the University will do all in its power to avoid any unnecessary future tuition increases.

Sincerely yours,

Robert M. Jones, President

RMJ:ti

LETTERHEAD

February 19, 19--

Dear Customer:

By now many of you are aware of the fact that we have asked
the Public Utilities Commission for authority to increase
our rates for gas and electric service. We have taken this
action reluctantly and hope that some of the following
information will explain why it was necessary.

There is little need to recite the effects of inflation
over the past decade. We encounter it every day - in our
business life as well as our personal life. For example,
we are serving 35% more electric customers and 41% more gas
customers today than we did ten years ago, and we're doing
with only 12% more employees. During that same period of
time, our wages have increased by 78% and our taxes by 80%.
These are factors over which you, individually, or we, as
a business, have little, if any, control.

During this same 10 years, however, we have avoided any
increase in electric rates and have had only one small
increase in natural gas rates. We have reached a point,
however, where inflationary pressures have outstripped
the economies we have gained from automation, more efficient
facilities and better efforts on the part of our employees.

In view of this unfortunate, yet inevitable, situation, our
only alternative is to seek an increase in rates. We have
filed an application with the Public Utilities Commission
which, if allowed, would result in an increase of about
8.0% in electric revenues and less than 2% in natural gas
revenues.

We must ask for this increase in order to continue to furnish
you wi the high quality of gas and electric service you have
every right to expect. I sincerely hope that this information
will help you to better understand our position.

Sincerely,

Robert M. Jones
President

RMJ:ti

Specimen/65

MEMORANDUM

MEMORANDUM

TO   Department Heads   DATE March 1, 19--

FROM   Robert Jones

SUBJECT Telephone Audit

The 10% budget reduction requires that the costs of our telephone service be examined.

As a routine matter we do conduct a premise check from time to time with representatives of the telephone company. This is done to insure that we are being charged properly, and only, for equipment we use.

There is, of course, an additional question about telephone equipment and that question is, "Is it necessary?", particularly in view of our budget problem.

We have asked the telephone company to furnish someone to conduct not only a "premise" check, but also a necessity or efficiency check, and as a result Mr. Don Thompson of Mid-States Telephone Company will be checking all telephone equipmentduring the next few weeks. We will appreciate your usual good cooperation in this endeavor.

RJ/ti

Specimen/66

MEMORANDUM

TO   ALL DIVISION HEADS   DATE March 1, 19--

FROM   ROBERT JONES, COMPTROLLER

SUBJECT 5% BUDGET REDUCTION

Because the company's revenues have been lower than anticipated at the beginning of the year, we are forced to cut every division budget 5%. You will take all necessary steps to reduce your operating funds by this amount. The company's survival is at stake. We are depending on you to do your part.

Give me by March 15 your specific plans to reduce your divisional budget by 5%.

450

Specimen/67

August 13, 19--

Mr. William S. Miller
1200 Central Avenue
Spencer, Transylvania 54321

Dear Mr. Miller:

Thank you for your employment inquiry.

Although it is difficult to predict future availability
of specific positions, we do have occasional openings for
Technologists with your background in our Department as
well as in other areas of research.

You will find enclosed some information which is not
intended arbitrarily to discourage further interest on
your part. However, we trust it will help to explain our
limitations in employment consideration of out-of-area
applicants until they are locally available for interviews
and referral to appropriate departments.

You may request an employment application if you decided
to come here at some future time for a firsthand exploration
of job opportunities in this area. This will enable us to
assemble, in advance of your arrival, more detailed
information concerning your qualifications.

Your inquiry is appreciated, and we hope you will be
successful in finding an employment opportunity consistent
with your interests and abilities.

Sincerely yours,

Robert M. Jones
Director of Personnel

rmj:ti

451

Specimen/68

May 27, 19--

Mr. William S. Miller
1200 Central Avenue
Spencer, Transylvania 54321

Dear Mr. Miller:

Thank you for your employment application.

Unfortunately, we haven't any current or
anticipated openings in your field of interest.
I wish I knew of some firm that could use a
person with your qualifications. However, I
know of none at present.

I do wish you every success in find a position
commensurate with your abilities.

Sincerely yours,

Robert M. Jones
Personnel Manager

R.M. Jones/ti

452

Specimen/69

February 28, 19--

Mr. William S. Miller
1200 Central Avenue
Spencer, Transylvania 54321

Dear Mr. Miller:

Thank you for your recent inquiry about transferring to City University.

Normally, transfer students are only considered for admission after they have completed one full year of college work. Since you have less than this, we cannot admit you.

Thank you again for your interest in City University. If we can be of further service, please let us know.

Sincerely yours,

Robert M. Jones
Director of Admissions

RMJ:ti

Specimen/70

LETTERHEAD

November 15, 19--

<u>Special Delivery</u>

Mr. William S. Miller
Star-X Painters
1200 Central Avenue
Spencer, Transylvania 54321

Dear Mr. Miller:

We appreciate your promptness in supplying the
requested credit information. We have carefully reviewed
the data and have communicated with all of the references
given.

We are always glad to give credit to people when
possible. In your case, however, there seems to be some
problem in meeting your short run obligations. In this
period of tight money, we must restrict our credit offerings
to those companies that meet their credit obligations in our
required 30 day period following issuance of statements.

We will be happy to furnish you materials and supplies
on a cash basis (C.O.D. or otherwise). This will allow you
to take advantage of a 2% discount, saving you considerable
money.

We look forward to serving you. We promise prompt
delivery and quality goods at fair prices.

Sincerely,

Robert M. Jones
Credit Manager

RMJ:ti

454

LETTERHEAD

June 10, 19--

Mr. Miller:

The attached request in my opinion reflects an imposition upon our time and energy that goes well beyond the limits of courtesy.

I suggest that filling in all the details you request would not benefit us in the least. Nor do I see any way in which it might benefit others. As you know we are engaged in a rather extensive research program. All our research is published and is available to your organization as well as to others through the usual channels.

R. M. Jones

Specimen/72

LETTERHEAD

TO: _____   DATE _____

      _____

      _____

          RELATIVE TO YOUR _____ DATED_____

          WE WISH TO ADVISE YOU OF THE FOLLOWING:

1.___ WE ARE REVIEWING THE ITEMS LISTED IN YOUR INQUIRY AND
      WILL ADVISE YOU OF OUR FINDINGS AS SOON AS WE HAVE
      COMPLETED OUR INVESTIGATION.

2.___ PLEASE PROVIDE ADDITIONAL INFORMATION RELATIVE TO THIS
      MATTER, INCLUDING OUR PURCHASE ORDER NUMBER.

3.___ YOUR INVOICE REFERENCED HAS NOT BEEN RECEIVED. PLEASE
      PREPARE AND FORWARD DUPLICATES.

4.___ COPY OF OUR DEBIT ATTACHED PER YOUR REQUEST.

5.___ THIS MATTER REFERRED TO _____
      FOR RESOLUTION. PLEASE REFER ALL INQUIRIES TO THAT OFFICE.

6.___ YOUR INVOICE RETURNED FOR THE FOLLOWING REASON:

7.___ WE ADJUSTED YOUR INVOICE _____ TO_____
      FOR THE FOLLOWING REASON:

                              VERY TRULY YOURS,

                              ACCOUNTS PAYABLE UNIT

                              BY_____

456

Specimen/73

April 15, 19--

Mr. William S. Miller
Assistant Dean
School of Business
City University
University Park, Nohio 98765

Dear Mr. Miller:

We thank you very much for your recent letter and the
interest you have expressed in our magazine.

Our magazine is made available, free of charge, to
students at our participating schools. Over the past
three years of our existence, we have been able to include
schools as participating schools upon request. At this
time, for purely economic reasons, we cannot add to our
free distribution. In the past three years, we have had
to turn down some twenty-two requests for participation.

I have added your name to our list of complimentary
subscribers in order that you may keep abreast of our
magazine's development for the remainder of this academic
year.

We appreciate your interest in us, and fully intend to
communicate to you the details of any revision in our
distribution plans. Please do not hesitate to contact us
on this or related subjects. We consider ourselves as a
communication medium between the student and the community
and have a keen desire to be responsive to their needs.

Sincerely yours,

Robert M. Jones
Managing Director

RMJ:ti

457

MEMORANDUM

TO   W.S. Miller

From   R.M. Jones

Subject   Job Termination

DATE   May 1, 19--

This will confirm our discussion of yesterday, in which I informed you that circumstances forced us to terminate your services as of June 1.

As we agreed, you will finish the project for Star-X Company, hopefully, before May 15. In this event, you may feel free to leave the firm at that time. In any event, you will be paid through June 1. Furthermore, you are entitled to all compensatory benefits including unemployment insurance and pay for any accrued vacation time.

May I wish you success in finding employment with another firm. As we discussed, Bill, your separation from our company was not due to your lack of ability, but to a special situation which prevented your continuing with the firm. Please feel free to give my name for reference purposes.

Specimen/75

June 30, 19--

Certified Mail

Mr. William S. Miller
1200 Central Avenue
Spencer, Transylvania 54321

Dear Mr. Miller:

After careful consideration of your entire academic
record and attendant circumstances, we regret that we
cannot permit you to register for the next academic year.
This action was taken by the Academic Standards Committee
because conditions in your case have not substantially
changed, and we feel that it is to your advantage to be
on suspension for one academic year. We hope that during
this year interval, you can do something about your
personal problems, so that you can reapply for the
following academic year with the assurance that external
pressures will not hamper your academic studies.

If you do wish to reapply, get your application for
readmission in by January 15, 19--.

Sincerely yours,

Robert M. Jones
Dean of Students

RMJ: ti

459

Specimen/76

April 27, 19--

CERTIFIED MAIL

Mr. William S. Miller
1200 Central Avenue
Spencer, Transylvania 54321

Dear Mr. Miller:

As you know, our contract which has been in existence
for more than five years, allows either party to cancel
our agreement by giving 30 days notice.

This letter is to inform you that we hereby cancel
the contract as of June 1, 19--.

Our repeated complaints about the quality of lumber
and timber and the delivery delays have beenfutile. You
can understand that we cannot tolerate such performance
because we cannot meet our production quality standards
and delivery schedules to our customers.

Sincerely yours,

Robert M. Jones
Purchasing Agent

RMJ:ti

460

Specimen/77

Dear Friend:

We're sorry to announce that Star-X Journal
ceases publication with this issue. Like
many other efforts these days, the Journal
has lost its final battle with rising over-
head costs.

The staff thanks all of you who have said so
many nice things about our work over the years.
We also plan to treasure the embarrassing
number of professional awards the Journal has
received during its 12-year career.

Most of all, we hope we have contributed
something worthwhile to the growth and understanding of significant developments in the
computer software field.

Star-X Journal Staff

Specimen/78

TO   Bill Miller

                                  DATE March 1, 19--

FROM   Bob Jones

SUBJECT   Faulty Computer Print Outs

We are again writing in an attempt to persuade you that it is most imperative that records be provided by the computer so that the Office of Accounts can carry on its day-to-day activities. A memo was sent to you February 23 requesting routine print outs and to this date the items received are not satisfactory, that is, some lists are not totaled, name fields are not adequate and we cannot post from such lists because of this. The daily totals of disbursements per the Computer come to $3,462,081.61; per the Bank Reconciliation listing and our Disbursements office the total should be $3,383,226.42, a difference of $78,855.19. The form, 'Request for Computer Run', has not been explained. Proper use of the revised "Daily Update Exceptions Corrections" form has not been explained.

Frankly, Bill, I'm more than a little disappointed. To 'sell' this program of computer accounting I advised my people to be at ease because they would still get the same information in the same format as they did in the past except that now it would come from the computer instead of from our own accounting machines. I honestly felt that this was the best way to reaffirm any sort of confidence in the capability of the computer after the state of mind it left our people in following last year's attempted change-over to the computer. In any event, failure to provide the needed accounting data as promised has done a considerable damage to the rapport between workers, and, worse, has broadened the gap between continuing the old system and really utilizing the computer to the maximum.

cc: Don' Thompson

462

Specimen/79

June 1, 19--

TO: ALL COMPANY EMPLOYEES

SUBJECT: ATTIRE AND APPEARANCE

Just last week I was shocked to see one of our salesmen dressed in what I call "hippie clothes." I am sure that I need not spell out what is meant by this term. Furthermore, the man's hair hung over his collar and was uncombed. Tragically, he was talking with a representative from the STAR-X Company, one of our best clients.

To my dismay, a quick survey of several departments in our company shows that this person is no isolated case. According to my findings, over one-third of our male employees are dressed in clothing which I consider to be beyond the mainstream of business attire. And, over one-half have hair longer than that acceptable to the traditional businessman.

I need not point out that most of our clients are basically conservative in their outlook and that this conservatism affects their perception of our company and its products. Any time that we offend their sensibilities by improper appearance, we adversely represent our firm, with attendant lost sales.

Effective immediately, I expect every manager of every division and department in this company to see that his employees dress properly and have conventional haircuts. Failure to do this will subject both the employee and his supervisor to immediate dismissal.

Robert M. Jones
President

RMJ/ti

Specimen/80

TO Systems and Procedures Department   DATE October 9, 19--

FROM Dean of Students

SUBJECT Two Cases

You apparently are gathering information about our services and systems through students, which I consider invalid and singularly inappropriate.

The two cases in point are the presumed investigation done by Mr. Thompson last year in which we were asked to indicate the amount of correspondence and contact we had with various offices in a given day. This was ridiculous. A given day does not provide any indication of either flow or volume in or out of the office. If such records are desired, we will be glad to have our secretaries keep track of memos, letters, phone calls, and other communications, if any, for a month or an over-all period of time which could be significant in connection with both volume and flow.

The second case in point is a study done by Verna Thomas for Dr. Browne which apparently is in your hands or has been in your hands. It concerns three forms used by our services. It deals with the most difficult one that we have had to struggle with which was, at the time Miss Thomas did her presumed investigation, in a state of flux, with plans to consolidate on to one page the content of several forms we had been using. It concluded with some blanket statements about the forms used in our area when in fact it concerned only three of many, many, many records which we keep and use, and related only to one segment of the total multitudinous processes in our office. I found myself quite offended to realize that what was done to help out a student trying to write a term paper has apparently been used in connection with administrative communication. As I said, I consider this invalid and singularly inappropriate and wonder how it could have occurred.

Therefore, I would like to suggest that information be gathered from the persons who are using forms or participating directly in processes--i.e., the appropriate administrative and secretarial personnel. It would seem to me that if you agree that this could be done we can make some real progress in relation to the matters which are of concern to all of us.

Specimen/81

June 18, 19--

Dear Bill:

Thank you very much for bringing me a copy
of the book authored by you. I also appreciate
the kind words you wrote to me on the inside
cover. It is always gratifying to me to see
that some of our best professors find the time
necessary to publish and to keep active in
their field.

I congratulate you.

Cordially,

Robert M. Jones
Vice President

Dr. William S. Miller
1200 Central Avenue
Spencer, Transylvania   54321

Specimen/82

October 9, 19--

Dear Mr. Miller:

This note is to acknowledge the generous donation of
your organization to the Ecological Preservation Society.
We have not only appreciated the loan of office furniture
which you've kindly provided over the past several years
but are now particularly grateful for your donating this
equipment to our organization. Understanding and support
such as you and your organization have provided have made
it possible for our non-profit service organization to
pass through the launching stage and develop to a point
where its stability and continued growth seems assured.

With sincere appreciation for your contribution and
personal best wishes, I am,

                                   Respectfully,

                                   Robert M. Jones
                                   Vice President
                                   Special Services

Mr. William S. Miller
1200 Central Avenue
Spencer, Transylvania

RMJ/ti

Specimen/83

LETTERHEAD

MEMORANDUM TO: All Employees

SUBJECT: Praise Memorandum

DATE: September 25, 19--

"You have been so very kind and patient with us
and our long-standing account. We do appreciate
it.

                "Thank you.

                "Verna Thomas"

Robert M. Jones
Credit Manager

RMJ/ti

Specimen/84

LETTERHEAD

Dear Customer,

We wish to thank you for your past patronage and we
    wish you a prosperous New Year.

Now's your chance to stock up on end-of-the-season specials
    during our giant semi-annual sale! You'll have your
    pick of our regular, high-quality merchandise at un-
    believably low prices. No items brought in just for
    sale. Get in on these fantastic savings.

For you, our preferred customer, the sale will run January
    14 and 15 and will be open to the general public on
    January 16. Don't miss this great opportunity!

                STAR-X MENS SHOP

COURTESY DAYS FOR OUR CUSTOMERS WILL BE JANUARY 14 and 15.

Specimen/85

LETTERHEAD

December 15, 19--

Mr. William S. Miller
1200 Central Avenue
Spencer, Transylvania 54321

Dear Mr. Miller:

I understand that you and your wife will celebrate
your twenty-fifth wedding next Saturday. Please accept
my own best wishes as well as those of the staff of
Star-X Company.

It has always been a pleasure for us to do business
with you. We would now like you to accept as a gift from
us a Star-X portable radio. We hope it will give you many
happy hours in the years ahead.

Congratulations!

Sincerely,

Robert M. Jones
Controller

RMJ:ti

Specimen/86

May 15, 19--

Mr. William S. Miller
1200 Central Avenue
Spencer, Transylvania 54321

Dear Mr. Miller:

I was sorry to learn that you are ill. My secretary
called the hospital this morning and was informed
that you are "resting comfortably."

I hope you will soon be your perky, efficient self
again. But do not return to work too quickly, because
we want you fit with a long, healthy, productive career
ahead of you.

Every best wish for a speedy recovery.

Sincerely,

Robert M. Jones
Vice President

RMJ:ti

*We deeply regret to announce the death
after a short illness of our
managing director Mr. Jack Bloom.*

*As he wished, the Company will continue
under the direction of his nephew
Mr. Ian Harris.*

N. Bloom & Son Ltd.

LETTERHEAD

Inter-Office Communication

TO: Admissions Office Personnel

FROM: Assistant Director

SUBJECT: Personnel Changes

DATE: December 12, 19--

Effective January 1, Mr. Donald B. Thompson, Admissions
Officer, will assume the position of Manager of the
Faculty Practice Fund.

Miss Verna Thomas, presently Manager of Central Services,
will assume the position of Admissions Officer, also
effective January 1.

We regret that Mr. Thompson is leaving the Admissions
Office. We are fortunate that he will remain with the
Medical Center and will, hopefully, be available for
an occasional consult.

Miss Thomas is a very capable individual, and I am sure
you will enjoy working with her.

                              Robert M. Jones

rmj:ti

DRUGS
DRUGS
DRUGS

For centuries, man has used drugs and narcotics in one form or another. Yet today, as never before, drugs and narcotics are being used[1] and abused[2] at an ever increasing rate. True, physicians are finding greater uses for drugs, but it is also true that drugs are being abused more than ever before on the college campuses throughout the nation. In part, the spread of drug abuse on the campus is due to ignorance—the ignorance of those who have no knowledge about the effects of drugs and narcotics.

It is not our purpose to pass judgment on those who use drugs; rather, this booklet has been assembled in the hope that it will serve to inform and make more aware those who contemplate the use of drugs. At least, after reading this booklet, the individual can make an *intelligent* decision . . . by himself . . . for himself.

For convenience, we have divided this booklet into four general categories: Hallucinogens, Narcotics, Stimulants, Depressants. Most of the information is presented in chart form for easy reference.

---

[1]*"USE" refers to the proper place of drugs or narcotics in medical practice.*
[2]*"ABUSE" refers to the self-administration of these drugs, without medical supervision. (Definitions from The Journal of the American Medical Association).*

LETTERHEAD

July, 19--

CLIENT NEWSLETTER

<u>Minimizing Death Costs Through Insurance Transfers</u>

Never before has the phrase"it's too expensive to die" been more
true. Death taxes and related costs seem to be ever increasing.
With the tax reform mood so prevalent in Congress, it seems a sure
bet that many devices previously available for minimizing death
taxes will soon be outlawed. Therefore, now is the time to review
your estate plan and take those death tax saving steps which may
not be available in the future!

In planning your estate you should consider lifetime gifts to
those who would normally receive your property upon your death.
In this way the property can be transferred without incurring any
death tax.

We recognize there is a natural reluctance to transfer control of
property during one's lifetime because we all want the everlasting
benefits of the property we own--it's mine, I earned it, and I'm
going to keep it" is a very normal response to a suggested lifetime
gift program. Insurance, however, is one type of asset where the
reluctance to make gifts seems somewhat unfounded. Insurance
provides its owner with very little in the way of lifetime benefits
--generally limited to borrowing or cashing in on the policy's cash
surrender value. However, upon death of the insured, the value of
the policy balloons tremendously and can cause a very substantial
death tax liability.

For this reason--the relatively minor lifetime benefit, but major
death tax cost--virtually every individual having potential death
tax problems should consider transferring ownership of his insurance
to his wife, children or other beneficiaries.

The lifetime benefits sacrificed by you will be minor--the death
tax savings to your heirs could be substantial. Consider the
possibility of such a tax savings device for your estate. We will
be happy to discuss the use of this type of transfer as well as
other estate tax savings devices with you.

Specimen/91

To provide students with the common body of knowledge in business and administration, programs shall include in their course of instruction the equivalent of at least one year of work comprising the following areas:

(a)   a background of the concepts, processes, and institutions in marketing and distribution, production, and financing functions of business enterprise;

(b)   a background of the economic and legal environment of business enterprise along with consideration of the social and political influences on business;

(c)   a basic understanding of the concepts and methods of accounting, quantitative methods, and information systems;

(d)   a study of organization theory, interpersonal relationships, control and motivation systems, and communications;

(e)   a study of administrative processes under conditions of uncertainty including integrating analysis and policy determination at the overall management level.

<u>MANAGEMENT GUIDE</u>

SUPERINTENDENT, PLANT NO. 1

I. FUNCTION

    As a line member of management, the Superintendent
of Plant No. 1 is charged with advising the General Manager
of the Manufacturing Division, and with conducting the
manufacturing, packaging, maintenance, and quality control
activities of the Company at Plant No. 1.

II. RESPONSIBILITIES AND AUTHORITY

    With the limits of his approved program, corporate
policies and control procedures, and Manufacturing Division
policies and procedures, the Superintendent of Plant No. 1
is responsible for, and has commensurate authority to
accomplish the fulfillment of the duties set forth below.
He may delegate to members of his section appropriate
portions of his responsibilities together with proportionate
authority for their fulfillment, but he may not delegate or
relinquish his over-all responsibility for results nor any
portion of his accountability.

III. OPERATIONS AND ACTIVITIES

    1. He will advise and assist the General Manager of
the Manufacturing Division in formulating proposals for
policies on, and will recommend procedures pertaining to,
manufacturing, packaging, maintenance, and quality control
activities, will administer such policies and procedures
when approved, and will conduct such activities at Plant
No 1.

    2. He will procure necessary transportation of supplies,
materials, and products in accordance with the Traffic Routing
Manual.

    3. He will buy necessary supplies, materials, and
services in accordance with the Buyers' Guide

    4. He will conduct necessary shipping and warehousing
activities in connection with the operation of Plant No. 1

                    . . .

YOUR CONDUCT AND APPEARANCE

The reputation of any company is dependent upon the conduct and appearance of its employees, both on and off the job. It is important that we reflect credit upon the Company as well as ourselves. To be courteous, cheerful, helpful, and as neat appearing as working conditions permit will be of great value in maintaining a good customer attitude toward us.

Of equal importance is the effect each of us has upon our fellow workers. Too much care cannot be given to matters of appearance, manners and personal cleanliness. Every detail is important -- the daily shave, care of teeth, clean clothing, etc. Moderation and good taste in dress and cosmetics are also important. If you work in an office, wear clothes that are appropriate for a business office. Remember that consideration and respect for the individual contribute to a more pleasant atmosphere in which to work.

The Company must maintain the highest standards of business ethics and as an employee, each of us is expected to observe strict rules of business conduct. To accomplish this objective it is necessary that every employee conduct himself, both on and off the job, so as to properly protect the interests of the Company. It must be further understood that these interests include not only those of the customers of the Company, but the stockholders, suppliers, and other employees as well.

Information concerning the accounts of customers, their names and addresses, or those of stockholders or employees whould not be given to unauthorized persons. Likewise, unauthorized use of Company information, property, or employees' working time is to be very carefully avoided.

The maintenance of this high standard of business conduct should also apply to any business relation an employee may enter into outside of the Company. Included in this category are employment, other than with the Company, and acceptance of gratuities or favors. These must be handled in such a manner as to avoid creating a conflict of interest with the employee's primary responsibility to the Company.

Whenever there is doubt as to what may be the right thing to do in any business relationship, your supervisor should be freely consulted. He has more experience in interpreting Company policy and will assist you in working out a satisfactory solution regarding your responsibility as an employee and your personal interests as related to Company objectives.

LETTERHEAD

NEW R. & D. DEPARTMENT OFFICE POLICIES

1. Office supplies are to be used <u>only</u> for official use.

2. All requests for secretarial time, beyond their regular duties, must be approved by their immediate superior.

3. All discussions, conferences, debates, etc. noisy enough to disturb office activities <u>must</u> be carried out <u>elsewhere</u>.

4. All books, papers, etc. in the laboratory and the library at the end of the work day will be discarded in a rubbish box.

5. If the director of a project is to be absent from the office for any length of time, they have a responsibility of seeing to it that their work is planned in advance.

6. Daily schedules (where you are and for what purpose) <u>must</u> be established by <u>all</u> personnel. The program secretary must be kept <u>informed</u> of these schedules and any changes.

Robert M. Jones
Director

November 14, 19--

EMPLOYEES' CREDIT UNION

This is an independent corporation organized by the employees of the Company under the banking laws of this state.

I. PURPOSE

To promote thrift among its members and to create for them a source of credit, at fair and reasonable rates of interest, to be used for provident and productive purposes.

II. MEMBERSHIP

Regular or retired employees of this Company are eligible for membership. New employees must have completed their probationary period to meet eligibility requirements. Prospective members shall subscribe to one or more $5.00 shares together with an entrance fee of twenty-five cents ($.25). Part time and temporary employees are not eligible for membership.

III. SHARES (SAVINGS)

A. Share savings may be made by cash or by payroll deduction. Minimum payment -- One Dollar ($1.00).

B. Shares may be withdrawn at any time unless pledged as security for a loan. A $5.00 share balance must be maintained for continuance of membership.

C. Maximum share holding of any member is $7,000.00.

D. Dividends: Dividends may be paid on all shares outstanding on June 30 and/or December 31 on the basis of the number of months of the year that shares have been fully paid. Shares fully paid on or before the tenth of the month earn for the full month. Dividends are declared either semi-annually or annually at the discretion of the Board of Directors. Upon the death of a member, the share balance may remain intact through the end of the current dividend period to avoid loss of dividend to the Joint Tenant.

Specimen/96

TYPES OF CASH BENEFITS

This table shows the principal types of payments and insured status needed for each.

Survivors

Monthly payments to your—   *If you are—*

*Widow 60 or over or disabled widow 50 or over _____ Fully insured.

*Widow (regardless of age) if caring for your child who is under 18 (or disabled) and is entitled to benefits __ Either fully or currently insured.

*(*Note: All types of widow's benefits may be paid to a surviving divorced wife under certain conditions.)*

Dependent children _____ Either fully or currently insured.

Dependent widower 62 or over, or disabled dependent widower 50 or over _____ Fully insured.

Dependent parent 62 or over _____ Fully insured.

Lump-sum death payment _____ Either fully or currently insured.

Disability

Monthly payments to—   *If—*

You as a disabled worker and your wife and children _____ You are fully insured and meet the special work requirements described on page 11.

Your child who became disabled before 18 and continues to be disabled after 18 _____ The parent receives retirement or disability benefits or the parent was fully or currently insured at death.

Specimen/97

TO: Director of Nursing
           Chief Pharmacist
           Administration

FROM: R. M. Jones, M.D.

DATE: September 17, 19--

SUBJECT: Questionable Drug Orders

From time to time questions have arisen concerning a drug
ordered for a patient. The questions have concerned the nature
or identity of the drug itself, the dosage, or the method of
administration. To be sure that such questionable drug orders
are checked, the following policy is herewith established:

    Whenever, for any reason, a drug order is questionable
    in the judgment of the pharmacist filling the order,
    it shall be the responsibility of the pharmacist to
    confirm the order with the physician concerned or to
    call the matter to the attention of the Nursing Super-
    visor before the drug is made available for delivery
    to the floor. If called to the attention of the
    Nursing Supervisor it shall be her responsibility to
    confirm the order with the physician concerned being
    sure that he understands the nature of the question;
    i.e. whether it relates to the drug itself, the dosage,
    or the method of administration.

Nothing in this policy shall be construed to mean that any
professional responsibility of any nurse or any pharmacist or
the doctor are intended to be changed or questioned in any way.
This policy is established to insure that unintentional
erroneous drug orders will not be administered to patients.

Specimen/98

December 7, 19--

Gentlemen:

As the Holiday Season approaches, we wish to again remind
our many suppliers and friends that it is the long-
established policy of Star-X Company to prohibit acceptance
of gifts and gratuities, in any form, by its employees.
Star-X is proud of the reputation it has built for fair
dealing and impartiality in its supplier relations, and
we know we can continue to count on your full cooperation
in this matter.

May we take this opportunity to express our sincere
appreciation to your Company for the fine support afforded
our vital defense program this past year, and we extend to
each and every one of your employees our very best wishes
for a Merry Christmas and prosperous New Year.

Very truly yours,

STAR-X COMPANY
Spencer Branch

Robert M. Jones
Director
Materiel

RMJ/ti

Specimen/99

MEMORANDUM

To   Everyone

FROM   Robert M. Jones, Administrator

DATE March 11, 19-1

ReIssue: April 24, 19-8

SUBJECT PUBLIC RELATIONS: On Being Available and Receptive

Recently we have had complaints (two in 19-1 and one in 19-8) with respect to how patients are received when they come into the Clinic.

May I make the following suggestions to you:

1. Stop conversation among yourselves or paper work when a patient comes to the reception counter, to your department, or reception area.

2. Greet the patient, by name if possible, using a pleasant voice which intimates that you are glad to see him again and that he is welcome. This establishes acceptance.

3. Don't ask how they are, but say something impersonal about the weather, the trees, the flowers, etc. Or simply say "hello" or "Hi" if you know the patient.

4. If the patient has not met the doctor, introduce them. Check the chart to be sure.

5. When patient leaves say a pleasant and courteous goodbye.

6. Don't forget to SMILE. This helps to establish the bond of acceptance.

7. You should always act as if you were a hostess at some important function. The very fact that the patient is coming into the Clinic is important to him or he wouldn't be coming, and it is important to us!

8. Not an attractive building, a beautiful stone wall or well constructed rooms, nor functional furniture and new equipment make a Clinic: <u>but men and women using their opportunity to serve people in a friendly manner.</u>

Specimen/100

MEMORANDUM

TO Offices of Admissions, Nursing   DATE January 1, 19--
        and Security

FROM R.M. Jones, Director of Hospitals

SUBJECT DANGEROUS WEAPON POLICY (Supplement to Directive No. 10)

On rare occasions, patients may bring in firearms or dangerous weapons at the time of their admission to City Memorial Hospital. The following procedures should be adhered to on such occasions.

1. Patients will be encouraged to give the weapon to a relative or friend to take home for safekeeping.

2. Should the patient insist on having the hospital take the weapon for safekeeping, it will be accepted in the same manner as any other valuable.

   a. A hospital security guard will be called immediately (Ext. 4112) to check out the weapon and make sure it is safe for handling by hospital personnel.

   b. The weapon will then be stored in the safe along with other valuables.

3. In the event a weapon is taken away from a patient, either for his own safety or because of some altercation, a hospital security guard will be notified immediately.

   a. The security guard will receipt the patient for his weapon.

   b. The Hospital Security Office will arrange for safekeeping of weapons, and return of such when appropriate, under these circumstances.

RMJ:ti

MEMORANDUM

TO   Department Heads   DATE June 1, 19--

FROM   R.M. Jones, Mail Service

SUBJECT New Postage Rates

As you know, postage rates have recently been increased. Below
are a few suggestions which will help reduce costs and still
maintain good service.

1. ZIP code all mail.

2. Address for the optical character reader machine. The
    address should be printed in a standard type font since an
    OCR machine has trouble with italics and artistic fonts.
    All lines should be flush left at the margin:
                      Name
                      Street, P.O. Box, or Rural Route
                      Room or Suite
                      City, State, ZIP Code

3. Limit the use of airmail postage. Most out of state, first
    class goes by airmail. Do not use airmail on Friday.

4. Whenever possible divide parcel post into small packages
    weighing less than one pound.

5. Take advantage of third and second class bulk rates. Contact
    the Mail Service department for information.

6. Avoid the use of large manila mailing envelopes. Whenever
    possible, fold an item and mail it in a No. 10 size envelope,
    (9 1/2" x 4"). Clearly identify how your mail is to be
    handled.

7. If you have a mailing list, keep it current. The Company
    is charged for all returns on bulk mailings.

8. Plan ahead; avoid rush jobs.

9. Whenever possible, pre-sort outgoing mail:
                Local
                Out of Town
                Air
                Third Class
                Pre-stamped

Please feel free to contact the Mail Service department at Ext. 5052
if you have questions on postage rates or procedures.

Specimen/102

MEMORANDUM

TO   All Research Staff   **DATE** June 1, 19--

FROM   R.M. Jones, Director

SUBJECT Research Laboratory Procedure Changes

The laboratory working hours are 8:00 a.m. to 5:-0 p.m. From 5:00 p.m. to midnight, laboratory service is provided by the technical staff of each major area, so that each member is responsible for five evenings of shift duty approximately eight times during the year.

Every attempt should be made to keep abreast of current developments, hence, many new techniques and types of equipment related to automated and semi-automated procedures should be utilized. Among the new techniques is on-line processing of certain chemical determinations by using a computer housed in the laboratory area. We encourage all research staff to use this facility.

Specimen/103

MEMORANDUM

TO Supervisors and Department Heads   **DATE** June 1, 19--

FROM Robert M. Jones, Safety Officer

SUBJECT Safety

Many of you have expressed your concern about the safety and well-being of all employees. In light of this, I have drawn up the following procedures which you may wish to post.

1. Exercise care and be alert to any unsafe conditions.

2. Report any unsafe condition to your Supervisor or Department Head.

3. Report near accidents so that the conditions can be corrected before actual accidents occur.

4. Make suggestions to your supervisors for any improvements which could reduce on the job accidents.

RMJ:ti

Specimen/104

NOTE: THE NEXT MEETING DATE IS SET FOR THURSDAY, MAY 12,
AT 2:30 PM IN CONFERENCE ROOM C IN THE STUDENT CENTER.

The lengthy meeting commenced with a lively discussion of
the ACRA Program. The program has been approved and will begin
in January in the Department of Psychology.

A draft of a proposal was presented to the Council by Bill
Brewer (a student at City University). The poorly-worded draft
outlined ways to change the present structure of courses at the
University. Mr. Brewer was adamant in stating that he would like
to see more interesting courses taught....also, a reduction in the
amount of disultory required courses. Dr. Jones suggested that
Mr. Brewer study articles regarding previous programs set up at
other universities. It was also suggested that the above ideas
be presented to the Deans of all Colleges to get their reactions.
There was heated conflict among discussants about this last point.

Dr. Thompson asked for suggestions to include in his report
to the general faculty....It was suggested that the ACRA program
be included, that the proposal of Mr. Brewer be mentioned, and
that the lack of suggestions coming into the Council be mentioned.
At times, bitter misunderstandings arose about the exact nature
of the ACRA program. In fact, anger was so intense that some
participants shouted at one another. Three stalked out of the
meeting.

It was mentioned by the students present that the establishment
of student groups in the various departments has not to date been
very successful.

The question was raised as to how to replace members of the
Council who are leaving the University.....should they be appointed
or voted in?

It was decided that the Council meet once a month in the
future instead of weekly. (This last point was hotly debated, but
after the chairman brought the group to order, a majority voted
in favor of the monthly over the weekly meetings.)

The meeting was finally adjourned at 6:30 p.m.

CITY UNIVERSITY

MINUTES OF MEETING OF GENERAL FACULTY

June 1, 19--

A special meeting of the General Faculty of City University was held in the Science Building Auditorium at 1:30 p.m. on Friday, June 1, 19--.

Permission for the press was approved.
Permission to televise was approved.

REPORT OF UNIVERSITY SENATE - Professor Donald Thompson

REPORT OF THE PRESIDENT

REMARKS OF VICE CHANCELLOR BROWNE

MOTION BY PROFESSOR ROBERT JONES

1.   That the University as presently constituted be kept open by whatever legal use of persuasion or force may be necessary.

2.   That official representatives of the administration and faculty meet at their earliest moment practicable with representative student leaders to plan a new and permanent center for open-forum education.

3.   That the several college faculties take an immediate inventory of their will and resources for contributing to such a center.

AMENDMENT TO JONES MOTION (Professor Thomas)

It was moved and seconded to add a motion of confidence in the University President.

AMENDMENT TO JONES MOTION (Professor Butler)

It was moved to delete that phrase "by whatever use of persuasion or force" so that it would read "this University as presently constituted will be kept open."

487

Specimen/105 (continued)

```
GENERAL FACULTY MEETING
June 1, 19--
Page Two
```

IT WAS VOTED to amend.

IT WAS VOTED to vote on the Jones proposal.

IT WAS VOTED to adopt the Jones proposal as amended.

Proposal, as amended, as follows:

JONES MOTION AS AMENDED

1. That the University as presently constituted will be kept open.

2. That official representatives of the administration and faculty meet at their earliest moment practicable with representative student leaders to plan a new and permanent center for open-forum education.

3. That the several college faculties take an immediate inventory of their will and resources for contributing to such a center.

MOTION CARRIED

MOTION ON "FACULTY SURVEY" (Professor Vance)

It was moved that this general faculty vote on the specific questions raised in the document entitled "Faculty Survey."

MOTION TO TEMPORARILY POSTPONE CONSIDERATION (Professor Clark)

It was moved and seconded that consideration of this instrument be temporarily postponed and that a committee be appointed to revise and report back to the General Faculty.

IT WAS VOTED to postpone (175 to 154)

Meeting adjourned at 3:30 p.m.

Verna Thomas
Secretary

488

Specimen/106

REPORT

of the

COMMUNICATIONS STUDY TASK FORCE

Assumptions and Basic Problems

One of the most important abilities a manager must possess is to make himself understood by his employees, superiors, other managers, and people outside the organization. In turn, he must be able to understand the meanings and ideas they attempt to convey to him. This two-way process is <u>communication</u>.

Within our organization are a multitude of communication problems that result in inefficiency, frustration, and a significant percent of "scrap" work. Of the ten problem areas identified by the Division of Operations, <u>communication responsibility</u> is the most critical. For example, frequent failures to "follow through" on and document essential communications weaken our management of all operational activities.

An Operational Definition of Communication Responsibility

Communication Responsibility

The manager and employee who exercises communication responsibility attempts to carry out the communication obligations of his job, and in doing so has a concern for effects and consequences of his communication. Specifically a responsible manager and employee does the following in his communication:

1. Documents important oral statements.
2. Follows through on essential communication until it is fully completed.
3. Gives prompt attention to communication when it is needed.
4. Makes his communication so clear that "foul-ups" are unlikely.
5. Plans and prepares communication so that it will be fully effective.
6. Makes himself competent to discharge communication duties.
7. Avoids waste of money, time, and effort on unneeded communication.
8. Makes sure he receives accurately the sender's intended message

Specimen/107

SYSTEMS NOTES - FALL REGISTRATION

Scope - Attack the "Processing" problems.
Accept, insofar as possible, previous input systems.
Observe input and communications for later improvement.
Build files of type to permit information retrieve for
all purposes.
Build the type of programs which would be open ended
(permit addition of tests and other criteria for admit
to a class without rewrite and reconstruct of the original
programs).
Place first priority on academic department and college
needs with the maximum number of students and variety
of problems as possible.

Limitations - Self imposed for this first registration.
Refrain from disturbing input systems necessary to maintain
the previous system. A reduced field house operation was
a known need the first time, consequently the requirement.
Reversal of plan to conduct a portion of registration by
remote terminal. Lack of information from the previous
registrations of students of one college taking courses
in another, removed the possibility of a "planned"
registration result.

Observations - Everything processed by the computer was done with
precise correctness. All errors were as a result of
maintaining previous manual systems and/or in manual
operations at check points established in the first attempt
at a computer registration.

All of the computer programs created are usable for subsequent
registrations. No single purpose or one-time programs were written,
consequently no wasted effort or funds have been encountered by this
office. Many programs were created. Notes on a few of these would
be of interest to the reader and provide a deeper insight into
what has been attained in the full scope of the undertaking, as well
as indicate the areas open for improvement.

Sectioning - Processes students course requests, creates files of
course sections recording each student with added information (from
another tape file) of class, college, and major. Checks student
information tape file for invalid student numbers and suspension,
rejects requests for courses not offered, builds a file of students
requesting overloads, builds a file of students requesting specific
permission courses, updates a status file of course offerings (supply
vs. demand) recording for later programs student stations available
or number oversubscribed. Processing time = 10 students per second.

Specimen/107 (continued)

Resectioning - Moves students from sections that are oversubscribed.
First sorts the students in the oversubscribed section to an array
according to class, college, major, and individual student preference.
Moves the students out with the lowest combination of priorities
first, checks and passes the student who may not be moved without
conflict of time. Updates the status file of available student
stations. The program automatically encodes the student class
record to record the resection action for later retrieve.
Processing time = 8 students per second.

Financial Billing and Course Schedule - Adds place, time, section,
instructor and credit hours from course offering file (the latter
a check on previous programs and to bring in later information).
Also, adds mailing address from another file. Calculates hourly
or regular tuition based on credit hours, calculates health charge
where applicable, checks files and adds dorm, fraternity, or
sorority housing charges, pulls in and adds various financial arrears,
adds special course fees, checks other files and adds credits for
scholarships and tuition waivers, under various rules and types
(percentage, various hours, or amount credits) limits credits
according to rules applying both to either specific charges or
total amounts and creates a tape file from which course schedules
and bills are printed and a file from which class schedules and
deans, advisors, and registrars cards are printed. Processing time
= 12 students per second.

These are but a few of the programs yet are "care" programs.
It is perhaps obvious to the reader that these programs, being
created as open ended, can have added tests. For example, the
"sectioning" program can have added provisions for restricting admit
of a student to "Tatting" to a female, age 21, junior with a GPA
of 2.85 or better. By the same token, we cannot add a provision to
a program, if the information is not on a file. The point is that
anything may be added where the data is in existence, reliable, and
current.

Each of the files has been created in a manner whereby they may
be loaded from the tapes to a disc and, therefore, would be
accessible from any part of the campus with a remote terminal.

During the period of work on the central registration system,
we have also with the great cooperation of the Institutional Research
Staff been developing a full computer record and system of space. One
of the three main purposes of this system is for use in registration
in class room assignments.

The above two points are the key to our direction and purpose
for future registrations.

Systems Notes - Page 3

Conclusion

We have placed first emphasis on the processing functions. We now must make these even more responsive to the college and department requirements. This requires two major areas of effort. Communication and criticism from every department head and Dean. Also, communication to the students of requirements which must be met to attain admission into a course. We should not program restrictions unless the students are aware their requests will be rejected without exception if requirements are not met.

Our major task ahead is to modernize the input systems. Previous systems concepts seem to have been the production of various forms of processed wood pulp with major menial clerical effort to be performed by professional and non-professional alike.

The admission systems must be modernized both to serve that department and to provide earlier and more complete information files of incoming transfer and new freshmen for the registration process.

Flow of information into the Finance Office as well as through it must be modernized. Previous applications converted data into a printed record which was used as a reference in a mass manual processing effort.

Classroom assignments, schedule preparation revision and student data recording in the Registrars function must be mechanized to reduce additional following manual operations in the registration process.

In all areas it is necessary to adopt the concept that menial clerical functions shall be performed by the computer and individuals, being free of these functions, can devote their time to service and decision processes. It is no small task to convince all those involved to adopt this concept. Some may never do so. It should be emphasized that the computer made no mistakes. All errors were human and for all I accept full responsibility.

It has been said we attempted too much. To have attempted less would have been just another patch on a proven inadequate system. We have proven the manual processing system can be computerized. A major effort is now required to prove that the same may be accomplished in the input systems.

We have just begun to do what is needed.

So many individuals have contributed help, suggestions and advice that to single out any might be considered a slight. With no such intention, I must acknowledge the outstanding help of Verna Thomas, Don Thompson, Bill Miller, and Jean Browne.

R. M. Jones

QUALIFICATIONS OF EXPERTS
NOT DOCUMENTED

Civil Service instructions require that an agency's files contain a standard application form for Government employment or another written statement showing the qualifications and background of the individual which satisfy requirements to employ him as an expert. To qualify as an expert under Civil Service instructions, an individual must possess skills superior to those possessed by persons with ordinary competence in that activity. In the case of the three persons employed as experts, HEW files contained documents evidencing their past work history, but the documents for two of the persons--experts 3 and 8--did not show that they possessed superior skills in their particular fields of endeavor. They had skills which HEW lacked, but their expertise in their fields was not established.

The files indicated that expert 3 had experience working with the aged, a skill which none of HEW's regular employees possessed and which HEW needed. Although the files showed that expert 3 was a competent individual in his field, they did not show that he possessed superior skills in this field. Moreover, his relatively few years of experience in the area of work involved would seem to raise doubt that he was an expert.

According to Social Security Administration personnel, expert 8 was hired because he had experience in insurance claims--a type of experience which the Administration lacked. Expert 8 described his duties as principally involving the negotiation of contracts and leases with Blue Cross associations and plans throughout the country. Although his file indicated that he was competent, it did not show that he possessed superior skill in his field.

In commenting on these cases, HEW acknowledged that there may be a question of whether the appointments of experts 3 and 8 were appropriate. It stated, however, that it considered their appointments necessary because their services were urgently needed.

We believe that HEW did not comply with Civil Service instructions in these cases because it did not document, as required, that these individuals were in fact experts as defined by Civil Service instructions. The fact that HEW may have needed these persons for urgent work would not seem to relieve HEW of the responsibility to comply with Civil Service instructions.

Specimen/109

DIGEST*

WHY THE REVIEW WAS MADE

(1)   The Chairman, Special Subcommittee on Alcoholism and Narcotics, Senate Committee on Labor and Public Welfare, asked the General Accounting Office (GAO) to make a study to determine the cost savings to the Government that might be brought about through a program aimed at identification, prevention, and treatment of alcoholism among Federal civilian employees.

(2)   The study was requested because of--
        The Subcommittee's concern about the growing impact of alcoholism upon our society,
        Strong congressional and public interest in this important health area,
        The Subcommittee's finding that treatment tied to employment personnel programs--under which alcoholism is dealt with in its early stages--ad brought about recoveries at rates much higher than those in clinics and hospitals unrelated to such an environ- ment.
        The cost savings achieved by private industry, as a result of alcoholism programs, and
        The existing potential for the Federal Government to implement, within its own administrative structure, a strong alcoholism program for its employees.

(3)   On August 10, 1970, the Senate passed a bill (S. 3835) that provides for a comprehensive Federal program for the prevention and treatment of alcohol abuse and alcoholism, including the development and maintenance of appropriate policies and services for Federal civilian employees.

FINDINGS AND CONCLUSIONS

(4)   Studies have shown that:
        Alcoholism is a disease, and the alcoholic is a sick person.
        The alcoholic can be helped and is worth helping.
        Alcoholism is a public health problem and therefore is a public responsibility.
        There is no immunity to alcoholism conferred by background, position in life, profession or occupation, or sex. (See pp. 4 and 5.)

(5)   Alcoholism has been hidden and denied for so long that no one really knows how many people are suffering from it. Estimates of the number of alcoholics in the United States are among the most publicized --and challenged--statistics on alcoholism.

---

*From Committee Print, Substantial Cost Savings From Establishment of Alcoholism Programs for Federal Civilian Employees, Comptroller General of the United States, October, 1970.

494

(6)   Therefore, in conducting its study, GAO relied on information
provided by individuals in Federal agencies, State governments, and
industry and by others who have studied the problem of alcoholism
to arrive at estimates of the prevalence of alcoholism in the Federal
Government, the costs incurred as a result thereof, and the cost
savings that might result from an effective Government-wide alcoholism
program.

(7)   GAO estimated the number of Federal civilian employees suffering
from alcoholism (at various assumed rates of prevalence ranging from
4 to 8 percent of the work force) and the resulting employer costs
to the Federal Government (based on a factor of about 25 percent of
average annual salary) as follows:

(Dollar amounts in millions)

(8)   Estimated prevalence of alcoholism among Federal civilian employees

Percent	Number of alcoholic employees	Estimated annual employer costs due to alcoholism
4 - - - - - - - - - - - -	112,000	$275
5 - - - - - - - - - - - -	140,000	345
6 - - - - - - - - - - - -	168,000	410
7 - - - - - - - - - - - -	196,000	480
8 - - - - - - - - - - - -	224,000	550

(9)   Authorities on alcoholism feel that about 54 of every 100 alcoholic
employees would be likely to recover as a result of an employer's
alcoholism program. Therefore the estimated annual employer costs
being incurred by the Government among its civilian employees might
be reduced by over 50 percent because of an alcoholism program. (See
p. 10.)

(10)   Deducting the estimated cost to the Federal Government of such a
program--$15 million annually--the net cost savings would range
from $135 million to $280 million annually. (See p. 12.)

(11)   An effective Government-wide alcoholism program, by helping reduce
the number of alcoholics and problem drinkers in the total population,
would also contribute to the economic and social benefits which the
Federal Government and society as a whole would obtain from alcoholism
programs in general. There would be reductions in--among other things
--traffic accidents, crime, and the need for welfare and medical
services attributable to the misuse of alcohol. (See p. 13.)

(12)   Finally, the program would attend to a part of one of the Nation's
major health problems and, at the same time, would give a group of sick
Federal employees a greater chance to recover and live decent lives.

495

STUDY OF MANAGEMENT AND COMMUNICATION PROBLEMS

BETWEEN HEADQUARTERS AND A BRANCH DIVISION

SYMPTOMS

PROBLEMS

Men in Headquarters responsible
for program reviews are unfamiliar
with Divisional work requirements.

Don't know who to talk with at
Headquarters about mutual problems

Reaction to question about turn
around time was "whose necks are
you going to cut off?"

A recent Headquarters memo on
new goals for Division was
completely unclear.

The Division is not assuming
the responsibility for getting
the information to and from
Headquarters regardless of
the obstacles involved.

Men in Headquarters responsible
for program reviews are unfamiliar
with Division work requirements.

The Division does not know
what Headquarters needs to
know about us.

A Deputy Director at Headquarters
did not send out a program review
because he didn't feel that anyone
would read the material. The
Division obtained a copy upon
request.

It took several weeks after Head-
quarters was notified for the
Division to learn that the ASCO
Project would be funded.

It took about three months after
Headquarters was notified for the
Division to learn that the CRB Pro-
ject would be funded.

The Division has not defined
which information from Headquarters is crucial and how
it should be communicated.

Specimen/111

ANALYZING OUTPUT SYSTEMS AT STAR-X COMMUNICATIONS

Each type of output system serves a different purpose, and they build upon one another. The performance and informative systems provide intraorganizational balance. Through the transactional system, the organization keeps in contact with other organizations. The innovative system is change, which it accomplishes by intervening into any of the other systems.

Why did Star-X Communications not do the job intended? We applied the output systems to communications hardward, and found the following: (1) that the wire service and the radio setup had been insufficient in the job that they did; (2) that internal balance had not been kept; (3) that these two kinds of hardware communications had been lacking in terms of the environment and other organizations; and that the equipment really had not been designed to accommodate all the jobs.

The solution to lessen the problem, or possibly get rid of it entirely, is to add an additional wire service, the AP, giving the news department more news and a wider scope of information. We also felt that if another radio band were installed, there would be less noise over the nets and the whole operation would become more efficient.

Specimen/112

TO Communication Seminar Participants   **DATE** July 10, 19--

FROM   Robert Jones, Management Analyst

SUBJECT   Information Related to Seminar

Attached are notes I prepared on the meeting of May 24.

I think you will also be interested in comments on the seminar
which occured while Dr. Miller, Dr. Thompson and I were
discussing External Communication on June 22.

In a brief discussion of the seminar, Dr. Miller made it
clear that he is extremely interested in the outcome of this
seminar. He hopes that it will have a strong beneficial
impact on the division. If the group would like, he would
be happy to meet with members to discuss any development they
would like him to comment on; he does not wish, however, to
force himself on the group.

During this discussion, Dr. Thompson said that he felt the
group had reached a point where it had formed opinions on the
writing policy of the Division, and that it had gone sufficiently
far in this direction to define these opinions as recommendations
to management. He believes, therefore, that the group should
consider doing the following:

1. Define what it has accomplished to date;

2. Recommend changes to management as appropriate;

3. Consider how best to communicate its findings to
    the rest of the staff;

4. Define its plans for the future: what it expects
    to accomplish, in what sequence, and by what dates.

BASIC CONCEPTS UNDERLYING VALIDITY STUDIES

Over a period of many years, research workers in the testing field have developed a uniform way of thinking about the design of validity studies and have adopted in most instances a standard set of statistical concepts and procedures for these studies.

The logic of validity studies requires that careful consideration be given to three basic issues. First, some measure of success must be identified. This measure should be acceptable to test users as a reasonable indicator of success. In validity study work, this measure is usually called the criterion. Many graduate schools have generally considered that first-year average grades constitute an acceptable criterion. Second, appropriate predictive measures must be identified. Extensive experience has shown that previous academic record makes an important contribution to prediction over and above that obtained from test scores. Accordingly, the validity study design includes some measure of undergraduate record whenever possible. Finally, the group of students on which the study is to be based must be carefully defined. In particular, it is important that the group be fairly large so that the statistical results may be interpreted with confidence.

The relation between the predictive measures and the criterion is expressed the form of a correlation coefficient, which is referred to in the validity study context as a validity coefficient.

Correlation Between Two Variables

Correlation is the tendency for two measures, such as height and weight, to vary together or be related for individuals in a group. If, as in the case with height and weight, one variable tends to go up as the other goes up, then the correlation is positive. On the other hand, months of practice and golf scores would have negative correlation, for ordinarily as the one variable increases the other tends to decrease. Correlation does not imply causation but only concomitance.

The <u>correlation</u> <u>coefficient</u> is the customary index for
expressing the degree of the relationship observed between
two sets of measures for the same group. The coefficient can
vary from -1.00, showing perfect negative correlation, through
zero, indicating no correlation, to +1.00, showing perfect
positive correlation.

If, for example, the correlation coefficient between
height and weight for a group of men were +1.00, one could,
knowing a man's height, predict his weight perfectly, that is,
without error. Another way of saying this is that all the
variation in the men's weight is accounted for by their
variation in height. A correlation of +1.00 would strongly
imply causation between the variables, though this would not
be a certainty since the apparent relation between the
variables being correlated might in actuality be caused by
a third variable.

On the other hand if the correlation coefficient between
height and weight were zero, one could not predict a man's
weight any more accurately knowing his height than not knowing
his height, and therefore the best guess as to his weight
would be the average weight of all the men in the group.

Most correlation coefficients fall somewhere between
zero and 1.00, which means that knowledge of an individual's
score on one variable enables one to predict his standing on
the other variable imperfectly but with greater accuracy
than if the correlation were zero. The higher the coefficient,
the less error there will be in making this prediction.

Specimen/114

SCHEDULE OF ANTICIPATED INCOME FROM MEMBERSHIP DUES

20 Patron members (+approx. 3) @ $25.00

```
39.4% of 20 =  8 Jan.  exp.  x $25.00  = $200.00
12.6% of 20 =  2 Apr.  exp.  x  18.75  =   37.50
23.8% of 20 =  5 July  exp.  x  12.50  =   62.50
24.2% of 20 =  5 Oct.  exp.  x   6.25  =   31.25
```
$ 331.25

200 Sustaining members (+approx. 22) @ $10.00

```
39.4% of 200 = 79 Jan.  exp. x $10.00  = $790.00
12.6% of 200 = 25 Apr.  exp. x   7.50  =  187.50
23.8% of 200 = 48 July  exp. x   5.00  =  240.00
24.2% of 200 = 48 Oct.  exp. x   2.50  =  120.00
```
1,337.50

650 Regular members (+approx. 70) @ $6.00

```
39.4% of 650 = 256 Jan.  exp. x $ 6.00  = $  6.00
12.6% of 650 =  82 Apr.  exp. x   4.50  =  369.00
23.8% of 650 = 155 July  exp. x   3.00  =  465.00
24.2% of 650 = 157 Oct.  exp. x   1.50  =  235.50
```
1,075.50

50 Student members (+approx. 2) @ $3.50

```
39.4% of 50 = 20 Jan.  exp.  x $ 3.50  = $ 70.00
12.6% of 50 =  6 Apr.  exp.  x   2.63  =   15.78
23.8% of 50 = 12 July  exp.  x   1.74  =   20.88
24.2% of 50 = 12 Oct.  exp.  x    .89  =   10.68
```
117.34

TOTAL ANTICIPATED INCOME $2,861.59

Specimen/115

The alarm was given at 10:08 a.m. by Mr. Thomas, who then wnt to the Emergency and triage area for observation.

Engineers responded and were on the spot at 10:09. The Laboratory personnel showed up at 10:09, and the Admissions people were at their duty sites at 10:10. Stretchers began arriving at 10:11, and within several minutes nine stretchers were in the area. Supply processing department arrived at 10:11. Four interns and residents reported and were given verbal instructions by Mr. Thomas as to which areas they should report to, and then told they could return to work. Oxygen therapy arrived at 10:14. It took a little while for the hand litters to arrive, but they were on site seven minutes after the initial alarm was given. All supply carts had arrived and were opened by 10:14.

Seven physicians responded within ten minutes of the initial alarm, which we think is remarkably good, considering that two or three of them had to come from their offices. Within a twelve-minute period of time all doctors on the call list had been reached by phone.

Physical Therapy Department appeared to be very well prepared to serve as a shock treatment area. Pharmacy people were in the emergency area rapidly.

Critique of Said Drill

The engineering department announced that they had not heard the buzzer; nor were they certain that they heard the alarm called initially. The p.a. system brought several complaint from different areas that could not hear it. The phone operators will be asked to precede each verbal announcement with a loud application of the buzzer. Dr. Thompson noted at the doctors' entrance that there was a sign saying "Area closed," and this might compel some incoming doctors to turn around and seek another exit. Dr. Browne suggested that we have a master chart with a layout of the disaster areas in the Hospital there so that when doctors arrive they can simply check that and see where they are assigned to work, whether it's major treatment or surgery or shock treatment, etc. The drill went off very well. The Hospital staff should feel proud.

Selected Bibliography

We include a listing of some of the more useful books on communications for organizations. Bear in mind that these are only a few out of the innumerable ones published. However, you may start with this listing and, from references given in each, expand your study into others of your choice.

For convenience, we list books under these headings and in this order: (1) Writing and Reading, (2) Speaking and Listening, (3) Organizational Communication, and (4) Management and Communication.

Writing and Reading

Aurner, R. *Effective Communications in Business*. Cincinnati: South-Western, 1958.

Bache, W.B. *Educator's Guide to Personalized Reading Instruction*. Englewood Cliffs, N.J.: Prentice-Hall, 1961.

Case, Keith E. and George T. Vardaman. *Mature Reading and Thinking*. Denver, Colo.: Communication Foundation, Inc., 1964.

Douglass, Paul. *Communication Through Reports*. Englewood Cliffs, N.J.: Prentice-Hall, 1957.

Himstreet, W.D. and W.M. Baty. *Business Communications*. Belmont, Calif.: Wadsworth, 1969.

Janis, Jack H. *Writing and Communicating in Business*. New York: Macmillan, 1964.

Keithley, Erwin M. and Margaret H. Thompson. *English for Modern Business*. Homewood, Ill.: Irwin, 1966.

Schutte, W. and E.R. Steinberg. *Communication in Business and Industry*. New York: Holt, Rinehart & Winston, 1962.

Shurter, Robert L. and J.P. Williamson. *Written Communication in Business*. New York: McGraw-Hill, 1964.

Strong, Ruth M. *Diagnostic Teaching of Reading*. New York: McGraw-Hill, 1964.

Strunk, W. and E.G. White. *The Elements of Style*. New York: Macmillan, 1959.

Tichy, H.J. *Effective Writing*. New York: John Wiley, 1968.

Vardaman, George T., Carroll C. Halterman, and Patricia B. Vardaman. *Cutting Communications Costs and Increasing Impacts*. New York: John Wiley, 1970.

Weisman, Herman M. *Basic Technical Writing*. Columbus, Ohio: Charles E. Merrill, 1969.

Witty, Paul A. *How to Improve Your Reading*. Chicago: Science Research Associates, 1963.

Speaking and Listening

Barrett, Harold. *Practical Methods in Speech*. New York: Holt, Rinehart & Winston, 1968.

Duker, Sam. *Listening: Readings*. New York: Scarecrow Press, 1966.

Harnack, R. Victor and Thorrel B. Fest. *Group Discussion Theory and Techniques*. New York: Appleton-Century-Crofts, 1964.

Larson, P. Merville, et al. *Communicating Effectively Through Speech*. Dubuque, Iowa: Kendall-Hunt, 1969.

Lee, Irving J. *How to Talk with People*. New York: Harper & Row, 1952.
Maier, Norman R.F. *Problem-Solving Discussions and Conferences*. New York: McGraw-Hill, 1963.
Nichols, Ralph G. and Leonard A. Stevens. *Are You Listening?* New York: McGraw-Hill, 1957.
Rogers, Carl R. and R.E. Farson. *Active Listening*. Chicago: Industrial Relations Center, University of Chicago, 1955.
Tannenbaum, Robert, et al. *Leadership and Organization*. New York: McGraw-Hill, 1961.
Vardaman, George T. *Effective Communication of Ideas*. New York: Van Nostrand Reinhold, 1970.

Organizational Communication

Barnard, Chester I. *The Functions of the Executive*. Cambridge, Mass.: Harvard University Press, 1938.
Haney, W.V. *Communication and Organizational Behavior*. Homewood, Ill.: Irwin, 1967.
Janis, Jack H. (ed.) *Business Communication Reader*. New York: Harper & Row, 1959.
Maier, Norman R.F., et al. *Communication in Organizations*. Ann Arbor, Michigan: Foundation for Research on Human Behavior, 1959.
Merrihue, Willard V. *Managing by Communication*. New York: McGraw-Hill, 1960.
Peters, Raymond W. *Communication within Industry*. New York: Harper & Row, 1950.
Raines, I.I. *Better Communications in Small Business*. Washington, D.C.: Small Business Administration, 1953.
Tannenbaum, Robert, et al. *Leadership and Organization*. New York: McGraw-Hill, 1961.
Thayer, Lee O. *Administrative Communication*. Homewood, Ill.: Irwin, 1961.
Vardaman, George T., Carroll C. Halterman, and Patricia B. Vardaman. *Cutting Communications Costs and Increasing Impacts*. New York: John Wiley, 1970.
Vardaman, Patricia B. *Forms for Better Communication*. New York: Van Nostrand Reinhold, 1971.
Wiener, Norbert. *The Human Use of Human Beings*. Boston: Houghton-Mifflin, 1950.

Management and Communication

Bergen, G.L. and W.V. Haney. *Organizational Relations and Management Action*. New York: McGraw-Hill, 1966.
Dale, Ernest. *Management Theory and Practice*. New York: McGraw-Hill, 1965.
Gellerman, Saul W. *The Management of Human Relations*. New York: Holt, Rinehart & Winston, 1966.
Herzberg, Frederick. *Work and the Nature of Man*. The World Publishing Company, 1966.
Leavitt, Harold J. *Managerial Psychology*. Chicago: University of Chicago Press, 1964.
Likert, Rensis. *New Patterns of Management*. New York: McGraw-Hill, 1961.
McGregor, Douglas. *The Human Side of Enterprise*. New York: McGraw-Hill, 1960.
Maslow, Abraham H. *Eupsychian Management*. Homewood, Ill.: Irwin and Dorsey, 1965.
Roethlisberger, Fritz J. *Management and Morale*. Cambridge, Mass.: Harvard University Press, 1950.
Sayles, Leonard R. *Managerial Behavior*. New York: McGraw-Hill, 1964.
Tannenbaum, Robert, et al. *Leadership and Organization*. New York: McGraw-Hill, 1961.
Thompson, Victor A. *Modern Organization*. New York: Alfred A. Knopf, 1961.
Vardaman, George T. and Carroll C. Halterman. *Managerial Control through Communication*. New York: John Wiley, 1968.

Index